The Lyle
official
ARTS
review

Converted at the rate of exchange on the day of sale.

SBN 0-902921-83-5

Copyright © Lyle Publications '78
Glenmayne, Galashiels, Scotland.

Printed by Apollo Press
Dominion Way, Worthing, Sussex, England.

Bound by Newdigate Press, Vincent Lane,
Dorking, Surrey, England.

Distributed in the U.S.A. by
Apollo, 391 South Road (U.S.9)
Poughkeepsie, New York 12601.

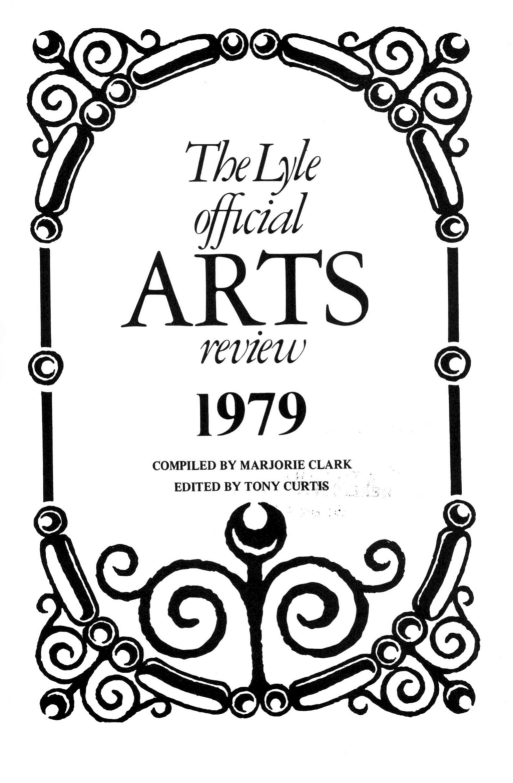

The Lyle official ARTS review

1979

COMPILED BY MARJORIE CLARK
EDITED BY TONY CURTIS

Auction Acknowledgements

Andrew, Hilditch & Son, *19 The Square, Sandbach, Cheshire.*
Auktionshaus Am Neumarkt, *Neumarkt 13, Zurich 8001, Switzerland.*
Australian Art Auctions, *11 Tradewinds Place, Kareela, Australia.*
Richard Baker & Baker, *9 Hamilton Street, Birkenhead.*
Bonham's, *Montpelier Galleries, Montpelier Street, London.*
Richard A. Bourne Co. Inc., *Box 141, Hyannis Port, Massachusets 02647.*
Brackett's, *27-29 High Street, Tunbridge Wells, Kent.*
E. J. Brooks & Son, *39 Park End Street, Oxford.*
Brown & Merry, *128 High Street, Berkhamsted, Herts.*
Buckell & Ballard, *1A Parsons Street, Banbury, Oxfordshire.*
Butler & Hatch Waterman, *Auctioneers, High Street, Tenterden, Kent.*
H. C. Chapman & Son, *North Street, Scarborough.*
Christie's, *8 King Street, St. James', London.*
Christie's, *South Kensington, 85 Old Brompton Road, London.*
Christie's, *502s Park Avenue, New York, N.Y. 10022.*
Dacre, Son & Hartley, *1-5 The Grove, Ilkley, West Yorkshire.*
Dee & Atkinson, *The Exchange, Driffield, East Yorkshire.*
Edmiston's, *The Mart, 164 Bath Street, Glasgow.*
Elliott & Green, *40 High Street, Lymington, Hants.*
J. Entwistle & Co., *The Galleries, Kingsway, Ansdell, Lytham St. Annes, Lancs.*
Foll & Parker, *9 High Street, Woburn Sands, Milton Keynes.*
John Francis, Thomas Jones & Sons, *The Mount, Carmarthen.*
Geering & Colyer, *Highgate, Hawkhurst, Kent.*
Stewart Gore, *95 High Street, Broadstairs, Kent.*
Goteborgs Auktionsverk, *Tredje Langgatan 7-9, 413 03 Goteborg, Sweden.*
Graves, Son & Pilcher, *71 Church Road, Hove.*
Gribble, Booth & Taylor, *West Street, Axminster, Devon.*
C. Wesley Haslam & Son, *St. Helens Place, High Street, Rhyl.*

Heathcote Ball & Co., *47 New Walk, Leicester.*
Husseys, *Alphin Brook Road, Exeter.*
G. A. Key, *Market Place, Aylsham, Norwich.*
King & Chasemore, *Station Road, Pulborough, West Sussex.*
Lalonde Bros. & Parham, *71 Oakfield Road, Bristol.*
T.R.G. Lawrence & Son (Fine Art), *19b Market Street, Crewkerne, Somerset.*
Thomas Love & Sons Ltd., *St. John's Place, Perth.*
Manchester Auction Mart, *2-4 Atkinson Street, Manchester.*
Morphets of Harrogate, *4-6 Albert Street, Harrogate.*
Neales of Nottingham, *192 Mansfield Road, Nottingham.*
D. M. Nesbit & Co., *7 Clarendon Road, Southsea, Hants.*
The Nottingham Auction Mart, *Byard Lane, Nottingham.*
Phillips, *The Old House, Knowle, Solihull.*
Christian Rosset, *29 Rue du Rhone, 3e Etage, Geneve.*
Smith, Woolley & Perry, *5 West Terrace, Folkestone.*
Sotheby Bearne, *3 Warren Road, Torquay, Devon.*
Sotheby's, *34/35 New Bond Street, London.*
Sotheby's Belgravia, *19 Motcomb Street, London.*
Sotheby's (Hong Kong) Ltd., *P.O. Box 83, Hong Kong.*
Spear & Sons, *The Hill, Wickham Market, Nr. Woodbridge, Suffolk.*
Henry Spencer & Sons, *20 The Square, Retford, Yorkshire.*
Staniland's, *York County Chambers, 50 Hall Gate, Doncaster.*
Swetenhams, *5 St. Werburgh Street, Chester.*
David Symonds, *High Street, Crediton, Devon.*
Walker, Barnett & Hill, *3-5 Waterloo Road, Wolverhampton.*
Wallis & Wallis, *Regency House, 1 Albion Street, Lewes, Sussex.*
Warner, Sheppard & Wade, *16/18 Halford Street, Leicester.*
Woolley & Wallis, *The Castle Auction Mart, Salisbury.*

ACKNOWLEDGEMENTS

The publishers wish to thank the following for their assistance
in the production of this volume.

**May Mutch Alison Morrison David Little Josephine McLaren
Nicky Park Janice Moncrieff Margot Rutherford Peter Hogley**

Introduction

Here is the fifth edition of the Lyle Official Arts Review. Beside details of many thousands of oil paintings, watercolours, drawings and prints, the 1979 edition of the Lyle Official Arts Review contains over 2,000 illustrations of selected pictures ranging in value from £1 to £1,000,000. These values are computed from auction results gathered over the past year.

Every entry is listed alphabetically under the Artist's name for easy reference and includes a description of the picture, its size, medium, auctioneer and the price fetched.

As regards authenticity of the works listed, this is often a delicate matter and throughout this book the conventional system has been observed:

The full Christian name(s) and surname of the artist denote that, in the opinion of the auctioneer listed, the work is by that artist.

The initials of the Christian name(s) and the surname denote that, in the opinion of the auctioneer listed, the work is of the period of the artist and may be wholly or partly his work.

The surname only of the artist denotes that, in the opinion of the auctioneer listed, the work is of the school or by one of the followers of the artist or painted in his style.

The word 'after' associated with the surname of the artist denotes that, in the opinion of the auctioneer listed, the picture is a copy of the work of the artist. The word 'signed' associated with the name of the artist denotes that, in the opinion of the auctioneer listed, the work bears a signature which is the signature of the artist.

The word 'bears signature' or 'traces of signature' denote that, in the opinion of the auctioneer listed, the work bears a signature or traces of a signature that may be that of the artist.

The word 'dated' denotes that the work is dated and, in the opinion of the auctioneer listed, was executed at that date.

9

ARTS REVIEW

If, as many people believe, the art market is an indication of the economic health of the country, Britain is beginning to feel a rising optimism — cautious, perhaps, in some sectors but nonetheless apparent all over the board.

Every area of the market is strong — "steady" is the most frequently used word among the experts — and some sectors are healthily flourishing. Old Masters for instance are demanding higher and higher prices as every month passes. The only problem for the auction houses is that there are fewer Old Masters coming up for sale than there has been for several years. The reason for this is the improved economic climate and the cautious optimism of the British who are now tending to hold onto their treasures rather than sell them as they often had to do up till as recently as a year ago. The hold-ing back of pictures does however mean that those which do come up for auction are fetching ever-rising prices. Even the experts have to admit that some prices made for Old Masters in the past year have been truly amazing. To make a spectacular price however the work of art has to be of super-lative quality because buyers have become more and more discriminating. The mass of "school" pictures which have been appearing on the market still demand fairly good prices but are not as hotly contested as the quality pictures.

The demand for quality above all else is reflected throughout the whole spectrum of the art world — whatever is good will sell well, be it Flemish, Victorian, 19th century Continental, Modern, a watercolour, a print or an etching. The insistence on excellence is welcomed as an encouraging trend in the art trade because as recently as a year ago auctioneers were saddened to watch the foreign buyers who had flooded the market paying grossly inflated prices for what could only be described as "rubbish". Since art experts know that prices begin at the bottom end of the market rather than the top, large prices going for low quality goods could only artificially elevate the prices of the better class items but with the signs of discrimination beginning to appear again, the market is settling down to a time of steady growth. Types of pictures which until only a year ago were in the doldrums are also beginning to show signs of rising optimism and this is nowhere more apparent than among Modern and contemporary paintings.

Another cheering sign is that foreign buyers, particularly Germans and Belgians who have for the last two years dominated the buying market, are beginning to give leeway to domestic purchasers and several auction houses report that while sixty per cent of their lots went abroad last year, the total is now down to forty per cent. Art exports however continue to reap a good reward for the Treasury and for our currency reserves — in 1977 they amounted to over £123.3 million, a rise of twenty-six per cent over the previous year. Foreign buyers were once again led by the Americans who bought £37.3 million worth of art in Britain — an eight per cent rise over 1976. The number of Swiss, French and Japanese buyers however dropped significantly — the Japanese by twenty-four per cent. Buyers from Holland, Germany, Spain and Canada all increased however, the Dutch by an amazing five hundred and

fifty per cent.

The most sought after type of picture over the year has of course been in the field of the Old Masters which can still demand almost any figure in the auction houses of Britain and America. Sotheby's gave dramatic evidence of this in June when they sold the Robert Von Hirsch collection in London. It was claimed that this was the finest collection ever to come up for auction, outclassing even the much publicised Mentmore sale. Among the Von Hirsch pictures which made high prices were a Madonna and Child painted in 1427 by Giovanni Di Paolo as part of the altar piece of a chapel in Sienna and an early El Greco, dated between 1565 and 1570, of "The Flight into Egypt". They were sold for £500,000 and £90,000 respectively.

The prices paid for these pictures only reflects the steadily growing momentum which Old Masters have shown throughout the year. Some astonishing prices have been paid for quality pictures like £190,000 for an Aert Van Der Neer. Pictures have been fetching two and three times the estimate placed on them and it is the general opinion that when a good picture comes up there is absolutely no limit to what buyers will give to secure it. They have, however, to be convinced of two things — the picture's quality and its authenticity. If these conditions are met, prices escalate. Works by Van Der Neer, Jan Van Goyen and still lifes, particularly flower pieces continue to hold their places as top favourites. Compared to Dutch and Flemish pictures, early Italian works from the 15th and 16th centuries look fairly cheap, especially if they are painted on panels which are

"The Branchini Madonna" - Giovanni Di Paolo
(Sotheby Parke Bernet & Co.) **$920,000 £500,000**

"The Flight Into Egypt" - El Greco
(Sotheby Parke Bernet & Co.) **$165,600 £90,000**

not popular because buyers worry about the condition of the wood and whether it would stand up to central heating. Canvasses are much preferred and this preference is reflected in the price. Because the works of early Italian painters are generally lower, some experts feel that this is an area where investors might search for possible gain in the future.

A problem which affects the whole of the selling market is the shortage of good pictures. As one dealer said "there are plenty of pot boilers about but the good pictures are becoming increasingly hard to find." People with good pictures are keeping them and so many have been already sold that the market is becoming very thin in the top areas. There are fortunately still some discoveries being made however. One of the employees of Spencer's of Retford found a small oil painting, only eight inches by ten inches, by the Dutch 17th century painter Jan Davidsz De Heem hanging on the wall of a terraced house in Yorkshire. It made the high price of £46,000 at auction and delighted its owners who were amazed to discover that their little painting was worth seven times more than their house.

Old Master drawings, prints and engravings too, have been showing a noticeable rise in prices over the year and there has been a considerable amount of American institutional buying in this field. At Christie's a 1517 drawing of the Prophet Matthew by Sebastiano Del Piombo made £104,000 the highest price ever for a drawing by that artist. Minor Veronese artist Farinato drawing sold for £5,000 and other drawings which have made high prices were a

Tiepolo which brought a bid of £7,000 from the National Gallery of South Australia, and a Mazzola Bedoli for which the British Museum gave £3,500. Renaissance and Old Master drawings are a good investment field because selective buyers with the time to attend London drawings sales can still find good ones priced between £100 and £1,000.

Apart from the Old Masters, decorative and topographical prints have also been in great demand with Swiss topographical prints fetching very high prices from Swiss collectors who do not appear to care very much if the prints are damaged or of fairly average quality. Prints of German views also sell well and there has been a great interest in views of the Middle East. English topographical prints of high quality and in good condition make excellent prices but Portuguese and Spanish views raise very little interest because few buyers from these countries have been in the sale rooms and some collectors feel that this is a market which could well be developed in the future.

Other prints much in demand are sporting prints, railway prints and modern prints in pristine condition — an important proviso for them. In the last few months prints by Matisse have made good prices and people are beginning to concentrate on artists like Nash who recently made over £2,000 for a print. The American buyers have so far shown little interest in this area of the market and prices are therefore fairly low still. Collectors with discrimination and low budgets can pick up a few bargains in prints.

Other areas which may be developed with profit are mezzotints, particularly portraits which are priced more cheaply today than they were at the beginning of the century when they were very popular. It is surprising that even when inflation is taken into account, mezzotints in 1910 made more money than they do in 1978. People collecting them should go for early states rather than blurred or worn impressions. Another good area for bargain searching is caricatures where artists like Rowlandson and Gilray can be picked up for between £10 and £15 at auction though they rarely sell for less than £50 in a dealer's showroom. The price of a caricature depends largely on the quality of the colouring and on the subject. Themes like the Salmon Bill which have long lost their historical importance for us make little but caricatures featuring well-known characters like George IV or Napoleon fetch top prices. Etchings too are beginning to make better prices than they have for a long time and Love's of Perth recently sold an etching by the Swedish artist Anders Zorn for £225. Dry point etchings by artists of the last century have all gone up noticeably — an etching and aquatint by R. Howell after James Pollard made £2,300 recently at Bonham's.

There has been a steady rise in appreciation amongst buyers also for Victorian British painters. Where the Old Master market is international, this market is strictly domestic with the rare exceptions of one or two watercolour painters like Edward Lear and David Roberts who are appreciated world wide.

As far as oil paintings are concerned however most auction houses report good trade for Victorian pictures, particularly of the "genre" type. Typical of this was the intriguingly titled "I Will Show Thee That Thou Hast Not Got Among Beggars" by George Lance which was recently sold by Boardmans in Suffolk for the world record price of £3,700. It showed literary characters Captain Orlando and Gil Blas standing in a cave full of treasures.

"Genre" pictures always sell well even if they are unsigned and the criteria for buyers are quality first and 'Prettiness' second. Of the Victorian pictures that come up for sale sixty per cent are catalogued as being "in the style of" rather than "by" but this has not stopped them, if good, making two and three times more than their estimates.

Good sales have been reported for Victorians all over the country. At Bonham's Alfred Joseph Woolmer's "Spring", a charming picture of a woman and children in an avenue of trees, made £2,100. A Keeley Halswell entitled "Roba di Roma" made £3,200. A Walter Hunt farmyard scene sold at Spencer's of Retford for £6,000, a price which has made the hitherto unregarded Walter almost as desirable as his more famous brother Edgar. Another painter who was previously not sought after but is now making high prices is William Holyoake whose 1880 drawing room interior "Divining the Future" recently made £3,500. J. F. Herring, Jnr, continues to make good prices and two farmyard scenes by him were sold in Sussex and in Suffolk for £3,800 and £3,400. King and Chasemore sold a study of a shorthorn cow by Albert Clark for £810, a painting of a mare

"I Will Show Thee That Thou Hast Not Got Among Beggars"
- **George Lance** *(Boardman's)* **$6,808 £3,700**

"Divining The Future" - William Holyoake
(Spencer's) **$6,440 £3,500**

"Study Of A Shorthorn Cow" - Albert Clark
(King and Chasemore) **$1,507 £810**

and foal by E. M. Fox for £1,100 and a landscape of North Wales by Thomas Creswick for £900. In Love's of Perth, a picture of "Sonning on Thames" by Henry H. Parker made £700. None of these artists had fetched comparable prices in any saleroom before. Size does not appear to be a criterion either because at Phillips in Edinburgh a small oil painting measuring eight inches by six inches painted by William Henry Knight in 1860 made £1,850. It has been noticeable that painters whose work was recently priced at about £200 are now making upwards of £1,000 but this does not mean that everything by that artist is taking a sharp rise because only the best work is fetching high prices and the general discrimination of the whole art market is particularly prominent among the Victorians. Generally speaking however anything decorative — good pictures of children, ships or interiors are selling well.

There is also a strong following for 'local boy' artists. In Scotland, Scots artists make the best prices and at Love's in Perth a very good price of £1,350 was paid for a landscape with crofters beside a loch by W. R. Geikie. Similarly in Birmingham people buy the work of a Victorian painter Vincent Clare who painted flowers and fruit but who does not sell anywhere else. George Lance was an Essex man and his record price was made in East Anglia. In Norwich another local painter E. R. Smythe who turned out canvasses of boys trapping sparrows in the snow and monkeys at the circus, is highly sought after. Of course, there are also the local "schools" which still demand support from the people living in that part of the country — the Newlyn School in Cornwall, the Glasgow School, the

"Study Of A Mare And Her Foal" - E. M. Fox
(King and Chasemore) **$2,046 £1,100**

Yorkshire School and the Huntingdonshire School to mention a few.

An increase of interest in painters from the early 20th century has also been noted — painters like Scots Joseph Milne, Grosvenor Thomas and George Boyle. Men of the Newlyn School — Thomas Cooper Gotch, Stanhope Forth and Harold Harvey have all been making money for some time but this movement has not been publicised. Pictures which it would have been fairly difficult to sell well before have all been showing increases and this spring Christie's had a great success with the sale of part of the collection of the late Edward Le Bas, himself an R.A. who made a collection of the works of his friends and contemporaries. His collection made fourteen world record prices including £16,000 for a Sir George Clausen for whom the previous highest price was £3,800. A pastel drawing by the same artist made £3,400 but both works were exceptional. A Charles Cundall was sold for £2,200; a Gilman oil for £18,000 with a drawing by him also making the enormous price of £1,900. Charles Ginner's "Flask Walk Under Snow" made £8,000; a Graham Bell, a member of the Euston Road School, made £12,000 and an Eric Ravilious made £16,000. A Matthew Smith nude painted in Paris in 1931 was sold for £5,000 and the record price of £2,000 was paid for a John Minton whose previous record price was £820.

Other oil paintings which have been selling noticeably well include works by foreign artists of the 19th and 20th centuries — the early 20th century Italian painter Antoine Buvard who painted Venetian canals for example. Another is Heinrich Zugal, a German animal painter whose work would only fetch about £500 if he was English but who makes upwards of £5,000 because of the foreign interest in him. A picture by the 19th century Belgian painter Emile Claus was bought for £1,600 recently at Boardman's in Suffolk where Belgian buyers are prominent because of the good ferry link with Harwich. The Ger German, Wilhelm Kunert fetched £8,000 for a painting of a pair of lions, an early 20th century portrait of a young woman by the Dutch artist D. Edzard made £240 though it was only nine inches by eight inches and in Perth a series of tiny landscape paintings, measuring between one and a quarter inches by two and a quarter inches and three and a quarter inches by five and a quarter inches done by Professor Karl Heffner made between £170 and £320 each.

Watercolours sell well in London but do less well in the provinces though even there a modest rise has been recently noted. In February Christie's had a considerable success selling the Hetherington watercolour collection but as far as British watercolour artists are concerned Turner is still top of the market and the most expensive English watercolour ever sold was a Turner at Sotheby's which made £85,000. Norms for this artist tend to run between £20,000 and £25,000. These prices should not however deter the small collector who will still be able to pick up a good watercolour for between £10 and £15 if he uses his eyes at auction sales.

As in oil paintings one of the most popular sections of this area of the art world are Victorian "genre" pictures and painters like E. K. Johnstone and

Richard Beavis have been very popular. A Johnstone of a woman in a rose garden recently made what was considered to be the amazing price of £880 and at Love's in Perth a pretty painting of a woman and children on a beach by Dutch artist Bernardis Johannes Blommers was sold for £3,200.

Bonham's have noticed a sharp rise in the watercolour market since last November which was particularly noticeable among Middle Eastern views by David Roberts and the hitherto unregarded Lamplough who is now making between £300 and £400 a picture. Edward Lear too is highly sought after for his views of the Near East, Greece and Italy. In mid summer however it was noticed that the Middle East market stopped rising because it was felt to have reached its peak.

The contemporary taste for pretty pictures however has given a big boost to the work of illustrators like Arthur Rackham, one of whose illustrations for Rip Van Winkle sold at Phillips in Edinburgh for £1,050 even though it was faded and in poor condition. The watercolour market looks like continuing its upward climb because that type of picture has always appealed to the British and also because watercolours are considerably cheaper than oils.

Finally the Modern and Contemporary paintings are beginning to pick themselves up after being in the doldrums for several years. In the past Modern paintings suffered from being dealt in rather like stocks and shares and suffered the vicissitudes of stock-market-type ups and downs. Outside buyers became wary of bidding when they suspected that certain artists were being

A Landscape by Edward Lear *(Spencer's)* **$1,288 £700**

"Portrait De Fortuné Marion" - Paul Cezanne
(Sotheby Parke Bernet & Co.) **$276,000 £150,000**

bid up by dealers who had an interest in them and a good deal of "horse trading" went on behind the scenes. Of all the sectors of the art market, the Moderns have had the worst time recently and it is cheering to see them having a new injection of interest. Prices are stabilising and experts are looking forward to a series of items coming up this summer which will set the trend for the future. One of these is a Derain at Christie's which is expected to make over £200,000 because it is one of the best examples to come on the market for some time. A Renoir is expected to make about the same and a very good Cezanne and a fine Soutine should both make over £100,000. Works of art which belonged to the Duchess of Marlborough are also to be sold at Christie's and they include Degas pastels, a Boldini portrait of the Duchess and a Rodin marble sculpture dedicated to her by the artist which is expect to make over £20,000.

Modern works sold this year include £6,000 for a Russell Flint watercolour of a reclining nude; £2,200 for a Nash watercolour; A 1911 Sickert drawing of a mother and child which was sold for £17,000; a watercolour by the Vienna Secessionist Schiele which made £12,000; a Cezanne watercolour which went for £20,000 and a Raoul Dufy watercolour of racehorses going to the start which was sold for £7,000.

Chagall's painting "Quai a Paris" was sold for £64,000 and £78,000 was made by a Pisarro. Buyers are also showing growing interest in the work of contemporary artists and £11,000 was

"A Model" - Sir William Russell Flint *(Christie's)* **$6,624 £3,600**

"Promenade Au Bord De La Mer; Le Havre" - Raoul Dufy
(Christie's) **$6,624 £3,600**

paid for a completely blue picture called "Monochrome in Blue" by Klein painted in 1961. A Peter Blacke made £10,000 and what was described as "an assemblage on panel" entitled "O.K. Dad Let's Get A T.V." by Arman made £7,500. A 1965 Dubuffet was bought for £10,000 and a Robert Ryman for £26,000.

None of the art experts see any prospect of the prices which have been recorded this year dropping in the future because of the general air of quiet optimism in the market and because of the stable attitude of the buyers. Altogether it looks as if investing in art, as many people are finding out, is a more profitable proposition than investing in the stock market but anyone starting out to buy art should always listen to the experts, take advice and avoid being rash. It is fatal to think that picture buying is easy and the general consensus of advice is to buy what you like and not because you think it will make a good investment.

LIZ TAYLOR

JOHN WHITE ABBOTT - On The Beach At Budleigh Salterton, Devon - inscribed and dated 1823 - pen and black ink, and watercolour - 5¼ x 7¼in.
(Sotheby's) $540 £300

J. T. ABELS - A Moonlit River Landscape With Fishing Vessels - on panel - 5¾ x 7¾in.
(Christie's) $450 £250

JOHN ABSOLON - Three Children Walking Through A Cornfield on a sunny day - signed - watercolour - 10½ x 14¾in.
(Sotheby Bearne) $396 £220

JOHN ABSOLON - Country Courting - heightened with white - 19½ x 15¼in.
(Sotheby's) $360 £200

ANDREAS ACHENBACH - A Fisherman - signed with initials - pencil - 31.5 x 19.4cm.
(Christie's) $63 £35

JOSEPH DENOVAN ADAM - Cattle Watering In The Shade - signed and dated 1873 - 11¼ x 17in.
(Sotheby's Belgravia) $396 £220

JOSEPH DENOVAN ADAM - Gypsy, a study of a terrier - signed - inscribed - dated 1927 - 13½ x 17½in.
(Sotheby's Belgravia) $68 £38

VALERIO ADAMI - La Sfinge - signed, inscribed and dated 26.8.70 on reverse - 28¾ x 23½ in.
(Christie's) $1,830 £1,000

ADMS

DOUGLAS ADAMS - Over The Butts
signed and dated 1898 - 30 x 48in.
(Sotheby's Belgravia)   **$1,980 £1,100**

JOHN CLAYTON ADAMS - A River
Of The South - signed and dated 1897 -
51½ x 77¾in.
(Christie's)   **$1,800 £1,000**

CHARLES W. ADDERTON - Flamborough
Fishermen - signed - 18½ x 28½in.
(Sotheby's Belgravia)   **$144 £80**

EVERT VAN AELST - Tulips, Roses, And
Other Flowers In A Glass Vase, on a stone
ledge - signed and dated 1653 - on panel -
13½ x 11in.
(Christie's)   **$6,840   £3,800**

JACQUES LAURENT AGASSE - George
Irving On Horseback in an extensive land-
scape - 34 x 43½in.
(Christie's)   **$5,040 £2,800**

CHRISTOPH LUDWIG AGRICOLA -
A Kingfisher On A Branch - bodycolour -
28.1 x 20.3cm.
(Christie's)   **$540   £300**

JAMES ALFRED AITKEN - In The
Black Mount - signed - 19 x 28½in.
(Sotheby's Belgravia)   **$81 £45**

AFRO - Fortune Teller - signed and
dated 1950 - oil - on panel - 21¾ x 11½in.
(Sotheby's)   **$2,196 £1,200**

FRANS VAN AKEN - The Interior Of
An Inn - signed - 18½ x 22½in.
(Christie's)   **$2,340 £1,300**

JOSEF ALBERS - Study For Homage To The Square - Confirming - signed with monogram - dated '71 - signed, titled, inscribed and dated 1971 on the reverse - oil on masonite - 31½ x 31½in.
(Sotheby's) **$19,215 £10,500**

JOSEF ALBERS - Structural Constellation "N N – 4" - signed - titled, inscribed and dated 1962 on the reverse - machine engraved formica - 19¾ x 26in.
(Sotheby's) **$4,941 £2,700**

PIETRO ALAMANNA - The Madonna And Child Enthroned - the Madonna with the infant Christ on her knee, an apple at her feet, angels on either side behind her - signed and dated - gold ground - on panel - 39¾ x 20in.
(Sotheby's) **$31,450 £17,000**

FREDERICK JAMES ALDRIDGE - Calm Sea with sailing barges and other ships off the coast - signed and dated '81 - 18 x 32in.
(Woolley & Wallis) **$450 £250**

FRANCESCO ALBANI, School of - The Sleep of Venus - 42 x 63in.
(Christie's N. York) **$1,760 £962**

ALEGIANI

FRANCESCO ALEGIANI - A Trompe L'Oeil of prints against a wood wall - signed and signed with initials - 39¼ x 29¼in.
(Christie's) $1,224 £680

EDWIN J. ALEXANDER - Harebells - signed with initials - on buff paper - heightened with bodycolour - 12¼ x 6½in.
(Sotheby's Belgravia) $810 £450

ROBERT ALEXANDER - Rabbit Fanciers - signed - 37 x 31in.
(Christie's) $540 £300

ROBERT L. ALEXANDER - Study Of A Hunter Outside A Stable - signed and dated 1886 - 13 x 18in.
(Sotheby's Belgravia) $396 £220

W. S. ALFRED - The 'Earl Of Zetland' Off The Coast - signed - inscribed 'Dunkirk' - dated 1884 - 24¼ x 36in.
(Sotheby's Belgravia) $540 £300

ALIENSE - The Resurrection - black chalk, pen and brown ink, brown wash - 31.5 x 22.5cm.
(Christie's) $144 £80

ALIGNON - The Faggot Gatherer - indistinctly signed - 15½ x 25¼in.
(Christie's) $900 £500

HENRY ALKEN - A Huntsman At Full Gallop; and A Jockey On A Grey At Full Gallop - the first inscribed 'Go Along' - pencil and watercolour - 5¾ x 9in. and smaller.
(Christie's) $720 £400 Two

HENRY ALKEN - A Tandem on a country road - signed - on board - 6½ x 13¼in.
(Sotheby's) **$1,080 £600**

SAMUEL ALKEN - A Chained Bear Attacked By Dogs - signed - on panel - 7 x 9¾in.
(Sotheby's) **$270 £150**

ALLAN - Budleigh Vale, South Devon - signed - inscribed - 13¾ x 20½in.
(Sotheby's Belgravia) **$108 £60**

SIR LAWRENCE ALMA-TADEMA - The Education Of The Children Of Clovis - signed and dated 1868 - on panel - 25 x 35½in.
(Christie's) **$18,525 £9,500**

ARCHIBALD RUSSELL WATSON ALLAN - Ploughers - signed - 72 x 72in.
(Sotheby's Belgravia) **$540 £300**

R. ALLAN - A Steamer And Other Ships Off The Coast - signed - 15¾ x 17½in.
(Sotheby's Belgravia) **$72 £40**

SIR WILLIAM ALLAN - The Spinner Surprised - signed and dated 1826 - on panel - 15¼ x 19¼in.
(Sotheby's) **$720 £400**

J. W. ALLEN - Fisher Boys By Eel Nets - signed - on board - 11¼ x 15¼in.
(Sotheby's Belgravia) **$68 £38**

THOMAS ALLOM - Queen Victoria With A Mounted Escort Arriving At Windsor Castle - pencil, brown washes, heightened with white - 7½ x 15½in.
(Sotheby's) **$720 £400**

THOMAS ALLOM - Ruins At Ephesus - signed, inscribed and dated 1846 - 5 x 8¼in.
(Sotheby's) **$180 £100**

R. ALLOTT - An Italian Lake Landscape - signed and dated 1897 - 28½ x 38½in.
(Christie's) **$1,620 £900**

SIR LAWRENCE ALMA-TADEMA - Classical Figures Mooring A Barge - inscribed with artist's name and the date 1870 by the artist's daughter - a sketch - on panel - 17¾ x 23in.
(Christie's) **$2,340 £1,300**

MICHAEL VAN ALPHEN - A Turkish Beauty - signed and dated 1874 - 26 x 21in.
(Christie's) **$1,260 £700**

27

WILLIAM ANDERSON - A View Of Greenwich From The River Thames With Shipping - 22 x 31in. *(Christie's)* **$1,530 £850**

ALBIN AMELIN - Portrait - signed - 58 x 44cm. *(Goteborgs Auktionsverk)* **$2,057 £1,143**

AMERICAN SCHOOL, 19th century - View Of A Brig under shortened sail - oil - on canvas - 14 x 18in. *(Richard A Bourne Co. Inc.)* **$550 £305**

WILLIAM ANDERSON - Coastal Scene With Dutch Fishing Boats in calm water - signed and dated 1920 - on panel - 10 x 13in. *(Sotheby Bearne)* **$4,680 £2,400**

TOM ANDERTON - Bringing Out The Horses, Early Morning; A Continental Riverside Tow - signed - 17½ x 22¾in. *(Sotheby's Belgravia)* **$25 £14 Two**

CUNO AMIET - Ferdinand Hodler - 104 x 101cm. *(Auktionshaus am Neumarkt)* **$38,430 £21,000**

J. AMIGONI - Suffer The Little Children To Come Unto Me - the mount inscribed 'Amigoni' - pen and brown ink, brown wash - 29.1 x 18.5cm. *(Christie's)* **$70 £50**

H. ANDREWS - The Winning Card - arched top - 31½ x 41in. *(Christie's S. Kensington)* **$3,060 £1,700**

HORST ANTES - Female Figure With Headband - signed and dated 10.1.66 - gouache and watercolour - on paper - 21 x 16½in.
(Sotheby's) **$2,013 £1,100**

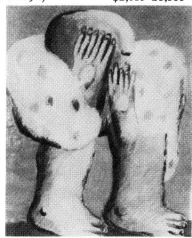

HENRY ANDREWS - Elegant Figures In A Formal Garden - signed - 42½ x 67in.
(Christie's) **$3,315 £1,700**

FILIPPO D'ANGELI - Saint Paul Shipwrecked - black chalk, pen and brown ink - 16 x 28cm.
(Christie's) **$90 £50**

R. ANSDELL - 'A Rest At The Drinking Trough' - signed - 11½ x 15½in.
(Sotheby Bearne) **$448 £230**

HORST ANTES - Figure In A Yellow Interior - signed - gouache and watercolour - on paper - 21 x 16½in.
(Sotheby's) **$3,111 £1,700**

HORST ANTES - Female Figure - signed and dated 7.2.66 - gouache, watercolour, Indian ink and charcoal - 21 x 16½in.
(Sotheby's) **$1,464 £800**

RICHARD ANSDELL - The Eagles' Eyrie - signed with monogram - on board - 17 x 37½in.
(Sotheby's Belgravia) **$810 £450**

RICHARD ANSDELL - Portrait Of A Gentleman, seated, small full length, wearing a blue coat and brown waistcoat - 14½ x 10¾in.
(Christie's) **$180 £100**

RICHARD ANSDELL - A Spaniel With A Dead Pheasant - signed with initials and dated 1860 - 26½ x 20in.
(Christie's) **$990 £550**

RICHARD ANSDELL and JOHN PHILLIP - The Fair At Seville - signed by both artists and dated 1857 - 43½ x 65½in.
(Christie's) **$2,925 £1,500**

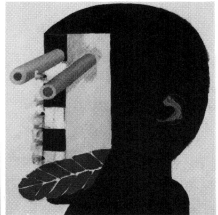

HORST ANTES - Preussischblauer Kopf Ohne Vase Mit 6 Federn - signed, inscribed with title and dated Aquatic 1971 on the reverse - 27½ x 23¾ in.
(Christie's) **$5,490 £3,000**

ANTOINE

ROBERT ANTOINE - Flowers - signed - oil
- on canvas - 55.5 x 46cm.
(Christian Rosset)   **$302 £165**

A. VAN ANTON - Extensive Landscape
with chickens and ducks by a pool -
signed and dated 1867 - panel - 7 x 9½in.
(H. Spencer & Sons)   **$342 £190**

J. VAN ANTROY - Poultry In A Field;
and Sheep In A Meadow - the former
signed and dated 1867 - oil - on panel -
7½ x 10in.
(Warner, Sheppard & Wade)
          $2,352 £1,200 Pair

SCHOOL OF ANTWERP, circa 1530 -
The Pieta - on panel - 28 x 20½in.
(Christie's)   **$9,100 £5,000**

KAREL APPEL - Deux Tetes - signed -
63¼ x 44¾ in.
(Christie's)   **$11,895 £6,500**

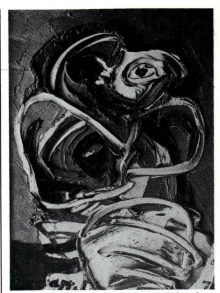

KAREL APPEL - Tete - signed and dated
'74 - 21½ x 15¼in.
(Christie's)   **$2,379 £1,300**

KAREL APPEL - Nu - signed and
dated 1960 - 77 x 51 in.
*(Christie's N. York)***$12,100 £6,722**

THOMAS VAN APSHOVEN - A River Landscape with peasants playing cards outside an inn - bears David Teniers signature - on panel - 14 x 20½in.
(Christie's) **$3,600 £2,000**

KAREL APPEL - Untitled Composition - signed and dated '58 - gouache and white chalk on paper - 19¼ x 25in.
(Sotheby's) **$2,196 £1,200**

APPIANI - A Classical Scene With Women Receiving Children - black chalk, pen and grey ink, grey wash - 33.2 x 41.4cm.
(Christie's) **$90 £50**

ANDREA APPIANI, Circle of - Portrait Of An Officer, three-quarter length, leaning on a parapet and holding a book, a landscape in the background - 39 x 30½in.
(Christie's N. York) **$715 £390**

THOMAS VAN APSHOVEN - A Wooded River Landscape with peasants outside an inn - on panel - 9 x 13in.
(Christie's) **$5,400 £3,000**

ALEXIS ARAPOFF - Paris At Night - signed and dated '28 - oil - on canvas - 54 x 81cm.
(Christian Rosset) **$878 £480**

THOMAS VAN APSHOVEN - A Kitchen Scene - a maid putting a bowl of strawberries on a counter on which are a lobster, game and a vase of flowers, on the ground fruit and vegetables - on metal - 10½ x 7in.
(Sotheby's) **$7,030 £3,800**

JAMES ARCHER - The Flower Pickers - signed with monogram and dated 1863 - 22 x 29½in.
(Christie's) **$3,600 £2,000**

ARCIMBOLDO

ARCIMBOLDO - An Anthropomorphic Portrait Of A Man, head and shoulders, made up of numerous birds - bears Hondecoeter signature - 35 x 27in.
(Christie's) **$5,400 £3,000**

JUAN DE ARELLANO - Flowers On A Ledge; and Flowers Fallen From A Pitcher - both signed and dated 1665 - 25 x 29¾in.
(Sotheby's) **$46,250 £25,000 Pair**

P. ARESI - An Italianate mountainous Wooded River Landscape, with figures on a path and buildings beyond - shaped top - 43 x 44in.
(Christie's) **$1,620 £900**

H. ARIYOSKI - Boathouse By A River - oil - 9 x 13in.
(G. A. Key) **$61 £34**

ARMAN - Untitled - signed and dated '73 - ink - 25½ x 20in.
(Christie's) **$1,006 £550**

ARMAN - Accumulation Informative - newspapers (New York Times) in a plexiglass box - 79¼ x 49½ x 4in.
(Christie's) **$7,320 £4,000**

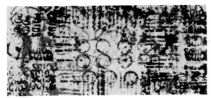

ARMAN - Orange And Blue - signed and dated 1958 - rubber stamps and paint traces - on board - 6 x 12¼in.
(Sotheby's) **$256 £140**

THOMAS W. ARMES - Autumn, farmland with figures - signed - oil - on canvas - 15 x 19½in.
(Neales of Nottingham) **$59 £32**

ARMFIELD - Three Sporting Dogs In A Highland Landscape - oil - on canvas - 13½in. diameter.
(Neales of Nottingham) **$154 £80**

EDWARD ARMFIELD - Spaniels Flushing Duck - signed - 11¾ x 15¼in.
(Sotheby's Belgravia) **$81 £45**

G. ARMFIELD - The Highland Shepherd's Home - bears other initials and date - bears inscription on the reverse - 16¼ x 22¼in.
(Sotheby's Belgravia) **$648 £360**

G. ARMFIELD - Terriers Chasing A Rat - 18 x 23½in.
(Sotheby's Belgravia) **$144 £80**

GEORGE ARMFIELD - A Hostile Encounter - signed and dated 1866 - 29½ x 39½in.
(Christie's) **$1,852 £950**

GEORGE ARMFIELD - Three Spaniels In A Wooded Landscape, putting up a cock pheasant - signed - 16½ x 20½in.
(Woolley & Wallis) **$342 £190**

GEORGE ARMFIELD - Five Terriers In A Stable - signed - 16½ x 20½in.
(Woolley & Wallis) **$486 £270**

GEORGE ARMFIELD - Dear Mrs George's Favourite - signed and inscribed - on board - 7 x 8¾in.
(Sotheby's Belgravia) **$198 £110**

GEORGE ARMFIELD - Rural Landscape - two English setters; and three Spaniels putting up a wild duck - signed - 11½ x 15½in.
(H. Spencer & Sons) **$486 £270 Pair**

GEORGE ARMFIELD - A Wooded River
Landscape - signed - 9½ x 11½in.
(Sotheby's Belgravia) **$468 £260**

MARY NICOL NEILL ARMOUR -
In Rassay - recto and verso - 10½ x
15¼in.
(Sotheby's Belgravia) **$216 £120**

MARY NICOL NEILL ARMOUR -
Flowers With Poppy - signed and dated
'71 - 19½ x 15¼in.
(Sotheby's Belgravia) **$360 £200**

GEORGE ARNALD - Village Crosses - one
signed and dated 1802 - 9¾ x 6¾in.
(Sotheby's) **$376 £220 Pair**
F. ARNOLD - Moonlight Scene With
Figure In Lane - watercolour - 9 x 14in.
(G. A. Key) **$76 £42**

HARRIET ARNOLD - Queen Victoria
with her children by a lake in the grounds
of Buckingham Palace - 23¼ x 35¼in.
(Christie's) **$2,340 £1,200**

JOSE GALLEGOS Y ARNOSA - The
Matador's Respite - signed and dated 1909 -
on panel - 9½ x 16in.
(Christie's) **$3,600 £2,000**
D'ARPINO - Venus And Adonis - red
chalk - 24.2 x 17.8cm.
(Christie's) **$135 £75**
IL CAVALIER D'ARPINO, Circle of -
The Lapidation Of Saint Stephen -
black chalk - 41.0 x 27.0cm.
(Christie's) **$99 £55**

JACQUES D'ARTHOIS - A Wooded Landscape with huntsmen and dogs on a path
by a pool - signed - 34 x 52in.
(Christie's) **$14,560 £8,000**

JACQUES D'ARTHOIS - A Wooded Landscape with a shepherd and sheep, and peasants by cottages beyond - signed - 18 x 21¼in.
(Christie's) **$4,680 £2,600**

EDMUND ASHFIELD - Portrait of the Duc de Rohan wearing a full wig, a lace collar and a red top coat - pastel - 10 x 8¼ in.
(Sotheby's) **$126 £70**

A. ASPERTINI - Head Of A Courtisan - inscribed and dated 1520 - on panel - 13 x 10in.
(Christie's) **$3,240 £1,800**

J. ASSELIJN - A Blasted Tree-Trunk in an Italianate landscape - on panel - 13¼ x 10in.
(Christie's) **$2,340 £1,300**

ASSELYN - A Landscape With Roman Ruins - pen and brown ink, grey wash - 20.0 x 19.8cm.
(Christie's) **$108 £60**

W. ASHFORD - A Rocky River Landscape, fishermen and other figures in the foreground, a ruin and castle beyond - 29¾ x 39in.
(Sotheby's) **$1,980 £1,100**

SIR WILLIAM ASHTON - Cattle By A River at evening - signed - oil - on panel - 7 x 10½in.
(Sotheby's) **$232 £120**

BALTHASAR VAN DER AST - Grapes, Apples, Peaches And Redcurrants in a Chinese blue-and-white deep dish with a gourd, a tulip and fruits on a stone ledge - on panel - 17½ x 23¼in.
(Christie's) **$12,740 £7,000**

CHARLES REGINALD ASTON - The
Head Of Loch Lomond - signed - 14½
x 27½in.
(Christie's) **$780 £400**

SAMUEL ATKINS - An English Two
Decker off the South coast, a frigate
anchored nearby - signed - watercolour,
watermark Strasburg Lily - 13¾ x 18¾in.
(Christie's) **$3,060 £1,700**
JOHN GUNSON ATKINSON - Fingal
Mill, Devon - signed - inscribed on the
reverse - 11½ x 9¼in.
(Sotheby's Belgravia) **$482 £268**

JEAN ATLAN - Composition - signed -
dated '54 - oil - on hessian - 39½ x 32in.
(Sotheby's) **$4,026 £2,200**

JEAN ATLAN - Personnages - signed and
dated '54 - oil - on hessian - 21¾ x 18in.
(Sotheby's) **$2,379 £1,300**
JEAN-MICHEL ATLAN - Untitled -
signed and dated '53 - coloured chalks -
16½ x 9¾in.
(Christie's) **$512 £280**

CHRISTIAN LUDWIG ATTERSEE - Drei
Katzenbocke - signed, inscribed with title
and dated 74 - watercolour - gouache and
black and coloured chalks - 17¼ x 12¼ in.
(Christie's) **$640 £350**

JAN ADRIAENSZ. VAN ATTEVELT - A Young Physician In His Laboratory - signed - 35½ x 44in.
(Christie's) $11,700 £6,500

MILTON AVERY - Mexican Washer-women - signed and dated 1946 - 28 x 36in.
(Christie's N. York) $17,600 £9,778

PETER VAN AVONT - The Madonna And Child With The Infant Saint John The Baptist and attendant angels in a landscape - signed - on panel - 15 x 21½in.
(Christie's) $3,060 £1,700

AULD - Another Drink, Please - signed - 12 x 10½in.
(Sotheby's Belgravia) $81 £45

A. AUSTEN - A Quiet Smoke - signed - 17½ x 13½in.
(Sotheby's Belgravia) $90 £50

ALEX AUSTEN - A Gentleman Lighting A Pipe and feeding a parrot respectively - signed - canvas - 12 x 8½in.
(Morphets of Harrogate) $414 £230 Pair

W. FRED AUSTIN - Turners Square, Norwich - watercolour - 13 x 17in.
(G. A. Key) $54 £30

AUSTRIAN SCHOOL, 17th century - A Market Scene - a crowd of elegantly dressed men and women, some with pages, some at table, others around tented booths and at stalls - 17½ x 24¼in.
(Sotheby's) $7,030 £3,800

THOMAS BRABAZON AYLMER - View From Near The Doge's Palace towards the Grand Canal - inscribed and dated May 1837 - pencil heightened with white - 10 x 14in.
(Christie's S. Kensington) $153 £85

W. AYRTON - Boathouse At Hickling - watercolour - 13 x 20in.
(G. A. Key) $90 £50

G. AYTOUN - A Loch Scene - signed and dated 1868 - 22½ x 35in.
(Sotheby's Belgravia) $180 £100

CORNELIS DE BAELLIEUR - The
Triumph Of David - on copper - 18½ x
24½in.
(Christie's) $7,644 £4,200

G. BAGLIONE - The Card Player - 32
x 28in.
(Christie's) $1,800 £1,000

F. V. BAILEY - Flowerpiece In The
Style Of Van Huysum - signed - oil -
23½ x 17½in.
(Graves, Son & Pilcher) $540 £300

BAIRD - Cutting Grass By The Sea -
9 x 11½in.
(Sotheby's Belgravia) $22 £12

S. H. BAKER - A Village Street -
15½ x 21½in.
(Sotheby's Belgravia) $198 £110

**HENDRIK VAN DE SANDE
BAKHUYZEN** - Skaters On A River Near
A Windmill - signed on the backing -
pencil, grey wash - 10.7 x 16.4cm.
(Christie's) $756 £420

L. BAKHUYZEN - Dutch Men-O'-War And
Other Sailing Vessels at anchor off a jetty -
bears signature - 38 x 55in.
(Christie's) $7,644 £4,200

T. C. BALE - Still Life Of Fruit And An Earthenware Jug - 11¾ x 23½in. *(Sotheby's Belgravia)* **$99 £55**

THOMAS C. BALE - Still Life Of Game And Fruit On A Wooden Ledge - signed - 23½ x 19½in. *(Sotheby's Belgravia)* **$360 £200**

BALE - Still Life Of Fruit On A Bank - oil - 8 x 12in. *(G. A. Key)* **$97 £54**

LUDOLF BAKHUYZEN - Seascape - oil - on canvas - 45.5 x 63cm. *(Christian Rosset)* **$1,823 £1,013**

HENDRIK VAN BALEN and JAN BRUEGHEL, THE YOUNGER - Diana And Her Nymphs After The Hunt, in a wooded river landscape - on panel - 23½ x 34½in. *(Christie's)* **$15,300 £8,500**

LUDOLF BAKHUYZEN - A State Yacht, Dutch Men-O'-War And Other Vessels in a stiff breeze offshore - signed and dated 1671 - 17¾ x 54¼in. *(Christie's)* **$68,400 £38,000**

T. C. BALE - Still Life Of Fruit And Game On A Ledge - bears monogram - 23¼ x 19¼in. *(Sotheby's Belgravia)* **$396 £220**

JAN VAN BALEN - The Madonna And Child with attendant angels making music - on panel - 37½ x 29in. *(Christie's)* **$1,080 £600**

ANTONIO BALESTRA, Circle of - Venus instructing Vulcan to make arms for Aeneas - 31 x 42½ in. *(Christie's N. York)* **$495 £270**

BALLANTINE

JOHN BALLANTINE - A Woman Of
Samaria - signed and dated 1875 -
23½ x 19½in.
(Sotheby's Belgravia) $162 £90

GEORGE BALMER - Dunnotar Castle
and cliff scene in storm - 6½ x 6½in.
(Brooks) $210 £110

ELIAS MOLLINEAUX BANCROFT -
Tangier - signed with initials and dated
1883 - on board - 9 x 13in.
(Sotheby's Belgravia) $128 £70

BANDINELLI - A Standing Man -
inscribed - black chalk - 40.7 x
26.8cm.
(Christie's) $45 £25

J. J. BANNATYNE - Coastal Scene -
A Summer Day - 33 x 58cm.
(Edmiston's) $378 £210

C. R. BANNER - Cottage Scenes - both
signed - one with initials - dated 1871 -
on board - 7¾ x 10¼in.
(Sotheby's Belgravia) $198 £110 Pair

MARCIANO A. BAPTISTA - A View
of Hong Kong, showing the Church and
Government House - signed - watercolour - 15 x 25½ in.
(Sotheby's, Hong Kong) $2,077 £1,154

MARCIANO A. BAPTISTA - A View
of Hong Kong seen from Morrison Hill
looking towards Central - watercolour -
14¾ x 25½ in.
(Sotheby's, Hong Kong) $311 £173

FILIPPO BARATTI - The Prisoner -
signed and dated Paris 1883 - signed,
inscribed and dated 1883 on the
reverse - 41 x 31in.
(Christie's) $9,900 £5,500

CHARLES BURTON BARBER - The Adventures Of Puncher - signed and inscribed - 14 x 10in.
(Sotheby's Belgravia) **$81 £45**

JAMES BARENGER - The Earl Of Derby's 'Opal' and foal - signed and inscribed - mixed media, oil and watercolour - on paper - 8½ x 11½in.
(Christie's) **$2,700 £1,500**

JAMES BARENGER - Lord Derby's Foxhounds - signed and dated 1809 - 24½ x 29½in.
(Christie's) **$8,100 £4,500**

JOHN BARKER - 'Christmas Eve'; and 'Going To School' - signed and dated 1860 - arched tops - 17½ x 23½in.
(Sotheby Bearne) **$2,430 £1,350 Pair**

JOHN WRIGHT BARKER - Highland Cattle - signed - 39½ x 57in.
(Sotheby's Belgravia) **$1,620 £900**

BARKER OF BATH - Two Pointers In A Wooded Landscape - on panel - 9¾ x 14¼in.
(Sotheby's) **$360 £200**

BENJAMIN BARKER OF BATH - A River Gorge - signed - 11¾ x 15¼in.
(Sotheby's) **$360 £200**

A. BARLAND - A Farmyard And Cattle On A Path with a view of York Minster beyond - 19¼ x 29½in.
(Christie's) **$990 £550**

FRANCIS BARLOW - A Landscape With Wild Birds, Lizard and A Frog - signed and dated 1650 - oil - on canvas - 30 x 25in.
(Bonham's) **$10,800 £6,000**

A. HARRISON BARNES - River Scene - signed - oil - 36 x 24in.
(J. Entwistle & Co.) **$231 £125**

E. C. BARNES - A Gypsy Fortune-Teller - oval - 13 x 10½in.
(Sotheby's Belgravia) **$58 £32**

E. C. BARNES - The Sleeping Beauty -
signed with monogram - dated 1856 -
23 x 19½in.
(Christie's) $18 £10

S. J. BARNES - A River Scene,
Evening - 12½ x 21½in.
(Sotheby's Belgravia) $234 £130 Pair

SAMUEL J. BARNES - Cattle On A
Hill Path - signed - 19½ x 29½in.
(Sotheby's Belgravia) $90 £50

JOSEPH BARNEY - Still Life In The
Dutch Manner, with a vase of flowers,
bird's nest and insects on a ledge - signed
and dated 1807 - on panel - 31½ x 21¾in.
(Sotheby Bearne) $6,045 £3,100

G. B. BARR - Summer Flowers - signed -
dated 1886 - 34½ x 27in.
(Sotheby's Belgravia) $684 £380

DIDIER BARRA, sometimes called Monsu
Desiderio - A View Of The Port And City
Of Naples with ships offshore, a storm
overhead illuminating the city with a flash
of lightning - with a coat-of-arms - 45 x
69in.
(Christie's) $43,200 £24,000

FRANCOIS BARRAUD, called Gustave
Francois - Landscape - signed - oil - on
canvas - 50.5 x 61.5cm.
(Christian Rosset) $201 £110

BARTOLINI

FRANCOIS BARRAUD, called Gustave
Francois - Nude From The Back - signed -
charcoal and watercolour - 43 x 35cm.
(Christian Rosset) **$102 £56**

WILLIAM BARRAUD - A Young Ghillie -
signed and dated 1840 - 16¾ x 20½in.
(Sotheby's Belgravia) **$1,800 £1,000**

HENRY BARRAUD - Queen Victoria
And The Duchess Of Kent Seated In A
Carriage, attended by the Duke of
Wellington, the Prince Consort, Sir Robert
Peel and noblemen and courtiers at a
harriers meeting in Windsor Great Park,
with courtiers and grooms in attendance -
signed and dated 1845 - 43 x 72in.
(Christie's) **$68,400 £38,000**

JULIAN BARROW - Tulchan Lodge,
On The Spey - signed and dated 1975 -
23½ x 35½in.
(Sotheby's Belgravia) **$162 £90**

HENRY BARRAUD - Portrait Of Horatio
Kemble seated holding a pheasant with his
two pointers and a retriever, taking a rest
from shooting - signed and dated 1846 -
24¼ x 29¼in.
(Sotheby's) **$3,420 £1,900**

FREDERIC AUGUSTE BARTHOLDI -
New York Harbour - the Statue of Liberty
dominating the scene - signed, inscribed
and dated 1889 - watercolour - 4 x 7in.
(Sotheby's) **$579 £300**

VALENTINE BARTHOLOMEW - A
Gothic Country Residence - signed -
inscribed 'original sketch' - dated 1825 -
on grey paper - pencil, heightened with
white - 9 x 13¾in.
(Sotheby's Belgravia) **$9 £5**

F. BARTOLINI - The Carpet Seller -
signed - watercolour - 21 x 14in.
(Christie's) **$396 £220**

43

BARTOLOZZI

F. BARTOLOZZI - The Adoration Of The Magi, in the manner of Guercino - black and white chalk on blue paper - 25.1 x 37.2cm.
(Christie's) **$180 £100**

JACOPO BASSANO, After - The Road To Calvary - on panel - 8¼ x 12in.
(Christie's) **$5,400 £3,000**

E. BASCHENIS - Musical Instruments on a draped table - 38¾ x 55½in.
(Christie's) **$14,400 £8,000 Pair**

BASSANO - Dives And Lazarus - 23½ x 39½in.
(Christie's) **$2,520 £1,400**

F. BASSANO - A Wooded Landscape with a peasant and cattle - 37 x 52½in.
(Christie's) **$3,600 £2,000**

L. BASSANO - Portrait Of An Old Man, three-quarter length, seated, wearing black costume - 52¼ x 38¼in.
(Christie's) **$2,520 £1,400**

C. BASSOLI - Peasants In A Piazza - signed, bodycolour - 13.5 x 17.8cm.
(Christie's) **$288 £160**

S. J. BATCHELDER - Broadland Scenes with wherries - watercolour - oval - 6 x 4in.
(G. A. Key) **$180 £100 Pair**

STEPHEN J. BATCHELDER - Diamond Jubilee, Norwich 1897, night landscape with extensive view of Norwich picked out by search lights - oil - 24 x 36in.
(G. A. Key) **$468 £260**

FRANCESCO BASSANO, THE YOUNGER - Noah's Ark - 53 x 71½in.
(Christie's) **$7,200 £4,000**

BATES - Eel Traps - 16 x 24in.
(Sotheby's Belgravia) **$126 £70**

DAVID BATES - Extensive Wooded Land-scape with figure and sheep - 28 x 38in. *(Christie's S. Kensington)* **$2,250 £1,250**

DAVID BATES - On Rydal Fell - signed and dated 1902 - on board - 9½ x 13½in. *(Sotheby's Belgravia)* **$846 £470**

DAVID BATES - A Wooded River Land-scape with faggot gatherers - signed and dated 1876 - 23¼ x 35¼in. *(Christie's)* **$2,145 £1,100**

GEORGE BATHGATE - The Seamstress - signed and dated 1885 - 16¾ x 22½in. *(Sotheby's Belgravia)* **$171 £95**

DAVID BATES - 'Mildenham Mill Near Worcester' - signed and dated 1874 - on canvas - 19 x 28in. *(King & Chasemore)* **$1,710 £950**

DAVID BATES - Near The Desert - signed and dated 1893-1903; signed, inscribed and dated 1893, retouched 1903 on the reverse - 24 x 39½in. *(Christie's)* **$1,710 £950**

POMPEO BATONI - Portrait Of Mrs. Sandilands, bust length wearing black lace dress and white turban - signed and dated Rome 1781 - framed as an oval - 27 x 22½in. *(Christie's)* **$16,200 £9,000**

BATONI

POMPEO BATONI - Portrait Of A Cavalry Officer In Walking-Out Dress, three-quarter length, leaning on a pedestal by a bust of Mars - signed and inscribed Romae 1774 - 38 x 39in.
(Christie's)   **$28,800**   **£16,000**

G. BATTISTA - Ponte Santa Trinita, Florence, in the rain - signed - body-colour - 33.1 x 48.8cm.
(Christie's)   **$216**   **£120**

GUSTAVE BAUERNFEIND - A Street Scene In Jaffa - signed and dated Munchen 1890 and inscribed Jaffa - 41 x 52½in.
(Christie's)   **$39,600 £22,000**

BAXTER - The Maid - oval - 35½ x 25in.
(Sotheby's Belgravia)   **$450 £250**

SARAH BAXTER - Portrait Of The Artist's Son; he is seen seated on a table surrounded by fruit and holding a bunch of grapes, watched by an Indian man-servant and his ayah, a mosque in the distance - 36¼ x 28½in.
(Sotheby's)   **$720**   **£400**

FRANCISCO BAYEU, Circle of - Portrait
Of Archbishop Pablo Garcia Abella,
seated, half length, wearing orders -
inscribed - 43¾ x 34in.
(Christie's N. York) **$1,650 £902**

RICHARD BEAVIS - A Mediterranean
Coaster Discharging Cargo - Catalan Bay -
signed and dated 1873 - signed and
inscribed on a label on the reverse - 30 x
44in.
(Christie's) **$1,710 £950**

BECKER - Landscape With Plough
Team - oil - 20 x 30in.
(G. A. Key) **$72 £40**

BECKER - The Smithy - oil - 20 x 30in.
(G. A. Key) **$61 £34**

F. Le B. BEDWELL - Imperialist Troops,
China; T'ai P'ing Rebels, China - signed
and dated 1861 - pencil and watercolour -
10 x 24 in.
(Sotheby's, Hong Kong) **$333 £185 Pair**

E. BEE - Landscape With Cottages And
Churchyard - watercolour - 11 x 8in.
(G. A. Key) **$9 £5**

JEAN BAZAINE - "Couple au bord de
l'eau, le soir" - signed and dated '43 -
inscribed and titled on the reverse - oil
- on canvas - 46 x 35in.
(Sotheby's) **$11,895 £6,500**

CLAUDIO FRANCESCO BEAUMONT -
Apollo And Allegorical Figures - a sketch
for a ceiling - 16½ x 22in.
(Christie's) **$2,340 £1,300**

RICHARD BEAVIS - Cattle Grazing -
Summer Afternoon - signed - signed
and inscribed on the reverse - on panel
- 9 x 13¾in.
(Christie's) **$126 £70**

RICHARD BEAVIS - Bulls Fighting -
signed - dated 1879 - 12¼ x 28in.
(Sotheby's Belgravia) **$324 £180**

GEORGE BEECHEY - Portrait Of A
Native, dressed in Indian costume, half
length - 29¼ x 24¼in.
(Christie's) **$5,400 £3,000**

RICHARD BRYDGES BEECHEY - The Battle Of Saint Vincent - signed, inscribed and dated 1881 - 30 x 45in.
(Christie's) **$5,184 £3,800**

CORNELIS BEELT - Figures On The Beach At Scheveningen with the Dutch fleet offshore - signed and dated 1659 - 27½ x 37½in.
(Christie's) **$8,640 £4,800**

RICHARD BRYDGES BEECHEY - Captain John Harvey's Action in the 'Brunswick', 1st June, 1794 - signed and dated 1886 - 30½ x 43½in.
(Christie's) **$2,880 £1,600**

J. DE BEER - The Crucifixion - on panel - 31 x 22½in.
(Christie's) **$5,400 £3,000**

ADRIAEN CORNELISZ. BEELDE-MAKER - Springer Spaniels In A Wooded Landscape with huntsmen and their dogs - signed and dated 1699 - 17¾ x 23¼in.
(Christie's) **$1,440 £800**

BEELICK - Landscape - signed - oil - on canvas - 41 x 23in.
(Stewart Gore) **$142 £75**

O. BEERT THE YOUNGER - Oysters, Pastry In A Wan Li Kraak Porcelain Bowl, a nautilus cup, plates of fruit with bread and an orange on a table - on canvas - on panel - 15¾ x 21in.
(Christie's) **$9,100 £5,000**

ROBERT BEESLEY - A Still Life Of
Mixed Fruit, including grapes, peaches,
strawberries and a melon - 20¾ x 25¾in.
(Sotheby's) **$288 £160**

ABRAHAM HENDRIK VAN BEESTEN -
An Allegory Of Plenty; and An Allegory
Of Love - both signed and dated 1765 -
on grisaille - 36 x 45in.
(Christie's) **$1,440 £800 Pair**

CORNELIS BEGA, Circle of - Peasants
Smoking By A Fireplace - on panel -
11 x 8¾in.
(Christie's N. York) **$660 £361**

SYBRAND VAN BEEST - A Village In
Winter with numerous figures on the ice
- on panel - 18 x 22½in.
(Christie's) **$13,650 £7,500**

A. BEGEYN - Goats By A Tree - 10½ x
14½in.
(Christie's) **$756 £420**

K. A. BEHENNA - Young Girl With
Kimono, Fan And Flowers - oil - 10 x 6in.
(G. A. Key) **$27 £15**

A. D. BELL - Fishing Boats Leaving
Harbour - watercolour - 10 x 14in.
(G. A. Key) **$54 £30**

ABRAHAM-HENDRIK VAN BEESTEN -
The Proposal For The Hand Of Sarte Jans;
and The Discovery Of Jan Claesz - both
signed and dated 1764 - 18¾ x 25¼in.
(Christie's) **$7,644 £4,200 Pair**

BELLE - Portrait Of A Gentleman, wearing
a brown velvet coat, standing, half length,
leaning on a stone ledge - 35 x 27in.
(Sotheby's) **$576 £320**

BELLINI

B. BELLOTTO - The Grand Canal, Venice, looking North-West from the Palazzo Corner to the Palazzo Contarini degli Scrigni - 19 x 26in.
(Christie's) **$6,300 £3,500**

BELLUCCI - Putti Presenting A Bas-Relief Of Charity - a sketch, paper - on canvas - arched top - 15¾ x 9½in.
(Christie's) **$468 £260**

GIOVANNI BELLINI, (and Studio) - The Madonna And Child With A Donor, a curtain and landscape beyond - signed - on panel - 33 x 26¾in.
(Christie's) **$108,000 £60,000**

ANTONIO BELLUCCI - A Woman Feeding A Dog - 28 x 21½in.
(Christie's) **$2,340 £1,300**

W. VON BEMMEL - An Italianate Landscape with peasants laundering - 19 x 15in.
(Christie's) **$810 £450**

THOMAS C. S. BENHAM - By The Bridge - signed and dated 1880 - canvas laid on panel - 15¼ x 19¼in.
(Sotheby's Belgravia) **$90 £50**

B. BELLOTTO - The Grand Canal, Venice, with the Rialto Bridge from the South - 21 x 28½in.
(Christie's) **$6,300 £3,500 Pair**

FRANK MOSS BENN - The Tobacco Seller - signed and dated 1938 - on board - 14 x 19½in.
(Christie's) **$624 £320**

ALFRED H. BENNETT - On The Sands, Mouth Of Conway, North Wales - inscribed, signed and dated 1888 - 19½ x 29½in.
(H. Spencer & Sons) **$540 £300**

F. M. BENNETT - Portrait Of An Eighteenth Century Gentleman - 29½ x 24½in.
(Sotheby's Belgravia) **$81 £45**

FRANK MOSS BENNETT - The Hunt Breakfast - signed and dated 1929 - on board - 13½ x 19¾in.
(Christie's) **$682 £350**

FRANK MOSS BENNETT - The Coachman's Story - signed and dated 1934 - 15¼ x 20½in.
(Christie's) **$6,240 £3,200**

FRANK MOSS BENNETT - The Ace Of Hearts - signed and dated 1922 - 13½ x 19¾in.
(Christie's) **$780 £400**

FRANK MOSS BENNETT - The Next Campaign - signed and dated 1928 - 14½ x 20½in.
(Christie's) **$682 £350**

GODWIN BENNETT - Figures By Ruins On The Nile - signed - heightened with bodycolour - 10½ x 14¾in.
(Sotheby's Belgravia) **$18 £10**

T. CAMPBELL BENNETT - Figure On A Road with Norwich Cathedral in background - watercolour - 5 x 7in.
(G. A. Key) **$27 £15**

WILLIAM BENNETT - The Deer Forest At Chatsworth - inscribed - 24¾ x 37¾in.
(Sotheby's) **$684 £380**

AMBROSIUS BENSON - The Madonna And Child with the Infant Baptist and two music making angels - on panel - 65 x 46in.
(Christie's) **$11,700 £6,500**

BENTABOLE

LOUIS BENTABOLE - View Of A Harbour Mouth with a paddle steamer and other shipping - signed and dated (18)58 - 16 x 22½in.
(Sotheby Bearne)   **$936 £480**

G. F. BENTLEY - "Near Betws-y-Coed, North Wales," a landscape with lake and figures in foreground, cottage and mountains in the distance - signed and dated 1872 - oil on canvas - 12 x 22in.
(H. C. Chapman & Son) **$234 £130**

E. BENVENUTI - Venetian Canals - both signed - watercolour - 6½ x 14½in.
(Sotheby's)   **$351 £190 Pair**

JOSEPH AUSTIN BENWELL - The Caravan - signed and dated 1878 - watercolour heightened with white - 22 x 15½in.
(Christie's)   **$468 £260**

JOSEPH AUSTIN BENWELL - The Head Of The Caravan - signed and dated 1880 - watercolour and body-colour - 12½ x 10in.
(Christie's)   **$756 £420**

JOSEPH AUSTIN BENWELL - Arabs Watering Their Camels By Ruins - signed and dated 1877 - pencil and watercolour heightened with white - 11 x 19in.
(Christie's)   **$360 £200**

JEAN BERAUD - La Pecheuse Parisienne - signed - on panel - 12 x 8in.
(Christie's)   **$576   £320**

BERCHEM - A Landscape With Peasants - pen and grey ink, grey wash - 31.1 x 22.9cm.
(Christie's)   **$108   £60**

BERCHEM - An Italianate Landscape with figures by a cascade and a town beyond - 49 x 38in.
(Christie's)   **$990 £550**

NICOLAES BERCHEM, Manner of - A Hunting Party By A Fountain - on panel - 22¼ x 21¼in.
(Christie's N. York)   **$605 £331**

NARCISSE BERCHERE - Ruined Temples With Buffalo Watering - signed - 33 x 48in.
(Christie's)   **$3,060 £1,700**

NARCISSE BERCHERE - A Camel Train Resting - signed - on panel - 10 x 14½in.
(Christie's)   **$1,620 £900**

BERGAMASQUE SCHOOL, About 1800 -
Design For The Decoration Of A Spandrel
With Saint John The Evangelist - pen and
brown ink, brown wash - 19.7 x 18cm.
(Christie's) **$153 £85**

ALFRED BERGSTROM - Path Through
A Forest - signed and dated 1901 - 66 x
46cm.
(Goteborgs Auktionsverk) **$1,543 £857**

FRANCESCO BERGAMINI - The Village
Schoolroom - signed and inscribed Roma -
oil - on canvas - 16 x 25in.
(Bonham's) **$2,520 £1,400**

DIRCK VAN BERGEN - A Wooded River
Landscape with peasants, cattle and sheep
by an urn, mountains beyond - bears signature - 14¾ x 18½in.
(Christie's) **$2,700 £1,500**

J. BERNARD - Two Classical Beauties
on a terrace - signed - on board - 22 x
14in.
(Phillips, Solihull) **$3,515 £1,900**

53

BERNARD

LOUIS MICHEL BERNARD - The Carpet Seller - signed - on panel - 22½ x 17in.
(Christie's) $900 £500

LOUIS MICHEL BERNARD - Arabs Gathered Round A Scribe In Tunis - signed - on panel - 22½ x 17in.
(Christie's) $270 £150

BERTRAND - A Trompe-L'Oeil of an engraving of Florence, drawings and playing cards - signed, dated 1767, inscribed and with dedication to John Dawson Esq. - pen and black ink, grey wash and watercolour - 32.5 x 45.5cm.
(Christie's) $252 £140

BALTHASAR BESCHEY - Putti With Spinning Tops in a wooded landscape - on panel - 13 x 10½in.
(Christie's) $2,520 £1,400

BETTERA - Still Lives Of Musical Instruments And Books on draped tables - both octagonal - 27 x 28in.
(Christie's) $9,000 £5,000 Pair

H. BETTERIDGE - A Donkey Ride - signed - 16 x 19½in.
(Sotheby's Belgravia) $39 £22

WILLIAM ROXBY BEVERLEY - Making For A Port, Heavy Weather Coming On - signed and inscribed on the reverse - 22¼ x 33¼in.
(Sotheby's) $540 £300

JAN DE BEYER - A Moated Chateau with figures on a foot bridge - pen and brown ink, watercolour - 13.7 x 21.0cm.
(Christie's) $180 £100

BIBIENA - Palatial Interiors: Stage Designs - one inscribed 'Bibiena' on the mount - pen and brown ink, grey and green wash - 26.2 x 15.0cm.
(Christie's) $90 £50 Pair

BIDDLE - A Still Life Of Flowers - bears a signature - 17½ x 23¼in.
(Sotheby's Belgravia) $63 £35

LAWRENCE BIDDLE - Still Life Of Pansies With A Japanese Ivory Carving - signed and dated '26 - on board - 9½ x 13½in.
(Sotheby's Belgravia) $810 £450

WILLIAM REDMORE BIGG - Portrait Of A Young Girl With Her Dog, full length, standing in a garden, a small pavilion beyond - 28¾ x 24¼in.
(Sotheby's) $900 £500

WILLIAM REDMORE BIGG - Portrait Of Langton Denshire, aged 15 - signed, inscribed and dated January 1791 on the reverse - painted oval - 29½ x 24in.
(Christie's) **$1,350 £750**

WILLIAM REDMORE BIGG, after - Arrest by Bailiffs; and The Father Released - coloured mezzotints - 45.5 x 60 cm
(Sotheby's Belgravia) **$99 £55 Pair**

JACOBUS BILTIUS - A Dead Hare, A Hunting Horn, A Game Bag and dead birds on a marble ledge - signed and dated 1659 - 37½ x 30½in.
(Christie's) **$3,420 £1,900**

TONY BINDER - Camel Drivers in the desert - signed - watercolour - 9¾ x 14¼in.
(Christie's) **$126 £70**

H. H. BINGLEY - Off To The Fishing Grounds; Thames Barges; Off Dover; Out Into The West - all signed - watercolour - 4 x 7in.
(Sotheby's Belgravia) **$234 £130 Four**

PETER BINOIT - Bunches Of Grapes In A Wan Li Kraak Porcelain Bowl, and bread and a knife on a pewter plate on a draped table - on copper - 20 x 27½in.
(Christie's) **$12,600 £7,000**

FELICE FORTUNATO BIGGI - Roses, Tulips and other flowers in a basket on a stone ledge - 27½ x 34½in.
(Christie's) **$7,200 £4,000**

BILBIE - Full-Length Portrait Of A Young Fair-Haired Girl, seated on a carved Jacobean chair - oil - on canvas - 37 x 29in.
(Neales of Nottingham) **$177 £95**

MAX BILL - Gelber Kern - signed twice and dated 1959-69 on the reverse - 22½in. diameter.
(Christie's) **$4,026 £2,200**

A. G. BIRCH - Still Life Mixed Fruit and an ewer and table - signed and dated - oil - on canvas - 14 x 18in.
(Butler & Hatch Waterman) **$58 £30**

BIRCH

DAVID BIRCH - A Crofter's Cottage
On The Coast - signed - on board -
8 x 10¼in.
(Sotheby's Belgravia) $72 £40

WILLIAM MINSHALL BIRCHALL -
Beatty's Battle Cruisers - signed -
inscribed and dated 1917 - heightened
with bodycolour - 8¼ x 12in.
(Sotheby's Belgravia) $45 £25

WILLIAM MINSHALL BIRCHALL -
Battle Of The River Plate - signed -
inscribed - heightened with bodycolour - 9½ x 13½in.
(Sotheby's Belgravia) $45 £25

D. BIRD - Nelson Directing The Fleet -
oil - 20 x 24in.
(G. A. Key) $18 £10

BISCAINO - The Adoration Of The Child
- pen and brown ink, brown wash - 31.6
x 20.6cm.
(Christie's) $90 £50

BARTOLOMEO BISCAINO -
Belshazzar's Feast - 30¾ x 22in.
(Christie's) $4,680 £2,600

DE BISSCHOP - View Of A Castle -
pen and brown ink, brown wash - 10.5
x 17.7cm.
(Christie's) $324 £180

ABRAHAM BISSCHOP - A Peacock,
Poultry And A Magpie In A Landscape -
signed and dated 1720 - 34½ x 35¼in.;
and A Goose, A Kingfisher And Other
Birds In A Landscape - 31 x 30¾in.
(Christie's) $6,370 £3,500 Two

ROGER BISSIERE - Sur Fond Noir -
signed and dated '57 - gouache and
watercolour - 16¾ x 21in.
(Christie's) $2,013 £1,100

JOSEPH BLACKBURN - Portrait Of An
Officer, three-quarter length, wearing
uniform, standing in a wooded landscape
- signed and dated 1773 - bears inscription
- 48½ x 39in.
(Christie's) **$2,520 £1,400**

EUGENE DE BLAAS - Study Of A
Young Woman - signed and dated 1887 -
watercolour - 34.0 x 24.2cm.
(Christie's) **$270 £150**

ANDREW BLACK - Dunnottar Castle -
signed - 15½ x 23½in.
(Sotheby's Belgravia) **$135 £75**

ANDREW BLACK - A Scottish
Fishing Village - signed - 29½ x 50in.
(Sotheby's Belgravia) **$864 £480**

THOMAS BROMLEY BLACKLOCK -
Picking Wild Flowers - signed and
dated 1901 - 17½ x 13½in.
(Sotheby's Belgravia) **$108 £60**

JOHN BLAIR - Children Fishing A Burn -
signed and dated 1878 - heightened with
bodycolour - 15 x 12¼in.
(Sotheby's Belgravia) **$180 £100**

BLAIR

JOHN BLAIR - A Scots Boy By A
Wooded Burn - signed - indistinctly
dated - heightened with bodycolour -
15¾ x 12¼in.
(Sotheby's Belgravia)   **$180 £100**

E. BLAIR-LEIGHTON - 'The Rose Arbour'
- signed and dated 1909 - oil - on board -
14 x 10in.
(Bonham's)   **$1,170 £650**

BENJAMIN BLAKE - A Pantry Still Life
including partridges, a snipe, a cock pheasant
and a hare - 13¼ x 17¼in.
(Sotheby's)   **$306   £170**

PETER BLAKE - Post Card, 1961 - on
board - 48 x 29¾in.
(Christie's)   **$18,300 £10,000**

PETER BLAKE - Woman In The Window,
1962 - mixed media - 44½ x 48¾ x 14in.
(Christie's)   **$15,555 £8,500**
PETER BLAKE - Lime Grove Baths - signed,
titled and dated January 31st, '61 - pencil
on paper - 4½ x 7in.
(Sotheby's)   **$549 £300**

WILLIAM BLAKE - Saul Confronted By The Vision Of Abraham Summoned By The Witch Of Endor - pencil - recto; Saul in Anguish as Abraham appears - pencil - verso - 6¼ x 9½in.
(Sotheby's) $1,656 £920

PETER BLAKE - Monochrome Gold Painting - signed and dated 1959 on the reverse - oil and gold leaves on panel - 19¾ x 18in.
(Christie's) $1,555 £850

RALPH ALBERT BLAKELOCK - A Mountain Stream at sunrise - oil - on canvas - 15½ x 23½in.
(Sotheby's) $2,316 £1,200

HENRI-JOSEPH VAN BLARENBERGHE - A Market Scene - a girl offering onions to a man standing by a barrow, to the left a woman at a vegetable stall being paid by a lady with a maid, other market women in the background - signed - on panel - 5¼ x 6½in.
(Sotheby's) $5,550 £3,000

PETER BLAKE - Postcard - signed - inscribed and dated 1968 - 24 x 15½in.
(Christie's) $1,372 £750

CHARLES BLATHERWICK - A Moorland Landscape - signed and dated 1872 - 23 x 35¼in.
(Sotheby's Belgravia) $54   £30

DIRCK BLEKER, Attributed to The Rape Of Europa - 20¼ x 25½in. *(Christie's N. York)* **$935 £511**

DAVID JOSEPH BLES - The Love Letter - signed - on panel - 12½ x 16¼in. *(Christie's)* **$3,600 £2,000**

JABEZ BLIGH - Mushrooms In A Basket; and Holly - both signed - watercolour heightened with white - 8¼ x 11¼in. and smaller. *(Christie's)* **$126 £70 Pair**

ALBERT BLIGNY - A Despatch From The Front - signed - on panel - 10 x 15¼in. *(Christie's)* **$756 £420**

THOMAS BLINKS - Hounds In A Churchyard 'Sanctuary' - signed and inscribed - watercolour - 14½ x 21½in. *(Heathcote Ball & Co)* **$238 £130**

THOMAS BLINKS - Over The Ditch - signed - 34½ x 48½in. *(Christie's)* **$6,300 £3,500**

THOMAS BLINKS - A Greyhound with a dead hare in an extensive landscape - signed - 35½ x 47½in. *(Christie's)* **$1,560 £800**

HENDRICK BLOEMAERT - A Woman Stealing Money From A Man At A Table - signed and dated 1632 - 49½ x 39½in. *(Christie's)* **$15,470 £8,500**

BLOEMAERT - An Allegorical Figure
With A Palm - grey wash - 23.5 x
16.4cm.
(Christie's)   **$81   £45**

VAN BLOEMEN - Travellers Near Roman
Ruins - black and red chalk - pen and
brown ink, grey wash, watermark - 29.2
x 38.8cm.
(Christie's)   **$216   £120**

BODDINGTON

JAN FRANS VAN BLOEMEN called
Orizzonte - An Italianate Garden with
figures by a classical urn - 38 x 28½in.
(Christie's)   **$4,320 £2,400**

H. FABER BLUHM - The Cross And The
Crescent - signed and dated 1879 - 27½ x
35½in.
(Christie's)   **$6,300 £3,500**

A. VAN BLYENBERCH - Portrait Of
Ben Jonson, standing three-quarter
length by a desk, wearing black costume
and holding a petition - 50 x 40in.
(Christie's)   **$2,520 £1,400**

FAUSTINO BOCCHI - The King And
Queen Of The Dwarfs In A Procession
To A Shrine - 28¼ x 39in.
(Christie's N. York)   **$3,520 £1,923**

E. H. BODDINGTON - Thames Scenes -
signed - oil - on canvas - 12 x 24in.
(D. M. Nesbit & Co.) **$579 £300 Pair**

61

BODDINGTON

EDWIN H. BODDINGTON - An Extensive Wooded River Landscape with cows - signed and dated 1865 - 11¾ x 21¾in.
(Christie's) **$576 £320**

EDWIN HENRY BODDINGTON - An Extensive Wooded River Landscape with figures and horses and cattle beyond - signed - 20 x 32in.
(Christie's) **$2,160 £1,200**

BODEN - Eel Catchers' huts on the Wensum behind Norwich Cathedral - watercolour - 10 x 13in.
(G. A. Key) **$50 £28**

GABRIEL BODENEHR, L'AINE - A Cavalry Skirmish - signed with monogram - grey wash heightened with white on blue paper - 27.1 x 42.0cm.
(Christie's) **$54 £30**

FREDERICK E. BODKIN - Coverack - signed - inscribed and dated 1886 - canvas - on board - 15½ x 29¼in.
(Sotheby's Belgravia) **$171 £95**

BOEL - River Scenes - on board - 9¼ x 15¼in.
(Sotheby's Belgravia) **$81 £45 Pair**

J. A. BOEL - Scottish River Scenes - signed with monogram - on board - 11½ x 6¾in.
(Sotheby's Belgravia) **$45 £25 Pair**

PIERRE LE BOEUFF - Continental Town Scenes - signed - watercolour - 15¼ x 11¼in.
(Brown & Merry) **$108 £60 Pair**

SEBASTIAAN THEODORUS VOORN BOERS - A Still Life With Grapes, Plums And Apples In A Basket By A Silver Ewer, With Figs And Other Fruit On A Ledge - signed - 17½ x 14½in.
(Christie's) **$1,620 £900**

FRANK MYERS BOGGS - Grand Camp - signed, inscribed and dated 1896 - watercolour - 10 x 15in.
(Sotheby's) **$328 £170**

WILLIAM BOISSEVAIN - "River In A Western Landscape" - oil - on board - 60 x 85.5cm.
(Australian Art Auctions) **$629 £346**

FRANCOIS BOITARD - Diana Parleying With Marine Deities - inscribed - pen and grey ink - 54.8 x 82.5cm.
(Christie's) **$396 £220**

GIOVANNI BOLDINI - La Place Pigalle, Paris - on board - 5½ x 5in.
(Christie's) **$1,800 £1,000**

H. BOLLONGIER - Tulips And Other Flowers in a vase, and insects on a ledge - on panel - 8½ x 6½in.
(Christie's) **$10,010 £5,500**

BOLOGNESE SCHOOL, 17th century - A Seated Peasant Covering His Eyes - indistinctly inscribed - red chalk - 17.0 x 18.8cm.
(Christie's) **$63 £35**

JOHANNES BOMAN - Still Life - signed with monogram and dated 1653 - oil - on panel - 35¼ x 32in.
(Bonham's) **$13,800 £7,500**

WILLIAM JOSEPH J. C. BOND - Figures Outside An Inn - signed - on board - circular - 5¼in. diameter.
(Sotheby's Belgravia) **$162 £90**

WILLIAM JOSEPH J. C. BOND - The Old Mill - signed - 19¾ x 23¾in.
(Sotheby's Belgravia) **$1,080 £600**

BONINGTON

R. P. BONINGTON - Shipping off the
Dutch Coast - 5 x 8½ in.
(Sotheby's) **$630 £350**

WALTER BOODLE - Borth Stream, N.
Wales - signed - 23½ x 17½in.
(Sotheby Bearne) **$185 £95**

E. C. BOOTH - Lowtide; Fisherfolk,
Scarborough - signed - inscribed and
dated 1891 - 10½ x 13¾in.
(Sotheby's Belgravia) **$86 £48 Pair**

SAMUEL LAWSON BOOTH - A Hill
Stream - signed and dated 1897 - 23½ x
35½in.
(Sotheby's Belgravia) **$180 £100**

JAN TER BORCH - A Young Artist
Drawing By Candlelight - signed with
monogram dated 1634 - 37 x 49½in.
(Christie's) **$36,400 £20,000**

EDWARD BOREIN - Mexican Cowboys
Driving Cattle Across An Arid Plain -
signed - watercolour, heightened with
bodycolour - 14½ x 19¾in.
(Sotheby's) **$9,650 £5,000**

EDWARD BOREIN - Cowboys Patrolling
A Herd Of Cattle - signed - watercolour -
15 x 19½in.
(Sotheby's) **$9,264 £4,800**

EDWARD BOREIN - Indian Chiefs
Carrying Ceremonial Standard riding
past wigwams - signed - watercolour,
heightened with bodycolour - 13¼ x
19¼in.
(Sotheby's) **$14,475 £7,500**

EDWARD BOREIN - A Mexican Rider
On His Palamino Horse - signed - watercolour, heightened with bodycolour -
15 x 18½in.
(Sotheby's) **$8,685 £4,500**

REV. WILLIAM BORLASE - The West View Of St Michael's Mount In Cornwall - signed with initials - inscribed and dated June 22 1738 - pencil, pen and black ink - 11 x 18½in.
(Sotheby's) $792 £440

J. BOSE - A Swan On A Woodland Pool - signed - black chalk, grey wash heightened with white - 28.4 x 26.4cm.
(Christie's) $72 £40

AMBROSIUS BOSSCHAERT THE YOUNGER - A Still Life Of Shells - on panel - 10¼ x 14in.
(Sotheby's) $9,250 £5,000

AMBROSIUS BOSSCHAERT THE YOUNGER - A Still Life Of Roses, Tulips and other flowers in a glass vase on a stone ledge - bears monogram - on panel - oval - 11 x 7½in.
(Christie's) $54,600 £30,000

AMBROSIUS BOSSCHAERT THE ELDER - A Rose, Iris, Tulips, Lily Of The Valley And Other Flowers In A Wan Li Bottle Jar on a ledge with a lizard and other insects - on copper - 12 x 8¾in.
(Christie's) $46,800 £26,000

BALTHASAR VAN DEN BOSSCHE - A Sculptor's Studio - signed and dated 1711 - 24¼ x 19in.
(Sotheby's) $5,475 £3,500

65

BOTERO

FERNANDO BOTERO - Il Nuncio - signed and dated - 56¼ x 46in.
(Christie's N. York) **$19,800 £11,000**

ANDREAS BOTH, Attributed to - Outside The Tavern - oil - on wood - 21.5 x 17cm.
(Christian Rosset) **$720 £400**

JAN BOTH, Manner of - A Wooded Italianate Landscape, with cattle and muleteers on a road - on panel - 18¼ x 21½in.
(Christie's N. York) **$770 £421**

GIOVANNI BOTTANI - The Migration Of Jacob - 37½ x 52½in.
(Christie's) **$5,460 £3,000**

BOUCHARDON - A Woman With A Tambourine - red chalk - 52.0 x 36.0cm.
(Christie's) **$117 £65**

BOUCHER - Venus And Cupid - 42¼ x 40¼in.
(Christie's) **$5,040 £2,800**

BOUCHER - Studies Of Hands - red and white chalk on grey paper - 25.1 x 18.0cm.
(Christie's) **$50 £28 Two**
BOUCHER - A Woman Attacked By A Man - red chalk, squared - 21.0 x 15.5cm.
(Christie's) **$50 £28**
BOUCHER - An Allegory Of Victory - black and white chalk - oval - 22.0 x 25.2cm.
(Christie's) **$153 £85**

FRANCOIS BOUCHER - An Italianate River Landscape with a ferry, country folk on a jetty, washerwomen nearby and a bridge beyond - grisaille - 21½ x 24in.
(Christie's) **$9,100 £5,000**

FRANCOIS BOUCHER - Head Of A Woman - signed - black stone with white highlights on blue paper - 19.5 x 18.5cm.
(Christian Rosset) **$2,160 £1,200**

BOUCKHORST - Revellers - pen and brown ink, brown wash, watermark - 20.9 x 31.3cm.
(Christie's) **$58 £32**

BOURDON

SAM BOUGH - "Morning, East Coast" - on board - 9½ x 15in.
(Morphets of Harrogate) **$405 £225**

PIERRE BOUDET - The Lieutenancy at Honfleur - signed and dated '69 - oil - 46 x 61cm.
(Christian Rosset) **$1,464 £800**

BOUDEWIJNS - Cavalry And A Wagon in a dune landscape - red chalk, watermark - 17.3 x 29.5cm.
(Christie's) **$117 £65**

ADRIAEN FRANS BOUDEWIJNS - A Wooded Landscape - a packman and another resting at the junction of two roads, a farm in the background - on panel - 8½ x 9¼in.
(Sotheby's) **$8,325 £4,500**

E. BOUDIN - The Beach Party - oil - 7 x 10in.
(G. A. Key) **$118 £66**

EUGENE-LOUIS BOUDIN - Four Large Ships Aground at low tide with horse-drawn wagon on the flats in the foreground - signed - oil - on canvas - 12¾ x 18½in.
(Richard A. Bourne Co. Inc.) **$31,000 £17,222**

SAMUEL BOUGH - A Distant View Of Edinburgh - signed - on board - 14 x 21½in.
(Sotheby's Belgravia) **$864 £480**

SAMUEL BOUGH - A Sunny Day In Iona - signed and dated 1871 - 32½ x 55½in.
(Sotheby's Belgravia) **$6,300 £3,500**

SAMUEL BOUGH - Muir O'Ord, Inverness-shire - signed and dated 1856 - heightened with white - 6¾ x 10¼in.
(Sotheby's Belgravia) **$90 £50**

WILLIAM ADOLPHE BOUGUEREAU - A Portrait Of The Model Antonia, small bust length, wearing Italian costume - bears inscription and the date 1875 - a sketch - paper laid down on canvas - 6 x 4¼in.
(Christie's) **$198 £110**

S. BOURDON, (After Poussin) - The Holy Family On The Steps - 15½ x 19½in.
(Christie's) **$3,060 £1,700**

BOURGAIN

GUSTAVE BOURGAIN - British Soldiers
In An Arab Market Place - signed and
signed on stretcher - 60 x 100in.
(Christie's) **$1,530 £850**

JAMES BOURNE - The Church At
Pulverback, with a girl on a path in
the foreground - signed and inscribed
on the reverse - pencil and watercolour - 9½ x 14in.
(Sotheby's) **$234 £130**

PIETER BOUT - A Wooded River Landscape with sportsmen resting by a
ruined monastery - 16 x 22½in.
(Christie's) **$8,100 £4,500**

FREDERIK BOUTTATS - Orpheus
Charming The Animals - on panel -
12¾ x 23¼in.
(Christie's) **$3,420 £1,900**

ANTOINE BOUVARD - A Venetian Canal
Scene - signed - 18¾ x 25in.
(Christie's) **$720 £400**

AUGUST BOUVARD - Venetian Canal
Scenes - signed - 18 x 24in.
(Christie's S. Kensington)
$4,680 £2,600 Pair

P. BOUYAPT - Gypsies Resting - 31 x
51cm.
(Edmiston's) **$558 £310**

BOWKETT - Head Study Of A Girl -
on board - 8 x 5¼in.
(Sotheby's Belgravia) **$25 £14**

ALICE BOYD - Hatton Smithy, May Day -
signed - inscribed and dated 1878 -
heightened with bodycolour - 11¾ x
17¾in.
(Sotheby's Belgravia) **$117 £65**

ALICE BOYD - An Elder Tree - signed
with monogram - inscribed - heightened
with bodycolour - 17¾ x 12in.
(Sotheby's Belgravia) **$32 £18**

THEODOR BOYERMANS - The Conversion Of Saint Paul - pen and brown and
grey ink, grey wash, octagonal - 14.2
x 13.2cm.
(Christie's) **$171 £95**

BOYLE - Figure Carrying Basket
In Wooded Landscape - oil - 17 x 11in.
(G. A. Key) **$72 £40**

THOMAS SHOTTER BOYS - A Distant
View of Notre Dame, Paris - Stormy
Weather - 6¾ x 9¾ in.
(Sotheby's) **$1,476 £820**

HERCULES BRABAZON BRABAZON -
A Study in Venice - pencil and watercolour heightened with white - 6½ x 9½
in.
(Sotheby's)   **$504   £280**

HERCULES BRABAZON BRABAZON -
The Steps Of The Great Mosque,
Kairouan, Tunisia - signed with initials
and inscribed on reverse - watercolour
and bodycolour - 6¾ x 9½in.
(Christie's)   **$324   £180**

LEONARD BRAMER - A Witch Fighting
With Demons - signed with an initial -
12 x 17¾in.
(Sotheby's)   **$2,775   £1,500**

THOMAS SHOTTER BOYS - Near The
Tuileries Gardens overlooking the Pont
de la Concorde towards L'Assemblee
Nationale, the Dome of Les Invalides in
the distance - signed and dated 1832 -
13¾ x 9½in.
(Sotheby's)   **$18,900   £10,500**

HERCULES BRABAZON BRABAZON -
On The Grand Canal, Venice - signed with
initials - pencil and watercolour heightened
with bodycolour on grey paper - 10 x 13½in.
(Sotheby's)   **$990   £550**

HERCULES BRABAZON BRABAZON -
A Street Scene In Cairo - signed with
initials and inscribed Cairo on the
reverse - watercolour and bodycolour -
9 x 6½in.
(Christie's)   **$576   £320**

ANTONIETTA BRANDEIS - The Castel
Dell'Ovo, Naples - signed with monogram -
8½ x 12½in.
(Christie's)   **$900   £500**

BRANDOIN - Figures Near An Italian
Lake - pen and brown ink and water-
colour - 18.3 x 26.7cm.
(Christie's)   **$108   £60**

BRANDOIN - A River Landscape In
Switzerland - pen and grey ink and
watercolour - 28.0 x 41.8cm.
(Christie's)   **$81   £45**

BRANGWYN - An Incident In The
Bazaar - bears monogram, and signature
on the reverse - on panel - 9¾ x 12¼in.
(Christie's)   **$216   £120**

BRANGWYN - Arab Musicians - bears
initials - 13 x 19in.
(Christie's)   **$252   £140**

ALFRED DE BREANSKI - The Kirk At
Arrochar, N.B. - signed - 30 x 50in.
(Lawrence) **$4,320 £2,400**

FRANK BRANGWYN - A Dockside Scene
- initialled and inscribed London 1900 -
oil - on canvas - 50 x 40in.
(King & Chasemore) **$2,700 £1,500**

ALFRED DE BREANSKI - "The
Tummel At Sunset", river and mountain
landscape - signed - 16 x 22in.
(Morphets of Harrogate) **$846 £470**

ADAM BRAUN - A Bacchante Reclining
Under A Canopy, in a landscape - signed
and dated 1805 - on copper - 17¼ x
23¼in.
(Christie's N. York) **$550 £300**

ALFRED DE BREANSKI - The Hills Of
Callander - signed and signed and inscribed
on the reverse - 19½ x 29¼in.
(Christie's) **$4,290 £2,200**

J. DE BRAY - Portrait Of A Lady, bust
length, wearing a dark dress with lace
collar and cap - on panel - shaped top
- 21½ x 15½in.
(Christie's) **$1,980 £1,100**

ALFRED DE BREANSKI - Cattle
Watering Near Snowdon, Wales -
signed - 29 x 49½in.
(Christie's) **$1,530 £850**

ALFRED DE BREANSKI - The Hills
Of Arran - signed on reverse - 23¼ x
35¼in.
(Christie's) **$99 £55**

ALFRED DE BREANSKI - A Highland
Loch Landscape with cattle watering -
signed - 23½ x 25½in.
(Christie's) **$3,120 £1,600**

ALFRED DE BREANSKI, SEN - 'Loch Awe from Brander' - signed and signed and inscribed on the reverse - 23¼ x 35¼in.
(Sotheby Bearne) **$2,880 £1,600**

ALFRED FONTVILLE DE BREANSKI - Evening On A Perthshire Loch - signed - 19½ x 29½in.
(Sotheby's Belgravia) **$1,530 £850**

ALFRED DE BREANSKI, SEN - 'The Vale Of Llangollen' - signed - 23¼ x 35½in.
(Sotheby Bearne) **$756 £420**

ALFRED DE BREANSKI, SEN - Ben Ledi - signed - inscribed and dated on the reverse - 15½ x 23¼in.
(Sotheby's Belgravia) **$1,530 £850**

ALFRED FONTVILLE DE BREANSKI - 'Autumn Evening', Burnham Beeches; and 'Early Morning', Clieveden - signed - 11¼ x 15¼in.
(Sotheby Bearne) **$2,047 £1,050 Pair**

GUSTAVE DE BREANSKI - Hay Barges - signed - 15½ x 23½in.
(Sotheby's Belgravia) **$207 £115**

JOSEPH VAN BREDAEL, Circle of - An Extensive Landscape, with peasants dancing by a ruin, numerous other figures, cattle and sheep, and a town beyond - 42½ x 67in.
(Christie's N. York) **$1,430 £781**

ALFRED DE BREANSKI, SEN - Evening At Invergarry - signed - inscribed on the reverse - 15½ x 23¼in.
(Sotheby's Belgravia) **$1,260 £700**

71

BREDAEL

KAREL VAN BREDAEL - A Cavalry
Engagement By A Tower - 15½ x 19¼in.
(Christie's) **$2,700 £1,500**

BARTHOLOMEUS BREENBERGH -
Landscape With Women Bathing - signed
in monogram - on panel - 6 x 9in.
(Sotheby's) **$9,250 £5,000**

**QUIRINGH GERRITSZ. VAN
BREKELENKAM** - Interior With A Lady
And Gentleman Drinking - inscribed - on
panel - 17¾ x 33¼in.
(Sotheby's) **$11,100 £6,000**

Q. V. BREKELENKAM, After - Woman
With A Jug, seated in an interior - on
panel - 18 x 13¾in.
(Sotheby's) **$144 £80**

JOHANN GEORG MEYER VON BREMEN -
Waiting For Supper - signed and dated 1851 -
12 x 9in.
(Christie's) **$1,170 £650**

THOMAS W. BRETLAND - A Bay
Hunter And A Chestnut Hunter in a
landscape - signed, inscribed and dated
Nottingham 1852 - 27 x 39in.
(Christie's) **$1,530 £850**

JOSEPH VAN BREYDEL - A Wooded
River Landscape with ferryboats and a
town beyond; and A River Landscape
with numerous figures by a quay,
ferries and a ruin nearby - 12¼ x 17in.
(Christie's) **$9,900 £5,500 Pair**

HARRY BRIGHT - Monkey Island:
many monkeys in XIX century costume,
river and trees in the distance - signed -
19 x 27in.
(H. Spencer & Sons) **$360 £200**

FREDERICK LEE BRIDELL - 'Belaggio
Rock, Lake Como' - signed and dated
1863 - oil - on canvas - 30 x 54in.
(Bonham's) **$4,680 £2,600**

HENRY BRIGHT - An Extensive Hilly
Landscape In Wales, with a figure by
a cottage - signed - 12¼ x 22¼in.
(Christie's) **$1,657 £850**

FREDERICK ARTHUR BRIDGMAN -
A Visit From The Chieftain - signed -
21 x 18in.
(Christie's) **$5,760 £3,200**

GIOVANNI FRANCESCO BRIGLIA -
Portrait Of A Gentleman, three-quarter
length, wearing a brown coat, with a
gold embroidered waistcoat, seated, his
arm resting on a book - inscribed 'Per
Anna Briglia' - dated 1768 - 44½ x
33½in.
(Christie's) **$1,620 £900**

FREDERICK ARTHUR BRIDGMAN -
Pouring Coffee - signed - 14 x 18in.
(Christie's) **$3,420 £1,900**

PAUL BRIL - A Cattle Market Among
Roman Ruins - copper - 8½ x 11¾in.
(Sotheby's) **$23,125 £12,500**

BRIL

BRIL - Romantic Landscapes With Cliffs and distant cliffs - pen and brown ink, brown wash, heightened with white - 29 x 21.8cm. and smaller.
(Christie's) **$396 £220 Two**

P. BRIL - The Temple Of Vesta And Santa Maria In Cosmedin, Rome - inscribed - pen and brown ink, brown wash - 18.3 x 30.3cm.
(Christie's) **$198 £110**

PHILIPP HIERONYMUS BRINKMANN - Haman Before Esther And Ahasuerus - signed with initials - on panel - 13 x 15½in.
(Christie's) **$2,700 £1,500**

E. E. BRISCOE - Axmouth Church And Village Church Scene - pencil - 10 x 14in. and 9 x 13in.
(G. A. Key) **$18 £10 Pair**

EDMUND BRISTOW - The Stubborn Donkey - signed and dated 1829 - 25¾ x 32in.
(Christie's) **$7,200 £4,000**

EDMUND BRISTOW - The Bone Of Contention - signed - on panel - 12 x 14in.
(Sotheby's Belgravia) **$828 £460**

CHARLES BRITTAN - 'Black Tor', Princetown - signed - watercolour - 12 x 14in.
(Hussey's) **$130 £72**

RICHARD HENRY BROCK - A Cottage At Shipworth - signed and inscribed on the reverse - on board - 10¾ x 7¾in.
(Sotheby's Belgravia) **$153 £85**

RICHARD HENRY BROCK - Cottages At Comberton And Teversham, Cambridgeshire - signed with initials - inscribed on the reverse - on board - 7¼ x 11¼in.
(Sotheby's Belgravia) **$414 £230 Two**

RICHARD HENRY BROCK - A Farmhouse At Haslingfield; Cottages At Triplow, Cambridgeshire - signed with initials - inscribed on the reverse - on board - 7 x 11¼in.
(Sotheby's Belgravia) **$414 £230 Pair**

JOHN LAMONT BRODIE - A Close Thing - signed and dated 1889 - 17½ x 23in.
(Sotheby's Belgravia) **$1,530 £850**

ELIAS VAN DEN BROECK - A Woodland Scene, with a snake devouring a lizard by a stream - signed - on canvas - on panel - 22¼ x 18½in.
(Christie's)   **$9,900 £5,500**

ELIAS VAN DEN BROECK - Poppies And Other Flowers in an urn, on a stone ledge - signed - 15½ x 12½in.
(Christie's)   **$8,640 £4,800**

ELIAS VAN DEN BROECK - Still Lifes Of Roses, Carnations And Other Flowers with lizards, snails and grasshoppers - both signed - 24 x 20in.
(Christie's)   **$21,840 £12,000 Pair**

W. BROMLEY - Three Children On River Bank Fishing, with wooded landscape, church and village in background - signed - oil - 18 x 24in.
(Richard Baker & Baker) **$2,880 £1,600**

PERCY BROOKE - Darwen Moor - signed - 9¾ x 13½in.
(Sotheby's Belgravia)   **$29 £16**

R. BROOKS - A group of figures under a tree at the edge of a village listening and watching whilst two gentlemen deep in conversation stand in front of them - signed and dated 1859 - 31 x 44in.
(H. Spencer & Sons)   **$1,170 £650**

H. BROOME - Sailing Vessels Offshore In A Breeze - signed and dated 1884 - canvas - on board - 19¼ x 29¾in.
(Christie's)   **$50 £28**

H. BROOME - Hulks And Sailing Vessels in a breeze - indistinctly signed - canvas - on board - 19½ x 29½in.
(Christie's)   **$1,620 £900**

ROBERT BROUGH - A Harbour Town - signed - grey wash, heightened with white - 3¾ x 4¾in.
(Sotheby's Belgravia)   **$14 £8**

A. BROUWER - A Man Reading - on panel - 7¼ x 6¼in.
(Christie's)   **$630 £350**

BROWER - An Archery Contest - oil - on panel - 15 x 19cm.
(King & Chasemore)   **$252 £140**

ARNESBY BROWN - 'Waiting To Hear The Result Of The Great Notts. v. Surrey Match, August 1892, in Nottingham' - signed - on panel - 8¾ x 9in.
(Elliott & Green)   **$302 £155**

CHARLES SIDNEY BROWN - A Faggot Gatherer Resting - signed - dated - on board - 11½ x 9¼in.
(Sotheby's Belgravia)   **$54 £30**

BROWN

J. MICHAEL BROWN - The Peat Gatherers - signed - 15½ x 23½in.
(Sotheby's Belgravia) **$864 £480**

JOHN BROWN - Portrait Of A Man, bust length, in half profile to the left - pencil - 23 x 16¾in.
(Christie's) **$540 £300**

JOHN BROWN - Portrait Of William Murray - inscribed on the reverse - pencil - oval - 20 x 16in.
(Sotheby's) **$72 £40**

MAYNARD BROWN - 'Spring' - signed - 23 x 16in.
(Sotheby Bearne) **$684 £380**

R. WOODLEY BROWN - A Wooded River Scene - signed and inscribed - dated 1851 on the reverse - 19½ x 23½in.
(Sotheby's Belgravia) **$234 £130**

KENNETH GEORGE BROWNE - Study Of A Negro, bust length - signed and dated Inings '44 - coloured chalks - 22½ x 17½in.
(Christie's) **$27 £15**

KENNETH GEORGE BROWNE - Study Of An Arab, bust length, from Desert Patrol, Arab Legion - signed and dated Amman '45 - coloured chalks - 23 x 18½in.
(Christie's) **$135 £75**

KENNETH GEORGE BROWNE - Askari Aid Kalid Of The Arab Legion Of Transjordan - signed and dated Amman '45 - inscribed on a label on the reverse - coloured chalks on brown paper - 17 x 18in.
(Christie's) **$108 £60**

KENNETH GEORGE BROWNE - Study Of Burnous - Tripoli - signed and inscribed - watercolour - 10 x 7¼in.
(Christie's) **$63 £35**

ABRAHAM BRUEGHEL, Attributed to - Grapes, Peaches, A Melon, Cherries, and other fruit in a landscape - 28 x 36in.
(Christie's N. York) **$6,600 £3,606**

J. BRUEGHEL, THE ELDER - A Village By A River with numerous figures, wagons, and a city in the distance - on panel - 12 x 18½in.
(Christie's) **$58,240 £32,000**

JAN BRUEGHEL, THE YOUNGER - A Windmill On A River with moored sailing boats and numerous figures - on copper - 6 x 8½in.
(Christie's) **$34,200 £19,000**

JAN BRUEGHEL II - Country Folk Dancing By A River - inscribed - on paper - 6 x 7¾in.
(Sotheby's) **$22,200 £12,000**

JAN BRUEGHEL, THE YOUNGER - A Village By A River with peasants, horses and carts on a road and figures on a ferry - on copper - 6 x 8½in.
(Christie's) **$14,400 £8,000**

JAN BRUEGHEL, THE YOUNGER - A Wooded Landscape with peasants in a cart on a track and cottages beyond - signed with initial - on copper - 7 x 5¾in.
(Christie's) **$43,680 £24,000**

JAN BRUEGHEL, THE ELDER - An Extensive Wooded Landscape with travellers on a path - on copper - 7 x 5¾in.
(Christie's) **$34,580 £19,000**

BRUEGHEL

JAN BRUEGHEL, THE ELDER - A Village with travellers and peasants at an inn - bears signature - on copper - 7 x 10¼in.
(Christie's)   **$99,000   £55,000**

PIETER BRUEGHEL, THE YOUNGER - A Wedding Procession in an extensive landscape - 55½ x 110¼in.
(Christie's)   **$54,600   £30,000**

PIETER BRUEGHEL, THE YOUNGER - Flemish Proverbs Illustrated In A Village Landscape - indistinctly signed and dated 1610 - 45 x 64¼in.
(Christie's)   **$162,000   £90,000**

PIETER BRUEGHEL, THE YOUNGER, Circle of - The Wedding Feast - 43½ x 76¼in.
(Christie's N. York)   **$2,200   £1,202**

G. BRUSAFERRO - The Deposition - black chalk, pen and grey ink, grey wash - 45.0 x 25.1cm.
(Christie's)   **$180   £100**

FRANCOIS BRUNERY - The Cardinal's Pet - signed - 17½ x 14½in.
(Christie's)   **$3,960   £2,200**

MME. ELISE BRUYERE - Portrait Of A Lady, half length, wearing a mauve dress - signed, and signed with initials - 28½ x 23¼in.
(Christie's)   **$1,080 £600**

HENRY CHARLES BRYANT - In The Farmyard - signed with initials and dated 1874 - on panel - 5 x 4in.
(Sotheby's Belgravia) **$179 £95**

ADAM BUCK - Girl In White Dress Sitting With Red Book - signed and dated 1828 - 8¾ x 7¾in.
(Sotheby's)   **$900 £500**

JOHN BUCKLER - Entrance to Cockermouth Castle, Cumberland - inscribed, signed and dated 1809 - 7½ x 5½ in.
(Sotheby's)   **$90 £50**

JOHN CHESSELL BUCKLER - Radford Abbey Gate, Nottinghamshire - inscribed, signed and dated 1813 - 8 x 12 in.
(Sotheby's)   **$162 £90**

C. F. BUCKLEY - Feeding The Swans - signed and dated 1867 - 13½ x 20¾in.
(Sotheby's Belgravia) **$129 £70**

FELIX BUHOT - Scene At Rotterdam With Fishing Boats; and Scene At The Old Hotel De Ville Ypres - watercolour - 25 x 15in.
(G. A. Key)   **$126   £70 Pair**

GERHARD BUKKERTI - Fruit On A Draped Table - signed and inscribed M - on board - 28 x 37in.
(Christie's) **$684   £380**

GEORGE LAWRENCE BULLEID - Springtime - signed and dated 1906 - 11¾ x 8in.
(Sotheby's Belgravia) **$324   £180**

RALPH BULLOCK - Pointers In Landscapes - both signed - dated '95 and '98 - 12½ x 18½in.
(Sotheby's Belgravia)   **$810 £450 Pair**

BURGARITZKY

HENRY WILLIAM BUNBURY - Horror At The Nurse's Arrival - pencil and watercolours, recto - 10 x 6¾in.
(Sotheby's)   **$72   £40**

JOHN WHARLTON BUNNEY - Holy Tintern, On The Wye, Monmouthshire - signed and dated - heightened with bodycolour - arched top - 21½ x 16¾in.
(Sotheby's Belgravia) **$117   £65**

HENDRICK VAN DER BURCH - Interior Of A Guardroom - on panel - 16¼ x 16in.
(Sotheby's)   **$5,920 £3,200**

JOSEPH BURGARITZKY - A Torrent In A Wooded Landscape - signed - 27 x 21¾in.
(Christie's)   **$900 £500**

BURNEY

EDWARD FRANCIS BURNEY - Designs for Decorations incorporating the signs of the zodiac and the constellations - pen and black ink and watercolour - 29¾ x 51½ in.
(Sotheby's) **$5,040 £2,800**

JOHN BURR - Grace Before Meat - signed and dated '82 - watercolour, heightened with bodycolour - 12 x 7½in.
(Sotheby's Belgravia) **$216 £120**

JAMES BURRELL - Fishing Vessels Offshore In A Choppy Sea - signed and dated 1868 - 29½ x 49½in.
(Christie's) **$234 £130**

BURRINI - The Adoration Of The Shepherds, the ox and ass emerging from a vault below - pen and brown ink, brown wash - 21.5 x 19.0cm.
(Christie's) **$99 £55**

ROBERT BURROWS - Figures By A Lake, Moonlight - signed - on panel - circular - 7½in. diameter.
(Sotheby's Belgravia) **$468 £260**

ROBERT BURROWS - On The Coast - signed with monogram - on board - 3¾ x 7¼in.
(Sotheby's Belgravia) **$76 £42**

AMES BURTON - A Chip Off The Old Block - signed and dated 1908 - inscribed on the reverse - 17½ x 23¼in.
(Sotheby's Belgravia) **$540 £300**

SIR FREDERICK WILLIAM BURTON - Portrait Of Miss Helen Faucit, late Lady Martin, wife of Sir Theodore Martin - signed with initials - inscribed - dated 1845 - 14½ x 11¼in.
(Sotheby's Belgravia) **$76 £42**

T. BURTON - Donkey With Goats In A Stable - signed - 14½ x 19¼in.
(Sotheby's Belgravia) **$81 £45**

BYRD

GIOVANNI BATTISTA BUSIRI - A Ruined Fortress - inscribed 'Gio Francesco' - black chalk, pen and brown ink - 19.2 x 26.0cm.
(Christie's) $90   £50

GIOVANNI BATTISTA BUSIRI - The Campo Vaccino, Rome - bodycolour - 22.5 x 33.2cm.
(Christie's) $900   £500

E. BUTLER - Wooded River Landscape With Figure Fishing And Children Nearby - oil - 34 x 42in.
(G. A. Key) $130   £72

THOMAS BUTLER - The Great Carriage Race - signed and inscribed 'Pall Mall, London' - 57½ x 95in.
(Sotheby's) $12,600   £7,000

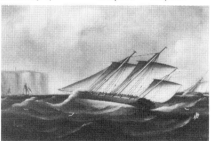

THOMAS BUTTERSWORTH - Boats In Heavy Seas - signed - oil - on canvas - 41 x 52cm.
(King & Chasemore) $1,176   £600

THOMAS BUTTERSWORTH - A British Man-Of-War And Other Shipping Off The Coast in choppy seas - signed - 17¼ x 23½in.
(Sotheby's) $1,890   £1,050

THOMAS BUTTERSWORTH - A Pilot Boat Sailing To Meet An Incoming Vessel off Dover; and A Pilot Boat Returning - signed - oil - on canvas - 14 x 18in.
(Bonham's) $6,840   £3,800 Pair

JACOB BUYS - A Woman Playing Patience - pen and brown ink and watercolour - 30.3 x 24.5cm.
(Christie's) $432   £240

PETER BYRD - A Coach And Four In The Snow - signed - heightened with bodycolour - 14¼ x 20in.
(Sotheby's Belgravia) $180   £100

81

IPPOLITO CAFFI - On A Venetian Canal - bodycolour - 16.5 x 13.0cm.
(Christie's) £110

M. CAFFI - Flowers In A Vase - 19¼ x 15in.
(Sotheby's) $10,175 £5,500

HECTOR CAFFIERI - Mother And Child seated by a window - signed - watercolour - 20 x 13¾in.
(Sotheby Bearne) $546 £280

W. W. CAFFYN - A Weedy Corner, Chilworth Pond, Surrey - 12 x 16in.
(G. A. Key) $79 £44

WALTER WALLOR CAFFYN - A Barge Moored By A House - signed and dated 1884 - 7½ x 11½in.
(Sotheby's Belgravia) $324 £180

JOHN CAIRNS - An Old Mill At Kilchrenan, Loch Awe - signed - inscribed and dated 1862 on the reverse - 17½ x 25in.
(Sotheby's Belgravia) $504 £280

SIR A. W. CALCOTT - Shipping Off A Continental Town, In Breezy Weather - 33½ x 52½in.
(Christie's) $72 £40

ALEXANDER CALDER - Sun And Moon, Birds In Space - signed and dated '63 - Indian ink and gouache - on paper - 29¾ x 21¼in.
(Sotheby's) $1,830 £1,000

CALLOW

ALEXANDER CALDER - Composition In Red, Black and Yellow - signed and dated '71 - gouache and Indian ink - 28¾ x 108in.
(Sotheby's) **$1,647 £900**

ALEXANDER CALDER - Landscape - signed and dated '65 - Indian ink and gouache - on paper - 29½ x 42½in.
(Sotheby's) **$1,830 £1,000**

PHILIP HERMOGENES CALDERON - 'The Betrayal' - oil - on panel - 38 x 28cm.
(King & Chasemore) **$396 £220**

WILLIAM FRANK CALDERON - A Hunt Terrier in an interior - signed and dated 1909 - 27½ x 35½in.
(Christie's) **$63 £35**

ALEXANDER CALDER - In The Orchid Room - signed and dated '64 - gouache and Indian ink - on paper - 42½ x 29½in.
(Sotheby's) **$2,470 £1,350**

WILLIAM J. CALLCOTT - The Castle Knell, Ischia, with shipping vessels on a stormy sea - signed - 17¼ x 31¼in.
(Christie's) **$975 £500**

ALEXANDER CALDER - "Batanus" - signed and dated 1962 - gouache - on paper - 29½ x 41½in.
(Sotheby's) **$2,287 £1,250**

GEORGE CALLOW - Off Flamborough Head - signed and inscribed - heightened with bodycolour - 9½ x 18¼in.
(Sotheby's Belgravia) **$32 £18**

CALLOW

JOHN CALLOW - A Fresh Breeze Off
Sheerness - signed and inscribed - 29½
x 49½in.
(Christie's)   **$108 £60**

WILLIAM CALLOW - Arona On The Lago
Maggiore - signed and dated 1866 - 13½ x
19¾in.
(Sotheby's)   **$2,520 £1,400**

WILLIAM CALLOW - Dutch Sailing
Vessel off the Coast - inscribed and dated
Aug. 1851 - 9½ x 13½ in.
(Sotheby's)   **$360 £200**

WILLIAM CALLOW - A View Of A
Church, with figures in the foreground -
signed and dated 1853 - 9 x 13in.
(H. Spencer & Sons)   **$414 £230**

WILLIAM CALLOW - Teatro Marcello -
signed and dated Roma 1877 - 9½ x
13½in.
(Christie's)   **$45 £25**

WILLIAM CALLOW - Riverside with
wooden quay and cottages - inscribed and
dated 1852 - 10 x 14 in.
(Sotheby's)   **$540 £300**

WILLIAM CALLOW - Taking Down
Sails In Port - pencil, heightened with
red bodycolour and white chalk on
buff paper - 4½ x 7¼in.
(Sotheby's)   **$288 £160**

WILLIAM CALLOW - A Path By A
Lake, fisherman in the foreground -
signed - pencil and watercolour -
9¾ x 13¾in.
(Sotheby's)   **$360 £200**

FREDERICK CALVERT - Coastal Scene
with shipping in a choppy sea - signed -
17½ x 23½in.
(Sotheby Bearne)   **$1,560 £800**

CAMBIASO - A Naiad With A Scroll
Riding A Dolphin And Putti - pen
and brown ink, brown wash - 38.3
x 28.6cm.
(Christie's)   **$72 £40**

L. CAMBIASO - Christ Bound To The
Column - black chalk, pen and brown
ink, brown wash - 30.9 x 14.0cm.
(Christie's)   **$144 £80**

L. CAMBIASO - The Reposo - pen and
brown ink, brown wash - 24.4 x 35.3cm.
(Christie's)   **$180 £100**

SIR DAVID YOUNG CAMERON -
The Sphinx By Moonlight - signed -
47½ x 35½in.
(Christie's)   **$1,440 £800**

SIR DAVID YOUNG CAMERON -
Near Stirling - signed - 18¾ x 28½in.
(Sotheby's Belgravia)   **$1,260 £700**

SIR DAVID YOUNG CAMERON -
Portrait Of A Man Seated, half-length -
signed with initials - 29¼ x 24¼in.
(Sotheby's Belgravia) **$171 £95**

SIR DAVID YOUNG CAMERON -
Sunset In Morvern - signed -
inscribed on the reverse - 16½ x 21¼in.
(Sotheby's Belgravia) **$900 £500**

KATHERINE CAMERON - A Famous
Harper Passing by; There Were Twa
Sisters Sat in a bower; - signed and
inscribed - all heightened with bodycolour - three in one frame - 14½ x
37in.
(Sotheby's Belgravia) **$1,116 £620**

CAMPAGNOLA - A River Landscape -
pen and black ink - 16.7 x 30.3cm.
(Christie's) **$54 £30**

RAIMONDO CAMPANILE - Monks Saying
Office In The Convent Dei Capuccini,
Rome - signed - 53½ x 39in.
(Christie's) **$360 £200**

JOCHEM GOVERTSZ. CAMPHUYSEN -
A Wooded Landscape With A Ruin - on
panel - 14½ x 22¼in.
(Sotheby's) **$10,175 £5,500**

CANALETTO, School of - The Bacino,
Venice, with gondolas and shipping -
20½ x 34in.
(Christie's N. York) **$880 £481**

DUNCAN CAMERON - Harvest Time,
A Lowland Village - signed - 25 x 40in.
(Sotheby's Belgravia) **$990 £550**

CANALETTO

CANALETTO SCHOOL - Grand Palais et place St. Marc - oil - on canvas - 39 x 54cm.
(Christian Rosset)   **$1,103 £613**

GIOVANNI ANTONIO CANAL, IL CANALETTO - The Church Of The Redentore, Venice with figures and gondolas - 23 x 36½in.
(Christie's)   **$100,100 £55,000**

LOUIS CANE - Composition - signed and dated Juin 1974 on the reverse - water-colour - 19¾ x 19¾in.
(Christie's)   **$586 £320**

S. CANTARINI - The Penitent Magdalene - red chalk - 21.7 x 17.0cm.
(Christie's)   **$72 £40**

BARTOLOMEO CAPORALI, Attributed to - The Entombment - on ogival shaped panel - 15 x 21in.
(Christie's N. York)   **$2,090 £1,142**

J. VAN DE CAPPELLE - Fishing Vessels Offshore in a calm sea - bears initials - on panel - 13¼ x 12¼in.
(Christie's)   **$10,800 £6,000**

VINCENZO CAPRILE - The Old Guitar Player - signed - 38¾ x 26in.
(Christie's)   **$3,240 £1,800**

GIOVANNI CARACCIOLO, Attributed to - The Holy Family - oil - on copper - dated 1640 - 17 x 22cm.
(Christian Rosset)   **$360 £200**

CARMICHAEL

CONSALVE CARELLI - The Piazza, Piacenza - signed and dated 'Piacenza 1875' - watercolour - 35.5 x 43.5cm.
(Christie's) **$504 £280**

GABRIELE CARELLI - A Neapolitan Boat, Vesuvius in the distance. and Shipping In The Bay Of Naples - both signed - watercolour - 17.5 x 13.0cm. and 12.5 x 17.6cm.
(Christie's) **$324 £180 Two**

GONSALVO CARELLI - Peasants Escorting A Priest On A Donkey - signed - watercolour - 26.0 x 27.8cm.
(Christie's) **$396 £220**

E. CARENGHI - The Snuffing Of The Candles - signed - watercolour - on board - 29½ x 21in.
(Christie's) **$576 £320**

LUCA CARLEVARIJS - The Molo, Venice, with the Doge's Palace, the Library, the mouth of the Grand Canal and the Church of Santa Maria della Salute - 37 x 78in.
(Christie's) **$136,500 £75,000**

CARLO CARLONE - Mercury And A Personification Of The Arts - a sketch - canvas - on panel - 7½ x 11½in.
(Christie's) **$1,440 £800**

MARGHERITA CARFI - A Still Life - oil - on canvas - 24 x 29in.
(Bonham's) **$4,320 £2,400**

L. CARLEVARIJS - The Bacino Di San Marco, Venice with galleys and numerous gondolas - 39¼ x 86¼in.
(Christie's) **$87,360 £48,000**

J. W. CARMICHAEL - 'Coastal Scene' - 17 x 24in.
(Staniland's) **$774 £430**

JAMES WILSON CARMICHAEL - A Coastal Scene, with fishermen near a rowing boat in the foreground, sailing barges and merchant vessels anchored in the distance - 21 x 29in.
(H. Spencer & Sons) **$1,170 £650**

JOHN WILSON CARMICHAEL - Moro Castle, Cuba, with a merchantman and a fishing vessel off the coast - signed and inscribed - 38 x 53½in.
(Christie's) **$2,880 £1,600**

JOHN WILSON CARMICHAEL - Sailing Vessels Offshore in a choppy sea - on board - 11½ x 14½in.
(Christie's) **$1,657 £850**

87

CARMICHAEL

JOHN WILSON CARMICHAEL - Fishing Vessels In A Calm, off Port Texel - signed and dated 1865 - 23½ x 35½in.
(Christie's) **$9,360 £4,800**

JOHN WILSON CARMICHAEL - Shipping On The Solent - signed and dated 1866 - 23½ x 35½in.
(Christie's) **$4,320 £2,400**

JOHN WILSON CARMICHAEL - A Wooded Coastal Landscape with a frigate at anchor, and a town beyond - signed and dated 1859 - 12 x 18¼in.
(Christie's) **$2,535 £1,300**

JOHN WILSON CARMICHAEL - H.M.S. Charlotte, Superb, Impregnable, Minden, Albion, Granigus, Leander, Hebrus and other frigates in a choppy sea - signed - 19½ x 35½in.
(Christie's) **$5,760 £3,200**

GIULIO CARMIGNANI - A Wooded Marsh Landscape At Sunset, with peasants and cattle - signed and dated 1869 - 42½ x 58in.
(Christie's) **$7,200 £4,000**

JOHN WILSON CARMICHAEL - H.M. Frigate 'George' and fishing vessels off Tynemouth - signed and dated 1846 - 34 x 50in.
(Christie's) **$12,675 £6,500**

JOHN WILSON CARMICHAEL - Salvaging A Wreck By Saint Michael's Mount - signed - 19½ x 29½in.
(Christie's) **$4,290 £2,200**

UGO DA CARPI - The Apostles Striking Ananie to death for lying to Saint Pierre - cameo drawing - 24 x 30cm.
(Christian Rosset) **$164 £91**

CARRACCI - The Martyrdom Of Saint Lawrence - pen and brown ink, grey wash - 32.3 x 23.6cm
(Christie's) $99 £55

ANNIBALE CARRACCI, Circle of - Travellers In A Southern Landscape - 41½ x 53in.
(Sotheby's) $13,875 £7,500

H. B. CARTER - "York" - a moorland landscape with a stone cross - water-colour - 4¾ x 6¾in.
(Warner, Sheppard & Wade) $33 £17

HENRY BARLOW CARTER - A Breezy Day Near Scarborough, seascape with ships caught in a storm off the coast - signed - 25 x 39½in.
(H. C. Chapman & Son) $324 £180

HENRY BARLOW CARTER - Near Whitby - 6 x 8½in.
(Sotheby's) $270 £150

J. H. CARVE - A Ranch In The Outback At Sunset - signed and dated 1884 - oil - on canvas - 12½ x 19¼in.
(Sotheby's) $2,123 £1,100

CASENTINO

CARUS - A View Of A German Town, with soldiers in the foreground - on panel 8 x 12in.
(Christie's) $288 £160

JEAN CARZOU - Venetian Canal Scene - signed - oil - on board - 6½ x 11¼in.
(Richard A Bourne Co. Inc.) $350 £194

JACOPO DEL CASENTINO - A Bishop Saint; St. John The Evangelist - gold ground - on panel - arched tops - 28¾ x 13¾in.
(Sotheby's) $20,350 £11,000 Pair

CASISSA

N. CASISSA - A Still Life, A Lobster,
A Basket, Oranges, Fish And Fungi On
A Ledge - 17 x 22in.
(Christie's)   **$3,240 £1,800**

F. W. CASSELL - Trapped - signed
- on board - 6¼ x 11in.
(Sotheby's Belgravia)   **$90 £50**

J. CASSELL - Missed; Trapped - one
signed - 11½ x 23¼in.
(Sotheby's Belgravia)   **$86 £48 Pair**

H. CASSIERS - Dutch Winter Landscape
and Coastal Scene - 19.5 x 40.5cm.
(Edmiston's)   **$180 £100 Pair**

GUSTAVE CASTAN - Hilly Landscape -
signed - oil - on panel - 33 x 51cm.
(Christian Rosset)   **$997 £545**

P. CASTEELS - Still Life: Vase of flowers
- signed and dated '27 - oil - on canvas -
45½ x 35½in.
(Richard A Bourne Co. Inc.)
               $11,750 £6,528

CASTEELS - Two Swans In Combat,
a third looking on - pen and brown ink,
watermark - 21.2 x 34.4cm.
(Christie's)   **$58 £32**

PIETER CASTEELS - A Heron, Duck,
Kingfisher And Other Birds by a
plinth in a landscape - 39 x 37¾in.
(Christie's)   **$5,760 £3,200**

V. CASTELLO - The Vision Of Saint
Anthony Of Padua - 15¼ x 8½in.
(Christie's)   **$1,080 £600**

ALESSANDRO CASTELLI - Mediterranean Coastal View with group of
peasants in woodland landscape overlooking a bay with hills in the distance -
signed and dated 1863 - oil - 39 x 63in.
(Graves, Son & Pilcher) **$2,880 £1,600**

LAUREYS A. CASTRO - Dutch Men-O'-
War And Other Vessels in a harbour -
signed - 45 x 54¼in.
(Christie's)   **$3,600 £2,000**

F. CATARIO - An Arab Street Scene -
signed - watercolour - 19 x 11¼in.
(Christie's)   **$54 £30**

FRANCESCO CASTIGLIONE - The
Death Of Dido - 29 x 23½in.
(Christie's)   **$4,320 £2,400**

FRANCESCO CASTIGLIONE - A
Sacrifice To Ceres - 29 x 23½in.
(Christie's)   **$4,320 £2,400**

T. CHARLES H. CASTLE - Portrait Of
A Lady Seated, half length - signed,
black chalk - 19¼ x 15¼in.
(Sotheby's Belgravia)   **$45 £25**

CASTRO - A Coastal Landscape with
figures loading barrels on a jetty, a
galley and men-o'-war offshore - 43½
x 78½in.
(Christie's)   **$1,980 £1,100**

L. A. CASTRO - A Coastal View With
Numerous Figures and shipping - on
panel - 11 x 16½in.
(Christie's)   **$1,980 £1,100**

CHARLES CATTERMOLE - Choosing
Fine Rugs In An Arab Palace - signed
and dated 1862 - 11¾ x 16in.
(Sotheby's)   **$1,980 £1,100**

CHARLES CATTERMOLE - An
Eastern Lady Reclining On A Couch -
signed and dated - 7 x 12½in.
(Sotheby's)   **$900 £500**

CAULLERY

L. DE CAULLERY - The Triumphant
Entry Of A King - on copper - on
panel - 11¾ x 14¾in.
(Christie's)   **$17,100 £9,500**

GIACOMO CAVEDONI - Jacob Mourning
Joseph - 38 x 30¼in.
(Sotheby's)   **$3,700 £2,000**

LOUIS DE CAULLERY - The Siege Of
Troy - on panel - 19½ x 25½in.
(Christie's)   **$5,824 £3,200**

P. LA CAVE - The Mill Stream - watercolour - 68 x 96cm.
(King & Chasemore)   **$549 £280**

PETER LA CAVE - Rustics And Their
Horses By A Stream - signed - on panel -
7 x 10in.
(Sotheby's)   **$450 £250**

NEVILLE WILLIAM CAYLEY - Yellow
Chats And Orange Chats - signed - 14¼ x
10½in.
(Sotheby's)   **$309 £160**

NEVILLE WILLIAM CAYLEY - Kooka-
burras On A Branch - signed - watercolour -
21¼ x 16¾in.
(Sotheby's) **$232 £120**

NEVILLE WILLIAM CAYLEY - A Lyre
Bird Perched On A Branch - signed -
watercolour - 23 x 15¾in.
(Sotheby's) **$482 £250**

NEVILLE WILLIAM CAYLEY - Flame
Robins And Hooded Robins - signed -
14½ x 10½in.
(Sotheby's) **$386 £200**
J. P. CAZES - Christ Among The
Doctors - 23 x 19in.
(Christie's N. York) **$660 £361**
MICHELANGELO CERQUOZZI,
Manner of - Peasants Round A Fire In
Winter - 13½ x 10in.
(Christie's N. York) **$198 £108**
GIOVANNI DOMENICO CERRINI,
Circle of - Saint Louis Receiving
Tribute - 46¼ x 37in.
(Christie's N. York) **$440 £240**

G. CERUTI - A Pastry Seller and other
youths playing cards in a landscape -
57 x 76in.
(Christie's) **$10,010 £5,500**

FEDERIGO CERVELLI - Venus And
Cupid - 34 x 28½in.
(Christie's) **$2,700 £1,500**

PAUL CHAIGNEAU - Le Retour Du
Troupeau, Coucher De Soleil, Plaine De
Barbizon - signed - 18 x 21½in.
(Christie's) **$468 £260**

F. CHALLA - Hambledon Common And
Wareham - signed - oil - 6½ x 8½in.
(Heathcote Ball & Co) **$329 £180 Pair**

CHALLE - The Atrium Of The
Colosseum - pen and brown ink, brown
wash heightened with white on blue
paper - 24.8 x 38.7cm.
(Christie's) **$144 £80**

J. B. C. CHALLE - A Classical Capriccio -
pen and brown ink, brown wash - 21.0 x
26.4cm.
(Christie's) **$81 £45**

G. CERUTI - The True Philosophy;
and The True Medicine - both inscribed -
paper - on panel - 15 x 10½in.
(Christie's) **$1,170 £650 Pair**

CERUTI - Portrait Of A Gentleman
wearing a yellow striped jacket and
matching hat with a boy, half length -
40 x 35in.
(Christie's) **$1,350 £750**

GEORGE PAUL CHALMERS - The
Legend, a sketch for the interior - 24½ x
29¼in.
(Sotheby's Belgravia) **$630 £350**

EVELYN CAROLINE CHALMERS - Portrait Of A Lady Reading, half length - signed - 25 x 30in.
(Sotheby's Belgravia) **$11 £6**

GEORGE CHAMBERS - Sailing Ships Off The South Coast - 6½ x 11¼in.
(Sotheby's) **$504 £280**

GEORGE CHAMBERS - Robin Hood's Bay, Near Whitby - 23½ x 32in.
(Christie's) **$4,680 £2,400**

HENRY BERNARD CHALON - Portrait Of A Bay Hunter and groom in a landscape - signed and dated 1807 - 19½ x 24¼in.
(Sotheby Bearne) **$5,265 £2,700**

GEORGE CHAMBERS - Haybarges offshore in a choppy sea - signed - 27¼ x 35in.
(Christie's) **$4,290 £2,200**

JOHN JAMES CHALON - A Wooded River Landscape with boys bathing and haymaking beyond - signed and dated 1810 - 41¾ x 35½in.
(Christie's) **$2,520 £1,400**

MASON CHAMBERLIN - Portrait Of Mr. Denshire, seated half length, wearing a blue jacket, buff waistcoat - inscribed on an old label on the stretcher - 29½ x 24¼in.
(Christie's) **$990 £550**

GEORGE CHAMBERS - A Collier Brig And Other Shipping in a choppy sea off Whitby - 17¼ x 23¼in.
(Christie's) **$3,120 £1,600**

GEORGE CHAMBERS - Shipping off
Sheerness - 7¼ x 10¼ in.
(Sotheby's) **$1,530 £850**
HENRI CHANET - Young Innocence -
signed - 24 x 18in.
(Christie's) **$504 £280**

JAMES CHARLES - In The Hayfield -
signed - 34½ x 47½in.
(Christie's) **$1,980 £1,100**
JAMES CHARLES - Selsey Bill -
signed - inscribed - 3¼ x 10¾in.
(Sotheby's Belgravia) **$135 £75**

JOHN CHARLTON - Summer - signed
with initials - dated 1909 - coloured
chalks on buff paper - 21½ x 33¼in.
(Sotheby's Belgravia) **$108 £60**
J. B. C. CHATELAIN - Lake Bolsena -
pen and brown ink, grey wash - 18.0 x
26.4cm.
(Christie's) **$54 £30**

CHARLES CHAPLIN - Lilac: a study of
a girl - signed - 16¾ x 13¼in.
(Christie's) **$2,880 £1,600**
JOHN WATKINS CHAPMAN - The
Bankrupt - signed and dated 1875 - on
board - 15½ x 12½in.
(Christie's) **$54 £30**
F. CHARDON - An Italian Capriccio With
Fishermen And Other Figures On Horseback
and at the water's edge in the foreground,
temples and churches beyond, and sailing
vessels in the distance - signed - on panel -
6 x 10½in.
(H. Spencer & Sons) **$360 £200**
ADOLPHE CHARLEMAGNE - A Carriage
In St. Petersburg - signed and dated 1864 -
silverpoint and watercolour heightened
with white - 18.8 x 29.2cm.
(Christie's) **$468 £260**

**VINCENT JEAN BAPTISTE
CHEVILLIARD** - The Bishop's Portrait -
signed - watercolour - 34.4 x 44.2cm.
(Christie's) **$234 £130**
CHIARI - The Pieta With An Angel -
black chalk - 27.8 x 20.7cm.
(Christie's) **$117 £65**

CHINESE SCHOOL

GIUSEPPE CHIARI, Attributed to - The Holy Family - 19¼ x 14¾in. *(Christie's N. York)* **$1,100 £601**

CHINESE SCHOOL, 19th century - 'Chow Tai', A British Steamer underway off the coast - 17¼ x 23in. *(Sotheby's, Hong Kong)* **$457 £254**

CHINESE SCHOOL, circa 1780 - The Waterfront At Canton showing the Danish, Austrian, Swedish, British and Dutch flags, junks and sampans offshore - 17 x 29in. *(Sotheby's, Hong Kong)* **$5,404 £3,002**

CHINESE SCHOOL, circa 1840 - Junks At Anchor By A Folly Fort - 17½ x 22½in. *(Sotheby's, Hong Kong)* **$623 £346**

CHINESE SCHOOL, circa 1830 - The Waterfront At Canton with the American, British and Dutch flags - 9½ x 11¾in. *(Sotheby's, Hong Kong)* **$1,975 £1,097**

CHINESE SCHOOL, circa 1880 - The 'Star Of Russia', A British Clipper In Full Sail - 25½ x 35½in. *(Sotheby's, Hong Kong)* **$1,350 £750**

CHINESE SCHOOL, circa 1830 - A View Of Macao And The Praya Grande - 17½ x 22¾in. *(Sotheby's, Hong Kong)* **$1,143 £635**
CHINESE SCHOOL, 19th century - A Junk Under Sail Off The Coast - 17½ x 23in. *(Sotheby's, Hong Kong)* **$292 £162**

CHINESE SCHOOL, circa 1890 - A View Of Hong Kong And The Harbour with British Naval vessels and French and British merchant ships at anchor - inscribed 'Hong Kong' - 16 x 21½in. *(Sotheby's, Hong Kong)* **$2,808 £1,560**

CHINNERY

CHINNERY - A View Of Macao, showing Leal Senada, with the fort in the background, two figures in the foreground - 7¼ x 10in.
(Sotheby's, Hong Kong) **$311 £173**

G. CHINNERY - A View of Hong Kong, with a flag pole on Pedder's Hill in the middle distance - watercolour - 9 x 13¾ in.
(Sotheby's, Hong Kong) **$1,143 £635**

GEORGE CHINNERY - A Chinese Fisherman Standing On Rocks in front of the Citadel and Franciscan Fort, Macao - pen and brown ink and watercolour - 5¼ x 6¾in.
(Christie's) **$2,340 £1,300**

GEORGE CHINNERY - Studies Of A Chinese Scribe - inscribed with the artist's shorthand and dated twice October 21st, '42 - pencil, pen and brown ink - 6¼ x 9½in.
(Christie's) **$324 £180**

GEORGE CHINNERY - Portrait Of A Gentleman, small bust length, wearing a dark coat - 9¾ x 8¼in.
(Christie's) **$3,600 £2,000**

GEORGE CHINNERY - Portrait Of A Gentleman, seated, small three-quarter length, wearing a dark coat and yellow waistcoat - 11½ x 10in.
(Christie's) **$3,600 £2,000**

GEORGE CHINNERY - The Citadel And Franciscan Fort, Macao - inscribed with the artist's shorthand - pencil, pen and brown ink, brown wash - 7 x 10¾in.
(Christie's) **$990 £550**

GEORGE CHINNERY - Tanka Boats Off He'-Ang Shan - inscribed on the reverse and numbered 77 - pen and brown ink and watercolour - 4½ x 5¾in.
(Christie's)   **$2,700 £1,500**

GEORGE CHINNERY - Portrait Of Margaret Erskine, afterwards Margaret Walton, three-quarter length, seated on a settee with a red curtain and a landscape through a window behind - 15½ x 12¼in.
(Sotheby's, Hong Kong) **$9,353 £5,196**

GEORGE CHINNERY - A Tanka Boat Girl - inscribed on the reverse - 8 x 6¼in.
(Christie's)   **$3,240 £1,800**

GEORGE CHINNERY - 'Alloy', A Tanka Boat Girl - 11 x 14½in.
(Christie's)   **$2,520 £1,400**

GEORGE CHINNERY - Self-Portrait Of The Artist Seated, three-quarter length, holding a brush and palette, with a subsidiary study upper left - inscribed with the artist's shorthand and dated 1848 - pencil, pen and brown ink - 5 x 4¼in.
(Christie's)   **$4,320 £2,400**

CHINNERY

GEORGE CHINNERY - Portrait Of A Lady, seated three-quarter length, wearing a white dress - 15 x 12½in.
(Christie's) **$9,000 £5,000**

D. CHODOWIECKI - Profile Study Of A Woman With Elaborately Dressed Hair - pencil and red chalk - 22.0 x 14.6cm.
(Christie's) **$81 £45**

RENE LOUIS CHRETIEN - A Still Life With A Dead Duck, a copper bowl, a basket and apples on a table - signed - 12¾ x 16in.
(Christie's) **$270 £150**

JAMES ELDER CHRISTIE - Hot Tea - signed with monogram and dated '91 - 26 x 19½in.
(Sotheby's Belgravia) **$540 £300**

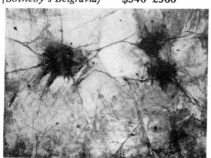

CHRISTO - Untitled - signed and dated 1960 - lacquered paper - 18 x 24½in.
(Christie's) **$915 £500**

CHRISTO - Packed Edition - signed and dated '63 - magasines, plastic and robe - 35¾ x 57¾in.
(Christie's) **$7,320 £4,000**

CHRISTO - Large Project For Valley Curtain - signed - titled - inscribed and dated - pencil, coloured chalks and coloured crayons - on paper - 35¾ x 60in.
(Sotheby's) **$12,810 £7,000**

CHRISTO - Untitled - signed and dated '60 - lacquered paper - 21¾ x 16¼in.
(Christie's) **$512 £280**

EMMA CIARDI - 'On The Garda Lake' - signed - oil - 18 x 22in.
(Hussey's) **$1,080 £600**

C. CIGNANI - Study Of A Putti With Upraised Arms - red chalk - 26.5 x 19.7cm.
(Christie's) **$108 £60**

CIGOLI - Studies For A Deposition - inscribed - black chalk - 18.2 x 27.7cm.
(Christie's) **$63 £35**

F. CIPOLLA - A North African Village
Square - signed and inscribed Roma -
16 x 23½in.
(Christie's)   **$900 £500**
CIPPER - An Old Lady, three-quarter
length, holding a candle - 31¼ x 25¼in.
(Christie's)   **$576 £320**
CIPPER - Portrait Of A Peasant Drinking
By Lamplight - 31¼ x 25¼in.
(Christie's)   **$360 £200**

P. CLAESZ. - A Peeled Lemon, A Ham,
Bread, A Bunch Of Grapes, An Upturned
Tazza And A Roemer On A Table - on
panel - 23 x 32½in.
(Christie's)   **$7,560 £4,200**

CIPRIANI - Children Depicted Representing
The Sciences Of Astronomy And Medicine -
30¾ x 45¾in.
(Sotheby's)   **$540 £300 Pair**
G. B. CIPRIANI - A Roman Emperor
Sacrificing In The Temple Of Vesta -
pen and grey ink, grey wash - 29.1 x
22.2cm.
(Christie's)   **$72 £40**
GIOVANNI BATTISTA CIPRIANI -
The Annunciation - black chalk -
16.9 x 15.0cm.
(Christie's)   **$58 £32**
GIOVANNI BATTISTA CIPRIANI -
Time And Beauty - red chalk - 22.5
x 17.3cm.
(Christie's)   **$99 £55**
PIER FRANCESCO CITTADINI, Manner
of - Portrait of a Lady in a red dress
holding a fan - 29 x 23½ in.
(Christie's, N. York)   **$440 £240**

PIETER CLAESZ. - A Still Life Of A
Crab, on a pewter plate, a basket of grapes,
a roemer, a salt, bread, a dish of olives and
lemons on a draped table - signed with
monogram and dated 1656 - on panel -
20 x 26½in.
(Christie's)   **$16,380 £9,000**

PIETER CLAESZ. - A Pewter Jug, A Bunch
Of Grapes, Peaches On A Plate, A Pie, And
A Roll With A Knife, A Parcel Gilt Spoon
And A Glass Of Wine On A Table Covered
With A White Cloth - signed with initials -
on panel - 18¾ x 27¼in.
(Christie's)   **$32,760 £18,000**

PIETER CLAESZ - A Still Life Of A Pewter Flagon, a pie on a pewter plate, a roemer, grapes, bread, a knife and a peeled lemon on a table - signed with monogram and dated 1632 - 16½ x 25in.
(Christie's) $145,600 £80,000

CLARE - Still Life Of Fruit In A Landscape - bears signature - on board - 6¾ x 9¾in.
(Sotheby's Belgravia) $58 £32

GEORGE CLARE - Apples, Gooseberries And Strawberries, on a mossy bank; and Blossom And A Bird's Nest by a mossy bank - both signed - 6 x 9in.
(Christie's) $1,260 £700 Pair

OLIVER CLARE - Still Life With Grapes, crab apples, strawberries on a mossy bank; and companion piece With Blossom, Mayflower and bird's nest - signed - oil - on canvas - 6 x 8in.
(Bonham's) $936 £520 Pair

GEORGE CLARE - Still Life Of Roses And Geraniums by a bank - indistinctly signed - signed on the reverse - 13½ x 21½in.
(Sotheby's Belgravia) $144 £80

OLIVER CLARE - Still Life Of Fruit On A Mossy Bank - signed and dated - 5½ x 8½in.
(Sotheby's Belgravia) $378 £210

OLIVER CLARE - Still Life Of Grapes, Peaches etc - signed and dated 1920 - oil - 14½ x 11½in.
(Phillips, Solihull) $784 £400

O. CLARE - Summer Fruits On A
Bank - oil - 14 x 10in.
(G. A. Key)   **$90 £50**

O. CLARE - Still Life Of Grapes, Strawberries And An Apple - bears signature -
8½ x 6½in.
(Sotheby's Belgravia)   **$117 £65**

OLIVER CLARE - Still Lifes Of Fruit
By Mossy Banks - signed - on board -
8¼ x 11in.
(Sotheby's Belgravia)   **$1,980 £1,100 Pair**

VINCENT CLARE - Primula And Lachen-
allia - signed - signed and inscribed on the
reverse - 17½ x 11½in.
(Christie's)   **$1,530 £850**

OLIVER CLARE - Still life with a bird's
nest and various flowers and grapes,
peach, greengages and other soft fruit
- signed - 9½ x 11½in.
(Sotheby Bearne)   **$1,620 £900 Pair**

VINCENT CLARE - Still Lifes Of
Fruit And Blossom - both signed -
10 x 12in.
(Sotheby's Belgravia)   **$2,520 £1,400 Pair**

103

CLARE

C. ALBERT CLARK - 'Pretty Polly', A Bay Filly in her stall - signed and dated 1905 - on canvas - 44 x 61cm.
(King & Chasemore)   **$288 £160**

J. CLARK - "Cats Cradle", study of two young children - canvas - 14 x 11in.
(Morphets of Harrogate)   **$594 £330**

VINCENT CLARE - Primulas, Violets, Blossom and a bird's nest on a mossy bank - signed - 11½ x 9½in.
(Christie's)   **$1,462 £750**

OCTAVIUS T. CLARK - River Landscapes - both signed - 19½ x 29½in.
(Sotheby's Belgravia)   **$1,170 £650 Pair**

ALBERT CLARK - 'Summering' - signed - 19 x 30in.
(Staniland's)   **$558 £310**

S. J. CLARK - A Farmyard Scene - bears a signature - 21 x 27¼in.
(Sotheby's Belgravia)   **$396 £220**

CLAUDE - A Mediterranean Seaport - pen and brown ink, brown wash - 18.5 x 25.6cm.
(Christie's)   **$54 £30**

ALBERT CLARK - Study Of A Short Horn Cow - signed - 50 x 61cm.
(King & Chasemore)   **$1,507 £810**

104

PIERRE DE CLAUSADE - An Extensive
Coastal Landscape, with three boats on
the shore - signed - 21¼ x 39¼in.
(Christie's)   **$810 £450**

H. CLAVEL - Tender Memories - signed -
18 x 26in.
(Christie's)   **$450 £250**

ROBERT CLEMINSON - On The Alert -
signed - 29½ x 25in.
(Sotheby's Belgravia)   **$198 £110**

ROBERT CLEMINSON - 19th century
Sporting Paintings of two setters on the
grouse moor; and two setters at the
edge of a copse awaiting pheasant to
fall to the ground - signed - oil on canvas
- 16 x 24in.
(H. C. Chapman & Son) **$396 £220 Pair**

HENDRICK DE CLERCK - The Infancy
Of Bacchus - on panel - 18½ x 24½in.
(Christie's)   **$14,400 £8,000**

HENDRICK DE CLERCK, Circle of - The
Feeding of the Five Thousand - 45 x 50 in.
(Christie's N. York)   **$880 £481**

JOOS VAN CLEVE, Manner of - Portrait
Of The Emperor Maxmillian Of Germany,
bust length, wearing the order of the
Golden Fleece - inscribed - on panel -
24¼ x 19in.
(Christie's N. York)   **$220 £120**

J. CLEVELEY - The Morning Gun At
Greenwich with sailing vessels and rowing
boats in the foreground - 33½ x 51¼in.
(Christie's)   **$7,560 £4,200**

JOHN CLEVELEY - A Marine Cutter
Towing A Dinghy and a man-o'-war
beyond - signed and dated 1773 - 13
x 16½in.
(Christie's)   **$5,040 £2,800**

105

CLEVELEY

JOHN CLEVELEY - Shipping Off The Needles, Isle of Wight - 5½ x 7½in.
(Sotheby's) $864 £480

DANIEL CLOWES - Coursing, a greyhound pursuing a hare - signed and dated 1814 - 19 x 23¼in.
(Sotheby's) $684 £380 ·

EDWARD JOHN COBBETT - The Reaper - signed and dated 1864 - on board - 17¾ x 14in.
(Christie's) $432 £240

FREDERICK SIMPSON COBURN - Winter Landscape with a logging team - signed and dated 1930 - oil - on canvas - 12 x 16in.
(Bonham's) $3,780 £2,100

LEONARDO COCCORANTE - Christ At The Pool Of Bethesda - 34½ x 46½in.
(Christie's) $3,240 £1,800

M. COCHRAN - Shipping Off The Coast - signed and dated 1859 - 12¼ x 15¼in.
(Sotheby's Belgravia) $117 £65

GEORGE COCKRAM - 'Llyn Ogwen' - signed - watercolour - card - 6½ x 10½in.
(Walker, Barnett & Hill) $63 £35

CODAZZI - Dido And Aeneas At Carthage - 37½ x 52¼in.
(Christie's) $1,710 £950

VIVIANO CODAZZI - An Architectural Cappricio with classical figures in the foreground and a lake beyond - signed with monogram and dated Roma 1665 - 37 x 52in.
(Christie's) $8,100 £4,500

J. COGHILL - By An Italian Lake - signed and dated 1893 - canvas laid on board - 13¼ x 19½in.
(Sotheby's Belgravia) $117 £65

A. B. COHEN - Reading A Letter - signed - 7½ x 9½in.
(Sotheby's Belgravia) $63 £35

GEORGE VICAT COLE - 'At Wargrave On Thames' - signed with monogram and dated 1876 - 23½ x 36in.
(Christie's) $2,340 £1,200

GEORGE VICAT COLE - 'Noon-day Rest' - signed with monogram - 22½ x 28½in.
(Sotheby Bearne) $1,764 £980

COLLINS

J. COLEMAN - Cottage Scenes - dated 1889 - watercolour - 12 x 9in.
(Andrew Hilditch & Son) **$29 £16 Pair**

GEORGE VICAT COLE - A Wooded River Landscape, with a figure and dog on a path and cattle watering - signed - 11½ x 9¾in.
(Christie's) **$180 £100**

EVERT COLLIER - A Vanitas Still Life with a Nautilus cup, a violin, a globe, a watch, and an open book resting against a lute on a draped table - inscribed - on panel - 19½ x 26½in.
(Christie's) **$10,440 £5,800**

GEORGE VICAT COLE - The End Of The Day - monogram and dated 1886 - oil - on canvas - 30 x 25in.
(Gribble, Booth & Taylor) **$3,780 £2,100**

GEORGE VICAT COLE - Arundel At Sunset - signed with monogram and dated 1873 - 22 x 36in.
(Christie's) **$36 £20**

A. COLLINS - The Sailing Ship 'Elizabeth' off our English port - oil - 27 x 40in.
(Bonham's) **$3,960 £2,200**

C. COLLINS - When The Tide Is Out - watercolour - 13 x 20in.
(G. A. Key) **$63 £35**

VICAT COLE - A River Tow Path with figures of children and barges - signed and dated 1880 - oil - 12 x 21in.
(Warner, Sheppard & Wade) **$4,312 £2,200**

CHARLES COLLINS - A Peacock, Chickens and other birds in a wooded landscape - signed and dated 1740 - 47½ x 49½in.
(Christie's) **$7,200 £4,000**

COLONIAL SCHOOL

COLONIAL SCHOOL, Early 19th century - Exterior Of A Javanese Palace with assembled troops and native ceremony in progress - watercolour - 16 x 21in.
(Christie's S. Kensington) **$396 £220**

COLONIAL SCHOOL, Attributed to Thomas Griffiths Wainewright - "Portrait Of A Colonial Lady" - crayon - oval - 46 x 37cm.
(Australian Art Auctions) **$540 £300**

CHARLES COMPTON - The First Parting - signed - inscribed on the reverse - 27 x 34in.
(Sotheby's Belgravia) **$900 £500**

EDWARD THEODORE COMPTON - Am Zeiger - signed with initials - inscribed and dated 1894 - heightened with bodycolour - 11¾ x 8½in.
(Sotheby's Belgravia) **$68 £38**

S. CONCA - A Capriccio: Mercury, Psyche And Cupid - on gold ground panel - 24¼ x 21½in.
(Christie's) **$2,002 £1,100**
CONDY - The Village Butcher's Shop - 13 x 11in.
(Sotheby's) **$252 £140**

NICHOLAS MATHEW CONDY - Study Of British Men-O'-War with other shipping - signed and dated 1836 - mill board - 11½ x 15¼in.
(Sotheby Bearne) **$4,680 £2,400**

NICHOLAS MATHEW CONDY - Coastal Scene, Plymouth, with British men-o'-war and fishermen in the foreground drawing a net - mill board - 11½ x 15¼in.
(Sotheby Bearne) **$5,265 £2,700**

GILLIS CONGNET - Mount Olympus - on panel - 33½ x 50in.
(Christie's) **$2,700 £1,500**

ALFRED CHARLES CONRADE - France - signed and dated 1918 - watercolour and bodycolour on grey paper - 33.5 x 29.0cm.
(Christie's) **$25 £14**

JOHN CONSTABLE - Flatford Mill From The Lock - inscribed and the date 1810 or 1811 - 10 x 12in.
(Christie's) **$99,000 £55,000**

JOHN CONSTABLE - In Richmond Park 1832 - watercolour sketch - 6 x 9in.
(H. Spencer & Sons) **$270 £150**

BENJAMIN CONSTANT - Favourites Of The Emir - signed and dated 1879 - 39 x 23½in.
(Christie's) **$6,840 £3,800**

BENJAMIN CONSTANT - 'Arab Desert Hunting Scene' - oil - on panel - 12 x 23¾in.
(Lalonde Bros. & Parham)
$2,379 £1,300

BENJAMIN CONSTANT - The Guard - signed - on panel - 17½ x 12in.
(Christie's) **$1,080 £600**

B. CONSTANT - Study Of A Seated Arab - 23½ x 19½in.
(Christie's) **$288 £160**

KAREL VAN CONTICH - The Way Home - signed and inscribed - oil - on canvas - 19 x 25¾in.
(Richard A Bourne Co. Inc.) **$700 £389**

HERBERT MOXON COOK - Moored Boats On An Estuary; By The Side Of A Loch - signed - one heightened with bodycolour - 7 x 19¾in.
(Sotheby's Belgravia) **$76 £42 Pair**

HERBERT MOXON COOK - On The Side Of A Lake - signed and dated 1880 - 6½ x 18¼in.
(Sotheby's Belgravia) **$50 £28**

JOHN COOK - On South Uist - signed - on board - 12½ x 14¾in.
(Sotheby's Belgravia) **$58 £32**

JOSHUA COOK, JUN - Still Life With Fruit - signed - 18¾ x 23¼in.
(Sotheby Bearne) **$162 £90**

COOK

M. T. C. COOK - That Orbed Maiden
With White Fire Laden - inscribed -
heightened with bodycolour and gold -
19½ x 16in.
(Sotheby's Belgravia)   **$50 £28**

E. W. COOKE - Figure On Horse and
other figures on seashore with yachts
in distance - oil - on panel - 10 x 14in.
(G. A. Key)   **$86 £48**

EDWARD WILLIAM COOKE - Portsmouth Harbour, a smack approaching a
hulk - signed and dated 1856 - inscribed
on the reverse - 14½ x 22½in.
(Sotheby's)   **$540   £300**

EDWARD WILLIAM COOKE - Interior
Of A Martello Tower, Pevensey, morning
after a capture of smugglers and their
tubs - signed - 16½ x 20¾in.
(Christie's)   **$720 £400**

EDWARD WILLIAM COOKE - A Traffic
Dahabeeah On The Nile - inscribed -
pencil and watercolour heightened with
white on blue paper - 9¼ x 13¾in.
(Christie's)   **$153 £85**

COOPER - Interior Scenes with figures
and Pets - signed - watercolour drawings -
9¾ x 13½in.
(J. Entwistle & Co.)   **$139 £77 Pair**

ABRAHAM COOPER - A Chestnut Racehorse With Jockey Up, in an open landscape - 27 x 35½in.
(Christie's)   **$5,760 £3,200**

ALFRED EGERTON COOPER - Epsom
Downs On Derby Day - signed - heightened with bodycolour - on grey paper -
11¼ x 14¼in.
(Sotheby's Belgravia)   **$36 £20**

J. COOPER - A Still Life Of Fruit,
including melon, grapes, peaches and figs -
indistinctly signed - 34½ x 49in.
(Sotheby's)   **$1,710 £950**

R. COOPER - By The Nile - signed - both
heightened with bodycolour - 10 x 14in.
(Sotheby's Belgravia)   **$22 £12 Pair**

T. S. COOPER - Cattle In A Farmyard -
bears signature and dated - 11½ x
15½in.
(Sotheby's Belgravia)   **$540 £300**

T. S. COOPER - Head Study Of A Cow -
on board - 6½ x 5¾in.
(Sotheby's Belgravia)   **$153 £85**

T. S. COOPER - Seven Huddled Sheep
On A Hillside, with storm clouds above
- dated 1874 - oil - 31 x 25½in.
(C. Wesley Haslam & Son)
     $1,125 £625

THOMAS SIDNEY COOPER - Sheep In A
Highland Landscape - signed and dated 1853
- watercolour - 19 x 27in.
(Christie's S. Kensington)   **$648 £360**

THOMAS SIDNEY COOPER - Three
Bulls in an extensive landscape - signed
and dated 1833 - on panel - 10¾ x 8¼in.
(Christie's)   **$81 £45**

THOMAS SIDNEY COOPER - Sheep
In An Extensive Landscape - signed
and dated 1865 - on panel - 7¾ x 12¼in.
(Christie's) **$396 £220**

THOMAS SIDNEY COOPER - Highland
Sheep Grouped On Hillside with rocky
craggs - signed - oil - on panel - 20 x
26½in.
(The Nottingham Auction Mart)
$2,798 £1,450

THOMAS SIDNEY COOPER - Sheep On
The Downs - signed and dated 1840 - on
canvas - 30 x 40cm.
(King & Chasemore) **$1,080 £600**

THOMAS SYDNEY COOPER - In
Canterbury Meadows: extensive landscape, six sheep rest near a pool while a
cow drinks, a herd grazes beyond under
a sky filling with rain clouds - signed
and dated 1893 - 17¾ x 24in.
(H. Spencer & Sons) **$1,224 £680**

THOMAS SIDNEY COOPER - Early
From Old Smithfield Market, 1832 -
signed and dated 1887 - 72 x 60in.
(Christie's) **$18,000 £10,000**

THOMAS SIDNEY COOPER - Sheep In
An Extensive Landscape - indistinctly
signed - 9½ x 15½in.
(Christie's) **$1,170 £650**

ADRIAEN S. COORTE - Asparagus And Red-
Currants On A Ledge - signed and dated 1696
- canvas - on panel - 12½ x 9in.
(Christie's) **$63,000 £35,000**

ALFRED CORBOULD - Returning From Her Majesty's Drawing Room - signed and dated 1853 - 19½ x 30in.
(Christie's) **$1,267 £650**

ADRIAEN S. COORTE - Wild Strawberries In A Bowl And Gooseberries On A Ledge - signed Corte and dated 1696 - canvas - on panel - 12½ x 9in.
(Christie's) **$63,000 £35,000**

GEORGES RICARD CORDINGLEY - Sundown At Sea - signed - dated - on panel - 14 x 26½in.
(Sotheby's Belgravia) **$342 £190**

JOHN CORDREY - The London-Coventry-Birmingham Royal Mail Fifteen Miles From London - signed and dated 1811 - 16¼ x 23½in.
(Christie's) **$2,700 £1,500**

FANNY CORBAUX - The Day Before Marriage - signed and dated 1849 - heightened with bodycolour - 14 x 10¼in.
(Sotheby's Belgravia) **$252 £140**

JOHN CORDREY - A Coachman and two bays with a curricle on a country road - signed and dated 1807 - oil - on canvas - 19 x 30in.
(Bonham's) **$3,420 £1,900**

CORNEILLE - The Good Samaritan -
pen and brown ink, grey and brown
wash - 27.4 x 18.2cm.
(Christie's)   **$90 £50**

PIERRE CORNU - Young Girl - signed -
oil - on canvas - 46 x 61cm.
(Christian Rosset)   **$1,025 £560**

CORREGGIO - The Madonna And Child
With Saint John The Baptist, the patron
of a town and a kneeling prelate -
inscribed 1525 - pen and brown ink,
brown wash - 32.7 x 23.8cm.
(Christie's)   **$72 £40**

ORESTE CORTAZZO - "The Banquet" -
on panel - 10 x 13in.
(Phillips, Solihull)   **$4,410 £2,450**

CORTONA - An Enthroned Emperor
And His Attendants Before A Portico -
black chalk, grey wash heightened with
white - 35.8 x 21.5cm.
(Christie's)   **$54 £30**

GIOVANNI COSTA - A Mediterranean
Coastal Landscape - on panel - 5½ x 9in.
(Christie's)   **$720£400**

GIOVANNI COSTA - A Mediterranean
Coastal Landscape with a peasant woman -
on panel - 8 x 14in.
(Christie's)   **$990 £550**

COSWAY - The Madonna And Child -
the mount inscribed followed by a
monogram - pen and brown ink, grey
wash - 19.1 x 14.4cm.
(Christie's)   **$117 £65**

PIERRE AUGUSTE COT - The Tambourine
Dancer - signed and dated 1873 - 83 x 44in.
(Christie's)   **$3,060 £1,700**

COTES

JOHN SELL COTMAN - The Castle Of Falaise - signed and dated 1820 - pen and brown ink, brown wash - 7¾ x 12in. *(Christie's)* **$810 £450**

FRANCIS COTES - Portrait Of Elizabeth Burdett, half length, wearing a floral dress, and blue ermine lined coat - 29½ x 24¼in. *(Christie's)* **$2,700 £1,500**

JOHN SELL COTMAN - A Gatehouse With Figures In The Foreground, a tower in the distance - signed in pencil and with initials - 8¼ x 6in. *(Sotheby's)* **$3,060 £1,700**

FRANCIS COTES - Portrait Of Dr. Connell, Husband Of Lady Philippa Hamilton, three-quarter length, wearing a blue coat and pink waistcoat, leaning against a tree - 49¼ x 39in. *(Christie's)* **$3,420 £1,900**

J. S. COTMAN - Church Interior - pencil drawing - 11 x 8in. *(G. A. Key)* **$43 £24**

JOHN SELL COTMAN - Boats Drawn Up By A Lake in a rocky highland landscape - signed and numbered 1470 - pencil and watercolour - 8½ x 12½in. *(Christie's)* **$2,700 £1,500**

JOHN SELL COTMAN - Clippersby Church, Norfolk - signed and numbered 466 - on buff paper - 7 x 10¾in. *(Sotheby's)* **$5,760 £3,200**

N. COUDY - View Of Coombe Cellar on the River Teiger - oil - on canvas - 28 x 22in.
(Butler & Hatch Waterman)
$1,320 £675

COURTOIS - The Aftermath Of A Battle - inscribed - black chalk, brown wash - 23.2 x 39.4cm.
(Christie's) $72 £40

J. COURTOIS - Horsemen Near A Fortified Bridge - black chalk - 19.4 x 26.6cm.
(Christie's) $90 £50

J. COURTOIS - A Cavalry Engagement - 16½ x 37in.
(Christie's) $1,350 £750

JACQUES COURTOIS, IL BORGOGNONE, Circle of - A Cavalry Battle - 48 x 50½in.
(Christie's N. York) $3,080 £1,683

JAN VAN COUVER - A Dutch River Estuary Scene With Shipping - signed - 23½ x 35½in.
(Christie's) $1,584 £880

ROBERT McGOWN COVENTRY - Quayside Fishing Boats - both signed - 14½ x 21½in.
(Sotheby's Belgravia) $720 £400 Pair

R. M. G. COVENTRY - Busy Harbour Scene - watercolour - 28 x 45cm.
(Edmiston's) $225 £125

LIONEL J. COWEN - Love's Letterbox - signed and dated '77 - 28 x 17½in.
(Christie's S. Kensington) $612 £340

WILHELM COWTH - The Toast - signed and dated 1889 - oil - on panel - 5¾ x 4¾in.
(Bonham's) $3,240 £1,800

DAVID COX - On the Shore near Calais - 6 x 8½ in.
(Sotheby's) $3,060 £1,700

DAVID COX - Bolton Woods, Yorkshire - signed and dated 1832 - 7¾ x 11in.
(Sotheby's) $2,340 £1,300

DAVID COX - Llanfair Church, N. Wales - inscribed on reverse - pencil and red chalk - 5¾ x 14¾in.
(Christie's) $198 £110

DAVID COX - Low Tide, Calais - signed and dated Oct. 22, 1834 - pencil and watercolour - 5 x 7in.
(Christie's) $2,520 £1,400

DAVID COX - A Young Boy Letting Hounds Off Their Leash below a castle - watercolour - 10¼ x 15¾in.
(Sotheby's) $576 £320

DAVID COX - Calais Pier - signed and dated 1831 - 8¾ x 12¼in.
(Sotheby's) $3,600 £2,000

DAVID COX - 'Kenilworth Castle' - figures on punt in river - signed - 8 x 10½in.
(Brooks) $558 £310

DAVID COX, JUN - A Landscape With Cows And A Village - signed and dated 1871 - watercolour - 33 x 53cm.
(King & Chasemore) $108 £60

DAVID COX, JUN - Border Farm, Adelaide's Seat, River Warfe, Yorkshire - oil - 14 x 17in.
(G. A. Key) $135 £75

D. COX - "Bolton Abbey", Yorkshire - signed - watercolour - 7¼ x 11¼in.
(Warner, Sheppard & Wade)
                                $1,029 £525

JACK COX - Ducks In Flight Over Marshes - oil - 20 x 30in.
(G. A. Key) $94 £52

R. G. COXON - A Scottish Trompe L'Oeil - signed and inscribed - 19¼ x 25½in.
(Sotheby's Belgravia) $396 £220

COYPEL - Venus And Adonis; and Venus And Mars - on copper - circular - 11¾in. diameter.
(Christie's) $2,700 £1,500 Pair

COYPEL - The Muses - three inscribed in French - black and red chalk - inscribed ovals - 17.4 x 14.2cm.
(Christie's) $1,368 £760 Four

COYPEL - A Nude Kneeling, His Wrists Tied - black and white chalk on blue paper - 32.1 x 20.8cm.
(Christie's) $63 £35

F. M. DE LA COZE - Shadows On The Water - signed - 21 x 28½in.
(Sotheby's Belgravia) $54 £30

ALEXANDER COZENS - A Classical Building By A Pool in a landscape - signed on the reverse - grey, black and brown wash - 6½ x 8½in.
(Sotheby's) $864 £480

ALEXANDER COZENS - Classical Buildings With A Mountain Behind - brown wash - 6¼ x 8¼in.
(Sotheby's) $540 £300

ALEXANDER COZENS - A Hill Top - signed - grey and brown wash - 8¾ x 12in.
(Sotheby's) $882 £490

JOHN ROBERT COZENS - Isola Bella, Lake Maggiore At Dusk, with figures in a boat covered with a striped awning approaching the island - 17¼ x 24¼in.
(Sotheby's) $41,400 £23,000

FRANCESCO COZZA, School of - Hagar And The Angel - 25 x 34in.
(Christie's N. York) $660 £361

CRAESBEECK - Peasants Eating And Drinking in an interior - on copper - 6½ x 8½in.
(Christie's) $1,116 £620

J. VAN CRAESBEECK - Tavern Interior With Numerous Figures Playing Cards, the domestics plucking poultry and cooking and with utensils, barrels and ewers loosely scattered - oil - 30 x 46in.
(Heathcote Ball & Co) $8,601 £4,700

WILLIAM MARSHALL CRAIG -
Powderham Castle on the Estuary of the
River Exe, Devon - signed - pencil and
watercolour - 11 x 15½ in.
(Sotheby's) $270 £150

WALTER CRANE - Eastern Broad -
signed with device - inscribed - dated
Sept. '86 - inscribed on the reverse -
6¾ x 10in.
(Sotheby's Belgravia) $72 £40

J. H. CRANSTOUN - Duchray Glen -
dated 1865 - oil - 16 x 24in.
(Thomas Love & Sons Ltd.)
                    $333 £185

EDMUND THORNTON CRAWFORD -
On The Thames - signed - 13¼ x 19¼in.
(Sotheby's Belgravia) $1,170 £650

W. CRAWHALL - The Thames At
Westminster with boat builders and
sailing barges - signed and dated 1859 -
25 x 41in.
(Christie's) $1,530 £850

CREDI - God The Father In Prayer -
grey wash heightened with white on
grey preparation - 25.2 x 17.2cm.
(Christie's) $180 £100

E. T. CRAWFORD - Fishing Boats Off
The Bass Rock - oil - on panel - 38 x 31cm.
(King & Chasemore) $171 £95

ROBERT CREE CRAWFORD - Sunset
Over The Sea - signed - dated 1874 -
22 x 40in.
(Sotheby's Belgravia) $144 £80

L. DI CREDI - The Madonna Adoring
The Infant Christ - on panel - circular -
34¾in. diameter.
(Sotheby's) $22,200 £12,000

G. M. CRESPI - The Madonna And Child With The Infant Saint John The Baptist - 18¾ x 14in.
(Christie's) **$1,620 £900**

GIUSEPPE MARIA CRESPI - Jupiter Among The Corybantes - 23 x 29in.
(Christie's) **$5,400 £3,000**

CRESWICK - Landing A Fish - bears signature - on board - 11½ x 15¼in.
(Sotheby's Belgravia) **$90 £50**

THOMAS CRESWICK - Fairy Glen, Near Whitby, Yorkshire - signed and dated 1857 - canvas - on board - 21½ x 25½in.
(Christie's) **$1,462 £750**

THOMAS CRESWICK - A Mountainous Wooded River Landscape, with cattle by a cascade - signed - shaped top - 17½ x 31½in.
(Christie's) **$108 £60**

CRETI - A King Kneeling In Prayer - the mount inscribed 'Guido Reni' - pen and brown ink - 15.1 x 12.8cm.
(Christie's) **$54 £30**

DONATO CRETI, Circle of - A Roman Hero Crowned By Fame - 57½ x 48in.
(Christie's N. York) **$275 £150**

A. H. CRICHTON - Street Scenes With Figures - signed - 11¾ x 8in.
(Buckell & Ballard) **$166 £92.50 Pair**

JOSHUA CRISTALL - The Judgement Of Paris - pencil and watercolour - 24 x 17½in.
(Christie's) **$684 £300**

GIOVANNI DI BARTOLOMEO CRISTIANI - The Coronation Of The Virgin - on gold ground panel - octagonal - 22 x 16½in.
(Christie's) **$50,960 £28,000**

ERNEST CROFTS - 'Napoleon And The Old Guard' - signed and dated 1880 - 13 x 18in.
(Christie's) **$1,260 £700**

CROME

J. B. CROME - Moonlight River Scene With Wherry, Mills and Figures - oil - 24 x 30in.
(G. A. Key) **$486 £270**

J. B. CROME - Fishing Boats Anchored On A River, a village with windmills beyond - 8¾ x 12¼in.
(Sotheby's) **$990 £550**

JOHN BERNAY CROME - Saint Martin, Norwich - on panel - 17½ x 14½in.
(Christie's) **$270 £150**

W. H. CROME - A River View Near Harwich - signed with initials - 9½ x 13½in.
(Sotheby's) **$576 £320**

THOMAS HARTLEY CROMEK - At Areopagus - signed inscribed and dated Nov. 1846 - 8¼ x 19 in.
(Sotheby's) **$630 £350**

THOMAS HARTLEY CROMEK - The West Front of San Marco, Venice, seen through Gothic Arches - signed and dated 1841 - 16¾ x 12¼ in.
(Sotheby's) **$306 £170**

H. CROMWELL - A View Of The Ruins Of Wovesley Castle - inscribed and dated 1797 - also inscribed on the reverse - pencil and watercolour - 15 x 21¾in.
(Sotheby's) **$126 £70**

RAY AUSTIN CROOKE - "Islanders" - oil - on canvas - 44 x 44cm.
(Australian Art Auctions) **$1,084 £602**

ANTHONY JANSZ. VAN CROOS - A River Landscape With Flooded Cottages - inscribed with initials and dated 1652 - on panel - 18¼ x 24½in.
(Sotheby's) **$12,025 £6,500**

CROSATO - A Frieze Of Figures - black chalk, grey wash heightened with white on grey paper - 10.2 x 24.0cm.
(Christie's) **$54 £30**

WILLIAM CROSBY - A Continental Village - signed - on board - 14½ x 17¾in.
(Sotheby's Belgravia) **$108 £60**

W. CRUIKSHANK - Still Lifes Of Birds' Nests - bear signatures - heightened with bodycolour - 8 x 11in.
(Sotheby's Belgravia) **$68 £38 Pair**

H. HADFIELD CUBLEY - A Spring Morning, Messley, Congleton with sheep on a hillside - signed - verso inscribed - oil - on board - 13½ x 21½in.
(Neales of Nottingham) **$97 £52**

GEORGE CUITT, JNR - A View Of Kelso - 17¼ x 23in.
(Sotheby's Belgravia) **$468 £260**

AELBERT CUYP, School of - Portrait Of A Lady, said to be Cornelia Bosman, half length, in a black dress and white ruff - bears signature and a date 1656 - on panel - 24 x 18½in.
(Christie's N. York) **$880 £481**

RICHARD DADD - Portrait Of The Artist - etching - inscribed in the plate 'Rd. Dadd se ipse fecit 1841' - rare, good impression with margins - 5¼ x 4½in. *(Sotheby's)* **$540 £300**

RICHARD DADD - The Sublime Porte, Constantinople - inscribed in pencil - pencil - on blue paper - 10 x 7in. *(Sotheby's)* **$144 £80**

RICHARD DADD - A Ming Jar, A Coffee Pot, A Glass Of Wine And A Knife On A Table - signed with initials and dated 1838 - on board - 3 x 4in. *(Christie's)* **$2,340 £1,300**

RICHARD DADD - A Bearded Arab, bust length, wearing a green turban - on panel - 12½ x 8½in. *(Christie's)* **$936 £520**

RICHARD DADD - The Castilian Spring At Delphi - inscribed on the verso - pencil and watercolour - 10¼ x 7in. *(Sotheby's)* **$990 £550**

RICHARD DADD - St. George After The Death Of The Dragon - pencil, brown wash - 7 x 9in. *(Sotheby's)* **$504 £280**

121

M. DAHL - Portrait Of A Gentleman, half length, wearing a blue cloak and white stock - canvas laid on panel - 29½ x 24½in. *(Sotheby's)* **$270 £150**

MICHAEL DAHL - Portrait Of A Lady, half length, wearing a white dress and holding a hat and an houlette - 30 x 25in. *(Sotheby's)* **$396 £220**

MICHAEL DAHL, Attributed to - Portrait Of A Gentleman, standing, three-quarter length, in a grey doublet and red cloak, wearing a sword, in a landscape - 49 x 40in. *(Christie's N. York)* **$550 £300**

DALBY - Full Cry, a painted papier-mache tray decorated with a gold border - area of painting approximately 16in. x 24in. *(Sotheby's)* **$360 £200**

DAVID DALBY - 'Priam', a bay racehorse with jockey up - 12 x 15½in. *(Christie's)* **$1,170 £650**

C. VAN DEN DAELE - The Doctor's Visit - signed and dated 1855 - on panel - 23¼ x 17½in.
(Christie's) **$1,890 £1,050**

DAVID DALBY OF YORK - A Bay Hunter And Two Couples Of Bedale Hounds outside a stable - signed and dated 1825 - 24½ x 29½in. *(Christie's)* **$3,060 £1,700**

DALMATIAN SCHOOL, circa 1500 - Saint Jerome Preaching In The Wilderness; on the reverse, The Imitation Of Christ - on panel - shaped top - 8 x 6¼in. *(Christie's)* **$1,980 £1,100**

C. VAN DEN DAELE - The Grandchildren's Visit - signed and dated 1856 - on panel - 29½ x 22¼in.
(Christie's) **$2,340 £1,300**

EMILE VAN DAMME-SYLVA - Study Of
A Girl and three cows at the edge of a
pond - signed - on panel - 10¾ x 15in.
(Sotheby Bearne)   **$1,287 £660**

T. T. M. DAMSCHRODER - Cottage
Interior With A Lady Seated Sewing
Beside A Table, an elderly man seated
in the corner, offering a toy sheep to
a young girl - signed - 25½ x 33in.
(H. Spencer & Sons)   **$2,250 £1,250**

FRANCIS DANBY - A Romantic Landscape
with snow-capped mountains and palm trees
near water - brown washes heightened with
white on grey paper - 14½ x 19¾in.
(Sotheby's)   **$126 £70**

SIR NATHANIEL DANCE - Portrait
Of Dr. Richard Terrick, Bishop Of
London (1764-77), half length - 29½
x 24½in.
(Christie's)   **$900 £500**

SIR NATHANIEL DANCE - Portrait Of
Christopher Norton, seated half length,
wearing a green coat and holding a brush
and palette - 25½ x 19½in.
(Christie's)   **$1,440 £800**

SIR N. DANCE - Portrait Of Two Young
Girls, one seated full length wearing a
white dress and holding a lamb, the other
standing full length wearing a maroon
dress - 59 x 47in.
(Christie's)   **$3,420 £1,900**

DANCE

THOMAS DANIELL - An Indian Mountainous Wooded River Landscape with figures in the foreground by a temple - signed - 42 x 55in.
(Christie's)   **$7,560 £4,200**

SIR NATHANIEL DANCE - Portrait Of A Lady, bust length, wearing blue dress - oval - 23 x 19in.
(Christie's)   **$900 £500**

WILLIAM DANIELL - A Coastal Scene with sailing vessels in a squall - signed and dated 1814 - 23 x 35in.
(Christie's)   **$2,700 £1,500**

WILLIAM DANIELL - A View Of Clovelly, North Devon - 16½ x 26¾in.
(Christie's)   **$1,350 £750**

CESARE DANDINI - Lucretia - 46 x 37in.
(Christie's)   **$2,700 £1,500**

OTTAVIO DANDINI - Studies Of Hands (recto); A Soldier (verso) - signed with initials - red chalk - 19.8 x 13.6cm.
(Christie's)   **$36 £20**

HENRI PIERRE DANLOUX, School of - Cephalus and Procris - on copper - 6¾ x 9 in.
(Christie's N. York)   **$495 £270**

ARTHUR E. DAVIES - View Of Norwich Cathedral from the river with bathers and fishing boat - oil - 15 x 19in.
(G. A. Key) $216 £120

ANDRE HENRI DARGELAS - 'Altering Time' - oil - on panel - 16 x 12in.
(Bonham's) $4,680 £2,600

A. DARVALL - 'Church Bells With A Sunset Harbour View in the distance' - signed and dated '81 - watercolour - 7 x 11¼in.
(The Manchester Auction Mart.) $25 £14

GUSTAVE DAVID - Amorous Scenes - both signed - watercolour heightened with white - 28.0 x 22.8cm.
(Christie's) $432 £240

ALAN DAVIE - "Shaman no. 5" - signed - titled and dated '69 - gouache - on paper - 22 x 30in.
(Sotheby's) $1,318 £720

ARTHUR E. DAVIES - Boats At Lowestoft - watercolour - 11 x 15in.
(G. A. Key) $324 £180

NORMAN PRESCOTT DAVIES - Classical Figures On Terraces - both signed and dated 1895 - 11¾ x 8¾in.
(Christie's) $108 £60 Pair

125

DAVIES

TYDDELSEY DAVIES - Samuel Beale, Huntsman To The Carew Family, mounted on a grey hunter, surrounded by hounds in a landscape - signed - indistinctly inscribed on reverse - 25 x 30in.
(Sotheby's)   **$2,520 £1,400**

ARTHUR H. DAVIS - River Landscape From Canford Mill, near Wimborne - signed - 30 x 18in.
(Elliott & Green)   **$198 £110**

C. DAVIS - Broadland Scenes with wherries - watercolour - oval - 7 x 9in.
(G. A. Key)   **$50 £28 Pair**

H. W. B. DAVIS - Twilight Grey - oil - 18 x 24in.
(G. A. Key)   **$50 £28**

HENRY WILLIAM BANKS DAVIS - The Picnic - signed and dated 1873/4 - inscribed on reverse - oil - on canvas - 44 x 72in.
(Bonham's)   **$2,340 £1,300**

JOHN SCARLETT DAVIS - Part Of The Palais De Justice, Paris - pen and brown ink - 6¾ x 3¾in.
(Sotheby's)   **$108 £60**

WILLIAM HENRY DAVIS - View Of The Duke Of Grafton's Hounds And Huntsmen taken from the kennel in Whittlebury Forest - signed, inscribed and dated 1815 and inscribed on the reverse - pencil and watercolour - 10¾ x 17¼in.
(Sotheby's)   **$432 £240**

HENRY DAWSON - A View Of Durham Cathedral from the river - signed and inscribed and dated 1876 on the reverse - 47¾ x 61½in.
(Christie's)   **$2,880 £1,600**

HENRY DAWSON - A Harbour Scene With A Man At A Water Pump, a woman and child walking along a path, boats in the distance and a town and hills beyond - signed and dated 1852 - 33½ x 48½in.
(H. Spencer & Sons)   **$468 £260**

EDWARD DAYES - Durham - signed - pencil and watercolour - 4½ x 6½in.
(Christie's)   **$11,70 £650**

EDWARD DAYES - Conisbrough Church, Yorkshire - pencil and watercolour - 7¼ x 9¼in.
(Sotheby's)   **$576 £320**

WILLIAM WOOD DEANE - A Piazza In Verona - signed and dated 1870 - heightened with bodycolour - 33½ x 38in.
(Sotheby's)   **$936 £520**

R. DEARN - Rocks Near Spanishead, Isle Of Man - signed - dated 1895 - inscribed on the reverse - 13½ x 23½in.
(Sotheby's Belgravia) **$9 £5**

PHILIBERT LOUIS DEBUCOURT - Scene De Carnaval - pen and brown ink and watercolour - 30.0 x 44.0cm.
(Christie's) **$720 £400**

GABRIEL-ALEXANDRE DECAMPS - A Harem - 16½ x 25in.
(Christie's) **$540 £300**

ALFRED DEHODENCQ - Studies Of Nubians - black chalk - 28.8 x 22.5cm.
(Christie's) **$99 £55**

E. DEKKERT - The Coast Of Fife - inscribed - on board - 12¼ x 15½in.
(Sotheby's Belgravia) **$162 £90**

J. C. DELAFOSSE - Designs For Andirons With Urns And Putti - black chalk, pen and grey ink, brown or grey wash - 43.5 x 34.0cm. and smaller.
(Christie's) **$216 £120 Two**

ALEXIS-AUGUSTE DELAHOGUE - An Arab Girl Seated by a tree - signed and dated 1907 - on canvas - on panel - 12¾ x 16in.
(Christie's) **$144 £80**

H. DELE - Norfolk Landscape With Mills - watercolour - 13 x 21in.
(G. A. Key) **$36 £20**

D. VAN DELEN - Figures In A Palatial Arcade - on panel - 14¾ x 18¾in.
(Christie's) **$1,440 £800**

DIRK VAN DELEN - An Architectural Capriccio with elegant figures promenading - signed and indistinctly dated 1636 - on panel - 19 x 21¼in.
(Christie's) **$10,920 £6,000**

ALBERT DELERIVE - A Punch And Judy Show; and A Fairground Scene - both signed - brown wash - 15.9 x 11.6cm.
(Christie's) **$81 £45 Pair**

J. W. DELFF - Portrait Of A Gentleman, bust length, wearing a dark coat with lace collar - on panel - 22½ x 17½in.
(Christie's) **$900 £500**

FREDERIC JEAN-BAPTISTE DESMARAIS - The Horatii - signed and dated Rome 1792 - framed in a shaped overmantel - 34 x 62½in.
(Christie's) **$11,830 £6,500**

ALEXANDRE FRANCOIS DESPORTES - A Pair Of Colourful Cockerels fighting in a farmyard, a pheasant and other poultry beyond - signed and dated 1713 - oil - 38 x 50in.
(Heathcote Ball & Co) **$6,588 £3,600**

T. DESSOULAVY - The Colosseum With Monks in the foreground - signed and dated Rome 1838 - pencil and brown wash - 30.5 x 49.0cm.
(Christie's) **$144 £80**

LUDWIG JULIUS CRISTIAN DETTMANN - A Sunlit Coastal Scene with a child paddling - signed - oil - on canvas - 34 x 49in.
(Bonham's) **$1,656 £900**

DEUTSCH

LUDWIG DEUTSCH - The Guards Of
The Harem - signed - on panel - 31 x 38in.
(Christie's) $9,900 £5,500

LUDWIG DEUTSCH - Two Arabs
Playing Chess - signed and dated Paris
1896 - 21 x 16in.
(Christie's) $13,500 £7,500

LUDWIG DEUTSCH - In The Mosque -
signed and dated Cairo 1898 - on panel -
26½ x 23in.
(Christie's) $11,700 £6,500

LUDWIG DEUTSCH - The Nubian Guard
- signed and dated Paris 1888 - 57 x 37in.
(Christie's) $27,000 £15,000

LUDWIG DEUTSCH - Outside The
Palace - signed - on panel - 27½ x 38in.
(Christie's) $31,500 £17,500

LUDWIG DEUTSCH - The Antique Dealers - signed - on panel - 28 x 32in.
(Christie's) **$3,600 £2,000**

LUDWIG DEUTSCH - A School In Cairo - signed and dated Paris 1890 - on panel - 31 x 39in.
(Christie's) **$11,700 £6,500**

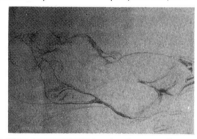

ACHILLE DEVERIA - An Outstretched Nude - signed - crayon drawing - 16.5 x 23cm.
(Christian Rosset) **$106 £59**

E. F. M. DEVERIA - Harlequin And Columbine; and A Girl With A Witch - both signed with initials - pencil and watercolour heightened with white - 18.8 x 16.3cm.
(Christie's) **$99 £55 Pair**

EUGENE DEVERIA - Young Girl - signed - drawing - 11.5 x 14cm.
(Christian Rosset) **$153 £85**

LUDWIG DEUTSCH - A Moorish Guard - signed - on panel - 11½ x 7½in.
(Christie's) **$2,700 £1,500**

LUDWIG DEUTSCH - An Arab Street Scene With A Procession - signed - 44 x 35in.
(Christie's) **$10,800 £6,000**

DEVIS

A. DEVIS - Portrait Of A Lady in a blue dress, seated with a dog in landscape - oil - 50 x 40in.
(Buckell & Ballard)   **$351 £195**

ARTHUR DEVIS - Portrait Of Alicia And Jane, daughters of Richard Clarke Esquire, Walford Church and Walford Court, Ross-on-Wye, can be seen beyond - signed - 36 x 28in.
(Sotheby's)   **$46,800 £26,000**

ARTHUR DEVIS - Portrait Of A Lady, small full length, wearing a white dress, seated by a table in an interior - 15½ x 12½in.
(Christie's)   **$3,060 £1,700**

ARTHUR DEVIS - Portrait Of Robert Banks Hodgkinson, full length, wearing a red suit and a blue coat, standing on a terrace - 22½ x 15½in.
(Sotheby's)   **$1,440 £800**

T. C. DIBBIN - Traders On The Seashore - watercolour - 8 x 12in.
(G. A. Key)   **$57 £32**

J. DIBDEN - 'Barges' - signed - oil sketch - 16 x 23in.
(Hussey's)   **$67 £37**

THOMAS COLMAN DIBDIN - A French Street Scene - signed and dated 1876 - heightened with white - 21 x 14½in.
(Sotheby's)   **$396 £220**

SIR FRANK DICKSEE - Daughters Of Eve - signed - signed, inscribed and dated 1925 on reverse - 34½ x 20½in.
(Christie's)   **$72 £40**

M. I. DICKSEE - "Thoughts" - Girl Sitting At Desk - watercolour - 6 x 5in.
(G. A. Key)   **$79 £44**

J. VAN DIEGEN - A Wooded Landscape With Sheep And A Goat; and A Wooded Landscape With Sheep, A Windmill beyond - both signed - on panel - 6½ x 9¼in.
(Christie's)   **$1,350 £750 Pair**

DIEPENBECK - An Angel Appearing To Saint Margaret - grey wash - 22.8 x 17.3cm.
(Christie's) $99 £55

DIES - San Lorenzo, Toscana - the mount inscribed - brown wash - 26.8 x 35.8cm.
(Christie's) $45 £25

ADRIAEN VAN DIEST - A Rocky Coastal Landscape with fisherfolk and sailing vessels beyond - signed - 14¼ x 19¼in.
(Christie's) $2,700 £1,500

HENDRIK JOSEPH DILLENS - In The Cornfield - signed and dated - on panel - 10½ x 9in.
(Christie's) $900 £500

FRANK DILLON - The Gourieh, Cairo signed and inscribed on the reverse - 15 x 11½in.
(Christie's) $1,620 £900

FRANK DILLON - An Arab Courtyard - 16½ x 11½in.
(Christie's) $810 £450

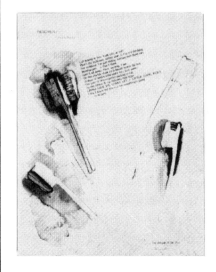

JIM DINE - Fragment - signed with initials - dedicated for Ted and dated 1969 - watercolour and toothpaste on print - 15¼ x 11¼in.
(Sotheby's) $622 £340

131

DIRIRE

H. **DIRIRE** - Still Life: Vase of flowers on window ledge - signed - oil - on canvas - 40 x 32½in.
(Richard A. Bourne Co. Inc.)
$1,000 £556

JEAN DISCART - The Blind Water-seller - inscribed Paris and signed - on panel - 8¼ x 6in.
(Christie's)
$1,350 £750

H. **DISNEY** - 'Sportsman's Paradise' - a composition of fantasies incorporating a circular panel depicting the pugilists Heenan and Sayers - signed and dated 1860 - 23¾ x 19¾in.
(Sotheby Bearne)
$409 £210

FREDERICK DIXEY - 'Temple Lock, The Thames' - signed - watercolour - 5 x 6in.
(Hussey's)
$47 £27

CHARLES DIXON - 'The Orontes' surrounded by numerous vessels - signed and dated '05 - watercolour - 21 x 31in.
(King & Chasemore)
$900 £500

CHARLES DIXON - Off Gibraltar - signed - inscribed and dated 1920 - heightened with bodycolour - 14 x 29½in.
(Sotheby's Belgravia)
$612 £340

CHARLES DIXON - A View Of Durham Cathedral From The Rooftops - signed and dated 1891 - heightened with white - 17 x 31in.
(Sotheby's Belgravia) **$135 £75**

ANTONIO DIZIANI, Attributed to - A Rocky Wooded River Landscape with figures by a cascade - 28½ x 36in.
(Christie's N. York) **$3,740 £2,044**

GASPARE DIZIANI - The Assumption Of The Virgin - 27¼ x 15½in.
(Sotheby's) **$12,950 £7,000**

H: J. DOBSON - News From Abroad - 40 x 50cm.
(Edmiston's) **$612 £340**

H. J. DOBSON - Rustic Politicians - 40 x 50cm.
(Edmiston's) **$667 £370**

RAEBURN DOBSON - Coiling A Rope - signed twice - once indistinctly - 11½ x 7¼in.
(Sotheby's Belgravia) **$68 £38**

ROBERT DOBSON - Early Morning On The River Conway, North Wales - signed - 29¼ x 19½in.
(Sotheby's Belgravia) **$45 £25**

W. DOBSON - Portrait Of A Lady, half length, wearing a low-cut brown dress - 29 x 24in.
(Sotheby's) **$504 £280**

A. BROWNLIE DOCHARTY - Ben Lui - 70 x 90cm.
(Edmiston's) **$504 £280**

ALEXANDER BROWNLIE DOCHARTY - Haymaking - signed - 13½ x 20in.
(Sotheby's Belgravia) **$684 £380**

DODD

SIMON VAN DER DOES - A Peasant
Woman And A Child, with cattle, sheep
and goats in a wooded landscape -
signed and dated 1707 - 37 x 31¼in.
(Christie's)   **$3,060 £1,700**

ARTHUR DODD - 'In Full Cry'; and 'The
End Of A Good Run' - signed and dated
1885 and 1886 - oil - 35½ x 23½in.
(Phillips, Solihull)   **$1,607 £820 Pair**

JACOB VAN DER DOES, Attributed
to - A Wooded Italianate Landscape,
with a shepherdess and cattle - 11¼ x
13in.
(Christie's N. York)   **$352 £192**

EDWIN DOLBY - Louviers; Burgos
Cathedral - signed and inscribed -
heightened with bodycolour - 26½
x 17½in.
(Sotheby's Belgravia)   **$396 £220 Pair**

EDWIN THOMAS DOLBY - Outside
Lambeth Palace Near Westminster
Bridge, a rowing match on the Thames -
11½ x 18in.
(Sotheby's)   **$360 £200**

C. DOLCI - Portrait Of A Man - black
and red chalk - 30.5 x 23.7cm.
(Christie's)   **$99 £55**

W. ANSTEY DOLLAND - The Marble
Balcony - signed - 10¼ x 13½in.
(Sotheby's Belgravia)   **$108 £60**

R. DOMEA - Venetian Scene - signed -
oil - on canvas - 23 x 13in.
(Stewart Gore)   **$380 £200**

PIETER CORNELIS DOMMERSEN - A
View In Coblenz, Germany - signed and
dated 1891 - inscribed on reverse - on
panel - 9½ x 7¾in.
(Christie's)   **$2,520 £1,400**

WILLIAM R. DOMMERSEN - The Town
Hall And Market Place, Tours - signed -
19¾ x 15¼in.
(Christie's)   **$1,260 £700**

WILLIAM R. DOMMERSEN - The Flower
Market At Nice - bears Koekkoek signature -
15½ x 11½in.
(Christie's)   **$540 £300**

W. ANSTEY DOLLAND - The Evening
Glow - signed - 17½ x 7¾in.
(Sotheby's Belgravia)   **$288 £160**

DOMMERSEN

WILLIAM R. DOMMERSEN - The Grande Place, Malines - signed and inscribed on the reverse - 23½ x 19½in.
(Christie's) **$2,340 £1,300**

WILLIAM R. DOMMERSEN - The Butter Hall, Louvain - signed and inscribed on the reverse - 23½ x 19½in.
(Christie's) **$2,250 £1,250**

MARTINO DEL DON - The Atrium Of San Marco, Venice - signed - watercolour and bodycolour - 33.0 x 26.2cm.
(Christie's) **$72 £40**

DAVID ABERCROMBIE DONALDSON - A Montrose Jug - signed - 29¼ x 29¼in.
(Sotheby's Belgravia) **$324 £180**

DIONYS VAN DONGEN - An Italianate Wooded River Landscape with peasants, cattle and sheep on a path by a ruin - indistinctly signed and dated 1798 - on panel - 18 x 22in.
(Christie's) **$2,700 £1,500**

GUSTAVE DORE - Alsace - signed and dated 1869 - 75½ x 50in.
(Christie's) **$4,500 £2,500**

136

GUSTAVE DORE - Lorraine - signed and dated 1869 - 75½ x 50in.
(Christie's) **$3,420 £1,900**

J. DORNER - St. Jerome In The Wilderness - signed and dated 1776 - on panel - 13½ x 10in.
(Dee & Atkinson) **$990 £550**

JACOB DORNER - A View Of Munich - signed - pencil and watercolour - 27.9 x 41.2cm.
(Christie's) **$1,260 £700**

EDWARD ALGERNON STUART DOUGLAS - 'In The Slips'; 'Slipping'; 'The Turn'; and 'The Kill' - signed and dated 1885 - oil - on board - 9 x 26in.
(Bonham's) **$7,650 £4,250 Four**

EDWARD ALGERNON STUART DOUGLAS - The Meet; and On The Scent - both signed and one dated 1918, the other 1917 - 15¾ x 23½in.
(Christie's) **$3,120 £1,600 Pair**

DOUGLAS

EDWARD A. S. DOUGLAS - The Kill - signed and dated 1912 - 7¾ x 13¼in.
(Sotheby's Belgravia) **$36 £20**

SIMON JOHANNES VAN DOUW - Italianate Landscapes with peasants and cattle by monuments - one indistinctly signed - on panel - 19¼ x 16¼in.
(Christie's) **$2,700 £1,500 Pair**

J. DOWNMAN - Portrait Of A Gentleman, wearing Windsor uniform, half length - 23 x 20in.
(Sotheby's) **$720 £400**

JOHN DOWNMAN - Portrait Of John Boyd Esq., M.P., half length, in profile to the left - signed, inscribed on the original mount and dated 1783 - stump and watercolour heightened with white - oval - 7½ x 6½in.
(Christie's) **$900 £500**

THOMAS MILLIE DOW - Flowers From The Hills - signed with initials - arched top - 86 x 27¾in.
(Sotheby's Belgravia) **$720 £400**

JOHN DOWNMAN - Portrait Of Charlotte Monro - signed with initals - inscribed on the reverse - oval - 8 x 7in.
(Sotheby's) **$396 £220**

J. C. DROOCHSLOOT - Peasants Merrymaking In An Interior - on panel - 12 x 19in.
(Christie's) $1,620 £900

RICHARD DOYLE - Midsummer's Night's Dream - inscribed on the reverse - pen and black ink heightened with red watercolour on buff paper - 13¼ x 16½in.
(Sotheby's) $1,170 £650

DOYLY-JOHN - 'Little Harbour, Cannes' - signed - oil - on canvas - 18 x 26in.
(Lalonde Bros. & Parham) $293 £160

ALFRED DE DREUX - Portrait Of Baron Jules Finot, head and shoulders - 24 x 19½in.
(Christie's) $360 £200

MARTIN DROLLING - A Boy With A Box (recto); A Woman In An Interior (verso) - black chalk - 19.1 x 15.6cm.
(Christie's) $234 £130

JOOST CORNELISZ. DROOCHSLOOT - Numerous Beggars By A Ruin In A Town - signed and dated 1643 - on panel - 17¾ x 34in.
(Christie's) $6,840 £3,800

JOOST CORNELISZ. DROOCHSLOOT - Peasants Merrymaking Outside A Village Inn - bears traces of signature - on panel - 29 x 41½in.
(Christie's) $7,200 £4,000

MICHEL-MARTIN DROLLING - A Little Boy With A Dog In A Park - signed and dated 1804 - 12¼ x 9¼in.
(Sotheby's) $7,030 £3,800

JOOST CORNELISZ. DROOCHSLOOT - Beggars Receiving Alms In A Village - bears monogram and dated 1648 - on panel - 16 x 23½in.
(Christie's) $6,840 £3,800

JAMES DRUMMOND - The Old Fisherman - signed and dated 1874 - 19¾ x 14¾in.
(Sotheby's Belgravia) $58 £32

JAMES DRUMMOND - Winter - signed with monogram and dated '63 - 26½ x 21¼in.
(Christie's) $72 £40

JEAN DUBUFFET - Chiffre Legendaire Du Lavabo - signed and dated '65 - signed again, inscribed and dated fevrier 65 on the reverse - 39¼ x 31¾in.
(Christie's) $18,000 £10,000

F. DUCALE - A Peasant Girl In A Cowshed - 40½ x 25½in.
(Christie's) $1,440 £800

ERNEST ANGE DUEZ - At The Window - signed - 41¼ x 19¼in.
(Christie's) $1,800 £1,000

WILLIAM DUFFIELD - A Young Woman In A Kitchen, standing by a table with dead game - signed and dated 1856 - 16¾ x 20¾in.
(Christie's) $1,170 £600

DUGHET - An Italianate Wooded Landscape with figures in the foreground and a house beyond - 38 x 49½in.
(Christie's) **$1,224 £680**

EDWARD DUNCAN - Near Shere - signed and dated 1878 - pencil and watercolour - 9¼ x 13¾in.
(Sotheby's) **$144 £80**

G. DUGHET - An Extensive Wooded River Landscape, with huntsmen and dogs by a river, a town beyond - 37 x 52in.
(Christie's) **$2,700 £1,500**

EDWARD DUNCAN - Skiddaw And Broadwater, Cumberland - signed - 29¾ x 51½in.
(Sotheby's) **$1,476 £820**

GASPARD DUGHET, School of - An Extensive Italianate River Landscape with Tobias and the Angel - 35¾ x 20¼ in.
(Christie's N. York) **$1,100 £601**

DUNCAN - A Petition To Mary, Queen Of Scots - 13 x 17½in.
(Sotheby's Belgravia) **$54 £30**

T. DUNCAN - A Young Man Resting With His Dog, a castle beyond - 39½ x 31¼in.
(Sotheby's Belgravia) **$288 £160**

EDWARD DUNCAN - Old Houses and Fishermen on the Kentish Coast - 14½ x 21¼ in.
(Sotheby's) **$810 £450**

JOHANNES BERTHOLOMAUS DUNTZE - A Frozen River Landscape With A Village - signed and dated 1864 - 25½ x 40in.
(Christie's) **$11,700 £6,500**

DUPLESSIS

C. MICHEL - H. DUPLESSIS - A Cavalry
Encampment; and A Wooded River Landscape with cavalry on the march - one
signed - on panel - 9 x 12¼in.
(Christie's)   **$5,040 £2,800 Pair**

GAINSBOROUGH DUPONT - A Portrait Of
William Thomas Lewis, The Comedian, half
length, wearing Van Dyck costume, a rapier
in his right hand - 27¼ x 23¾in.
(Sotheby's)   **$5,400 £3,000**

JULES DUPRE - French Landscape -
signed - oil - on canvas - 18¾ x 26in.
(Richard A. Bourne Co. Inc.)
                                 $500 £278
DURER, After - The Madonna And
Child - on panel - 6 x 4¾in.
(Christie's)   **$4,320 £2,400**

DUTCH SCHOOL, 18th century -
Still Life Of Fruit, falling from an
upturned basket, set in an open landscape
- 18 x 36in.
(Morphets of Harrogate)
                                 $1,404 £780

**DUTCH SCHOOL, Second Half of the
18th century** - A Winter River Landscape, with figures skating and a town
beyond - signed with initials - 13 x
15½in.
(Christie's)   **$3,960 £2,200**
DUTCH SCHOOL - Fruit And Still Life
- 69 x 88cm.
(Edmiston's)   **$972 £540**

DUTCH SCHOOL, 19th century - Harbour Mouth Scene with shipping in a choppy sea and figures by the quayside - 25 x 47in.
(Sotheby Bearne) **$2,340 £1,200**

DUTCH SCHOOL, 17th century - A Fortified Roman Gateway - inscribed - dated 1622 - black chalk, grey wash - 12.7 x 18.5cm.
(Christie's) **$81 £45**

DUTCH SCHOOL, 18th century - Dido Receiving Aeneas At Carthage - black chalk, pen and brown ink, brown wash - 13.1 x 20.7cm.
(Christie's) **$63 £35**

DUTCH SCHOOL, 18th century - Dutch Men-O'-War In A Calm - bears Van de Velde II's initial - pencil and watercolour - 20.8 x 32.4cm.
(Christie's) **$108 £60**

DUTCH SCHOOL, 19th century - A Vase Of Flowers - oil - on canvas - 69 x 50cm.
(King & Chasemore) **$521 £270**

DUTCH SCHOOL, 18th century - Sportsmen Near A Hide - grey wash - 28.7 x 34.4cm.
(Christie's) **$45 £25**

DUTCH SCHOOL, 17th century - A Seated Peasant With A Pipe - red chalk, watermark Arms of Amsterdam - 21.9 x 15.5cm.
(Christie's) **$90 £50**

DUTCH SCHOOL, early 17th century - Two Brigs At Anchor, A Rowing Boat in the foreground - black chalk - 17 x 26cm.
(Christie's) **$216 £120**

J. DUVAL - Girl With A Pitcher, a girl with her dog collecting water, in a landscape - 12 x 9½in.
(H. Spencer & Sons) **$432 £240**

JEAN F. DUVAL - A Country Boy With His Pet Guinea Pig And White Mouse - signed oil - on canvas - 13½ x 11½in.
(Neales of Nottingham) **$560 £290**

VAN DYCK - Studies Of Hands And Of The Head Of An Old Man, possibly for a Saint Christopher - pen and brown ink - 15.5 x 15.2cm.
(Christie's) **$36 £20**

VAN DYCK - Studies Of A Hand Holding A Staff And Of The Lower Part Of A Draped Figure - black and white chalk on grey paper - 38.3 x 27.3cm.
(Christie's) **$153 £85**

PHILIP VAN DYK - A Man And Woman Making Music On A Stone Balcony, with a boy holding a birdcage - signed with initials - on panel - 14¼ x 12¼in.
(Christie's) **$43,200 £24,000**

JOAN EARDLEY - Hillside Village -
pen, watercolour and crayon - 47 x
60cm.
(Edmiston's)   **$756 £420**

**JOAN KATHLEEN HARDING
EARDLEY** - Study Of A Young Girl -
coloured chalks - 11½ x 6in.
(Sotheby's Belgravia)   **$432 £240**

MAUD EARL - A Collie With A Covey
Of Grouse in the background - signed -
45¾ x 16¾in.
(Sotheby's Belgravia)   **$360 £200**

MAUD EARL - The Lap Of Luxury - signed - 21½ x 29½in.
(Christie's) **$684 £380**

THOMAS EARL - A Terrier With A Hare - signed and dated '63 - 19½ x 23½in.
(Sotheby's Belgravia) **$1,170 £650**

EDEMA - A Woody River Landscape with peasants, cattle and sheep in the foreground and a cottage beyond - 23 x 46in.
(Christie's) **$720 £400**

GERARD VAN EDEMA, School of - A Wooded River Landscape, with peasants in the foreground - 22¼ x 31½in.
(Christie's N. York) **$990 £541**

ALFRED S. EDWARD - Off The Harbour Arm - signed - 24 x 36in.
(Lawrence) **$1,008 £560**

DENIS WILLIAM EDEN - 'To Live Is Happy' - signed, inscribed and dated 1906 - signed and inscribed on the reverse - 27 x 23¼in.
(Christie's) **$1,260 £700**

E. M. EDMOND - Swans And Punt On River Severn - oil - 12 x 18in.
(G. A. Key) **$36 £20**

G. VAN DEN EECKHOUT - Portrait Of A Bearded Old Man, small bust length, wearing dark robes and cap - on panel - 15½ x 12in.
(Christie's) **$1,620 £900**

W. EGGINGTON - 'Dartmoor Landscape' - signed - watercolour - 14 x 17in.
(Hussey's) **$54 £30**

W. M. EGLEY - The Slave Market - bears Roberts signature - 27 x 35½in.
(Christie's) **$810 £450**

EGLINGTON - The Cotter's Family - 13½ x 17in.
(Sotheby's Belgravia) **$468 £260**

EHRENBERG

WILHELM VAN EHRENBERG - Figures Outside A Palace - indistinctly signed - 25¾ x 35in.
(Sotheby's) **$5,550 £3,000**

WILLEM SCHUBERT VON EHRENBERG - Figures By Classical Ruins in an extensive river landscape - signed and dated 1678 - 32¾ x 53¾in.
(Christie's) **$2,520 £1,400**

GEORG DIONYSIUS EHRET - Ervitamia - signed, inscribed 'Ahovai Plum' and dated 1753 - watercolour and bodycolour on vellum - 10 x 6¾in.
(Christie's) **$630 £350**

S. T. EINGRUBIL - Sportsmen Near A Lake - signed and dated 1838 - watercolour - 23.3 x 35.4cm.
(Christie's) **$2,340 £1,300**

PER EKSTROM - Landscape - signed - 80 x 110cm.
(Goteborgs Auktionsverk) **$5,400 £3,000**

FRANCOIS EISEN - Peasants Merry-making Outside An Inn with a church in an extensive landscape beyond - signed - 42 x 34in.
(Christie's) **$2,880 £1,600**

KNUT EKWALL - Old Man Reading To A Young Girl - signed - 35 x 26cm.
(Goteborgs Auktionsverk) **$4,243 £2,357**

JEAN FRANCOIS ELIAERTS - Roses, Carnations and other flowers in an urn with plums, grapes and cherries on a stone ledge; and Roses, Chrysanthemums and other flowers in an urn with grapes, peaches and plums on a stone ledge - 22 x 18in.
(Christie's) **$9,100 £5,000 Pair**

OTTMAR ELLIGER - Roses, Carnations, Sweet Peas and other flowers in a glass vase on a ledge - 18½ x 12in.
(Christie's) **$13,650 £7,500**

OTTMAR ELLIGER - Design For A Frontispiece With King William Of Orange And Queen Mary - pencil, grey wash, watermark Arms of Amsterdam - 28.4 x 18.8cm.
(Christie's) **$504 £280**

THOMAS ELLIOTT - A View Of Portsmouth Harbour with a man-o'-war under sail and the fleet at anchor off Spithead - 33½ x 54½in.
(Christie's) **$3,060 £1,700**

EDWIN ELLIS - A Coastal Scene With Fisherfolk - signed - 17½ x 32¾in.
(Christie's) **$540 £300**

ALFRED W. ELMORE - The Gaming Table - on board - 7¼ x 6in.
(Christie's) **$324 £180**

LOUWYS AERNOUTS ELSEVIER - A Carcass Of Meat Hanging In A Barn - signed and indistinctly dated 1641 - on panel - 18¼ x 23¼in.
(Christie's N. York) **$1,760 £962**

ELSHEIMER

ELSHEIMER - An Allegory Of Creation - pen and brown ink, brown wash heightened with white - 8.9 x 10.8cm.
(Christie's) **$81 £45**

F. EMMANUEL - Afternoon Shadows - 14½ x 22in.
(Sotheby's Belgravia) **$36 £20**

JOHN EMMS - After The Chase - signed and dated '78 - 37¾ x 51¼in.
(Christie's) **$4,320 £2,400**

JOHN EMMS - 'Rocking Joe' - signed and dated 1899 - 27 x 35in.
(Sotheby Bearne) **$2,632 £1,350**

JOHN EMMS - The Hunt Terrier's Litter - signed - 19½ x 25½in.
(Christie's) **$2,160 £1,200**

JOHN EMMS - A Hound And Puppies in an interior - signed - 17½ x 23½in.
(Christie's) **$2,340 £1,300**

JOHN EMMS - A Bay And A Chestnut Hunter in a field, with a magpie - signed - 24¼ x 37½in.
(Christie's) **$1,080 £600**

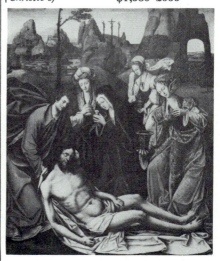

C. ENGELBRECHTSZ. - The Lamentation - on panel - 59 x 43¼in.
(Sotheby's) **$14,800 £8,000**

ENGLISH SCHOOL, 19th century - Travellers On A Heath in the Wouwerman style - panel - 14½ x 12in.
(Sotheby Bearne) **$540 £300**

ENGLISH SCHOOL, early 19th century - River Landscape - canvas - on board - 8 x 11in.
(Sotheby Bearne) **$429 £220**

ENGLISH SCHOOL, late 19th century - Country Landscape with a horse-drawn cart and figures near a homestead - 25 x 40in.
(Sotheby Bearne) **$1,890 £1,050**

ENGLISH SCHOOL, Late 16th century, Attributed to - Portrait Of Admiral Lord Howard Of Effingham, bust length, in armour, wearing the insignia of the Order of the Garter - 26½ x 19¼in.
(Christie's N. York) **$715 £391**

ENGLISH SCHOOL, 16th century - Queen Elizabeth I in her Coronation Robes - on panel - 50 x 39½in.
(Sotheby's) **$64,750 £35,000**

ENGLISH SCHOOL, late 18th century - The York Regiment Stationed In The Garden Of Montague House, London, during the Gordon riots - pen and black ink - water-colour - 11½ x 17¼in.
(Sotheby's)   **$270 £150**

ENGLISH SCHOOL, circa 1740 - A View Looking Along Broad Quay To St. Michael's Hill And Church, Bristol - 37 x 46½in.
(Christie's)   **$9,900 £5,500**

ENGLISH SCHOOL, circa 1850 - Portrait Of A Gentleman; and Portrait Of A Lady, seated three-quarter length, in an interior - 49½ x 39½in.
(Christie's)   **$2,730 £1,400 Pair**

ENGLISH SCHOOL, 19th century - Coastal Scene with a ruined Abbey and shipping in a choppy sea - indistinctly signed and dated 1855 - 17½ x 32¾in.
(Sotheby Bearne)   **$1,560 £800**

ENGLISH SCHOOL - Members Of A Family in an interior architectural setting - on canvas - 46 x 43in.
(King & Chasemore)   **$1,800 £1,000**

ENGLISH SCHOOL, circa 1802 - The Battle Of Copenhagen, the British fleet grouped in the centre, the Danish fleet and the town of Copenhagen seen beyond - 33 x 45in.
(Sotheby's) **$1,440£800**

ENGLISH SCHOOL, Mid 16th century - John Sydenham of Coombe, as a youth, wearing Tudor riding dress - on panel - 35½ x 29in.
(Lawrence) **$4,860 £2,700**

ENGLISH SCHOOL - Portrait Of A Gentleman, half-length, said to be a member of the Coleridge family - inscribed and dated 1840 - pastel - 15½ x 12¾in.
(Sotheby's) **$270 £150**

ENGLISH SCHOOL, 19th century - A Farmer With Donkey In A Wooded Landscape with figures in the background - oil on canvas - 42 x 38in.
(H. C. Chapman & Son) **$351 £195**

ENGLISH SCHOOL, mid 19th century - A Young South American Indian Boy sitting by an open door - watercolour - 12¼ x 17¾in.
(Sotheby's) **$425 £220**

ENGLISH SCHOOL

ENGLISH SCHOOL, mid 18th century - Admiral Boscowan Taking Louisberg From The French on 25th January 1758, The Prudente burning in the middle of the harbour, The Bienfascente being towed out of harbour - oil - on canvas - 24¼ x 26¼in.
(Sotheby's)   **$579 £300**

ENGLISH SCHOOL, circa 1850 - A Visit To Grandpapa's, with children playing at the foot of a stone staircase - oil - on canvas - 22½ x 18½in.
(Neales of Nottingham) **$4,150 £2,150**

ENGLISH SCHOOL - Dhows On The Nile - watercolour heightened with white - 6½ x 9½in.
(Christie's)   **$81 £45**

ENGLISH SCHOOL, circa 1870 - Sydney From Lavender Bay, sailing ships in the water and the city in the distance - watercolour - 17½ x 24in.
(Sotheby's)   **$1,351 £700**

ENGLISH SCHOOL, 20th century - Cattle At Sunset - oil - on canvas - 87 x 11.3cm.
(King & Chasemore)   **$386 £200**

IGNAZ EPPER - Frauenakt - 48 x 43cm.
(Auktionshaus am Neumarkt)
     $1,517 £829

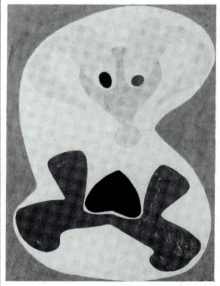

MAX ERNST - Insect - 31.5 x 23.5cm.
(Auktionshaus am Neumarkt)
     $19,215 £10,500

RUDOLF ERNST - An Arab Guard Outside A Mosque - 14¾ x 11in.
(Christie's)   **$2,160 £1,200**

RUDOLF ERNST - The Servant's
Greeting - signed - on panel - 28 x 35½in.
(Christie's) **$10,800 £6,000**

RUDOLF ERNST - The Coffee Seller -
signed - on panel - 21½ x 17½in.
(Christie's) **$6,840 £3,800**

RUDOLF ERNST - After Prayer - signed -
on panel - 35½ x 28in.
(Christie's) **$27,900 £15,500**

RUDOLF ERNST - The Money Lender -
signed - on panel - 24½ x 32in.
(Christie's) **$9,000 £5,000**

RUDOLF ERNST - Arab Merchants On A
Quayside - signed - on panel - 28½ x 36in.
(Christie's) **$3,960 £2,200**

RUDOLF ERNST - Two Arabs In An
Interior - signed - on panel - 28½ x 36in.
(Christie's) **$10,800 £6,000**

ERTVELT

A. VAN ERTVELT - Dutch Sailing Ships Offshore In a rough sea - 20 x 23½in.
(Christie's) **$1,800 £1,000**

JACOB VAN ES - Oysters On A Plate with a roemer and a lemon on a table - on panel - 9¾ x 13½in.
(Christie's) **$9,000 £5,000**

JACOB FOPPENS VAN ES - A Bowl Of Strawberries, A Basket Of Mulberries, With Artichokes, Two Roemers And A Roemer-Holder on a table - signed - on panel - 17¾ x 28½in.
(Christie's) **$5,760 £3,200**

J. F. VAN ES - Bunches Of Grapes in a porcelain bowl and nuts on a table - on copper - on panel - 9 x 12½in.
(Christie's) **$1,530 £850**

GEORGES D'ESPAGNAT - Le Repos de Mme. d'Espagnat - 73 x 92cm.
(Auktionshaus am Neumarkt) **$15,165 £8,287**

C. ESCHARD - A Mill Near Woods - pen and grey ink, grey wash - 20.0 x 31.4cm.
(Christie's) **$58 £32**

IGNACIO LEON Y ESCOSURA - 'The Pearl Necklace' - signed and dated 1870 - on panel - 5¾ x 3¾in.
(Sotheby Bearne) **$540 £972**

D'ESPOSITO - View Of Valletta Harbour with shipping - watercolour - 3 x 6in.
(G. A. Key) **$40 £22**

RICHARD HAMILTON ESSEX - The Duke Of York's Monument And Carlton House Terrace From St. James' Park - signed and inscribed on the reverse - 8½ x 12¾in.
(Sotheby's) **$396 £220**

WILLIAM ETTY - The Farewell - on board - 19¼ x 26in.
(Christie's) **$864 £480**

WILLIAM ETTY - A Study Of A Nude, small half length - inscribed and dated Nov. 1837 - on board - on panel - 15 x 13in.
(Christie's) **$1,260 £700**

WILLIAM EVANS OF ETON - Windsor From The Lock, figures and horses in the foreground - pencil and watercolour - 13½ x 17½in.
(Sotheby's) **$756 £420**

C. EVERARD - Flowers And Still Life On A Table - oils - 8 x 5in.
(G. A. Key) **$18 £10 Pair**

ALLAERT VAN EVERDINGEN - A Wooded Scandinavian Landscape with a sawmill by a cascade - 29½ x 24in.
(Christie's) **$2,700 £1,500**

PIETER VAN EVERDINGEN - Men-O'-War And Fishing Smacks At Sea - signed on the reverse - grey wash, watermark Arms Of Amsterdam - 20.3 x 32.4cm.
(Christie's) **$198 £110**

EWBANK - Figures On A Loch - 21½ x 26in.
(Sotheby's Belgravia) **$108 £60**

GASPAR VAN EYCK - A Mediterranean Coastal Scene with a galley firing a salute and men-o'-war moored offshore - bears indistinct signature and date - 41½ x 53½in.
(Christie's) **$6,300 £3,500**

J. FAANMAN - A Girl Ironing - signed -
15 x 11½in.
(Christie's) $810 £450

B. V. FABELLICKY - Venice, The Grand
Canal With St Mark's Square and the
Doge's Palace - signed and inscribed Vienna
- oil - 19½ x 32in.
(Heathcote Ball & Co) $732 £400

JOHN FAED - Rosalind and Orlando
in a wooded glade with roses and hollyhocks - signed and dated '65 - 26 x 19in.
(Woolley & Wallis) $1,584 £880

JOHN FAED - The Slave Girl - on board -
17 x 24in.
(Christie's) $11,700 £6,500

JOHN FAED - A View Of Gatehouse,
seen through an archway flanked by
bronze statues - signed and dated 1885 -
41 x 30in.
(Christie's) $1,710 £950

THOMAS FAED - The Music Lesson, the
old music master seated at ease, his atten-
tive girl student seated at his feet, an open
book on her lap and a cello by her side -
signed and dated 1853 - oil - on canvas -
24½ x 30in.
(Neales of Nottingham) $1,004 £520

THOMAS FAED - A Peasant Washer Woman by a stream and a child reclining on the bank - signed and dated 1883 - oil - 9¾ x 13¼in.
(Warner, Sheppard & Wade) **$1,666 £850**

THOMAS FAED - A Kitchen Interior - signed and dated 1863 - 15½ x 21in.
(Christie's) **$342 £190**

ELEANOR FAIRLAM - A Nook Of The Thames - signed and inscribed on the reverse - 11½ x 19½in.
(Christie's) **$1,365 £700**

J. FAIRLESS - A View Of Corbridge, Northumberland - signed - dated 1843 - on board - 19 x 29in.
(Sotheby's Belgravia) **$198 £110**

FANCELLI - A Sacrifice To Diana - black chalk, pen and brown ink, brown and grey wash - 31.4 x 22.8cm.
(Christie's) **$90£50**

FARINATO - Saint Jerome - black chalk, pen and brown ink, brown wash heightened with white, squared in black chalk, on blue paper - 26.8 x 17.6cm.
(Christie's) **$144 £80**

DAVID FARQUHARSON - Haymaking, Holland - signed and dated '84 - 17½ x 29½in.
(Sotheby's Belgravia) **$1,620 £900**

DAVID FARQUHARSON - The River Doon, Ayrshire - signed and dated 1898 - 8¼ x 11½in.
(Sotheby's Belgravia) **$504 £280**

DAVID FARQUHARSON - Noonday Shelter - signed and dated 1879 - 19½ x 35½in.
(Sotheby's Belgravia) **$2,520 £1,400**

DAVID FARQUHARSON - Autumn Pastures Above The Tarn; The Errant Calf - both signed and dated '87 - 20 x 29½in.
(Sotheby's Belgravia) **$6,300 £3,500 Pair**

FARQUHARSON

J. FARQUHARSON - An Approaching
Storm - 9½ x 11½in.
(Sotheby's Belgravia)   **$36 £20**

JOSEPH FARQUHARSON - Harvesting
On The Coast Of Scotland - signed -
33½ x 59½in.
(Christie's)   **$1,170 £600**

JOSEPH FARQUHARSON - Highland
Cattle On A Beach - signed - 17 x 35¼in.
(Sotheby's Belgravia)   **$720 £400**

G. A. FASOLA - Design For A Decorative
Panel - inscribed - pen and brown ink and
watercolour - 11.8 x 17.9cm.
(Christie's)   **$45£25**

JOHANN ADAM FASSAUER - Poultry In
Wooded Landscapes - both on panel - 6½ x
8½in.
(Christie's)   **$1,044 £580 Pair**

G. FATTORI - A Mounted Cavalry
Man in a landscape - bears signature -
7 x 15in.
(Christie's)   **$576£320**

JEAN FAUTRIER - Composition - signed
with initials and dated '60 - pen, ink and
wash - on paper - 20 x 25½in.
(Sotheby's)   **$1,921 £1,050**

GIACOMO LA FAVRETTO - Italian
Girls And A Man Admiring An
Umbrella - signed - watercolour -
26.0 x 38.8cm.
(Christie's)   **$1,440 £800**

FENWICK - In The Lake District -
25½ x 32½in.
(Sotheby's Belgravia)   **$360£200**

FRANZ DE PAULA FERG - An Italianate
Market Place With Strolling Players -
signed - on copper - 10¼ x 12¾in.
(Christie's)   **$7,644 £4,200**

FRANZ DE PAULA FERG - Peasants
Merrymaking By A Fountain with a mountainous landscape beyond - signed - on
copper - 10¼ x 12¾in.
(Christie's)   **$10,010 £5,500**

FRANZ DE PAULA FERG - A Winter Landscape with figures on a frozen waterway near a farm - signed - on copper - 8½ x 11¼in.
(Christie's)   **$11,830 £6,500**

JOHN DUNCAN FERGUSSON - Woman On A Bench - on board - 9¼ x 7¼in.
(Sotheby's Belgravia)   **$630 £350**

JOHN DUNCAN FERGUSSON - Thorenc - Afternoon 1929 - 76 x 66cm.
(Edmiston's)   **$2,610 £1,450**

JOHN DUNCAN FERGUSSON - Les Tilleuls, Becheron - dated 1932 - 65 x 54cm.
(Edmiston's)   **$810£450**

FERNELEY - A Bull with a herdsman outside a shed - 28 x 36in.
(Sotheby's)   **$810 £450**

JOHN FERNELEY, JUN - 'Styrrup', a chestnut hunter in an extensive landscape - signed, inscribed and dated 1860 - 27¼ x 35¼in.
(Christie's)   **$990 £550**

JOHN FERNELEY, SEN - General Chasse, A Bay Racehorse, standing in a field - signed - 9½ x 11½in.
(Sotheby's)   **$900 £500**

SCHOOL OF FERRARA, circa 1480 - The Flight Into Egypt - on panel - 14 x 21in.
(Christie's)   **$9,000 £5,000**

GIOVANNI ANDREA DE FERRARI - The Madonna And Child Appearing To Saint Peter, Saint Paul And Saint John The Evangelist - 56½ x 66in.
(Christie's)   **$5,460 £3,000**

FERRARI

GIUSEPPE FERRARI - Arabs At Prayer in an extensive desert landscape - signed and dated Roma 1884 - water-colour - 53 x 96in.
(Christie's)   **$108 £60**

ORAZIO DE FERRARI - The Tribute Money - 44½ x 54in.
(Christie's)   **$5,400 £3,000**

E. FICHEL - Le Tasse Du Cafe - signed and dated 1882 - oil - on panel - 13 x 18in.
(Bonham's)   **$6,300 £3,500**

E. FICHEL - The Spinner - on panel - 10¾ x 8½in.
(Christie's)   **$684 £380**

EUGENE FICHEL - The Library - signed and dated 1865 - on panel - 15 x 18in.
(Christie's)   **$2,160 £1,200**

COPLEY FIELDING - A Fenland Scene With Boats - signed and dated 1824 - 24 x 37cm.
(King & Chasemore)   **$144 £80**

ANTHONY VANDYKE COPLEY FIELDING - A Distant View Of Cardiff - signed with initials - inscribed and dated 1829 - 7½ x 11½in.
(Sotheby's)   **$270 £150**

ANTHONY VAN DYKE COPLEY FIELDING - A Highland Scene - signed and dated 1828 - oil - on canvas - 11½ x 9½in.
(King & Chasemore)   **$1,440 £800**

ANTHONY VANDYKE COPLEY FIELDING - Distant View Of Chepstow Castle, Monmouthshire - signed and dated 1832 - 10 x 12¾in.
(Sotheby's)   **$1,800 £1,000**

ANTHONY VANDYKE COPLEY FIELDING - The Beach At Dover, Kent - signed - 11 x 14¾in.
(Sotheby's)   **$3,240 £1,800**

ANTHONY VANDYKE COPLEY FIELDING - A View Of Durham Cathedral from the South - 8½ x 10½in.
(Sotheby's)   **$324 £180**

FIGINO - The Rape Of The Sabines with A Ploughman and buildings under construction - black chalk, pen and brown ink - 8.8 x 21.1cm.
(Christie's)   **$117 £65**

FRANCIS OLIVER FINCH - A Romantic Landscape with a traveller by a waterfall - heightened with bodycolour - 17½ x 24 in.
(Sotheby's)   **$288 £160**

M. DEL FIORE - Roses, Tulips, And Other Flowers In Urns - 18½ x 10in.
(Christie's)   **$2,340 £1,300 Pair**

F. FISCHETTI - The Horses Of Apollo - pen and brown ink, grey wash - 18.8 x 15.4cm.
(Christie's)   **$63 £35**

FEDELE FISCHETTI - Four Girls In A Garden With A Fountain, a stag in the distance - pen and brown ink, grey wash - 19.7 x 24.7cm.
(Christie's)   **$135 £75**

FEDELE FISCHETTI, Attributed to - The Trinity In Glory - on oval panel - 10 x 7¼in.
(Christie's N. York)   **$330 £180**

MAJOR GENERAL SIR GEORGE BULTEEL FISHER - Near Killarney - pencil and watercolour - 14 x 19¼ in.
(Sotheby's)   **$180 £100**

J. FITZ-MARSHALL - Portrait Of A Fox Terrier In A Landscape - signed and dated 1909 - inscribed on the reverse - 13½ x 17¼in.
(Sotheby's Belgravia)   **$117 £65**

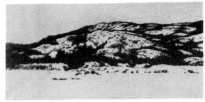

GUSTAF FJAESTAD - Winterlandscape - signed - 90 x 150cm.
(Goteborgs Auktionsverk)   **$4,114 £2,286**

GUSTAVE FLASSCHOEN - The Round Up, a South American Gaucho pursuing a herd of horses - signed - 14½ x 17¼in.
(Sotheby's)   **$425 £220**

DAN FLAVIN - Untitled - fluorescent light (yellow, red) - length 94½in.
(Christie's)   **$5,490 £3,000**

J. FLEMING - A View Of The Lake Of Menteith With Stirling Castle In The Distance - 27 x 36in.
(Sotheby's Belgravia)   **$2,700 £1,500**

FLEMISH SCHOOL

FLEMISH SCHOOL, 17th century -The Miraculous Draught Of Fishes - 34 x 42¾in.
(Sotheby's) **$10,175 £5,500**

FLEMISH SCHOOL, 17th century - Three Men Leaning On A Balustrade - pen drawing - 32 x 20cm.
(Christian Rosset) **$347 £193**

FLEMISH SCHOOL, circa 1625 - Alexander And The Body Of Darius - 49 x 64½in.
(Christie's) **$2,880 £1,600**

FLEMISH SCHOOL, circa 1700 - Wooded River Landscapes with peasants outside cottages and fishing vessels beyond - one indistinctly signed with initials - on panel - 7¼ x 9½in.
(Christie's) **$3,640 £2,000 Pair**

FLEMISH SCHOOL, 17th century - The Offering - oil - on wood panel - 25.5 x 33.5cm.
(Christian Rosset) **$239 £133**

FLEMISH SCHOOL, Late 16th century - The Adoration Of The Magi - 31 x 40in.
(Christie's N. York) **$660 £361**

C. FLETCHER - Coaching Scenes - signed - on panel - 9¾ x 12in.
(Sotheby's Belgravia) **$756 £420 Pair**

HARRY BENTON FLETCHER - The Temple Of Luxor, Sunset - signed with monogram and signed and inscribed on the reverse - watercolour - 17½ x 11in.
(Christie's) **$72 £40**

SIR WILLIAM RUSSELL FLINT - 'Melody' - signed - sepia crayon - 12 x 7¾in.
(Sotheby Bearne) **$468 £240**

J. V. DE FLEURY - A Gypsy Encampment - indistinctly signed and dated - 13¼ x 17in.
(Sotheby Bearne) **$270 £150**

GOVAERT FLINCK - Cupid Asleep in a wooded landscape, with nymphs bathing beyond - signed and dated 1655 - 26 x 32in.
(Christie's) **$6,370 £3,500**

SIR WILLIAM RUSSELL FLINT - Tristan and Isolda - signed and dated MCMX - watercolour - 28 x 22cm.
(Edmiston's) **$756 £420**

FLINT

SIR WILLIAM RUSSELL FLINT -
In The Hills - signed - 10 x 14½in.
(Sotheby's Belgravia) **$540 £300**

SIR WILLIAM RUSSELL FLINT -
Above A Loch - signed - 10 x 14¼in.
(Sotheby's Belgravia) **$396 £220**
MARY SARGANT FLORENCE - Truth
And Beauty - tempera - on panel -
27½ x 69in.
(Sotheby's Belgravia) **$27 £15**

FLORENTINE SCHOOL, Early 16th
century - Portrait Of A Young Man
Wearing A Red Hat - inscribed - oil -
on panel - 24 x 17in.
(Phillips, Solihull) **$666 £340**

F. FLORIS - The Triumph Of Judas
Maccabees - bears inscription - on
panel - 52¾ x 82½in.
(Christie's) **$3,420 £1,900**
FOCQUELER, 18th century - Martinique
Harbour with sailing ships and rowing
boat, Negro and Negress with fruit vendors
- signed - oil - on canvas - 19 x 11in.
(Stewart Gore) **$617 £325**

HENRY FOLLENFANT - Village Scenes
- signed and dated - 20 x 29½in.
(Sotheby's Belgravia) **$1,044 £580 Pair**
LAI FONG - A British Clipper Under
Sail - signed - inscribed 'Calcutta' and
dated 1894 - 11½ x 15½in.
(Sotheby's, Hong Kong) **$3.060 £1,700**

LAVINIA FONTANA, Circle of - Portrait
of a Lady as Saint Ursula, standing full
length in a river landscape with a town
in the background - 82½ x 49½ in.
(Christie's N. York) **$6,050 £3,306**

FONTEBASSO - Studies Of Three Nymphs Supporting Cushions - pen and brown ink, brown wash on brown paper - 19.9 x 20.6cm.
(Christie's) **$90 £50**
BELIN DE FONTENAY - Roses, Tulips And Other Flowers In A Sculptured Urn on a ledge - 24½ x 18½in.
(Christie's) **$1,620 £900**
GIROLAMO FORABOSCO, Attributed to - A Lady In Red And Yellow Dress, small bust length - 6 x 5in.
(Christie's N. York) **$220 £120**

T. FORD - An Exotic Still Life - signed - inscribed and dated May 1874 - heightened with bodycolour - 20½ x 15¼in.
(Sotheby's Belgravia) **$270 £150**

JEAN-LOUIS FORAIN - The Blond Hair - 70 x 59cm.
(Auktionshaus am Neumarkt) **$4,802 £2,624**

CAPTAIN JOHN HAUGHTON FORREST - A Steam Yacht In A Choppy Sea - signed and inscribed Cowes - 29½ x 46½in.
(Christie's) **$3,705 £1,900**

N. FORCELLA - The Hookah - signed - 27½ x 18in.
(Christie's) **$1,350 £750**

G. FORSTER - A Street Scene In Enfield - on board - 10½ x 17½in.
(Sotheby's Belgravia) **$540 £300**

MARIO FORTUNY - Head Of A
Cavalier - signed and dated 1867 - on
panel - 8 x 5½in.
(Christie's) **$1,530 £850**

MARIO FORTUNY - A Roman Lady,
standing small three-quarter length
wearing black - signed and inscribed
Rome - on board - 11½ x 8in.
(Christie's) **$1,350 £750**

FOSCHI - A Winter River Landscape
with travellers on a path and a village
beyond - 28½ x 36in.
(Christie's) **$990 £550**

FOSTER - Playing With Toy Boats -
bears monogram - heightened with white -
9 x 14in.
(Sotheby's Belgravia) **$126 £70**

HERBERT WILSON FOSTER - Wild
Flowers, Fresh And Free - signed -
heightened with bodycolour - 23½
x 19¾in.
(Sotheby's Belgravia) **$576 £320**

MYLES BIRKET FOSTER - Rio Ognisanti,
Venice - signed with monogram - water-
colour heightened with white - 5½ x 3¾in.
(Christie's) **$1,044 £580**

MYLES BIRKET FOSTER - Cadenabbia - signed with monogram - watercolour heightened with white - 4¾ x 7¼in.
(Christie's) **$1,260 £700**

VERNON FOSTER - River Scene With Cottage And Figures on the Downs - watercolour - 10 x 14in.
(G. A. Key) **$32 £18**

TSUGHOUHARU FOUJITA - Self-Portrait with cat - 44 x 34.5cm.
(Auktionshaus am Neumarkt) **$1,213 £663**

J. A. FOUND - Snipe Shooting And Duck Shooting - oil - 9 x 12in.
(Buckell & Ballard) **$90 £50 Pair**

THEODORE FOURMOIS - A Wooded Landscape with a figure in the foreground and a cottage byond - canvas laid down on panel - 7½ x 9¾in.
(Christie's) **$378 £210**

W. FOWLER - Landscape With Fisherman - signed - oil - 7 x 11in.
(Hussey's) **$155 £86**

FRANCES

C. J. FOX - Drover And Cattle At A Ford - watercolour - 8 x 12in.
(G. A. Key) **$36 £20**

E. M. FOX - Study Of A Mare and her foal - signed and dated 1839 - oil - on canvas - 63 x 78cm.
(King & Chasemore) **$2,046 £1,100**

HENRY CHARLES FOX - Driving Sheep Along A Country Lane - signed and dated 1919 - heightened with bodycolour - 14 x 20¾in.
(Sotheby's Belgravia) **$104 £58**

HENRY CHARLES FOX - In Early Spring - signed and dated 1910 - heightened with bodycolour - 25¼ x 39in.
(Sotheby's Belgravia) **$198 £110**

HENRY JAMES FOX - Cattle Watering - signed - watercolour - 13 x 20in.
(Hussey's) **$230 £128**

J. FRANCES - Cavaliers Drinking Outside An Inn - signed - 31¾ x 25in.
(Christie's) **$2,160 £1,200**

FRANCOIS LOUIS THOMAS FRANCIA - Entering Harbour at Calais - signed - 11 x 17¼ in.
(Sotheby's) $1,170 £650

FRANCOIS LOUIS THOMAS FRANCIA - The Royal Observatory, Greenwich, with the Artist sketching on the hillside - signed and dated 1828 - 10¾ x 17 in.
(Sotheby's) $1,530 £850

GIACOMO FRANCIA - The Madonna And Child With Saint Francis And Saint Catherine - on panel - 26 x 22in.
(Christie's) $8,190 £4,500

SAM FRANCIS - Blue 1960 - acrylic on paper - 19¾ x 26 in.
(Christie's) $5,124 £2,800

SAM FRANCIS - Untitled Composition - signed on the reverse - gouache - on paper - 15 x 11in.
(Sotheby's) $2,928 £1,600

SAM FRANCIS - Symbols and Spaces - watercolour - 42 x 73 in.
(Christie's N. York)$15,400 £8,555

**F. FRANCKEN THE YOUNGER AND
J. VAN KESSEL** - Saint Hubert And
Saint Anthony Abbot - on copper - on
panel - 6½ x 9in.
(Christie's) $2,340 £1,300

FRANS FRANCKEN THE YOUNGER -
The Presentation Of The Virgin - signed
and dated 1640 - on copper - 14¾ x
19¼in.
(Christie's) $2,700 £1,500

F. FRANCKEN THE YOUNGER -
Minerva The Protectress Of The Arts
And Sciences - on panel - 28½ x 41in.
(Christie's) $28,800 £16,000

FRANCO-FLEMISH SCHOOL, circa 1720 -
The Rape Of Europe - red chalk, pen and
brown ink, grey wash, watermark Arms of
Amsterdam - 27.4 x 34.8cm.
(Christie's) $126 £70

FRANS FRANCKEN, Attributed to -
Ecce Homo - oil - on copper - 18 x
14.5cm.
(Christian Rosset) $383 £213

FRANS FRANCKEN - Visitors In An Artist's
Gallery Of Pictures, with an allegorical scene
to the right - 20¾ x 29¼in.
(Christie's) $14,040 £7,800

ALBERT J. FRANKE - A Conversation
By The Well - signed and dated Munchen
'86 - on panel - 13 x 10½in.
(Christie's) $1,440 £800

169

FRANKENTHALER

HELEN FRANKENTHALER - Swan Lake No. 2 - signed - inscribed and dated 1961 - acrylic on canvas - 93 x 93½ in.
(Christie's N. York) **$45,100 £25,055**

JOSE FRAPPA - A Theological Dispute - signed - 21 x 25in.
(Christie's) **$756 £420**

A. FRASER - A Rural Landscape With Horses Drinking at a duckpond and boys fishing - signed - oil - on canvas - 16 x 24in.
(Warner, Sheppard & Wade) **$1,960 £1,000**

ALEXANDER FRASER - On Holmwood Common, Surrey - signed - inscribed on the reverse - 15½ x 23¼in.
(Sotheby's Belgravia) **$864 £480**

ALEXANDER FRASER - A View Of Kilchurn Castle, Argyllshire with crofters, cattle, sheep and goats in the foreground - signed - 29 x 40½in.
(Christie's) **$1,440 £800**

A. ANDERSON FRASER - A Quiet River Scene - signed with monogram - dated 1886 - heightened with body-colour - 18 x 27in.
(Sotheby's Belgravia) **$153 £85**

F. G. FRASER - Broadland Scenes - watercolour - 7 x 14in.
(G. A. Key) **$36 £20 Pair**

ROBERT W. FRASER - Punting On A River - signed with initials - heightened with bodycolour - 7½ x 15in.
(Sotheby's Belgravia) **$99 £55**

ALEXANDER FRAZER, SEN - The Bugler - signed and dated 1843 - 15¾ x 11½in.
(Christie's) **$720 £400**

WILLIAM MILLER FRAZER - The Tay
Near Newburgh - signed - 13½ x 21½in.
(Sotheby's Belgravia) **$504 £280**

WILLIAM MILLER FRAZER - Near
Huntingdon - signed - 11½ x 13½in.
(Sotheby's Belgravia) **$252 £140**

WILLIAM MILLER FRAZER -
Animals Grazing By A Mill - signed
and dated '03 - 24½ x 29½in.
(Sotheby's Belgravia) **$540 £300**

FRENCH SCHOOL - A Traveller By A
Fallen Column Near Rome - the mount
inscribed 'hors de Rome. 1756' - pencil,
pen and grey ink and watercolour -
35.4 x 48.4cm.
(Christie's) **$54 £30**

FRENCH SCHOOL, 18th century - The
Dice Player - watercolour on vellum -
25.2 x 20.0cm.
(Christie's) **$27 £15**

**FRENCH PROVINCIAL SCHOOL, 19th
century** - The Horses of Diomedes - oil -
on canvas - 51 x 60cm.
(King & Chasemore) **$412 £210**

FRENCH SCHOOL, 19th century -
Flowers - oil - on canvas - 61 x 46cm.
(Christian Rosset) **$527 £293**

FRENCH SCHOOL, 17th century -
Diana And Actaeon - oil - on canvas -
30 x 47cm.
(King & Chasemore) **$206 £105**

171

FRENCH SCHOOL

FRENCH SCHOOL - Christ Raising The Daughter Of Jairus - dated 1815 - pencil, grey wash, heightened with white - 38.0 x 25.4cm.
(Christie's)   **$117 £65**

FRENCH SCHOOL, circa 1730 - Lady At Her Toilette taking a letter from a black pageboy; and A Lady Drinking Chocolate - one signed with initials and dated 1730 - both on copper - 17 x 12½in.
(Christie's)   **$5,460 £3,000 Pair**

FRENCH SCHOOL - Study Of A Seated Woman - pastel - 66.0 x 54.0cm.
(Christie's)   **$81 £45**

FRENCH SCHOOL, late 19th century - A Group Of Four Ladies in a woodland glade - on panel - 10 x 14¼in.
(Sotheby Bearne)   **$225 £125**

FRENCH SCHOOL, 19th century - A Provencal Farm - oil - on panel - 24 x 18cm.
(King & Chasemore)   **$108 £55**

FRENCH SCHOOL, 18th century - Two Young Women Looking Upwards - red chalk - 18.5 x 24cm.
(Christian Rosset)   **$576 £320**

FRENCH SCHOOL, 18th century - A Lady Dressed A La Turque - pen and grey ink, grey wash - 26.4 x 18.8cm.
(Christie's)   **$90 £50**

THEODORE FRERE - Arabs At An Oasis - signed - on panel - 10 x 17in.
(Christie's) **$504 £280**

WASHINGTON F. FRIEND - The Falls At Niagara - signed - watercolour, heightened with white - 10¼ x 14¼in.
(Sotheby's) **$386 £200**

EMILE OTHON FRIESZ - Still Life With Apples and flowers - 38.5 x 46cm.
(Auktionshaus am Neumarkt) **$6,066 £3,315**

ALFRED DOWNING FRIPP - The Fisherfolks' Home - signed and dated 1889 - heightened with bodycolour - 21½ x 27½in.
(Sotheby's Belgravia) **$360 £200**

ALFRED DOWNING FRIPP - The Sailor's Departure - signed - heightened with bodycolour - 21½ x 27½in.
(Sotheby's Belgravia) **$576 £320**

GEORGE ARTHUR FRIPP - St. Vincent Rocks, Clifton, Bristol - signed and dated 1840 - inscribed on old label pasted to the reverse - 14½ x 24¼in.
(Sotheby's) **$2,520 £1,400**

GEORGE ARTHUR FRIPP - River And Mountain Landscape with figures and goats on a path - oil - on board - 8¼ x 11½in.
(Buckell & Ballard) **$243 £135**

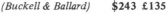

EUGENE FROMENTIN - Thieves Of The Night - signed and dated 1865 - 51¾ x 80¼in.
(Christie's) **$23,400 £13,000**

WILLIAM EDWARD FROST - The Spell - heightened with bodycolour - circular - diameter 8¾in.
(Sotheby's Belgravia) **$54 £30**

HARRY WINDSOR FRY - 'St. Christopher' - signed - arched top - 57 x 34¼in.
(Sotheby Bearne) $234 £130

THOMAS FRYE - Portrait Of A Man, bust length, wearing a turban, his hands resting on a chair - black and white chalk on brown paper - 17 x 13¼in.
(Christie's) $468 £260

ERNST FUCHS - Medusa-Look - signed and dated 1968 - acrylic and coloured chalks - 21 x 16½ in.
(Christie's) $2,745 £1,500

JOHANN HEINRICH FUSELI - A Sheet Of Figure Studies - inscribed - pen and brown ink - 7½ x 8in.
(Sotheby's) $3,960 £2,200

J. FYT - A Still Life Of A Dead Hare, partridges and other birds on a stone ledge - 14½ x 21½in.
(Christie's) $990 £550

J. FYT - A Still Life With A Parrot, Chickens, A Turkey And A Dead Hare And Snipe in a landscape - bears signature - 24¾ x 35½in.
(Christie's) $2,520 £1,400

GIUSEPPE GABANI - A North African
Street Scene - signed and inscribed Roma -
on board - 11 x 18¼in.
(Christie's)   **$1,710 £950**

DOMENICO GABBIANI - A Mother
And Child - inscribed - red chalk,
pen and brown ink, brown wash -
16.7 x 11.4cm.
(Christie's)   **$216 £120**

GAGEN - The Amethyst Falls, The
Mackenzie River, Thunder Bay, Ontario,
with fishermen in the foreground - oil -
on canvas - 27¾ x 20½in.
(Sotheby's)   **$888 £460**

THOMAS GAINSBOROUGH - Study of
a Cow - black and white chalks on brown
paper - 5½ x 7 in.
(Sotheby's)   **$1,980 £1,100**

THOMAS GAINSBOROUGH - Woodland
Pools - pen with brown ink, brown and
grey wash - 7¾ x 9½ in.
(Sotheby's)   **$3,420 £1,900**

THOMAS GAINSBOROUGH - A
Wooded Landscape with horsemen,
figures and ruined buildings, black and
grey chalk, grey wash, oil - 7¾ x 11½in.
(Sotheby's)   **$3,330 £1,850**

THOMAS GAINSBOROUGH - A Wooded
Landscape with herdsmen, cattle and
sheep by a pond - 46½ x 58½in.
(Christie's)   **$324,000 £180,000**

THOMAS GAINSBOROUGH - A Wooded Landscape With Village Scene, figures in the foreground, a church with steeple in the distance - pen and black ink, watercolour and oil on reddish-brown toned paper, varnished, mounted on canvas - 16 x 21in.
(Sotheby's) **$30,600 £17,000**

THOMAS GAINSBOROUGH - A Peasant Girl Gathering Faggots, 66½ x 48½in.
(Sotheby's) **$165,600 £92,000**

ROBERT GALLON - Shipping On The Thames - signed and dated (18)87 - 11½ x 35½in.
(Sotheby Bearne) **$1,287 £660**

ROBERT GALLON - On The Severn Near Worcester - signed - 23½ x 35½in.
(Christie's) **$3,060 £1,700**

ROBERT GALLON - A Landscape With A Village And Figures - signed - oil - on canvas - 20 x 30in.
(Bonham's) **$2,340 £1,300**

HERBERT REGINALD GALLOP - "Bridge Building" - 1927 - oil - on board - 45 x 60cm.
(Australian Art Auctions) **$596 £331**

GANDOLFI - Head Of A Girl - red chalk - 35.8 x 26.2cm.
(Christie's) **$180 £100**

RAFFAELLINO DEL GARBO - The Madonna And Child With Angels - on panel - circular - 37in. diameter.
(Sotheby's) **$40,700 £22,000**

GEORGE GARDINER - River Scene, View Of The Steam Packet - watercolour - 7 x 10in.
(G. A. Key) **$14 £8**

SID GARDNER - Feeding The Chickens, a street scene in Wilford with thatched cottages - signed - oil - on board - 9½ x 13¼in.
(Neales of Nottingham) **$87 £45**

H. GARLAND - Highland Drove - signed and dated 1895 - signed and dated on the reverse - 29¼ x 49½in.
(Christie's) **$900 £500**

W. F. GARDEN - Wooded River Land-scapes - signed and dated '93 - 7½ x 10¾in.
(Lawrence) **$1,188 £660 Four**

H. GARNIER - Street Scene In Cairo and companion - signed - 12 x 7in.
(Phillips, Solihull) **$1,073 £580 Pair**

WILLIAM FRAZER GARDEN - Evening, Sunset - signed and dated - heightened with bodycolour - 6½ x 10½in.
(Sotheby's Belgravia) **$522 £290**

LUCAS GASSEL - A Mountainous Land-scape With The Magdalen - signed in mono-gram and dated 1539 - on panel - 18¾ x 22in.
(Sotheby's) **$31,450 £17,000**

GAUERMANN

FRIEDRICH GAUERMANN - An Austrian Wooded River Mountain Landscape with mill and stag in the foreground - signed and dated 1835 - oil - on paper - 19½ x 15in.
(Bonham's) **$11,160 £6,200**

GAUFFIER - Figures Promenading In A Classical Landscape - 13 x 20in.
(Christie's) **$810 £450**

LOUIS GAUFFIER - A View Of Baiae - black chalk - 24.7 x 37.7cm.
(Christie's) **$108 £60**

GOLTZIUS GELDORP - Venus Holding The Golden Apple - signed with initials and dated 1616 - on panel - 25½ x 19¾in.
(Christie's) **$1,260 £700**

BENEDETTO GENNARI - Rinaldo Bewitched By Love For Armida - 97 x 63in.
(Sotheby's) **$6,475 £3,500**

F. GEERTY - A Domestic Interior With Two Peasant Children And A Cat - signed and dated 1865 - 29 x 25in.
(H. Spencer & Sons) **$414 £230**

PAUL GEN - The Violinist Noceti - signed and dated 15.11.30 - watercolour - 61 x 42cm.
(Christian Rosset) **$2,928 £1,600**

PAUL GEN - Fille de Delattre - 73 x 60cm.
(Auktionshaus am Neumarkt) **$9,606 £5,249**

ARTEMISIA GENTILESCHI, Attributed to - The Holy Family And Saint Anne, with a dove - 34 x 37½in.
(Christie's N. York)   **$418 £228**

M. GERARD - The Family Reunion - on panel - 17 x 14½in.
(Christie's)   **$3,060 £1,700**

JEAN LEON GEROME - The Call To Prayer - signed - on panel - 15½ x 11½in.
(Christie's)   **$23,400 £13,000**

GESSNITZER - 19th century Dutch Canal Scene - signed - canvas - 19 x 31½in.
(Morphets of Harrogate) **$648 £360**

GHEERAERTS - Portrait Of A Gentleman, thought to be John Dudley, Duke of Northumberland, half length, wearing armour and a ruff, a coat of arms of lozenges to his right - bears date '1594' - 23½ x 19½in.
(Sotheby's)   **$396 £220**

GHEERAERTS, THE YOUNGER - Portrait Of Sir Thomas Fleming at the age of 64, three-quarter length, wearing his robes of office and holding a parchment - dated 1608 - inscribed - on panel - 35¼ x 25¾in.
(Sotheby's)   **$504 £280**

P. L GHEZZI - Dwarfs In A Stable: The Arrival Of A Dignitary - inscribed - red chalk - 20.7 x 49.6cm.
(Christie's)   **$342 £190**

AUGUSTO GIACOMETTI - Laubbaume bei San Domenico - 25 x 34cm.
(Auktionshaus am Neumarkt)
$4,549 £2,486

GIAMPETRINO, Attributed to - Head Of The Virgin - en grisaille - 11 x 8in.
(Christie's N. York)   **$2,420 £1,322**

GIUSEPPE GIANNI - H.M.S. Helicon Anchored At Malta - on board - 12½ x 20¼in.
(Christie's)   **$720£400**

M. GIANNI - Neapolitan Scenes - signed - gouache - watercolour - 11 x 19in.
(Heathcote Ball & Co) **$101 £55 Pair**

GIAQUINTO - God The Father, in glory - on panel - circular - 5in. diameter.
(Christie's)   **$180 £100**

R. GIBBONS - 'Farmyard Scene' - signed - oil - 24 x 20in.
(J. Entwistle & Co.) **$277 £150**

THOMAS GIBSON - Portrait Of Elizabeth Hickes, later Mrs. George Somerville, depicted as a shepherdess against landscape background - signed and dated 1724 - 49 x 39¼in.
(Sotheby Bearne) **$780 £400**

WILLIAM ALFRED GIBSON - On The Moor - signed - 27½ x 35½in.
(Sotheby's Belgravia) **$324 £180**

THOMAS GIBSON - Three-quarter length portrait of Edwin Yate - 49 x 39in.
(Sotheby Bearne) **$507 £260**

W. A. GIBSON - Landscape with figures and buildings - oil - 9¾ x 15in.
(Thomas Love & Sons Ltd.) **$342 £190**

W. A. GIBSON - Meeting The Boats - 27 x 35cm.
(Edmiston's) **$558 £310**

JOSEPH W. GIES - Practising The French Horn - signed, inscribed and dated 1889 - oil - on panel - 15 x 12in.
(Bonham's) **$1,710 £950**

R. GIFFINGER - A Moonlight View Of A Harbour - signed - on panel - 20 x 15¾in.
(Christie's) **$720 £400**

JOHN GIFFORD - Two Gun Dogs With A Pheasant rising in woodland setting - signed - oil - 24 x 36in.
(Richard Baker & Baker) **$540 £300**

JOHN GIFFORD - Companion picture to previous lot, depicting two Gun Dogs Resting By Day's Catch in moorland setting - signed - oil.
(Richard Baker & Baker) **$486 £270**

ARTHUR GILBERT - Llanberis Pass -
signed and dated 1892 - inscribed on a
label on the reverse - 23½ x 35¾in.
(Christie's)   **$1,620 £900**

SIR JOHN GILBERT - Tales Of The
Sword - signed - heightened with body-
colour - arched top - 8½ x 10½in.
(Sotheby's Belgravia)   **$117 £65**

JOSEPH FRANCIS GILBERT - A Wooded
River Landscape, cattle and a figure in the
foreground and mountains beyond - signed,
inscribed 'Rochester' and dated June 30th
1829 - canvas - on panel - 13 x 19½in.
(Sotheby's)   **$648 £360**

JAMES GILES - Deer By A Loch,
Evening - signed and dated 1850,
heightened with bodycolour - 12
x 17¾in.
(Sotheby's Belgravia)   **$234 £130**

JAMES GILES - The Temple Of The Sybil
At Tivoli with figures and goats in the
foreground - signed and dated 1838 - on
panel - 17½ x 13½in.
(Sotheby's)   **$450 £250**

J. W. GILES - Stalkers - 18½ x 25½in.
(Sotheby's Belgravia)   **$360 £200**

JAMES WILLIAM GILES - Highland
Felicity, Benclibrick In The Distance,
Sutherland - signed and dated 1860 -
27¼ x 35¼in.
(Sotheby's Belgravia)   **$1,620 £900**

JAMES WILLIAM GILES - A Study On
A Highland Braeside - signed and dated
1867 - on board - 17½ x 23½in.
(Sotheby's Belgravia)   **$864 £480**

EDMUND GILL - On The River Dochart,
Killin, Scotland - signed and dated 1871
- 21½ x 29¼in.
(Christie's)   **$50 £28**

H. GILL - Still Life Of Fruit And A
Glass On A Table - signed - 9½ x 13¾in.
(Sotheby's Belgravia)   **$63 £35**

GILL

R. A. GILL - Italian Lake Scene with chalets and mountain background - watercolour - 9 x 15in.
(G. A. Key)   **$14 £8**

VAN GILL - London Dockland Scene with public house and fishing boats beached - watercolour - 14 x 20in.
(G. A. Key)   **$47 £26**

W. GILL - Figures By A Mill - 6¾ x 10¼in.
(Sotheby's Belgravia)   **$324 £180**

S. GILPIN - Study Of Two Horses - black chalk, a drawing of a landscape on the reverse - 20.0 x 29.5cm.
(Christie's)   **$27 £15**

SAWREY GILPIN - A Study Of Fighting Stallions - inscribed - pencil and coloured wash, heightened with white on buff paper - 16 x 33in.
(Sotheby's)   **$450 £250**

GIACINTO GIMIGNANI, Circle of - A Scene From Roman History - 59½ x 59½in.
(Christie's N. York)   **$1,760 £962**

BALDOMERO GALOFRE Y GIMINEZ - A Landscape With Horsemen - signed and inscribed Toledo - watercolour - 20.1 x 40.4cm.
(Christie's)   **$216 £120**

L. GIORDANO - The Adoration Of The Shepherds - 53 x 81¾in.
(Christie's)   **$3,960 £2,200**

LUCA GIORDANO - Saint Anne And The Infant Virgin In Glory, with Saint Sebastian, Saint James, Saint Ignatius Loyola and Saint Gregory below, and God the Father with the Dove and Angels above - 49½ x 26in.
(Christie's)   **$17,100 £9,500**

LUCA GIORDANO - The Annunciation -
oil - on copper - 23 x 21cm.
(Christian Rosset) **$383 £213**

GIORDANO - The Adoration Of The
Magi - 71 x 39½in.
(Christie's) **$1,350 £750**

GIOTTO, Close Follower of - The Last
Supper; and Saint Francis Receiving The
Stigmata - on gold ground panel - 13 x 6in.
(Christie's) **$11,700 £6,500 Pair**

PALMA GIOVANE, After - Apollo Flaying
Marsyas - on panel - 6 x 8½in.
(Christie's) **$1,530 £850**

PALMA GIOVANE - Study Of A Hand -
inscribed on the reverse - black chalk on
blue paper - 8.1 x 11.9cm.
(Christie's) **$54 £30**

APOLLONIO DI GIOVANNI, Circle of -
A Cassone: the front panel depicting a
triumphal procession; the end panels
Aristotle and Campaspe, and Samson and
Delilah - front panel 14¾ x 53in. end
panels 15 x 19in.
(Christie's) **$34,580 £19,000**

THOMAS GIRTIN - A River Valley
With Cattle And Sheep on a tree
covered bank - pencil and watercolour - 4¾ x 6in.
(Sotheby's) **$1,620 £900**

GIRTIN

THOMAS GIRTIN - Belle Vue And Pont De Sevres From St. Cloud - hand coloured soft ground etching - 5½ x 18in.
(Sotheby's) **$756 £420**

HUGH DE GLAZENBURGH - Portrait Of A Young Boy Seated - signed and dated 1948 - 64½ x 36in.
(Sotheby's Belgravia) **$324 £180**

HENRY GILLARD GLINDONI - The Interior Of A 16th century Room, with a man dancing with a small girl, a lady seated at a table playing a lute and singing - signed and dated 1885 - on panel - 9¾ x 11¾in.
(H. Spencer & Sons) **$504 £280**

HENRY GILLARD GLINDONI - A Park Scene With Two Young Ladies and an officer holding a cocked hat sitting on a bench - signed and dated 1887 - on panel - 9¾ x 11¾in.
(H. Spencer & Sons) **$864 £480**

HENRY GILLARD GLINDONI - A Warming Fire - signed and dated 1877 - on panel - 9½ x 7½in.
(Christie's) **$576 £320**

JOHN GLOVER - A Rocky Highland Landscape with figures on a track - watercolour heightened with white - 26½ x 40½in.
(Christie's) **$1,080 £600**

JOHN GLOVER - The Temple Of The Sybil At Tivoli - signed and inscribed on the reverse - watercolour - 19½ x 27¼in.
(Christie's) **$1,980 £1,100**

JOHN GLOVER - A Farm above Ullswater - 9¾ x 14 in.
(Sotheby's) **$108 £60**

DOMENICO GNOLI - Roman Dreamer - signed and dated '59 - brown and black ink - on paper - 26½ x 23½in.
(Sotheby's) **$3,843 £2,100**

GODCHAUX - An Extensive River Landscape with two figures in the foreground and a range of snowcapped mountains in the distance - signed - 15¼ x 25in.
(Sotheby Bearne) **$522 £290**

EDWARD ANGELO GOODALL - A Street in Cairo near Coppersmiths' Bazaar - 20½ x 14¼in.
(Sotheby's) **$630 £350**

JOHN WILLIAM GODWARD - Nerissa - signed and dated 1906 - 60 x 32in.
(Christie's) **$684 £380**

JAN GOEREE - Saint Hilary; and Saint Cyril - inscribed respectively 'Hilarius' and 'Cyrillus' - pen and brown ink, grey wash - 14.7 x 11.4cm.
(Christie's) **$50 £28 Two**

SIGISMUND GOETZE - The Crown Of England Being Offered To Richard, Duke Of Gloucester, at Baynards Castle, 1483 - 35½ x 23in.
(Sotheby's Belgravia) **$117 £65**

COLONEL ROBERT CHARLES GOFF - A Busy Harbour - signed with initials - 15 x 24in.
(Sotheby's Belgravia) **$63 £35**

T. S. GOOD - A Scottish Tavern - on board - 13½ x 18in.
(Sotheby's Belgravia) **$68 £38**

GOODALL

GOODALL - Blind Man's Buff In The Harem - 22 x 29in.
(Sotheby's Belgravia) $81 £45

EDWARD ANGELO GOODALL - Arabs On A Raft In A River Landscape with the Pyramids beyond - signed - watercolour - 13 x 25½in.
(Christie's) $504 £280

F. GOODALL - Shepherds And Their Flocks near the Pyramids - bears monogram - 11 x 21in.
(Christie's) $270 £150

FREDERICK GOODALL - The Blind Faker - signed with monogram and dated 1887 - watercolour heightened with white - 6¾ x 11½in.
(Christie's) $108 £60

FREDERICK GOODALL - Arabs And Camels At A Well near a desert town - signed with monogram - 24 x 49in.
(Christie's) $135 £75

FREDERICK GOODALL - A Well Near Cairo - signed and dated 1862 - watercolour heightened with white - 14 x 21in.
(Christie's) $180 £100

FREDERICK GOODALL - An Arab Encampment - signed with monogram and dated 1885 - 14½ x 35½in.
(Christie's) $900 £500

J. GOODE - Drawing Cover; Tally Ho; Over The Water; and The Kill - 6 x 11½in;
(Christie's) $990 £550 Four

HARRY GOODWIN - A View On The Grand Canal, Venice - signed with monogram and dated '78 - 29¾ x 46½in.
(Christie's) $1,440 £800

SIDNEY GOODWIN - Cottage Under The South Downes - watercolour - 10 x 14in.
(G. A. Key) $90 £50

J. GOODY - A Bunch Of Grapes - signed and dated 1889 - 13½ x 12in.
(Sotheby's Belgravia) $40 £22

JAN GOSSAERT, called Mabuse - The Virgin And Child With Saints - on panel - 33¼ x 27¼in.
(Sotheby's) $111,000 £60,000

ADOLPH GOTTLIEB - Totem - signed - oil and sand on canvas - 48 x 36 in.
(Christie's N. York) $15,950 £8,861

ANTONI GOUBAU - A Market Scene In Rome Near Trajan's Column - 40½ x 45½in.
(Christie's) $6,840 £3,800

RUVERIO GOUMA - Three Magpies Squabbling over a deserted picnic lunch - signed and dated 1878 - oil - 36 x 28in.
(Heathcote Ball & Co) $421 £230

JAN VAN GOYEN - An Extensive Land-scape with peasants and a horse-drawn cart - signed and dated 1654 - paper laid down on canvas - 9½ x 13½in.
(Christie's) **$32,400 £18,000**

JAMES GOW - 'The Advertisement - Wanted the Next of Kin' - signed and dated 1866 - oil - on canvas - 32 x 23in.
(Bonham's) **$1,350 £750**

JAN VAN GOYEN - A Wooded River Landscape with a ferry and a man fishing in the foreground - signed with initials and dated 1652 - on panel - 13 x 16in.
(Christie's) **$39,600 £22,000**

F. DE GOYA - An Inquisition Scene - 17¾ x 19¾in.
(Sotheby's) **$15,725 £8,500**

JAN VAN GOYEN - A River Landscape with a windmill and a tower - on panel - 23 x 32½in.
(Sotheby's) **$85,100 £46,000**

JAN VAN GOYEN, Manner of - A River Landscape, with a ferry near a village - bears monogram and a date 1640 - on panel - 22¾ x 32¾in.
(Christie's N. York) **$770 £421**

JAN VAN GOYEN - Sailing Vessels In A Squall Off Dordrecht - signed and dated 1641 - on panel - 17 x 30in.
(Christie's) **$171,000 £95,000**

GOZZOLI

GOZZOLI - The Pieta - on panel - 16 x 13in.
(Christie's)   **$900 £500**

BAREND GRAAT - The Pieta - signed or inscribed and numbered - red chalk - 9.9 x 29.7cm.
(Christie's)   **$99 £55**

J. E. GRACE - Wooded Landscape With Lake And Ducks - dated 1897 - oil - on canvas - 19½ x 25½in.
(Brackett's)   **$366 £200**

COLIN GRAEME - A Spaniel With A Hare - signed - 27 x 19¾in.
(Sotheby's Belgravia)   **$252 £140**

PETER GRAHAM - A Nesting Place - signed and dated 1904 - 52 x 35in.
(Sotheby's Belgravia)   **$2,700 £1,500**

LOUIS EMILE PINEL DE GRANDCHAMP - An Arab Boy With A Donkey - on board - 15 x 12in.
(Christie's)   **$1,530 £850**

EUGENE GRANDIN - 'Ship Emma, Capn; Geo. Agry', a full rigged black-hulled with sails set and the American flag streaming aft - signed and dated 1856 - watercolour - 16½ x 20½in.
(Richard A. Bourne Co. Inc.)   **$1,100 £611**

SIR FRANCIS GRANT - Portrait Of Jane Woolley, Nee Coape, small full length, seated, wearing a white dress, on a terrace - 28¼ x 34½in.
(Christie's)   **$756 £420**

SIR FRANCIS GRANT - Portrait Of The Artist's Daughter, Mary Isabella, half length, wearing a black dress, a pendant on a chain around her neck - 25 x 20½in.
(Sotheby's)   **$540 £300**

WILLIAM GREEN - Windermere From Belmont Grove - 14 x 19¼in.
(Sotheby's) **$396 £220**

SIR FRANCIS GRANT - Mrs. Roller On A Grey Hunter, riding side-saddle, with a Dalmation nearby - 55¾ x 67½in.
(Christie's) **$11,700 £6,000**

JOHN GREENHILL - Portrait Of Philip Woollrich, bust length, in armour, his head turned to the left - black chalk and pastel - on buff paper - 12¼ x 10¼in.
(Christie's) **$4,680 £2,600**

A. E. GRANT - A Winter Landscape At Sunset, hares in the foreground in snow covered dell, a lake in the distance - signed and dated '79 - oil - on canvas - 29 x 24in.
(Sotheby's) **$502 £260**

ALFRED H. GREEN - The Cotter's Delight - signed - 29½ x 24½in.
(Sotheby's Belgravia) **$54 £30**

G. GREEN - A rabbit with four young eating cabbage leaves in a grassy landscape - signed and dated December 1855 - 30 x 25in.
(H. Spencer & Sons) **$414 £230**

ROLAND GREEN - Rising Pintails - watercolour - 15 x 22in.
(G. A. Key) **$94 £52**

JAMES GREENLEES - Bringing Home the cattle - signed and dated 1885 - 19½ x 29½in.
(Sotheby's Belgravia) **$342 £190**

CHAS. GREGORY - 'Dordrecht' - signed - card - 20 x 15in.
(Walker, Barnett & Hill) **$270 £150**

J. S. GRESLEY - Beeston Meadows - watercolour - 12 x 17in.
(G. A. Key) **$54 £30**

J. B. GREUZE, Attributed to - "Smiling Youth" - signed - oil - on canvas - 39.5 x 30cm.
(Australian Art Auctions) **$14 £8**

ORAZIO GREVENBROECK - Capriccio Mediterranean Harbour Scenes - both signed - on copper - 6¾ x 13¼in.
(Christie's) **$8,190 £4,500 Pair**

EDITH GREY - Portrait Of A Farmer with an earthenware jug - signed and dated - heightened with white - 14 x 23in.
(Sotheby's Belgravia) **$50 £28**

ROBERT GRIFFIER and DIRK DALENS III - A Rhine Landscape - signed by both artists - on metal - 7½ x 10¾in.
(Sotheby's) **$12,950 £7,050**

MOSES GRIFFITH - A South Prospect of Fountains Abbey, Yorkshire - signed and dated 1777 - pencil, pen and black ink and watercolour - 13½ x 19¾in.
(Sotheby's) **$990 £550**

MOSES GRIFFITH - Tintern Abbey, Monmouthshire, the interior looking east across the transept - pen and black ink and watercolour - 10¾ x 15in.
(Sotheby's) **$684 £380**

MOSES GRIFFITH - The Bell Tower And Two Churches At Evesham, Worcestershire From The Avon - 9¾ x 7½in.
(Sotheby's) **$360 £200**

MOSES GRIFFITH - The Dropping Well at Knaresborough, Yorkshire - signed and dated 1777 - pencil, pen and ink and watercolour - 12¾ x 17¼in.
(Sotheby's) **$720 £400**

MOSES GRIFFITH - The Welsh Bridge, Shrewsbury, sailing barges in the foreground signed and dated 1776 - pencil, pen and black ink and watercolour - 12 x 19 in.
(Sotheby's)   **$1,170 £650**

MOSES GRIFFITH - Moelwyn Mountain, South West, Merionethshire - signed, inscribed and dated 1805 - 11 x 16½ in.
(Sotheby's)   **$576 £320**

GRIMALDI - A Fortified Palace On A River - pen and black ink, brown wash heightened with white on light brown paper - 24.8 x 40.5cm.
(Christie's)   **$126 £70**

ABEL GRIMMER - Landscape With Travellers By A Bridge; and Landscape With Travellers By A River - one signed and dated 1608, the other signed - on panel - circular - 4¾in. diameter.
(Sotheby's)   **$37,000 £20,000 Pair**

ABEL GRIMMER - A Village with peasants, cattle and sheep, and a manor house beyond a stream - on panel - 13¾ x 20¾in.
(Christie's)   **$9,900 £5,500**

ALEXIS GRIMOU, Circle of - A Boy, Bust Length, wearing a feathered hat - 16 x 12in.
(Christie's N. York)   **$195 £108**

GRIMSHAW - A Yorkshire Village By The Sea, By Moonlight - bears signature - 29¾ x 49¼in.
(Christie's)   **$540 £300**

ATKINSON GRIMSHAW - In The Pleasaunce, the artist's wife seated in their garden - signed and dated 1875 - 18½ x 29½in.
(Christie's)   **$14,040 £7,200**

ATKINSON GRIMSHAW - Chilworth Common, Oxfordshire - signed and dated 1868 - mixed media on paper - 14 x 19¾in.
(Christie's)   **$2,880 £1,600**

ATKINSON GRIMSHAW - Summer - signed and dated 1875 - signed and inscribed Knostrop Hall, Leeds on the stretcher - 24½ x 29½in.
(Christie's) **$46,800 £26,000**

ATKINSON GRIMSHAW - A View Of A House By Moonlight - signed and dated 1883 - 29¼ x 24½in.
(Christie's) **$4,680 £2,600**

ATKINSON GRIMSHAW - A Street Scene In Scarborough - signed and dated 1874 - on board - 21¾ x 17½in.
(Christie's) **$3,600 £2,000**

ATKINSON GRIMSHAW - A View Of Glasgow By Night - signed, and signed and inscribed Glasgow on the reverse - 24 x 35¾in.
(Christie's) **$5,040 £2,800**

ATKINSON GRIMSHAW - Under The Hollies, Roundhay Park - signed and dated 2.8.72 - signed and inscribed on the reverse - on board - 21½ x 17¼in.
(Christie's) **$5,850 £3,000**

ATKINSON GRIMSHAW - A Woman Walking Down A Moonlit Street - signed and dated 1880 - board - on panel - 21½ x 17in.
(Christie's) **$5,850 £3,000**

ATKINSON GRIMSHAW - Autumn - signed
- on board - 18½ x 14in.
(Christie's) **$3,960 £2,200**

JOHN ATKINSON GRIMSHAW - The
Clyde, Glasgow - signed and dated 1879 -
on board - 10½ x 16½in.
(Christie's S. Kensington) **$1,980 £1,100**

LOUIS GRIMSHAW - Old Chelsea - signed
- on panel - 11 x 16¾in.
(Christie's) **$4,680 £2,400**

CHARLES JOSEPH GRIPPS - Kitchen
Interior - signed and dated 1868 - oil -
on panel - 18 x 22in.
(Bonham's) **$10,440 £5,800**

THEODOR GROLL - The Roman Forum
With Children - signed and inscribed - 31 x
40½in.
(Christie's) **$10,800 £6,000**

WILLIAM GROOMBRIDGE - Fishermen
By A River below a ruined castle - signed
and dated 1782 - oil - 29 x 47in.
(Heathcote Ball & Co) **$3,202 £1,750**

A. DE GROOTE - Dutch Winter Scene
with skaters - signed - on panel - 17 x
25½in.
(Sotheby Bearne) **$972 £540**

A. DE GROOTE - View Of A Dutch Town with a church and barges on a canal - signed - on panel - 14¼ x 20½in.
(Sotheby Bearne) **$720 £400**

ROBERT E. GROVES - The Guard At The Gate - signed and dated 1918 - on board - 11¼ x 9½in.
(Christie's) **$144 £80**

CARLO GRUBACS - The Bacino Di San Marco, Venice - signed - 12½ x 17¾in.
(Christie's) **$2,880 £1,600**

CARLO GRUBACS - The Entrance To The Grand Canal, Venice With The Church Of Santa Maria Della Salute - signed - 12¼ x 17¾in.
(Christie's) **$2,520 £1,400**

ISAAC GRUNEWALD - Books And Vase Of Flowers - signed - 64 x 54cm.
(Goteborgs Auktionsverk) **$11,828 £6,571**

ADRIAEN DE GRYEFF - Hounds And Spaniels with dead game in landscapes - one signed - 13¼ x 17¼in.
(Christie's) **$5,040 £2,800 Pair**

ADRIAEN DE GRYEFF - A Wooded Landscape with dogs and dead game in the foreground and sportsmen beyond - on panel - 15 x 21in.
(Christie's) $2,700 £1,500

FRANCESCO GUARDI - The Isola Di San Giorgio Maggiore, Venice, with the Punta della Giudecca, the Churches of San Giovanni Battista and of the Zitelle, and with numerous vessels in the foreground - 13½ x 20½in.
(Christie's) $198,000 £110,000

ANTONIO GUARDI - The Sultan Receiving A Delegation Of Merchants - 17½ x 24½in.
(Christie's) $12,740 £7,000

F. GUARDI - A Capriccio Mediterranean Harbour Scene with figures and vessels - 14¾ x 20¼in.
(Christie's) $2,520 £1,400

F. GUARDI - The Fire At San Marcuola, Venice - 6¼ x 5¼in.
(Christie's) $5,040 £2,800

FRANCESCO GUARDI - The Isola Di San Giorgio Maggiore, Venice, with the Punta della Giudecca and the Church of San Giovanni Battista and with numerous vessels in the foreground - 16 x 25in.
(Christie's) $21,600 £12,000

GUARDI

FRANCESCO GUARDI - An Architectural Cappriccio with figures near a ruined arch, a church beyond - on panel - 7½ x 5¾in.
(Christie's) **$28,800 £16,000**

FRANCESCO GUARDI - A Lagoon By Moonlight with fisherfolk in the foreground and fishing vessels offshore - 11½ x 17½in.
(Christie's) **$18,200 £10,000**

F. GUARDI - A Moonlit Coastal Landscape with fishing vessels offshore - 8 x 10½in.
(Christie's) **$5,040 £2,800**

FRANCESCO GUARDI - A Capriccio with figures on a bridge by ruins - on panel - 6½ x 4 in.
(Christie's N. York) **$33,000 £18,030**

FRANCESCO GUARDI - A Capriccio with figures by a ruined arch - on panel - 6½ x 4 in.
(Christie's N. York) **$24,200 £13,225**

MAX GUBLER - Fish - 73 x 116cm.
(Auktionshaus am Neumarkt)
$14,155 £7,735

JEAN LE GUENNEC - The Seashore In Brittany - signed - gouache - 33 x 49cm.
(Christian Rosset) **$192 £105**

GUERCINO - Hercules - red chalk - 41.5 x 27.8cm.
(Christie's) **$72 £40**

GUERCINO - A Landscape With A Bridge - inscribed - pen and brown ink - 21.2 x 37.2cm.
(Christie's) **$108 £60**

GUGI - Venice, The Grand Canal busy with gondolas - signed - oil - on canvas - 31 x 23in.
(Neales of Nottingham) **$77 £40**

PAUL GUTSCHER - The Capuccini Convent Garden, Albano, By Moonlight - signed - on board - 10¾ x 13¾in.
(Christie's) **$153 £85**

ALBERT E. GYNGELL - Cottage by a Stream - signed and dated 1884 - 8 x 15½ in.
(Sotheby's Belgravia) **$288 £160**

CARL HAAG - On The Alert - signed - inscribed and dated 1876 - watercolour heightened with white - 20½ x 15in.
(Christie's) **$630 £350**

CARL HAAG - An Italian Girl in Regional Dress - signed and dated 1857 - watercolour - 12¼ x 8½ in
(Christie's) **$180 £100**

STEPHEN DE HAAN - A Winter Landscape With Skaters On A Frozen River - signed - 23¼ x 35¼in.
(Christie's) **$468 £260**

CORNELIS CORNELISZ. VAN HAARLEM - A Smoker - signed in monogram - on panel - 9 x 6½in.
(Sotheby's) **$5,550 £3,000**

DE HAAS - Cattle by a river - signed - oil - on canvas - 24 x 18in.
(Stewart Gore) **$400 £210**

LOUIS HACHE - The Village Blacksmith - sketch - on board - 15 x 9¾ in.
(Sotheby's) **$126 £70**

HACKAERT - A Bridge in an Italian Landscape - pencil and brown ink - 37.1 x 52.1 cm.
(Christie's) **$805 £40**

JAN HACKAERT and ADRIAEN VAN DER VELDE - A Hawking Party On A Road with birch trees by a pool - 26 x 22in.
(Christie's) **$32,400£18,000**

ARTHUR HACKER - The Evening Prayer - signed and dated 1881 - on panel - 15¾ x 12¼in.
(Christie's) **$144 £80**

JACOB PHILIP HACKERT, Circle of - A View Of An Italian Hilltown - bodycolour - 42.0 x 58.2cm.
(Christie's) **$630£350**

HACKERT - An Italian Landscape with a wayside fountain - pen and brown ink - 23.7 x 38.0cm.
(Christie's) **$63 £35**

JOHANN GOTTLIEB HACKERT -
Peasants And Their Animals Crossing A
Ford - signed and dated 1770 - water-
colour - 8¼ x 10½in.
(Christie's S. Kensington) **$612 £340**

LOUIS HAGHE - Council Of War At
Courtrai - signed - oil - on canvas -
40 x 45in.
(Swetenham's) **$5,700 £3,000**
LOUIS HAGHE - A Lady Reading A
Letter In An Interior - signed - 17¼ x
22¾in.
(Sotheby's Belgravia) **$58 £32**

GEORGE CHARLES HAITE - In The
Meadows, Holland - signed - indistinctly
inscribed on the reverse - on board -
10¾ x 15in.
(Sotheby's Belgravia) **$270 £150**

GEORGE CHARLES HAITE - A Dutch
Riverside Town - 15 x 11¼in.
(Sotheby's Belgravia) **$270 £150**

GEORGE CHARLES HAITE - The
Fishmarket - 15 x 11¼in.
(Sotheby's Belgravia) **$540 £300**

GEORGE CHARLES HAITE - By A
Dutch Canal - indistinctly inscribed on
the reverse - on board - 11½ x 17½in.
(Sotheby's Belgravia) **$153 £85**

PETER HALCOMBE - Arab Warriors
Riding In The Desert - both signed
with initials - on panel - 7½ x 9¾in.
(Christie's)   **$45   £25 Pair**
W. HALE - Coastal Scenes - signed -
on board - 7½ x 15½in.
(Sotheby's Belgravia)   **$90 £50 Pair**

HARRY HALL - 'Bend Or', a chestnut
racehorse with Fred Archer up, in a wooded
landscape - signed and dated 1881 - 27½ x
35in.
(Christie's)   **$2,520 £1,400**

HARRY HALL - A pair of Chestnut
Hunters - both signed and dated 1863 -
oil on canvas - 17½ x 21in.
(King & Chasemore)   **$1,296 £720 Pair**

HARRY HALL - A Chestnut Racehorse,
with jockey up, in an extensive landscape
- signed - 27 x 35¼in.
(Christie's)   **$1,620 £900**

HARRY HALL - 'Lord Lyon', a horse's head
- signed with initials, inscribed and dated
1866 - oil on canvas - 8 x 10in.
(King & Chasemore)   **$198 £110**
H. H. HALL - Highland Cattle Grazing -
oil - 24 x 20in.
(G. A. Key)   **$54 £30**

WESTALL HALL - A Game Of Chess -
signed - 15½ x 19½in.
(Sotheby's Belgravia)   **$90 £50**

HARRY HALL - 'Sunbeam', a bay racehorse, in a stable - signed and dated 1858
- 27½ x 35½in.
(Christie's)   **$2,160 £1,200**

J. P. HALL - Race Day, a young orange seller and her companion resting by a milestone, a race meeting beyond - signed - oil - on canvas - 13½ x 17½in.
(Neales of Nottingham) **$2,123 £1,100**

M. E. HALL - Still Life Of Wild Flowers In Jugs - signed and dated 1885 - 11¾ x 7¾in.
(Sotheby's Belgravia) **$90 £50 Pair**

T. M. HALL - Rural Landscape with two figures by cottage in lane - oil - 10 x 18in.
(G. A. Key) **$76 £42**

HALLE - The Three Graces - pencil and brown wash - 23.1 x 36.7cm.
(Christie's) **$90 £50**

HUGH DOUGLAS HAMILTON - Portrait Of James Byres Of Tonley, half length, seated - the sitter identified on a contemporary label on the backing - pastel - oval - 11 x 9¼in.
(Christie's) **$1,980 £1,100**

HUGH DOUGLAS HAMILTON - Portrait Of Christopher Norton, half length - the sitter identified on a contemporary label on the backing - pastel - an inscribed oval - 11 x 9½in.
(Christie's) **$810 £450**

RICHARD HAMILTON - "I'm Dreaming Of A White Christmas" - signed - numbered - dye transfer on special dye transfer paper mounted on board - 14¼ x 21¼in.
(Sotheby's) **$6,405 £3,500**

WILLIAM HAMILTON - Portrait Of Sarah Siddons As Katherine Of Aragon, half length, in a black dress - 29¼ x 24¼in.
(Christie's) **$990 £550**

WILLIAM HAMILTON - Hero And Leander - signed and dated 1801 - 16¾ x 10¾in.
(Sotheby's) **$162 £90**

GERTRUDE DEMAIN HAMMOND - A Proposal - signed - grey wash - 12 x 8½in.
(Sotheby's Belgravia) **$21 £12**

CHARLES HANCOCK - A Rural Landscape With A Shepherd And A Dog, a flock of sheep and cows in the foreground, trees and a river beyond, mountains in the distance - signed and dated 1879 - 13½ x 17¼in.
(H. Spencer & Sons) **$306 £170**

HANS HANSEN - In The Souk - signed - 20½ x 13¾in.
(Sotheby's Belgravia) **$22 £12**

HANS HANSEN - A Moorish Dance - signed - heightened with bodycolour - 9 x 9½in.
(Sotheby's Belgravia) **$126 £70**

PIETER HARBIME - Still Life With Flowers In A Vase - oil - on canvas - 27 x 22in.
(Bonham's) **$7,200 £4,000**

CHARLES MARTIN HARDIE - Outside A Dutch Village - signed with initials - dated '94 - on panel - 9½ x 13½in.
(Sotheby's Belgravia) **$504 £280**

HARDING - A Spanish Riverside Town - bears signature and date - 9¼ x 13½in.
(Sotheby's Belgravia) **$22 £12**

GEORGE PERFECT HARDING - Prince Henry And Mary Queen Of Scots - inscribed - pen and black ink and grey wash - 11¼ x 9½in.
(Sotheby's) **$50 £28**

T. P. HARDY - 'Seascape' - signed - watercolour - 14¾ x 8¾in.
(J. Entwistle & Co.) **$148 £80**

FREDERICK DANIEL HARDY - A Lady Writing A Letter - signed and dated 1878 - on panel - 12 x 9½in.
(Christie's) **$864 £480**

DUDLEY HARDY - Arab Warriors Resting In A Courtyard - signed - 13 x 20in.
(Christie's) **$252 £140**

DUDLEY HARDY - The Outpost - signed - 11½ x 17½in.
(Christie's) **$126 £70**

GEORGE HARDY - Welcome Footsteps - signed and dated 1890 - on panel - 17½ x 13½in.
(Christie's) **$3,705 £1,900**

HARDY

DUDLEY HARDY - Outposts - signed - watercolour and bodycolour - 9¾ x 13½in.
(Christie's) $126 £70

HEYWOOD HARDY - Head Study Of A Terrier - signed and dated 1898 - on panel - 7½ x 6¼in.
(Sotheby's Belgravia) $171 £95

HEYWOOD HARDY - The Elopement - signed and dated 1885 - 33 x 51¼in.
(Christie's) $171 £95

HEYWOOD HARDY - A Scottish Country House - signed and dated 1897 - 19¼ x 23¼in.
(Sotheby's Belgravia) $720 £400

T. B. HARDY - "Off Ambliteuse" - signed and dated 1896 - watercolour - 9½ x 18in.
(Warner, Sheppard & Wade) $549 £280

W. HARDY - The Return Of The Fleet - signed - 5½ x 10¼in.
(Sotheby's Belgravia) $25 £14

W. J. HARDY - A Gypsy Encampment near Caister Castle - watercolour - 5 x 7in.
(G. A. Key) $47 £26

EDWARD HARGITT - A Sutherland Deer Forest - watercolour - 19 x 28in.
(G. A. Key) $351 £195

ALEXI HARLAMOFF - A Study Of A Young Girl Sewing - signed - on canvas - 83 x 106cm.
(King & Chasemore) **$11,700 £6,500**

THOMAS J. HARPER - Still Lifes Of Fruit On A Ledge - both signed - 9½ x 13½in.
(Sotheby's Belgravia) $288 £160 Pair

EDWIN HARRIS - Norfolk Landscape With Sheep Grazing in foreground and church in middle distance - watercolour - 17 x 23in.
(G. A. Key) $40 £22

F. H. HOWARD HARRIS - 'A Nice Quiet Spot' - signed - watercolour - card - 18 x 29in.
(Walker, Barnett & Hill) $126 £70

C. H. HARRISON - Moonlight Broadland Scene - watercolour - 5 x 11in.
(G. A. Key) $140 £78

CHARLES HARMONY HARRISON - A Path Through The Dunes with distant view of sea - watercolour - 9 x 13in.
(G. A. Key) $68 £38

J. G. HARRISON - Harbour Scene - watercolour - 7 x 10in.
(G. A. Key) $13 £7

ARTHUR HARTLAND - River Landscape with a reed gatherer and punt - signed - 30 x 49in.
(Elliott & Green) $576 £320

HANS HARTUNG - Composition in Black, Brown and Yellow - signed and dated '51 - coloured chalks and crayons - on paper - 18¾ x 27¾in.
(Sotheby's) **$3,477 £1,900**

HANS HARTUNG - Composition - signed and dated '49 - coloured crayons, Indian ink and pencil on heavy paper - 19½ x 15½in.
(Sotheby's) **$4,026 £2,200**

HANS HARTUNG - T49-15 - signed and dated '49 - 15 x 21¼in.
(Christie's) **$8,052 £4,400**

A. W. HARVEY - Views On Wroxham And Oulton Broads - oil - 10 x 16in.
(G. A. Key) **$47 £26 Pair**

EDMUND HAVELL - A Groom With Two Horses and a dog outside a lodge gate - signed and dated 1842 - oil - on canvas - 28 x 36in.
(Bonham's) **$2,520 £1,400**

WILLIAM HAVELL - Classical Figures Resting Beneath A Tree beside a torrent in a mountain landscape - signed and dated 1805 - pencil and watercolour - 24 x 20¼in.
(Christie's) **$504 £280**

WILLIAM HAVELL - An Extensive View Of Paestum - signed - 27 x 49in.
(Christie's) **$1,657 £850**

J. H. HAWKSWORTH - Winter Fuel - signed - on board - 14¾ x 19in.
(Sotheby's Belgravia)   **$198 £110**

B. R. HAYDON - Falstaff Awaking - a sketch - 20¼ x 18¼in.
(Sotheby's)   **$1,620 £900**

HAYES - Fishing Boats Off The Coast - 16 x 22in.
(Sotheby's Belgravia)   **$72 £40**

EDWIN HAYES - A Beach Scene, South Wales - on board - 6½ x 10¾in.
(Sotheby's Belgravia)   **$81 £45**

GEORGE HAYES - Conway - signed and inscribed - 9 x 13in.
(Sotheby's Belgravia)   **$22 £12**

SIDNEY HAYES - Sheep Grazing On The Scottish Coast - signed - 14 x 20in.
(Sotheby's Belgravia)   **$68 £38**

JESSICA HAYLLAR - The Return From Confirmation - signed and dated 1888 - 19½ x 25½in.
(Christie's)   **$16,575 £8,500**

FRANCIS HAYMAN - Cupid Shooting His Love Dart - signed - pen and black ink, grey washes - oval - 7 x 5¾in.
(Sotheby's)   **$144 £80**

FRANCIS HAYMAN - The Good Samaritan - 78¼ x 48in.
(Sotheby's)   **$2,880 £1,600**

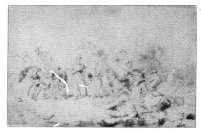

SIR GEORGE HAYTER - A Circassian Woman Taken As A Hostage By Georgians - signed, inscribed and dated - pencil and sepia wash - 21½ x 27½in.
(Sotheby's)   **$180 £100**

SIR GEORGE HAYTER - Christ Betrayed By Judas - signed - inscribed Paris and dated 1831 - on panel - 9½ x 8¼in.
(Sotheby's)   **$126 £70**

SIR GEORGE HAYTER - Costume Studies - 5¼ x 8½in.
(Sotheby's)   **$153 £85**

THOMAS HEAPHY - Portrait Of Miss Godfrey with her dog - signed, inscribed and dated 1802 - also inscribed with the sitter's name on the reverse - pencil and coloured washes on buff paper - 10 x 7¾in.
(Sotheby's) **$324 £180**

RALPH HEDLEY - The Days Catch, a young angler with his terrier sitting on a kitchen bench - signed and dated 1911 - oil - on canvas - 17½ x 13¼in.
(Neales of Nottingham) **$205 £110**

HEEM - A Still Life Of A Cut Melon, Plums, Grapes, Tomatoes And A Pear - 25¼ x 30in.
(H. Spencer & Sons) **$576 £320**

CLAES DIRCKSZ. VAN DER HECK - Saint Francis Receiving The Stigmata - signed and dated 1630 - 8½ x 12in.
(Christie's) **$1,800 £1,000**

CORNELIS DE HEEM - A Still Life Of Fruit - signed - 16 x 22in.
(Sotheby's) **$48,100 £26,000**

W. C. HEDA - A Still Life Of Oysters On Pewter Plates, a tiger ware jug, a facon-de-venise wine glass, and a silver salt on a draped table - bears signature and date 165? - on panel - 21 x 28in.
(Christie's) **$5,760 £3,200**

W. W. HEDGES - Figures Outside A Farmhouse - signed - 19½ x 29½in.
(Sotheby's Belgravia) **$171 £95**

CORNELIS DE HEEM - A Garland Of Roses, Poppies And Other Flowers, with a peeled lemon, a nectarine, and strawberries in a Delft plate, on a plinth - signed - 25 x 19¼in.
(Christie's) **$47,320 £26,000**

JAN DAVIDSZ. DE HEEM - A Still Life
Of Figs In A Bowl, nuts on a box, bread,
a peeled lemon an an ewer, and two glasses
of wine on a draped table - signed and
inscribed - 16 x 21¾in.
(Christie's) **$81,900 £45,000**

JAN DAVIDSZ. DE HEEM - A Still Life
Of Fruit - signed - on panel - 12 x 16¾in.
(Sotheby's) **$85,100 £46,000**

EGBERT VAN HEEMSKERK - The
Schoolmaster - signed - 10 x 11in.
(Christie's N. York) **$3,520 £1,923**

EGBERT VAN HEEMSKERK - Peasants
Merrymaking In An Inn - signed with
monogram - 31¼ x 42in.
(Christie's) **$8,736 £4,800**

EGBERT VAN HEEMSKERK -
Peasants In An Interior - 11½ x 9½in.
(Christie's) **$1,170 £650**

EGBERT VAN HEEMSKERK - Peasants
Drinking In An Interior - signed - on
panel - 5 x 4in.
(Christie's) **$2,340 £1,300**

**EGBERT VAN HEEMSKERK,
Attributed to** - A Peasant Family In An
Interior - 9¾ x 11½in.
(Christie's N. York) **$1,210 £661**

**EGBERT VAN HEEMSKERK, School
of** - The Doctor's Visit - 16¼ x 20½in.
(Christie's N. York) **$935 £511**

**EGBERT VAN HEEMSKERK,
Attributed to** - Peasants In A Tavern -
on panel - 10 x 12½in.
(Christie's N. York) **$770 £421**

**MARTIN VAN HEEMSKERK, School
of** - A Trial By Fire - 15¼ x 11½in.
(Christie's N. York) **$660 £361**

MARGARETA DE HEER - A Satyr
Uncovering The Sleeping Diana - signed -
bodycolour on vellum - 34.6 x 26.4cm.
(Christie's) **$180 £100**

KARL HEFFNER - Windsor Castle
from the river - signed - oil - 22 x 29in.
(Warner, Sheppard & Wade)
$5,292 £2,700

JOHANN KASPAR HEILMANN - A
Well - signed - black and white chalk
on blue paper - 21.2 x 21.6cm.
(Christie's) **$32 £18**

HEINTZ - A Turbaned Man Slaying
A Woman - pen and brown ink, brown
wash - 13.3 x 14.8cm.
(Christie's) **$90 £50**

W. HEMMING - Tired Out - signed -
inscribed and dated on the reverse -
on board - 8¾ x 11½in.
(Sotheby's Belgravia) **$252 £140**

WILLIAM HEMSLEY - Playing Leap
Frog - 39½ x 49in.
(Sotheby's Belgravia)   **$4,680 £2,600**

WILLIAM HEMSLEY - A Difficulty -
signed - heightened with bodycolour -
circular - diameter 9in.
(Sotheby's Belgravia)   **$306 £170**

BERNARD BENEDICT HEMY -
Fishermen In A Stiff Breeze - signed -
23¼ x 35¼in.
(Sotheby's Belgravia)   **$216 £120**

BERNARD BENEDICT HEMY - Venice -
signed - 23½ x 35½in.
(Sotheby's Belgravia)   **$342 £190**

CHARLES COOPER HENDERSON -
Hard Labour - signed with monogram -
pencil and watercolour - 8 x 14¼in.
(Sotheby's)   **$216 £120**

JOSEPH HENDERSON - Coast Scene
With Children and a distant headland -
45 x 60cm.
(Edmiston's)   **$648 £360**

JOSEPH HENDERSON - Off Ailsa
Craig - 47 x 60cm.
(Edmiston's)   **$270 £150**

JOSEPH MORRIS HENDERSON -
Overlooking A Loch - signed - 19¾ x
36in.
(Sotheby's Belgravia)   **$180 £100**

ADRIAEN DE HENNIN - The Rape Of
Europa - signed - 33½ x 50¼in.
(Christie's)   **$1,980 £1,100**

HENRY

B. B. HENRY - 'Coastal Scene With Coastguard Station, sailing ship at anchor and three figures standing beside a beached rowing boat' - oil - on canvas - 20 x 30¼in.
(Lalonde Bros. & Parham) **$293 £160**

FREDERICK HENRY HENSHAW - A Rest During Haymaking - signed with initials - oil - on canvas - 22 x 30in.
(Bonham's) **$4,140 £2,300**

JOHN ROGERS HERBERT - An Arab On A Camel In A Landscape - traces of a signature - 12 x 17½in.
(Christie's) **$576 £320**

JAMES G. SYDNEY HERBERT - Sketch Of The Lac De Gaube, Morning, The Pyrenees - signed - signed, inscribed and dated 1865 on the reverse - 13¼ x 23¼in.
(Sotheby's Belgravia) **$144 £80**

SYDNEY HERBERT - Mount Etna, Near Catania, Sicily - signed and dated 1871 - 23½ x 35½in.
(Christie's) **$2,340 £1,200**

E. B. HERBERTE - Hunting Scenes - signed and dated 1800 - 13½ x 17½in.
(Sotheby Bearne) **$1,008 £560 Pair**

ADOLF HERBST - The Little Princess - 62 x 47cm.
(Auktionshaus am Neumarkt) **$5,563 £3,040**

ROBERT HERDMAN - A Highland
Lassie - signed with monogram and
dated 1880 - 15½ x 11½in.
(Sotheby's Belgravia) **$432 £240**

ROBERT HERDMAN - The Fruit Seller -
signed with initials - inscribed and dated
Dec. 55 - heightened with bodycolour -
14½ x 10½in.
(Sotheby's Belgravia) **$63 £35**

HERING - Continental Landscapes -
both on board - circular - 5in. diameter.
(Sotheby's Belgravia) **$108 £60 Pair**

GEORGE HERIOT - Oystermouth Castle,
Glamorganshire - inscribed - pencil and
watercolour - 14¼ x 21 in.
(Sotheby's) **$720 £400**

L'HERMITTE - Haystooks - bears signature
- 7½ x 12¾in.
(Christie's) **$153 £85**

LUDWIG HERMANN - The Grand Canal,
Venice, With Santa Maria Della Salute -
signed and indistinctly dated 1876 - 35 x
56in.
(Christie's) **$5,040 £2,800**

J. F. HERRING - Ducks And Ducklings
in a landscape - 1o¾ x 14½in.
(Sotheby Bearne) **$207 £115**

JOHN FREDERICK HERRING - Wooded
Landscape with cattle proceeding in the
distance, the foreground group of horses,
foal, goat and kid - signed - oil - on canvas
- 19½ x 30in.
(The Nottingham Auction Mart.)
$3,052 £1,650

J. F. HERRING, JUN - Farmyard Friends,
horses, poultry and ducks beside a pond -
bearing signature - oil - on canvas - 9¼ x
13½in.
(Neales of Nottingham) **$298 £160**

JOHN FREDERICK HERRING, JUN -
Farmyard Scene with three horses and
other farm animals - signed - 13½ x 19½in.
(Sotheby Bearne)   **$2,925 £1,500**

JOHN FREDERICK HERRING, JUN -
Farmyard Scenes With Horses, pigs and
poultry - one signed - 11½ x 15½in.
(Sotheby Bearne)   **$5,220 £2,900 Pair**

JOHN FREDERICK HERRING, JUN -
An Extensive Landscape with the York -
London carrier's waggon and a hunt
drawing cover beyond - signed - 27½ x
35¼in.
(Christie's)   **$7,200 £4,000**

JOHN FREDERICK HERRING, JUN -
Hunters, Poultry And Pigs In A Field,
with a hunt beyond - signed - 15¾ x 23¾in.
(Christie's)   **$2,730 £1,400**

JOHN FREDERICK HERRING, JUN -
Loading The Log-Wagon - signed - 11½
x 17¾in.
(Christie's)   **$5,460 £2,800**

JOHN FREDERICK HERRING, JUN -
Pigs And Poultry In A Farmyard - 16 x
16in.
(Christie's)   **$2,700 £1,500**

JOHN FREDERICK HERRING, SEN -
'The Pets' - signed and dated 1860 - on
panel - 9¼ x 11¼in.
(Sotheby Bearne) **$875 £486**

JOHN FREDERICK HERRING, SEN -
A Greyhound In A Landscape - signed and
dated 1855 - 15½ x 19¾in.
(Sotheby's) **$3,600 £2,000**

JOHN FREDERICK HERRING, SEN -
A Black Hunter fully saddled and standing
in a stable, the owner to the right - signed
and dated 1845 - 50 x 38in.
(Sotheby's) **$5,040 £2,800**

JOHN FREDERICK HERRING, SEN -
Pyrrhus 1st, a chestnut racehorse standing
in his stall - inscribed and signed and dated
1846 - on panel - 9¾ x 12in.
(Sotheby's) **$5,400 £3,000**

JOHN FREDERICK HERRING, SEN -
Cart Horses Watering At A Stream - signed
and dated 1853 - 14½ x 18¼in.
(Christie's) **$3,120 £1,600**

JOHN FREDERICK HERRING, SEN -
Mendicant, a dark bay racehorse in a stable -
inscribed - signed and dated 1846 - on panel
- 9¾ x 12in.
(Sotheby's) **$5,400 £3,000**

211

JOHN FREDERICK HERRING, SEN -
Waiting For Master - signed - on panel - 14¼
x 18¼in.
(Sotheby's)   **$4,320 £2,400**

JOHN FREDERICK HERRING, SEN - A
Study Of A Hunter in a landscape - signed
and dated 1829 - oil - on canvas - 24 x 30in.
(King & Chasemore)   **$2,700 £1,500**

JOHN FREDERICK HERRING, SEN -
'Charles XII', and another racehorse
(possibly 'Euclid') with jockeys up, on
a racecourse - signed and dated 1839 -
11½ x 16in.
(Christie's)   **$5,400 £3,000**

JOHN FREDERICK HERRING, SEN -
Study Of The Heads Of A Dark Bay And
A Grey Pony, with a cockerel - signed -
on board - 5¾ x 7¾in.
(Christie's)   **$2,340 £1,200**

JOHN FREDERICK HERRING, SEN -
Hop Pickers In An Extensive Landscape -
signed and dated 1854-1860 - 25 x 43in.
(Christie's)   **$12,600 £7,000**

J. F. HERRING - Study Of A Hunter
in a landscape - oil - 20 x 24in.
(G. A. Key)   **$468 £260**

JOHN FREDERICK HERRING, SEN -
'Walton', a bay racehorse by a wall -
signed, inscribed and dated 1819 - 17½
x 23½in.
(Christie's)   **$11,700 £6,500**

DE HEUSCH - A Wooded Landscape
with travellers resting by a river - bears
initials - on panel - 24½ x 18in.
(Christie's)   **$864 £480**

JACOB DE HEUSCH, School of - A Wooded Italianate River Landscape, with drovers, and peasants in the foreground - 37 x 68in.
(Christie's N. York) **$770 £421**

WILLEM DE HEUSCH, Manner of - A Wooded Italianate Landscape, with travellers on a road near a lake - 21 x 28¾in.
(Christie's N York) **$550 £300**

JAN VAN DER HEYDEN - A View In Amsterdam - on panel - 15¼ x 15¾in.
(Sotheby's) **$51,800 £28,000**

FRIEDRICH JOSEPH NICOLAI HEYDENDAHL - Rohrender Hirsch - 80 x 120.5cm.
(Auktionshaus am Neumarkt) **$1,010 £552**

G. HICKIN - A Hilly Landscape With Ducks in the foreground - signed - 11½ x 17½in.
(Sotheby's Belgravia) **$32 £18**

GEORGE ELGAR HICKS - 'The Traitor' - signed and dated 1902 - 12 x 27in.
(Sotheby Bearne) **$1,131 £580**

J. HIGHMORE - Portrait Of A Gentleman, three-quarter length, standing, wearing a grey coat and waistcoat and a white stock - canvas - on board - 49½ x 39½in.
(Sotheby's) **$396 £220**

HILDER - A Woodland Stream - inscribed - on panel - 19 x 24in.
(Sotheby's) **$864 £480**

RICHARD HILDER - A Wooded Lake Landscape with figures on a path - signed - on panel - 11½ x 15½in.
(Christie's) **$126 £70**

RICHARD HILDER - A Wooded River Landscape with figures on a path and a cottage beyond - on panel - 13½ x 17½in.
(Christie's) **$1,620 £900**

213

RICHARD HILDER - A Wooded River Landscape with fishermen and figure on a bridge - on panel - 13½ x 17½in.
(Christie's)　　　**$1,620 £900**

RICHARD HILDER - Figures And Cattle In Extensive Landscapes - on panel - 11¾ x 16in.
(Sotheby's)　　**$5,040　　£2,800 Pair**

RICHARD HILDER - A Wooded River Landscape with a cottage - 20¼ x 29¼in.
(Christie's)　　　**$1,440 £800**

FRANK HILDER - A Pastoral Scene Of Cows, Cottages And River, trees and fields in the background - signed and dated 1897 - oil on canvas - 29 x 50in.
(H. C. Chapman & Son) **$378 £210**

B. HILES - Girl Sitting On Bank watching fishing boats on river - watercolour - 10 x 7in.
(G. A. Key)　　　**$32 £18**

BARTRAM HILES - A Shipyard - signed - heightened with bodycolour - 9¾ x 7¼in.
(Sotheby's Belgravia)　　**$90 £50**

C. STEWART HILL - A Continental Bay, Evening - signed - on board - 14 x 17in.
(Sotheby's Belgravia)　　**$32　£18**

DAVID OCTAVIUS HILL - Thewes Castle, Kirkcudbright; Above A Loch - both signed - one with initials - on panel - 11¾ x 17¾in.
(Sotheby's Belgravia)　　**$720 £400 Pair**

JAMES JOHN HILL - Nymphs Bathing In A Stream - signed - circular - 22in. diameter.
(Christie's)　　　**$198 £110**

JAMES JOHN HILL - The Lark - signed - on board - 15¼ x 11½in.
(Christie's)　　　**$468 £260**

THOMAS HILL - A New Moon - signed with initials - watercolour heightened with bodycolour - 10½ x 16½in.
(Sotheby's Belgravia)　**$25　£14**

ROBERT ALEXANDER HILLINGFORD - Waterloo, 18th June, 1815 - Wellington encouraging a British Infantry Square - signed - 34½ x 54in.
(Christie's)　　　**$15,600 £8,000**

214

FREDERICK HINES - Feeding The Ducks - signed and dated 1908 - heightened with bodycolour - 14½ x 10in.
(Sotheby's Belgravia)   **$68 £38**

THEO HINES - The Brook At Sunset - oil - 13 x 9in.
(G. A. Key)   **$36 £20**

THEODORE HINES - Cliveden On Thames - signed - inscribed on the reverse - 19½ x 29½in.
(Sotheby's Belgravia)   **$990 £550**

THEODORE HINES - On Loch Achray - signed - canvas laid on board - 18 x 13¾in.
(Sotheby's Belgravia)   **$270 £150**

ANDREW HISLOP - On Loch Lomond - signed - inscribed - 13½ x 20½in.
(Sotheby's Belgravia)   **$153 £85**

L. S. HITCHCOCK - Old Man And Boat On Marshes - oil - 7 x 9in.
(G. A. Key)   **$36 £20**

OLLE HJORTZBERG - Flowers On A Table with books and a tray - signed - 65 x 54cm.
(Goteborgs Auktionsverk) **$7,200 £4,000**

MEINDERT HOBBEMA, Manner of - A Woody Landscape, with cottages and a farm in the distance - bears signature - on panel - 23¼ x 33¼in.
(Christie's N. York)   **$825 £451**

DAVID HOCKNEY - K's For King - 31½ x 22½in.
(Christie's)   **$7,686 £4,200**

215

DAVID HODGSON, Attributed to - Horses, Pigs And Poultry In A Farmyard - on panel - 15½ x 20½in.
(Christie's) **$252 £140**

FRANZ HOEPFNER - Figures On The Coast - signed and dated - 19½ x 29½in.
(Sotheby's Belgravia) **$270 £150**

HANS HOFMANN - Blue in Blue - signed, inscribed and dated 1954 - 50 x 40 in.
(Christie's N. York) **$46,200 £25,666**

FRANZ HOEPFNER - Vale Of Bettews Garmon, North Wales - signed and dated 1881 - signed, inscribed and dated on the reverse - 52 x 74in.
(Christie's) **$1,980 £1,100**

THOMAS CHRISTOPHER HOFLAND - Castellamare: Taken From The New Road Leading To Sorrento, figures with cattle and sheep in the foreground - 52¾ x 72½in.
(Sotheby's) **$16,200 £9,000**

HOGARTH - Interior Of A Gentlemen's Club with revellers - oil - 15 x 19in.
(Heathcote Ball & Co) **$897 £490**

WILLIAM HOGARTH - Portrait of H.R.H. William Augustus, Duke Of Cumberland, full length, wearing a scarlet coat and breeches, a green waistcoat trimmed with gold and a blue sash, a soldier with standards and drums beyond - dated 1732 - 17¾ x 13½in.
(Sotheby's) **$117,000 £65,000**

**HANS HOLBEIN THE YOUNGER,
Manner of** - Portrait Of Thomas Cromwell,
small half length, in a dark fur-lined coat
and hat - on panel - 14¼ x 12in.
(Christie's N. York) **$2,530 £1,382**

B. L. HOLD - Partridge And Grouse On
A Moor - both signed and dated '96 -
19½ x 29½in.
(Sotheby's Belgravia) **$1,530 £850 Pair**

J. HOLLAND - Figures Outside A
Village - 23½ x 19¼in.
(Sotheby's Belgravia) **$342 £190**

TOM HOLD - Partridge On The Alert;
King Of The Woods - both signed - 9½
x 11¼in.
(Sotheby's Belgravia) **$810 £450 Pair**

JAMES HOLLAND - A Venetian Canal -
signed with initals, inscribed 'Venice',
and dated 1857 - pencil and watercolour - 10¾ x 7½in.
(Sotheby's) **$1,692 £940**

217

JAMES HOLLAND - The Forum With Trajan's Column, and the Church of Sante Maria De Loretto - signed with monogram - 10¾ x 14½in.
(Christie's)   **$720 £400**

JAMES HOLLAND - A View In Venice - signed and dated 1844 on the reverse - 20 x 24in.
(Christie's)   **$1,710 £950**

JAMES HOLLAND - The Coast At Lynmouth, North Devon - signed and inscribed - 23½ x 35½in.
(Christie's)   **$1,800 £1,000**

JAMES HOLLAND - San Giovannie Paolo, Venice - signed, inscribed and dated 1835 pencil and watercolour heightened with white - 13½ x 9¾ in.
(Sotheby's)   **$900 £500**

JAMES HOLLAND - The Salute From The Doge's Palace - signed with monogram and dated - pencil and watercolour - 9¾ x 6¾in.
(Sotheby's)   **$1,710 £950**

JOHN HOLLAND - A Bunch Of Flowers - signed - 29¾ x 24½in.
(Sotheby's Belgravia)   **$234 £130**

JOHN HOLLAND - A Village In Galway - signed - 17¼ x 23¼in.
(Sotheby's Belgravia)   **$432 £240**

EDWARD HOLMES - A Girl And Small Child drinking by a stream - signed - 19th century - oil - 18¼ x 26in.
(The Manchester Auction Mart.)
$564 £310

JAMES HOLMES - Near Margate - inscribed and dated 1838 - 8¼ x 6½in.
(Sotheby's Belgravia) **$16 £9**

LAURITS HOLST - "The Revenge" and "The Rosario" - 19½ x 36in.
(Phillips, Solihull) **$1,044 £580**

E. F. HOLT - A Sportsman With A Pointer And A Setter Shooting Pheasants In A Corn Field - signed and dated 1865 - 25 x 29½in.
(Christie's) **$162 £90**

G. VAN HONTHORST - Christ Disputing With The Rabbies - oil - on canvas - 78 x 58in.
(Bonham's) **$10,672 £5,800**

ERNEST B. HOOD - Brass Toddy Kettle And Roses - 38 x 48cm.
(Edmiston's) **$324 £180**

HENDRICK HOOGERS - Study Of A Woman - signed - black and white chalk on grey-blue paper - 32.0 x 26.3cm.
(Christie's) **$36 £20**

HOOGSTRATEN - The Angel Appearing To Hagar - pen and brown ink - 19.5 x 24.2cm.
(Christie's) **$72 £40**

JAMES CLARKE HOOK - Milk For The Schooner - signed with monogram and dated 1864 - 26¾ x 41¾in.
(Christie's) **$117 £65**

HOOPER - Interior Scenes With Cavaliers - signed - on canvas - 10 x 14in.
(Morphets of Harrogate) **$306 £170**

JOHN HORACE HOOPER - 'Near Shiplake On Thames' - signed and signed and inscribed on the reverse - 23¼ x 41¼in.
(Sotheby Bearne) **$936 £520**

JOHN HORACE HOOPER - Evening At The Lock - signed - 15½ x 25¼in.
(Sotheby's Belgravia) **$576 £320**

HOPPNER

JOHN HOPPNER - Portrait Of Lady Arundel Of Wardour, three-quarter length, holding a folio, sitting in a landscape - 50 x 39in.
(Christie's)   **$6,300 £3,500**

JOHN HOPPNER - A Rustic Family Outside A Cottage - pencil and black chalk, heightened with white chalk on grey paper - 15 x 16in.
(Sotheby's)   **$234**   **£130**

HOREMANS - A Seated Woman With A Mug - black chalk, grey wash, watermark - 15.1 x 14.8cm.
(Christie's)   **$63**   **£35**

JAN JOSEF HOREMANS - A Courtyard Scene of an inn with figures conversing, drinking and playing Tric Trac, in the foreground a little girl plays with a spaniel - oil - on canvas - 26 x 32½in.
(Bonham's)   **$5,520 £3,000**

JAN JOSEF HOREMANS THE YOUNGER - Elegant figures refreshing themselves by a Portico in a Park - bears Lancret signature - 22 x 33 in.
(Christie's N. York)   **$1,650 £902**

GEORGE W. HORLOR - Going To The Fair - signed and inscribed on the reverse - 35¼ x 65¼in.
(Christie's)   **$11,700 £6,000**

JOSEPH HORLOR - Extensive Landscapes - on board - 11 x 17½in.
(Sotheby's Belgravia)   **$396 £220 Pair**

JOSEPH HORLOR - A Fishing Village - bears another signature and dated - 27½ x 45in.
(Sotheby's Belgravia)   **$648**   **£360**

J. HORLOR - A Bridge Over A River -
7½ x 9½in.
(Sotheby's Belgravia)   **$58**   **£32**

J. HORLOR, Attributed to - Landscapes -
4½ x 6½in.
(Elliott & Green)   **$180 £100 Pair**

T. L. HORNBROOK - A View In The
Mediterranean, An English Brig, A
Spanish Barque And A Gunboat - 25
x 33in.
(Phillips, Solihull)   **$1,467 £815**ʼ

EDWARD ATKINSON HORNEL -
At The Time Of The Singing Of The
Birds - signed and dated 1919 - 24 x
29¼in.
(Sotheby's Belgravia)   **$4,320 £2,400**

EDWARD ATKINSON HORNEL - In
The Wood - three girls picking flowers -
dated 1911 - 73 x 61cm.
(Edmiston's)   **$6,840   £3,800**

A. HORNUNG - Akt, 1916 - 81 x 65cm.
Auktionshaus am Neumarkt)
$1,517 £829

J. C. HORSLEY - Fair Students - 40 x
50in.
(Christie's)   **$1,800 £1,000**

B. HORWITZ - Extensive River Scene
At Llangollen, Wales - watercolour -
14 x 21in.
(G. A. Key)   **$40 £22**

GERRIT HOUCKGEEST - The Tomb Of The
Prince Of Orange In The New Church In
Delft - signed with monogram and dated
1650 - on panel - 20 x 16½in.
(Christie's)   **$9,000   £5,000**

GERRIT VAN HOUCKGEEST - The
Interior Of A Church, with a woman,
children and dogs - on panel - painted
arched top - 17¾ x 14¼in.
(Christie's)   **$4,500 £2,500**

JEAN PIERRE HOUEL - Peasants At
A Stream - signed and dated - pen and
grey ink, grey wash - 8.8 x 16.5cm.
(Christie's)   **$126   £70**

HOUGHTON
ARTHUR BOYD HOUGHTON - A
Mediaeval Landscape - 9¼ x 12in.
(Sotheby's Belgravia) **$180 £100**

GEORGE HOUSTON - Neidpath
Castle - signed - 27 x 35in.
(Sotheby's Belgravia) **$630 £350**

GEORGE HOUSTON - Figures On
The Bank Of A River, Summertime -
signed - 17½ x 23½in.
(Sotheby's Belgravia) **$396 £220**

GEORGE HOUSTON - On The Edge
Of A Loch - signed - 17¼ x 22¼in.
(Sotheby's Belgravia) **$432 £240**

GEORGE HOUSTON - Afton Water,
Ayrshire - signed - 27½ x 35½in.
(Sotheby's Belgravia) **$684 £380**

JOHN A. HOUSTON - River Pool With
Overhanging Rocks And Figures in the
foreground - dated 1857 - oil - 9½ x
13½in.
(Thomas Love & Sons Ltd.)
$288 £160
JOHN K. HOUSTON - The Truant -
signed - 11½ x 9¾in.
(Sotheby's Belgravia) **$99 £55**

ROBERT HOUSTON - On The West
Coast - signed - 27½ x 35½in.
(Sotheby's Belgravia) **$630 £350**

SAMUEL HOWITT - A Herd Of Deer
Watering in a stream - signed and dated
1792 - pen and grey ink and watercolour -
8¼ x 10¾in.
(Christie's) **$864 £480**

E. HUBER - Arabs At An Oasis - signed -
on panel - 6 x 8in.
(Christie's) **$90 £50**

WOLFGANG HUBER - A Village Scene
with peasants outside a tavern - signed -
black chalk, brown wash and bodycolour
- 17.7 x 25.3cm.
(Christie's) **$216 £120**

J. VAN HUCHTENBURG - A Cavalry
Engagement in an extensive landscape
with a town on a hill beyond - 32½ x
58in.
(Christie's) **$2,160 £1,200**

J. VAN HUCHTENBURG - A Cavalry Engagement In A Wooded Landscape - on panel - 20 x 27in.
(Christie's) **$1,260 £700**

JAN VAN HUCHTENBURG - A Caravan On The Move; and The Triumphant Entry Of An Oriental Army - 24½ x 54½in.
(Christie's) **$9,900 £5,500 Pair**

THOMAS HUDSON - Portrait Of A Gentleman, Said To Be A Member Of The Drake Family, three-quarter length, wearing a grey jacket and blue embroidered waistcoat - 49½ x 37½in.
(Christie's) **$2,700 £1,500**

THOMAS HUDSON - Constance Lucy Of Charlecote, wife of Sir John Burboyne, three-quarter length - oil - 49 x 39in.
(Heathcote Ball & Co) **$2,287 £1,250**

THOMAS HUDSON - Three-quarter Length Portrait Of Viscount Maynard Of Much Easton, Essex, in a landscape - oil - 49 x 39in.
(Heathcote Ball & Co) **$6,405 £3,500**

THOMAS HUDSON - Portrait Of A Young Lady, half length, wearing a pink and blue dress - 28¾ x 23¾in.
(Christie's) **$5,400 £3,000**

HUET - A Classical Landscape with a shepherd, shepherdess and cattle - 35½ x 52½in.
(Christie's) **$1,800 £1,000**

HUET

JEAN-BAPTISTE HUET - A Wooded
Landscape with a peasant and cattle in
the foreground and a cottage beyond -
signed and inscribed IX - 18 x 25½in.
(Christie's) **$5,040 £2,800**

JEAN-BAPTISTE HUET - A Wooded
Landscape with a shepherdess, sheep
and cattle - signed and inscribed IX -
18 x 25½in.
(Christie's) **$3,960 £2,200**

J. B. HUET - A Farm Surrounded By
Trees - inscribed 'J. Huet, 1762' - black
and white chalk on blue paper - 34.1 x
43.0cm.
(Christie's) **$216 £120**

WILLIAM HUGGINS - Giraffes In A
Landscape - signed and dated 1861 -
35 x 27½in.
(Christie's) **$10,800 £6,000**

WILLIAM HUGGINS - A Leopard,
seated - signed and dated 1873 - on
board - 15¾ x 11½in.
(Christie's) **$63 £35**

A. HUGHES - A Wooded Landscape with
figures by a stream - 20 x 26½in.
(Christie's) **$1,980 £1,100**

ARTHUR HUGHES - 'At Midnight
The Moon Cometh' - signed and
inscribed on the reverse - on panel -
11 x 15¼in.
(Christie's) **$45 £25**

EDWARD ROBERT HUGHES -
Female Nude Study, half length - signed -
black chalk - 13 x 10in.
(Sotheby's Belgravia) **$32 £18**

224

TALBOT HUGHES - The Rose Gatherer; and Waiting - signed and dated 1892 and 1896 - on panels - 8½ x 6¾in.
(Christie's S. Kensington) **$684 £380 Pair**

EDWARD HUGHES - A Welcome Gift - signed and dated 1865 - oil - on canvas - 18 x 14in.
(Bonham's) **$2,340 £1,300**

GODFREY HUGHES - Sunday School - signed twice - dated 1912 - 14 x 19in.
(Sotheby's Belgravia) **$58 £32**

J. J. HUGHES - View Of Bridgnorth - signed - 15½ x 25¼in.
(Sotheby Bearne) **$331 £170**

J. J. HUGHES - A Mountainous Wooded River Landscape, with peasants by a cottage - signed - 23½ x 35½in.
(Christie's) **$99 £55**

WILLIAM HUGHES - Still Life, a mallard, game birds and vegetables beside a copper preserving pan - signed and dated 1871 - 27½ x 35½in.
(Sotheby Bearne) **$585 £300**

WILLIAM HUGHES - A Dead Partridge, Apples, A Bunch Of Grapes And A Pottery Jug; and A Dead Grouse, Apples, Grapes And A Pottery Jug - both signed and dated 1866 - one on board - 14 x 17¾in.
(Christie's) **$1,462 £750 Pair**

VICTOR PIERRE HUGUET - The
Caravan - signed - 39 x 31in.
(Christie's) $3,060 £1,700

ABRAHAM HULK - Fishing Boats Off A
Jetty In A Choppy Sea - signed - on panel
- 6½ x 9in.
(Christie's) $2,700   £1,500

ABRAHAM HULK - A Fresh Breeze On
The Scheldt - signed - 16 x 24in.
(Christie's S. Kensington) $2,160 £1,200

VICTOR PIERRE HUGUET - Arabs
Outside A Mosque - signed - 33 x 25in.
(Christie's) $7,560 £4,200

HULK - Figures Near A Winding
River - 14¾ x 30in.
(Sotheby's Belgravia) $77 £42

ABRAHAM HULK, JUN - Figures In
Landscapes - signed - 29¾ x 19¾in.
(Sotheby's Belgravia) $576   £320 **Pair**

ABRAHAM HULK, JUN - Amongst
Corn Stooks - signed - 24 x 16in.
(Sotheby's Belgravia) **$216 £120**

F. MARTINUS HULK - The Mellow
Year Is Hastening To Its Close - signed -
29½ x 19½in.
(Sotheby's Belgravia) **$234 £130**

J. HULK - Dutch Street Scene - signed -
on panel - 16¾ x 13½in.
(Sotheby Bearne) **$1,482 £760**

W. F. HULK - Cattle With River In
Background - signed - board - 19 x 15in.
(Morphets of Harrogate) **$270 £150**

WILLIAM FREDERICK HULK - Cattle
Watering In A Landscape - signed - 11 x 9in.
(Christie's) **$216 £120**

W. J. HULK - Dutch Girl With Cattle -
30 x 24cm.
(Edmiston's) **$522 £290**

H. HULLEY - A Rocky Wooded Landscape With Travellers in a horse-drawn
cart - signed - inscribed - 21¾ x 31½in.
(Lawrence) **$1,224 £680**

FREDERICK WILLIAM HULME - A
Lane Near Ripley - signed and dated
1866 - 29½ x 49½in.
(Christie's) **$5,760 £3,200**

FREDERICK WILLIAM HULME -
Bramshott, Hampshire - signed,
inscribed and dated 1880 - 19¼ x
29½in.
(Christie's) **$1,440 £800**

JACOB VAN HULSDONCK - Plums In A
Bowl with plums and cherries on a table -
signed with monogram - on panel - 10½ x
15in.
(Christie's) **$57,600 £32,000**

CHARLES HUMBERT - Cow Drinking -
signed - oil - on panel - 40.5 x 23.5cm.
(Christian Rosset) **$293 £160**

HUMPHRY

A. HUMPHRY - Shepherd And Flock - oil - 10 x 23in.
(G. A. Key) **$40 £22**

HUNT - Landscape With Girl Feeding Geese centre foreground - signed - oil - on canvas - 29 x 20in.
(Stewart Gore) **$161 £85**

CHARLES HUNT - Dancing A Jig - signed and dated '93 - canvas - on board - 15½ x 19½in.
(Christie's) **$126 £70**

EDGAR HUNT - A Hen Coop with puppies, hens, a bantam cock and chicks - signed and dated '97 - 51 x 76cm.
(Phillips, Solihull) **$6,300 £3,500**

REUBEN HUNT - Children And Donkey In A Wooded Landscape, a young boy seated on a stool sketching, a donkey, with a young girl looking on - signed and dated - on canvas - 17½ x 23½in.
(Morphets of Harrogate) **$1,260 £700**

E. HUNT - A Cockerel, Hen, Rabbit And Two Hamsters near a hutch in a stone set yard - signed and dated 1908 - oil - 10 x 14in.
(Richard Baker & Baker) **$612 £340**

WALTER HUNT - A Promising Litter - signed and dated '84 - 17½ x 13½in.
(Christie's) **$4,290 £2,200**

WALTER HUNT - Shepherd Boy Asleep beside his dog in a meadow with sheep, ducks and a cow - signed and dated '96 - 29 x 41½in.
(Phillips, Solihull) **$6,660 £3,600**

WALTER HUNT - A Farmyard Scene With Two Calves, a girl with a collie puppy, a cockerel, two hens and chickens in the foreground, sheep and a thatched cottage in the distance - signed and dated 1923 - 19¾ x 29½in.
(H. Spencer & Sons) **$6,300 £3,500**

WILLIAM HENRY HUNT - A Token Of Love - signed - 15¼ x 11in.
(Sotheby's) **$792 £440**

GEORGE LESLIE HUNTER - A Mediterranean Town - signed - pen and ink and coloured chalks - 12¼ x 15½in.
(Sotheby's Belgravia) **$396 £220**

GEORGE LESLIE HUNTER - The French Market, New Orleans - signed - coloured chalks - 11½ x 9¼in.
(Sotheby's Belgravia) **$1,260 £700**

GEORGE SHERWOOD HUNTER - Shrimpers On A Beach - signed and dated 1885 - 15 x 29in.
(Christie's) **$432 £240**

GEORGE SHERWOOD HUNTER - On The Banks Of The Tiber - inscribed and dated Rome January 1876 on the reverse - 19 x 45in.
(Christie's) **$810 £450**

GEORGE SHERWOOD HUNTER - Fisherfolk On A Jetty - signed and dated 1880 - 24 x 19in.
(Christie's) **$780 £400**

GEORGE SHERWOOD HUNTER - Emptying A Salmon Net - 40 x 29¾in.
(Christie's) **$720 £400**

GEORGE SHERWOOD HUNTER - The Venetian Lagoon — A Last Crossing - 19 x 44¾in.
(Christie's)　　**$540 £300**

GEORGE SHERWOOD HUNTER - Fisherfolk On The Beach, Aberdeen - signed and dated 1880 - inscribed on reverse - 15 x 29¾in.
(Christie's)　　**$810 £450**

LOUIS BOSWORTH HURT - A Highland Drover At The Entrance To Glencoe - signed and dated 1882 - inscribed on the reverse - 23¼ x 35in.
(Sotheby's Belgravia)　　**$2,700 £1,500**

LOUIS BOSWORTH HURT - By A Highland Stream - signed and dated 1903 - 24 x 40in.
(Lawrence)　　**$3,600 £2,000**

LOUIS BOSWORTH HURT - 'In A Northern Glen By Peaceful Loch And Mist-Wreathed Hill' - signed - 23½ x 39½in.
(Christie's)　　**$6,825 £3,500**

LOUIS BOSWORTH HURT - In Glencoe - signed - inscribed on the reverse - 11½ x 17¼in.
(Sotheby's Belgravia)　　**$684 £380**

LOUIS BOSWORTH HURT - A Highland Drover - signed and dated 1882 - 11½ x 17¼in.
(Sotheby's Belgravia)　　**$360 £200**

HUSSAIN - The Blind Beggar; An Eastern Girl - signed and dated 1971 - canvas - on board - 23 x 18in.
(Sotheby's Belgravia)　　**$68　£38 Pair**

GEORGE WILEY HUTCHINSON - Cottages Near Ipswich - watercolour - 5 x 7in.
(G. A. Key)　　**$27　£15 ·**

HUTCHISON - Farm Lad With A Cow
in a stable - 17¼ x 28½in.
(Sotheby's Belgravia)   **$45 £25**

ROBERT GEMMEL HUTCHISON -
Children Playing On The Coast -
signed - 9½ x 11½in.
(Sotheby's Belgravia)   **$648 £360**

ROBERT GEMMEL HUTCHISON -
A Fresh Breeze - signed - on board -
7 x 9½in.
(Sotheby's Belgravia)   **$1,350 £750**

ROBERT GEMMEL HUTCHISON -
The Lost Ball - signed - inscribed -
heightened with bodycolour - 17½ x
23½in.
(Sotheby's Belgravia)   **$1,980 £1,100**

ROBERT GEMMEL HUTCHISON -
Young Peasant Girl reclining in corn-
field - oil - on canvas - 19 x 14½in.
(The Nottingham Auction Mart) **$2,316 £1,200**

ROBERT GEMMEL HUTCHISON - Portrait Of Nan, The Artist's Daughter -
signed - 35½ x 21½in.
(Sotheby's Belgravia)   **$396 £220**

J. B. HUYSMANS - A Wooded River
Landscape with travellers and hills
beyond - bears monogram - 19 x 22½in.
(Christie's)   **$1,350 £750**

LA HYRE - The Finding Of Moses - 42½
x 48in.
(Christie's)   **$1,080 £600**

231

J. C. IBBETSON - Sheltering From The Storm - on panel - 11 x 15in.
(Sotheby's) **$450 £250**

JULIUS CAESAR IBBETSON - A Rocky Landscape in North Wales, with figures on a path - on panel - 11½ x 15½in.
(Christie's) **$684 £380**

JULIUS CAESAR IBBETSON - The Pass At Borrowdale - 37 x 50¼in.
(Christie's) **$990 £550**

JULIUS CAESAR IBBETSON - Portrait Of A Young Boy, half length, wearing a blue jacket and white collar - 18½ x 15¾in.
(Christie's) **$1,350 £750**

JULIUS CAESAR IBBETSON - A Wooded Landscape, a horseman driving cattle across a ford to the left, a woman and child with two donkeys to the right, a cottage and ruins beyond - 16½ x 20½in.
(Sotheby's) **$1,170 £650**

IBBETSON - A Lake View, figures, boats and animals in the foreground - 8½ x 11½in.
(Sotheby's) **$180 £100**

IBBETSON - A Drover And His Flock On A Country Road - 22½ x 35½in.
(Sotheby's) **$396 £220**

IBBETSON - A River Scene, Anglers in the foreground and a castle and cottage on the far bank - on board - 11½ x 15¼in.
(Sotheby's) **$72 £40**

HENRI-GABRIEL IBELS - La Grand-mere Assise - signed - pastel - 12 x 8¾in.
(Sotheby's) **$146 £80**

HENRI-GABRIEL IBELS - Jeune Femme Assise Pres De La Fenetre - signed - pastel - 12 x 8¾in.
(Sotheby's) **$146 £80**
J. M. INCE - Road And Cottages Above A Welsh Estuary - inscribed - 15 x 19¼in.
(Sotheby's) **$270 £150**

DANIEL IHLY - Woman Sitting On A Balcony - 60 x 49cm.
(Auktionshaus am Neumarkt) **$1,213 £663**
JOHN WILLIAM INCHBOLD - Evening 1849: a study of trees by a pool - signed and inscribed - watercolour - 10¾ x 8½in.
(Christie's) **$92 £50**

BERNARDINO INDIA - A Female Saint in a niche - black chalk, pen and brown ink, brown wash - 18.3 x 7.7cm.
(Christie's) **$306 £170**

INDONI

FILIPPO INDONI - A Lady By An Arch - signed - watercolour - 19 x 11¾in.
(Sotheby's) **$463 £240**

WILLIAM INGHAM - Still Life Of A Hare and pheasants - signed and dated 6.3.16 - 31½ x 17½in.
(Sotheby's Belgravia) **$251 £130**

INGRUNI - The Goatherd - indistinctly signed and dated 1842 - 14¾ x 11¼in.
(Sotheby's) **$360 £200**

IRISH PROVINCIAL SCHOOL, Circa 1855 - A Farm Labourer's Family - 27 x 35in.
(Sotheby's Belgravia) **$1,072 £550**

IRISH PROVINCIAL SCHOOL, circa 1860 - Goughanbarre, source of the River Lee, Éire - heightened with body-colour - 26 x 39in.
(Sotheby's Belgravia) **$81 £42**

THOMAS TAYLOR IRELAND - Silver Birches - signed - 14 x 10in.
(Sotheby's Belgravia) **$68 £38**

THOMAS TAYLOR IRELAND - A Fishing Pool shaped by Silver Birches - signed and dated '99 - 35 x 23½in.
(Sotheby's Belgravia) **$978 £520**

ISRAELS - Evening Contemplation - 10¼ x 13in.
(Sotheby's) **$144 £80**

JOSEF ISRAELS - The Pet Lamb - signed - canvas - on panel - 5½ x 9in.
(Sotheby's) **$810 £450**

ITALIAN SCHOOL, NORTH - A Kneeling Female Saint - black chalk, pen and brown ink, brown wash - 14.4 x 7.2cm.
(Christie's) **$216 £120**

ITALIAN SCHOOL, 19th century - The Artistic Chambermaid - on panel - 12½ x 6in.
(Sotheby's) **$126 £70**

ITALIAN SCHOOL, 19th century - Figures In A Classical Landscape - on panel - 13¾ x 17¾in.
(Sotheby's) **$252 £140**

ITALIAN SCHOOL, 19th century - Portrait Of A Lady, small full length, in Italian peasant costume standing in a landscape - 32 x 30¼in.
(Christie's) **$270 £150**

ITALIAN SCHOOL, late 18th century - Flora - oval - 12½ x 10½in.
(Sotheby's) **$360 £200**

ITALIAN SCHOOL, 19th century - Bath Time - 28 x 35in.
(Christie's) **$3,420 £1,900**

ITALIAN SCHOOL, 19th century - Reading The Illustrated News - 31¼ x 25¼in.
(Christie's) **$2,880 £1,600**

ITALIAN SCHOOL, 18th century - Female Saint In A Cave, wearing pink and white draperies, seated on a rock, her hand on a human skull, a cross before her, two cherubim in the air above - 53 x 38in.
(H. Spencer & Sons) **$360 £200**

ITALIAN SCHOOL - Sappho With Her Lyre; Venus With A Looking Glass - inscribed on the reverse - on board - 14¾ x 9½in.
(Sotheby's) **$81 £45 Pair**

ITALIAN SCHOOL, 18th century - Belshazzar's Feast - on panel - 18½ x 29½in.
(Christie's N. York) **$220 £120**

ITALIAN SCHOOL - L'education de la Vierge par sainte Anne - oil - on canvas - 70 x 59cm.
(Christian Rosset) **$1,679 £933**

SEBASTIANO ITTAR - A View In Malta with M'dina in the distance - pencil and sepia wash - 6 x 9½in.
(Christie's) **$45 £25**

IVAN ALEXEIEVITCH IVANOW - Vue des Montes de Caucase - signed and inscribed - pencil and watercolour - 7 x 13in.
(Sotheby's) **$425 £220**

JOHN IVORY - View Over Acle Marshes - oil - 4 x 7in.
(G. A. Key) **$27 £15**

J

A. JACKSON - Hare Shooting On The Moors - oil - 18 x 30in.
(G. A. Key)   **$36**   **£20**

MONTAGUE JACKSON - L'Heure Divine - signed and inscribed - heightened with bodycolour - 20½ x 13¾in.
(Sotheby's Belgravia)   **$18**   **£10**

SAMUEL PHILLIPS JACKSON - Penolver Point; Lion Rock, Kynance - heightened with white - 4¾ x 6¾in.
(Sotheby's Belgravia)   **$45**   **£25 Pair**

PETER FRANS JACOBS - The Approach To La Riccia - signed and inscribed 'La Riccia' - pencil, grey and brown wash heightened with white on brown paper - 27.0 x 42.5cm.
(Christie's)   **$54**   **£30**

ANTONIO JACOBSEN - The Critic At Sea in full sails and driven by steam - signed, inscribed and dated 1889 - oil - on canvas - 21½ x 35½in.
(Sotheby's)   **$1,833 £950**

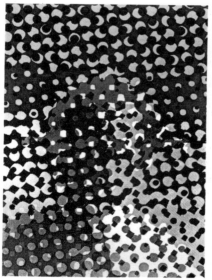

ALAIN JACQUET - Portrait Of A Man - signed and dated '64 - silkscreen - 63¾ x 44¾in.
(Christie's)   **$1,189 £650**

DAVID JAMES - 'Boats Going Out, Cornish Coast' - signed and dated (18)90 and inscribed - signed and dated on the reverse - 24¼ x 49¼in.
(Sotheby Bearne)   **$2,160 £1,200**

W. JAMES - A Faggot-Gatherer On A Cart Track - signed and dated - 39½ x 29½in.
(Sotheby's Belgravia)   **$288**   **£160**

W. JAMES - The Bacino Di San Marco, Venice, with the Dogana and the Church of Santa Maria della Salute - 24½ x 39½in.
(Christie's)   **$2,160 £1,200**

W. JAMES - The Piazza San Marco, Venice, with the Torre dell'Orologio - 24½ x 39½in.
(Christie's)   **$2,340 £1,300**

W. JAMES - The Canale Di Santa Chiara, Venice, with the mountains beyond - 24½ x 39½in.
(Christie's) **$1,800 £1,000**

W. JAMES - The Bacino Di San Marco, Venice, with the Doge's Palace and the Church of Santa Maria della Salute - 24½ x 39½in.
(Christie's) **$1,800 £1,000**

W. JAMES - A View On The Grand Canal, Venice, looking east from the Campo San Vio - 24½ x 39½in.
(Christie's) **$2,160 £1,200**

ALEXANDER JAMIESON - At The Seaside - on panel - 11½ x 15½in.
(Sotheby's Belgravia) **$684 £380**

BIDDY MacDONALD JAMIESON - On The Thames - on board - 10¾ x 14½in.
(Sotheby's Belgravia) **$22 £12**

F. E. JAMIESON - Highland Loch Scenes - oil - 16 x 24in.
(G. A. Key) **$126 £70 Pair**

F. E. JAMIESON - A Landscape; The Old Mill Brora, Sutherland - signed - 19½ x 29½in.
(Sotheby's Belgravia) **$180 £100 Pair**

F. E. JAMIESON - A Highland Loch Scene - signed - 15½ x 23½in.
(Sotheby's Belgravia) **$99 £55**

F. E. JAMIESON - Glen Goil; Argyllshire; Evening Glow, Glen Sheel, Ross-shire - both signed - inscribed on the reverse - 18¼ x 28¼in.
(Sotheby's Belgravia) **$288 £160 Pair**

F. W. JANKOWSKI - Grand Canal Venice, with the Doge's Palace, the Mola and Santa Maria della Salute - signed - 14½ x 22¾in.
(Sotheby's) **$630 £350**

F.-C. JANNECK - A Visit To The Money-Lender - on panel - 12½ x 17¼in.
(Christie's) **$4,680 £2,600**

FRANZ CHRISTOPH JANNECK - Elegant Figures Feasting In An Interior - signed - on copper - 16½ x 23½in.
(Christie's) **$40,040 £22,000**

W. G. F. JANSEN - An Extensive Coastal Landscape - bears signature - canvas on board - 14½ x 18½in.
(Christie's) **$198 £110**

WILLEM GEORGE FREDERICK JANSEN - A Canal Scene With A Man Towing A Barge - signed - on board - 15½ x 21in.
(Christie's) **$2,340 £1,300**

J. JANSON - Street Scene In Amsterdam with figures selling fish in the foreground - oil - on canvas - 26 x 32in.
(Bonham's)   **$4,416 £2,400**

CORNELIUS JANSSENS - Portrait Of Robert, First Lord Digby, half length, wearing a black cloak and white lace collar - 27¼ x 23¾in.
(Sotheby's)   **$630   £350**

HIERONYMUS JANSSENS - A Family Group in an elegant interior - 25½ x 34¾in.
(Christie's)   **$11,830 £6,500**

HIERONYMUS JANSSENS - A Gentleman Welcoming A Masked Couple at the steps of a Venetian palazzo - 32 x 40in.
(Christie's)   **$2,548 £1,400**

HIERONYMUS JANSSENS - An Interior With Figures Feasting And Making Music - on copper - 21 x 28¼in.
(Christie's)   **$3,060 £1,700**

VICTOR JANSSENS - Saint Cecilia with attendant music-making angels - 34½ x 48½in.
(Christie's)   **$2,340 £1,300**

JANSSENS - Portrait Of A Gentleman, half length, in black with a white lace ruff, a coat of arms to the left - inscribed with a quotation and dated 1622 - 29¼ x 24½in.
(Sotheby's)   **$450   £250**

ROBERT JEANNISSON - Cafe du Coin -
signed and dated 1936 - oil - on canvas -
25½ x 19½in.
(Sotheby's)   **$72 £40**

GEORGE H. JENKINS - Rivert Dart and
Dartmoor Landscapes - signed and dated
1875 - oil - 17¾ x 26in.
(Buckell & Ballard)   **$270 £150 Pair**

PAUL JENKINS - Phenomenon High
Vortex - signed - signed again, inscribed
and dated 1966 on the reverse - 48 x
50in.
(Christie's N. York)   **$4,400 £2,444**

WALTER JENNER - Naval Activity -
signed with monogram - dated and bears
another date - 17 x 23¼in.
(Sotheby's Belgravia) **$135   £75**

FRANCIS JOHNSON - Otago Or Attago,
A Chief At Amsterdam; A Warrior - both
signed and numbered - grey and brown
washes - 10½ x 8¼in.
(Sotheby's)   **$289 £150 Pair**

SIDNEY YATES JOHNSON - A River
Scene, Evening; Ducks By A Bridge -
one signed - one bears another signature -
11¾ x 17½in.
(Sotheby's Belgravia) **$144   £80 Pair**

HENRY L LE JEUNE - The Archers -
on panel - 5¾ x 7¾in.
(Sotheby's Belgravia) **$576   £320**

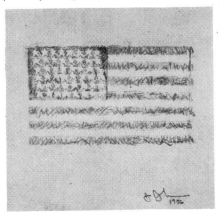

JASPER JOHNS - Small Flag -
signed and dated 1956 - coloured
chalks on grey paper - 4¼ x 4¼ in.
*(Christie's N.York)***$10,450 £5,805**

ALEXANDER JOHNSTON - Peggy And
Jenny, from the Gentle Shepherd -
signed with initials - on board - 9 x 8¾in.
(Sotheby's Belgravia)   **$504 £280**

ALEXANDER JOHNSTON - The Braw Wooer — "he spak o' the darts in my bonny black een, etc." — Burns - 28 x 36in.
(Lawrence)   **$1,080 £600**

JOLI - A Capriccio With Classical And Gothic Ruins - inscribed on the reverse - pen and brown ink, grey wash - 41.2 x 30.0cm.
(Christie's)   **$126**   **£70**

A. JOLI - A View Of Isola Bella - 22 x 4in.
(Christie's)   **$4,320 £2,400**

A. JOLI - A North Italian Lake with a port and shipping - 36 x 51½in.
(Christie's)   **$2,520 £1,400**

ANTONIO JOLI - A View Of Paestum from the South - 29 x 39¼in.
(Sotheby's)   **$6,475 £3,500**

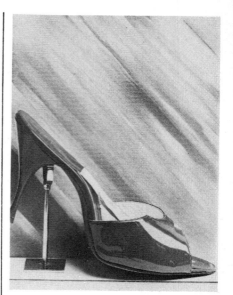

ALLEN JONES - Red Blue White Shoe - signed and dated '66 on the reverse - oil on canvas and shoe on stand - 10½ x 8 x 4in.
(Christie's)   **$1,244 £680**

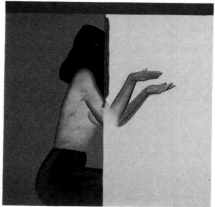

ALLEN JONES - Red Latex Suit - signed - dated '73 on the canvas overlap - oil and latex on linen - 48 x 48in.
(Christie's)   **$5,490 £3,000**

CHARLES JONES - Study Of Grazing Sheep in an open landscape - signed - inscribed and dated 1882 on reverse - 11½ x 19½in.
(Phillips, Solihull)   **$1,008 £560**

CHARLES JONES - A River Landscape - signed with monogram - dated 1880 - inscribed on the reverse - on paper - 13¾ x 19½in.
(Sotheby's Belgravia) **$180 £100**

CHARLES JONES - Cattle And Sheep In An Extensive Landscape - signed with monogram and dated 1879 - signed and dated 1879 on the reverse - 23¾ x 37½in.
(Christie's) **$1,852 £950**

CHARLES JONES - Eventide By The River Kennet - signed with monogram and dated 1874 - signed and dated 1874 and inscribed on an old label on the reverse - 35½ x 60in.
(Christie's) **$1,755 £900**

CHARLES JONES - Sheep In A Snowy Landscape - signed with monogram and dated '76 - signed and dated on the reverse - 21¾ x 37½in.
(Christie's) **$2,535 £1,300**

HUBERT JOHN JONES - Famous Cheshire Horses - signed and dated 1901, 1930, 1931, - oil - on canvas - 18 x 17in.
(Andrew Hilditch & Son) **$504 £280 Three**

PAUL JONES - Waiting - signed - 7¾ x 9½in.
(Sotheby's Belgravia) **$288 £160**

RICHARD JONES - A Dark Bay Hunter with a retriever and a terrier in a landscape - 27½ x 35¼in.
(Christie's) **$2,520 £1,400**

S. J. E. JONES - Duck Shooting; Snipe Shooting; Pheasant Shooting; Partridge Shooting - 7¾ x 10¾in.
(Christie's) **$15,300 £8,500 Four**

JAN MARTENS DE JONGE - A Cavalry Skirmish - on panel - 20 x 32¾in.
(Christie's) **$3,060 £1,700**

JONGKIND

JOHAN JONGKIND - The Port Of
Rotterdam - signed - oil - on canvas -
46 x 27cm.
(Christian Rosset) $5,760 £3,200
JORDAENS - Saint Peter Healing The
Cripple At The Gate Of The Temple -
black chalk, pen and brown ink,
brown wash - 17.7 x 26.5cm.
(Christie's) $81 £45

JACOB JORDAENS - Susannah And
The Elders - 82½ x 71in.
(Christie's) $9,000 £5,000

ASGER JORN - Untitled - signed and
dated '61 - gouache, watercolour, pen
and black ink - 14½ x 20in.
(Christie's) $1,006 £550

ASGER JORN - Untitled - signed and
dated '69 - collage - 15½ x 12¾ in.
(Christie's) $1,281 £700

ASGER JORN - "En allant a la Fete" -
signed - oil - on canvas - 33 x 37¾in.
(Sotheby's) $13,176 £7,200

ASGER JORN - A sort of bird's eye view
from slightly above - signed, inscribed in
Danish and dated 1963 - 21¼ x 25½ in.
(Christie's) $6,954 £3,800

ASGER JORN - Victoire Anglaise Sur
Mer - signed - signed, inscribed with
title in French and English and dated
'60 on the reverse - 27 x 21in.
(Christie's) $7,320 £4,000

ASGER JORN - A Dents Serrees - signed -
signed, inscribed and dated '60 on the
reverse - 25½ x 31¾in.
(Christie's) **$8,235 £4,500**

ASGER JORN - Untitled - signed and
dated Paris 1937 - oil on board - 20½ x
21½ in.
(Christie's) **$2,745 £1,500**

JOHN CANTILOE JOY - The 'Revenge'
at Spithead in 1837 - 11 x 17¼ in.
(Sotheby's) **$2,340 £1,300**

WILLIAM JOY - Yarmouth Jetty -
watercolour - 9 x 13in.
(G. A. Key) **$112 £62**

WILLIAM CANTILOE JOY - Fishing Boats
and other vessels in a choppy sea - signed -
watercolour - 12½ x 18¾in.
(Sotheby Bearne) **$1,521 £780**

WILLIAM CANTILOE JOY - The
Cutter Greyhound With Two Sailing
Ships - pencil and watercolour - 8 x
11½in.
(Sotheby's) **$1,404 £780**

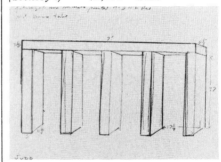

DONALD JUDD - Untitled - signed and
inscribed - pencil - 12½ x 15¾in.
(Christie's) **$1,098 £600**

DONALD JUDD - Untitled (Progression) -
blue lacquer on aluminium and brass -
160½ x 8¼ x 8in.
(Christie's) **$11,895 £6,500**

KADEZ - Portrait Of A Girl In Edwardian
Dress on edge of a wood - oil - 26 x 20½in.
(Buckell & Ballard)   **$171 £95**

FRANZ KAISERMANN - Vue Du Monte
Caliglio A Tivoli Et La Riviere De La
Thene Prise Au Lac Du Voleux - inscribed
on the reverse - pen and brown ink and
watercolour - 36.5 x 52.3cm.
(Christie's)   **$360   £200**

WILLEM KALF - A Peasant Woman peeling
vegetables in a kitchen - indistinctly signed
and dated 1643 - on copper - 6½ x 5¼in.
(Christie's)   **$5,824 £3,200**

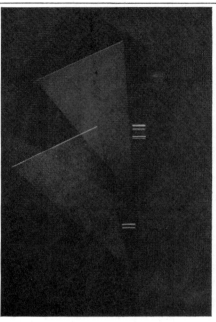

WASSILY KANDINSKY - Composition
Of Triangles - 48 x 31cm.
(Auktionshaus am Neumarkt) **$7,834 £4,281**

CHRISTIAN CORNELIS KANNEMANS -
Sailing Vessels In A Choppy Sea At Night -
signed and dated 1854 - 47 x 63½in.
(Christie's)   **$5,040   £2,800**

MARIE TEN KATE - A Seashore Scene with children with the catch - signed and dated 1850 - oil - on canvas - 16 x 19in.
(Warner, Sheppard & Wade)
$8,232 £4,200

MARIE TEN KATE - Three Children Poaching A Pheasant by a hedgerow - signed - coloured washes - 10 x 14in.
(Phillips, Solihull) **$720 £400**

KAUFMANN, late 19th century - A Windswept Coastal Scene with village and fisherfolk - oil - on canvas - 16½ x 53in.
(The Manchester Auction Mart.)
$136 £75

ON KAWARA - Mar. 17. 1972 - signed on the reverse - liquitex on canvas in a cardboard box with newspaper - 10¼ x 13in.
(Christie's) **$3,477 £1,900**

ARCHIBALD KAY - Cattle Resting - signed - indistinctly inscribed - 9½ x 13¼in.
(Sotheby's Belgravia) **$162 £90**

JAMES KAY - A Scottish Harbour Scene - signed and dated '95 - 17¾ x 26¾in.
(Sotheby's Belgravia) **$360 £200**

JAMES KAY - Rothesay Bay - signed - on board - 21½ x 31¼in.
(Sotheby's Belgravia) **$576 £320**

JAMES KAY - An Ayrshire Landscape - signed - on board - 21¼ x 31¼in.
(Sotheby's Belgravia) **$360 £200**

JAMES KAY - Figures Above The Seine - signed - on board - 22 x 33½in.
(Sotheby's Belgravia) **$1,980 £1,100**

KAY

JAMES KAY - Portincaple, Loch Long -
signed - on panel - 9½ x 13½in.
(Sotheby's Belgravia)   **$468 £260**

JAMES KAY - Yachting - oil - 10 x 14in.
(Thomas Love & Sons) **$558 £310**

JAMES KAY - Winter In The Highlands -
gouache - 50 x 60cm.
(Edmiston's)   **$630 £350**

C. J. KEATS - Busy Market Scene With
Many Figures At Bruges - signed - water-
colour - 28 x 20in.
(Richard Baker & Baker) **$180 £100**

ALEXANDER KEIRINCX - Diana And
Her Nymphs After The Chase in a wooded
river landscape - bears signature and
dated 1640 - on panel - 31¼ x 48½in.
(Christie's)   **$10,800 £6,000**

ELLSWORTH KELLY - Chatham X -
acrylic - on two panels - 108 x 95¾in.
(Christie's)   **$21,960 £12,000**

R. TALBOT KELLY - 'Karnak' - signed -
watercolour - 26 x 40in.
(Hussey's)   **$504 £280**

RICHARD GEORGE TALBOT KELLY -
Under The Eastern Sun - signed and dated
1909 - watercolour - 18¼ x 29¼in.
(Christie's)   **$864 £480**

R. JOSEPH KELSALL - Clipper Ship
And Cargo Steamer homeward bound -
watercolour - 13 x 19in.
(G. A. Key)   **$50 £28**

JENO KEMENEDY - 'The Bibliophiles' -
signed - dated Munchen 1886 - on panel -
7½ x 9¾in.
(Lawrence)   **$16,200 £9,000**

ROBERT KEMM, after Rosa Bonheur -
'Labourage Nivernais': Teams Of Oxen
Ploughing - signed and dated Paris 1860 -
51 x 102in.
(Christie's)   **$1,440 £800**

FLORENCE KENNEDY - Shielding Her
Son - signed and dated 1883 - 30¼ x
23in.
(Sotheby's Belgravia)   **$468 £260**

FLORENCE KENNEDY - The Love
Letter - 17½ x 23½in.
(Sotheby's Belgravia) **$162 £90**

W. KENNEDY - Portrait Of The Paddle
Steamer "Oregon" - oil - 11 x 23in.
(G. A. Key) **$72 £40**

WILLIAM KENNEDY - A Farmstead -
signed - 15½ x 23¼in.
(Sotheby's Belgravia) **$468 £260**

J. VAN KESSEL - An Assembly Of Birds -
many birds gathered around an open book -
on panel - 5¾ x 7½in.
(Sotheby's) **$27,750 £15,000**

JAN VAN KESSEL - A Concert Of Birds -
signed with monogram - on panel - 5 x
7½in.
(Christie's) **$25,200 £14,000**

JAN VAN KESSEL - Fish On The Bank
Of An Estuary; and A Still Life Of Fruit
In A Landscape - one signed - on copper -
5½ x 7½in.
(Sotheby's) **$17,575 £9,500 Pair**

JAN VAN KESSEL - Vulcan's Forge -
perhaps indistinctly dated 1660 (?) -
on panel - 21 x 36½in.
(Christie's) **$16,380 £9,000**

J. VAN KESSEL - A Still Life with
dishes of raspberries, bread and pastry -
5¼ x 8in.
(Christie's) **$4,320 £2,400**

247

KESSEL

J. VAN KESSEL - A Bowl Of Grapes
And Apples, with a glass of wine and
other fruit on a table - 5¼ x 8in.
(Christie's)   **$3,420 £1,900**

JAN VAN KESSEL - A Concert Of Birds -
on panel - 10½ x 14½in.
(Christie's)   **$16,200   £9,000**

JAN VAN KESSEL - A Concert Of Birds -
on panel - 6¾ x 9¾in.
(Christie's)   **$9,100 £5,000**

LEONARD KESTER - Clown - signed -
oil - on canvas - 51.5 x 41cm.
(Christian Rosset)   **$311 £170**

TILLY KETTLE - Portrait of Lieutenant
James Mayaffre, of the Indian Army,
standing three-quarter length, in a landscape wearing uniform - signed and dated
1773 - 49 x 39¼ in.
(Christie's)   **$4,320 £2,400**

KERSTIAEN DE KEUNINCK - A
Wooded Landscape With A Village -
on panel - 16 x 27½in.
(Christie's)   **$3,960 £2,200**

T. DE KEYSER - Portrait Of A Lady,
Aged 69, seated, three-quarter length,
wearing black dress and white collar
and cap - inscribed and dated 1646 - on
panel - 44 x 37in.
(Christie's)   **$5,400 £3,000**

WILLIAM KIDNER - Chartered Mercan-
tile Bank of India, London and China,
possibly in Shanghai, Chinese figures with
various forms of transport at the water's
edge in the foreground - signed and dated
1878 - watercolour - 21 x 25 in.
(Sotheby's, Hong Kong) **$4,986 £2,770**

BENJAMIN KILLINGBECK - A Dark Bay Racehorse and groom, by a stable, and an extensive landscape beyond - 39½ x 49½in.
(Christie's) **$2,700 £1,500**

GEORGE GOODWIN KILBURNE - The Best Man - signed and dated 1901 - on panel - 12¾ x 7¾in.
(Christie's) **$1,080 £600**

BENJAMIN KILLINGBECK - A Grey Arab Stallion and a groom, with a racecourse beyond - signed and dated 1774 - 39½ x 50½in.
(Christie's) **$6,300 £3,500**

GEORGE GOODWIN KILBURNE - The Goodbye - signed - heightened with body-colour - 6¾ x 11½in.
(Sotheby's Belgravia) **$198 £110**

BENJAMIN KILLINGBECK - A Bay Racehorse and groom by a stable, in an extensive landscape, with a country house beyond - 39½ x 50½in.
(Christie's) **$3,420 £1,900**

A. K. KIMM - A Highland Stream - indistinctly signed - dated 1920 - 42 x 28in.
(Sotheby's Belgravia) **$36 £20**

BENJAMIN KILLINGBECK - A Bay Racehorse and groom, by a stable, with an extensive river landscape beyond - 39½ x 49½in.
(Christie's) **$5,400 £3,000**

KING

BARAGWANATH KING - Evening, On A Loch - signed - heightened with body-colour - 18 x 28in.
(Sotheby's Belgravia) $99   £55

CECIL KING - The Red Gate - signed - 23 x 19in.
(Sotheby's, Hong Kong) $270 £150

JESSIE MARION KING - The Wish, Hope to sing through all the days - signed and inscribed - on vellum - pen and ink and watercolour - 9 x 6in.
(Sotheby's Belgravia) $1,800 £1,000

JESSIE M. KING - The Wee People - watercolour - 32 x 43cm.
(Edmiston's) $720 £400

JOHN YEEND KING - After A Shower - signed - on board - 6¾ x 9½in.
(Sotheby's Belgravia) $144   £80

YEEND KING - Shepherd And Sheep On A Country Lane, farm building nearby - signed - oil on canvas - 20 x 30in.
(Christie's S. Kensington) $720 £400

W. GUNNING KING - 'This Is My Wife, Quoth He, That Standeth Here ...' - signed and dated 1882 - 49½ x 75in.
(Christie's) $72 £40

YVES KLEIN - Monochrome Blue - signed and dated 1961 on the reverse - mixed media on canvas - on panel - 28¾ x 21¼in.
(Christie's) $20,130 £11,000

YVES KLEIN - Monopink - mixed media on canvas - on panel - 15¾ x 13¾in.
(Christie's) $9,150 £5,000

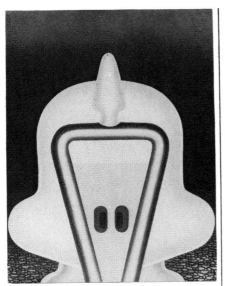

FRANZ KLINE - Untitled - signed and
dated '55 on the reverse - oil - on canvas -
50¾ x 86¾in.
(Sotheby's)   **$64,050 £35,000**

KONRAD KLAPHECK - Le Temoin -
signed, inscribed amd dated 1962 on the
reverse - 32½ x 22¾ in.
(Christie's)   **$4,209 £2,300**

GEORGE KNAPTON, Attributed to -
Portrait Of A Gentleman, bust length, in
a green coat, holding a book - 25¼ x 19¼in.
(Christie's N. York)   **$880 £481**

GUSTAV KLIMT - Jurisprudenz - 44.5
x 31cm.
(Auktionshaus am Neumarkt)
          $6,066 £3,315

WILLIAM ADOLPHUS KNELL -
Sailing Vessels Offshore In A Breeze -
signed - on panel - 15 x 23in.
(Christie's)   **$1,620 £900**

251

KNELL

WILLIAM ADOLPHUS KNELL - Shipping
In Portsmouth Harbour - signed - water-
colour heightened with white - 8¾ x 13½in.
(Sotheby's) **$720 £400**

WILLIAM CALLCOTT KNELL - 'Early
Morning on the River Medway' - signed
and dated 1863 - inscribed on the reverse ·
17½ x 29½in.
(Sotheby Bearne) **$1,692 £940**

WILLIAM CALLCOTT KNELL - Fishing
Boats Off Brixham - signed and dated
1870 - signed and inscribed on the reverse
- 32 x 42in.
(Christie's) **$900 £500**

WILLIAM CALCOTT KNELL - 'Wreck
Off The Caskets' - signed and dated 1876 -
signed, dated and titled on reverse - 40 x
57in.
(Lawrence) **$2,160 £1,200**

WILLIAM CALCOTT KNELL - Shipping
In Rough Seas Off The Coast - signed
and dated 1862 - 7½ x 14½in.
(Sotheby's Belgravia) **$135 £75**

G. KNELLER - Portrait Of A Young
Woman in a white dress with blue wrap -
28½ x 24in.
(Sotheby Bearne) **$468 £240**

SIR GODFREY KNELLER - Portrait
Of A Young Nobleman, standing, full
length, in peers' robes, wearing the
order of the garter, in a portico - 94 x
58in.
(Christie's N. York) **$3,520 £1,923**

SIR GODFREY KNELLER, School of -
Portrait Of A Man, half length, in a red
cloak - oval - 29¾ x 24¼in.
(Christie's N. York) **$352 £192**

GEORGE KNIGHT - Fishing Boats Off
The Coast - signed - 15¼ x 23½in.
(Sotheby's Belgravia) **$450 £250**

J. BUXTON KNIGHT - A Country
Village - signed - watercolour - 13 x
19in.
(The Manchester Auction Mart.)
$62 £34

DAME LAURA KNIGHT - A Portrait Of
Felicity - signed - inscribed on verso - 11½ x
9½in.
(H. Spencer & Sons) **$306 £170**

G. J. KNOX - Shipping At Sunset -
heightened with bodycolour - 12 x 25½in.
(Sotheby's Belgravia) **$90 £50**

JOHN KNOX - The Nelson Monument
On Glasgow Green Struck By Lightning
- 26½ x 35½in.
(Christie's) **$4,680 £2,600**

W. KNOX - 'On The Crest Of The Waves';
'In The Atlantic'; and 'Homeward Bound'
- signed and dated 1915 and 1916 - 10 x
14in.
(Phillips, Solihull) **$213 £115 Three**

FRANZ KOBELL - Waterfall - drawing -
11.5 x 16.5cm.
(Christian Rosset) **$553 £307**

KOEKKOEK

KOBELL - A Peasant Directing Soldiers
To A Ruined Castle - pen and grey ink,
brown wash - 30.7 x 46.8cm.
(Christie's) **$72 £40**

HENDRIK KOBELL - Men-O'-War Off A
Coast with a tower - pen and brown ink,
brown wash - 14.0 x 16.8cm.
(Christie's) **$252 £140**

HENDRICK WILHELM KOBELL -
Vessels Off The Dutch Coast - pen and
brown ink, grey wash - 18.5 x 22.9cm.
(Christie's) **$306 £170**

JOHANN BAPTISTE KOBELL -
Travellers On A Road at the edge of a
road - signed - grey and brown wash -
20.3 x 27.4cm.
(Christie's) **$126 £70**

HENDRIK BAREND KOEKKOEK - A
Wooded Winter Landscape With Figures On
A Path, A Cottage Nearby - signed - 39 x
29in.
(Christie's) **$1,710 £950**

HERMANUS KOEKKOEK - Dutch Sailing
Barges In A Calm Offshore - signed and
dated 1857 - 21½ x 29in.
(Christie's) **$10,800 £6,000**

JAN HERMANUS KOEKKOEK - 'On
The Scheldt, Holland' - signed and dated
1821 - wood panel - 7½ x 9½in.
(Morphets of Harrogate)
$3,610 £1,900

MARINUS ADRIANUS KOEKKOEK - A Wooded Hillside, figures in the foreground gathering kindling and a thatched dwelling in the background - signed - on canvas - 22 x 26in.
(Morphets of Harrogate)
$3,230 £1,700

MARINUS ADRIANUS KOEKKOEK - A Wooded Landscape With Peasants Pulling A Cart Across A Bridge - 16 x 24in.
(Christie's) $8,640 £4,800

JIRI KOLAR - Composition With Mondrian And Picasso - signed with initials and dated '71 - signed - inscribed and dated '71 on the reverse - collage on board - 12 x 15in.
(Sotheby's) $457 £250

PAUL KOLB - A View Of A Rocky Coast - signed and dated 1635 on the back - 10 x 14¼in.
(Sotheby's) $4,070 £2,200

H. KOLVE - A Mountain Stream - signed - 20 x 16in.
(Sotheby's Belgravia) $162 £90

PHILIPS KONINCK - An Extensive Wooded Landscape with a traveller and beggars on a path and shipping on a river nearby - signed - 32 x 43¼in.
(Christie's) $216,000 £120,000

EVERHARDUS KOSTER - 'Windmills On The Spaarne' - signed - 15½ x 22in.
(Lawrence) **$3,780 £2,100**

JOSEPH KOSUTH - Puzzle - Art As Idea As Idea - photographic blow-up on panel - 48 x 48in.
(Christie's) **$2,745 £1,500**

ALBERT KRAFT - Mary Magdalen - oil - on canvas - 46 x 35.5cm.
(Christian Rosset) **$239 £133**

JOHANN VICTOR KRAMER - A Felach, head and shoulders - signed and dated 1900 - inscribed Betsamur - 18 x 14½in.
(Christie's) **$450 £250**

JOHAN KROUTHEN - Summer Landscape - signed and dated 1921 - 80 x 110cm.
(Goteborgs Auktionsverk) **$7,071 £3,929**

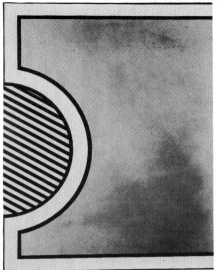

NICHOLAS KRUSHENICK - Ping Pong Coke (Right Element) - signed and dated Feb. 1970 on the reverse) - 40 x 30in.
(Christie's N. York) **$1,540 £855**

H. KUKSA - Still Life Of Roses - signed - oil - on canvas - 18 x 21½in.
(Neales of Nottingham) **$63 £34**

REINHOLD KUNDIG - Hirzel Im Winter - 45 x 49cm.
(Auktionshaus am Neumarkt) **$2,780 £1,519**

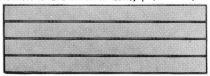

TADAAKI KUWAYAMA - Yellow with Chrome - signed on the reverse - 36¼ x 46¾ in.
(Christie's) **$1,281 £700**

CARLO LABRUZZI - The Transfiguration
- signed and indistinctly dated - 26½ x
17½in.
(Christie's)   **$1,080 £600**

**CHARLES F. DE LACROIX DE
MARSEILLE** - A Capriccio Mediterranean
Harbour at night with fisherfolk in the fore-
ground and a volcano erupting beyond -
signed and dated 1767 - 19½ x 29¼in.
(Christie's)   **$9,100 £5,000**

C. F. LACROIX DE MARSEILLE - A
Capriccio Mediterranean Coastal Landscape with sailors unloading a boat -
34¾ x 45½in.
(Christie's)   **$1,350 £750**

C. F. LACROIX DE MARSEILLE - A
Capriccio Mediterranean Harbour Scene
At Sunset, with numerous figures on a
quay - 34¾ x 45½in.
(Christie's)   **$1,350 £750**

H. LADBROOKE - Sketch Of Horsepond
In Westcliff Lane, Horsey - oil - 9 x 13in.
(G. A. Key)   **$22 £12**

HENRY LADBROOKE - A Wooded River
Landscape including a donkey and a figure
seated under a tree - circular - diameter
22in.
(Sotheby's)   **$1,080   £600**

J. B. LADBROOKE - Wooded Landscape
With Figure In Lane - oil - 12 x 17in.
(G. A. Key)   **$36 £20**

EDWARD LADELL - A Still Life Of Roses,
Bunches Of Grapes, Pansies And A Peach
on a marble ledge - signed with monogram -
16½ x 13¼in.
(Christie's)   **$5,070 £2,600**

P. DE LAEZLA - 'Italian Girl With Flowers'
- signed - oil - 14 x 12in.
(Hussey's)   **$148 £82**

GIUSEPPE LAEZZA - An Extensive
Italian Coastal Landscape with
fisherfolk on the shore - signed and
dated - 22½ x 46½in.
(Christie's) **$1,080 £600**

R. LAFAGE - The Apotheosis Of A
Warrior - pen and grey ink, grey wash -
35.8 x 49.6cm.
(Christie's) **$180 £100**

LOUIS JEAN FRANCOIS LAGRENEE -
An Allegory Of Wisdom - black and white
chalk on brown paper - 31.0 x 41.5cm.
(Christie's) **$288 £160**

F. J. LAING - Shipping In An Estuary -
signed - on board - 4¾ x 8¼in.
(Sotheby's Belgravia) **$135 £75**

LAIRESSE - A Roman Sacrifice - grey
wash - 36.2 x 46.2cm.
(Christie's) **$144 £80**

GERARD DE LAIRESSE, Circle of -
An Allegory Of Power - 35½ x 49½in.
(Christie's N. York) **$462 £252**

G. DE LAIRESSE - The Sacrifice Of
Iphigenia - 35¼ x 28¼in.
(Christie's) **$1,080 £600**

J. B. LALLEMAND - A Ruined Roman
Mausoleum - black chalk - 23.7 x
39.1cm.
(Christie's) **$216 £120**

LAMBERT - A River Landscape, figures and
animals in the foreground, a country house
on the far bank, classical ruins on a hillside
to the left; An Extensive Coastal Scene,
figures loading a boat in the foreground, a
man-of-war near a fort beyond - 27 x 39½in.
(Sotheby's) **$1,890 £1,050 Pair**

JAMES LAMBERT, JUN - Rocks At
Tunbridge Wells - signed, inscribed
and dated 1786 - in a painted oval -
10 x 14in.
(Sotheby's) **$198 £110**

JAN BAPTIST LAMBRECHTS -
Figures Drinking Outside An Inn - on
panel - 12¼ x 9¼in.
(Christie's) **$1,620 £900**

EUGENE LAMI - Studies Of Figures In
18th Century Costume - signed and
inscribed 'Louis XV' - pencil - 31.3 x
25.0cm.
(Christie's) **$27 £15**

WILLIAM B. LAMOND - Outside A
Fisherman's Cottage - signed - canvas
laid on board - 8½ x 10½in.
(Sotheby's Belgravia) **$306 £170**

AUGUSTUS OSBORNE LAMPLOUGH -
On The Nile - signed - watercolour -
10 x 18in.
(Christie's S. Kensington) **$216 £120**

AUGUSTUS OSBORNE LAMPLOUGH -
Sunset On The Nile - signed - watercolour -
20¼ x 29½in.
(Christie's) **$162 £90**

AUGUSTUS OSBORNE LAMPLOUGH -
A Scene On The Nile - signed and dated
1914 - watercolour - 9½ x 22¾in.
(Christie's) **$99 £55**

AUGUSTUS LAMPLOUGH - A Coastal
Scene with Arab sailing boats - signed -
14 x 21in.
(The Manchester Auction Mart.)
$524 £200

AUGUSTUS LAMPLOUGH - 'The Nile
Valley' - 17¾ x 28½in.
(The Manchester Auction Mart.)
$475 £250

VICTOR LAMPLOUGH - Arabs On
Camels outside a desert town - signed
and dated 1907 - watercolour - 10¼
x 19¼in.
(Christie's) **$36 £20**

MARK LANCASTER - Houston, Charleston
- signed - titled and dated '73 on the reverse
- acrylic on canvas - 68 x 102in.
(Sotheby's) **$1,647 £900**

GEORGE LANCE - Still Life - signed and
dated 1850 - oil - on canvas - 28 x 36in.
(Bonham's) **$3,960 £2,200**

GEORGE LANCE - A Still Life Of
Bunches of Grapes, a basket of apples,
a pumpkin, peaches and a pineapple in
a landscape - bears monogram - on board
- arched top - 23¾ x 18⅜in.
(Christie's) **$135 £75**

AUGUST ANDRE LANCON - Scenes From
Military Life - all inscribed and variously
dated and with the artist's studio stamp - pen
and brown ink - 153 x 231mm.
(Christie's) $91 £50 **Three**

NICOLAS LANCRET, Attributed to -
The Fire At Saint-Jean - oil - on canvas -
81 x 100cm.
(Christian Rosset) **$7,200 £4,000**

NICOLAS LANCRET - La Toilette - 27½ x
21½in.
(Christie's) **$36,000 £20,000**

NICOLAS LANCRET, Manner of -
Fetes Champetres - shaped - 37 x 42½in.
(Christie's N. York) **$990 £541 Pair**

JOHN LANDAVER - Midland Railway
Locomotive Engine - signed and inscribed
with title and 'Driven by John Hickinbotham,
Leicester' - 20¾ x 37¾in.
(Sotheby's) **$400 £220**

GENNARO LANDI - Athena - black
chalk, pen and brown ink - 28.0 x
17.4cm.
(Christie's) **$117 £65**

ANDREA LANDINI - A Good Vintage -
signed - 17¾ x 14½in.
(Christie's) **$3,150 £1,750**

ANDREA LANDINI - After Dinner -
signed - 17½ x 14½in.
(Christie's) **$3,150 £1,750**

J. LANDMANN - A Fortified Bridge -
signed and dated 1739 - grey and brown
wash - 26.8 x 37.8cm.
(Christie's) **$63 £35**

SIR EDWIN HENRY LANDSEER -
Male Nude Figure Studies - both
pencil - 7¼ x 3¾in. and 4 x 7½in.
(Sotheby's Belgravia) **$27 £15 Two**

LANDSEER

SIR EDWIN LANDSEER - The Hawk
Trainer - on panel - 9 x 11½in.
(Christie's)   **$11,700 £6,500**

SIR EDWIN LANDSEER - An Extensive
Highland Landscape - on board - 8 x 9½in.
(Christie's)   **$15,300 £8,500**

LANDSEER - Baby Minders - 29 x 24in.
(Sotheby's Belgravia)   **$612 £340**

LANDSEER - The Rescue; Desperate
Plight - both on metal - 6¾ x 8in.
(Sotheby's)   **$90 £50 Pair**

HENRY BOWER LANE - 'The St. Lawrence'
from a window in Rewco's Hotel - signed
with initials - dated 1841 - 6¾ x 9¼in.
(Lawrence)   **$900 £500**

GIOVANNI LANFRANCO - The Incredu-
lity Of Saint Thomas - 38 x 52½in.
(Christie's)   **$6,916 £3,800**

DIRK LANGENDIJK - The Return Of
The Hawking Party - signed and dated
1774 - on copper - 24½ x 32½in.
(Christie's)   **$30,940 £17,000**

ANDRE LANSKOY - La Croisiere dans le Correze - signed and dated 1960 - oil - on canvas - 28¾ x 39½in.
(Sotheby's) **$5,673 £3,100**

HIERONYMUS LAPIS - A Seated Academic Nude - signed - black chalk - 34.0 x 28.5cm.
(Christie's) **$63 £35**

GEORGE HENRY LAPORTE - Sir J. Hawley's 'Beadsman' Beating Lord Derby's 'Toxopholite' - signed and dated 1858 - inscribed on an old label on the reverse - 20¾ x 35½in.
(Christie's) **$2,340 £1,300**

GEORGE HENRY LAPORTE - Turks Training Arab Horses In Constantinople, with a mosque in the background - signed and dated 1853 - 27 x 32in.
(Christie's) **$4,860 £2,700**

GIOVANNI BATTISTA LANGETTI - A Philosopher - 36½ x 30½in.
(Christie's) **$4,320 £2,400**

WALTER LANGLEY - Portrait Of A Chelsea Pensioner - signed and dated - 13½ x 13in.
(Sotheby's Belgravia) **$135 £75**

MARK W. LANGLOIS - Outside The Fisherman's Cottage - signed - 20½ x 16¼in.
(Sotheby's Belgravia) **$540 £300**

LAPORTE

J. LAPORTE - Figures By A Farmhouse In A Wooded Landscape, cattle watering by a stream in the foreground - 15¼ x 20½in.
(Sotheby's)   **$504**   **£280**

WILLEM JOSEPH LAQUY - Feeding The Bird - signed - on panel - 16 x 14in.
(Christie's)   **$5,040 £2,800**

ERNEST LARA - By A Stream - signed - on board - 16¼ x 22½in.
(Sotheby's Belgravia)   **$270**   **£150**

ERNEST LARA - Village Scenes - signed with monogram and dated 1876 - 9¼ x 17¼in.
(Sotheby's Belgravia)   **$1,224**   **£680 Pair**

G. LARA - Outside The Cock Inn - 6½ x 9½in.
(Sotheby's Belgravia)   **$1,404**   **£780**

EDOUARD LARCHE - The Death Of General Marceau - signed - oil - on lined canvas - 37.5 x 45.5cm.
(Christian Rosset)   **$481**   **£267**

N. DE LARGILLIERRE - Portrait Of A Lady, Said To Be Madame De Noermont, As Diana, seated three-quarter length in a landscape - 54 x 41in.
(Christie's)   **$9,900**   **£5,500**

CARL LARSSON - Old Lady Under A Tree - 127 x 190cm.
(Goteborgs Auktionsverk)
       $19,543   **£10,857**

LASTMAN - Two Old Men At A Table - pen and brown ink - 18.2 x 14.6cm.
(Christie's)   **$153**   **£85**

PHILIP ALEXIUS DE LASZLO - Selling Primroses - signed and dated 1891 - heightened with white - 10 x 6½in.
(Sotheby's Belgravia)   **$128**   **£70**

CHARLES JAMES LAUDER - Still Life
Of Wild Flowers - signed - 29½ x 17½in.
(Sotheby's Belgravia) **$288 £160**

F. LAURI - A Bacchanal in a wooded
landscape - 17 x 25½in.
(Christie's) **$1,350 £750**

FILIPPO LAURI - The Ecstasy Of
Saint Francis - 18 x 15in.
(Christie's) **$2,880 £1,600**

SIR JOHN LAVERY - Portrait Of Lady
Young - signed and inscribed - oil - on
canvas - 45 x 26cm.
(King & Chasemore) **$707 £380**

SIR JOHN LAVERY - Portrait Of An
Arab Girl, small half length - signed
and dated '94 - 9¾ x 7¾in.
(Christie's) **$810 £450**

SIR JOHN LAVERY - A Connoisseur -
signed - indistinctly dated - black chalk -
10 x 13in.
(Sotheby's Belgravia) **$153 £85**

SIR THOMAS LAWRENCE - Portrait Of
A Lady, half length, in a white dress with
a rose - black and red chalk heightened
with white - oval - 29 x 24in.
(Christie's) **$1,710 £950**

SIR THOMAS LAWRENCE, Studio of -
Portrait Of King George IV, standing,
full length, in garter robes, before a red
curtain - 78 x 49in.
(Christie's N. York) **$3,300 £1,803**

HIPPOLYTE LAZERGES - The Siesta -
signed and dated Alger 1878 - on panel -
14 x 21in.
(Christie's) **$576 £320**

B. W. LEADER - "Evening on a Welsh
River" - signed and dated 1907 - oil -
9 x 14in.
(Warner, Sheppard & Wade)
$1,225 £625

B. W. LEADER - An English Hayfield -
signed and dated 1879 - oil - on canvas - 20
x 30in.
(Bonham's) **$7,728 £4,200**

B. W. LEADER - Tintern Abbey - signed
and dated 1873 - oil - 15½ x 23½in.
(Richard Baker & Baker) **$1,440 £800**

BENJAMIN WILLIAMS LEADER -
An Old House Near Ludlow - signed
and inscribed on the reverse - on board -
13½ x 17½in.
(Christie's) **$54 £30**

BENJAMIN WILLIAMS LEADER - Saint
Michael's Mount, Cornwall - signed and
dated 1877 - 17½ x 25½in.
(Christie's) **$2,145 £1,100**

BENJAMIN WILLIAMS LEADER - A
Highland River Landscape with cattle
watering at sunset - signed and dated
1866-1896 - 28 x 40¼in.
(Christie's) **$4,290 £2,200**

BENJAMIN WILLIAMS LEADER - A
View Of Worcester Cathedral - signed and
dated 1897 - signed and inscribed on the
stretcher - 15½ x 23¾in.
(Christie's) **$5,070 £2,600**

BENJAMIN WILLIAMS LEADER - A
View Of Burrows Cross, Surrey, At Sunset
- signed and dated 1897 - inscribed on the
reverse - 11½ x 17½in.
(Christie's) **$4,680 £2,400**

BENJAMIN WILLIAMS LEADER -
A Man In A Boat Near Sonning -
signed and dated 1910 - 13½ x 25½in.
(Christie's) **$171 £95**

JUAN DE VALDES LEAL - David And
Goliath - 57½ x 42¼in.
(Christie's) **$6,840 £3,800**

EDWARD LEAR - Constantinople, Ayoub
inscribed and dated 1848 - pencil, pen and
brown ink and watercolour - 12¾ x 20½ in.
(Sotheby's) **$3,420 £1,900**

EDWARD LEAR - Hebron - signed and
inscribed - pen and brown ink, watercolour -
6 x 9 in.
(Sotheby's) **$2,340 £1,300**

EDWARD LEAR - Civita-Castellana - signed and dated Roma 1844 - 14½ x 22in.
(Christie's)   **$5,400 £3,000**

EDWARD LEAR - The Lonely Valley Of Zebbug - extensively inscribed, dated March 28, 1866 - pencil, pen and brown ink and watercolour - 7½ x 18½in.
(Christie's)   **$1,440 £800**

EDWARD LEAR - The Dead Sea And Hingedi From Masada - signed, inscribed and dated April 1858 - watercolour heightened with white - on buff paper - 11½ x 18in.
(Christie's)   **$1,800 £1,000**

EDWARD LEAR - St. Julian's Bay; Malta; Valetta At Dusk - both signed with monogram - 3¾ x 7¾in.
(Sotheby's)   **$936   £520 Pair**

EDWARD LEAR - A View Of Mount Blanc From Pont Pelissier - signed with monogram - 13¼ x 21in.
(Christie's)   **$5,070 £2,600**

EDWARD LEAR - Athens - inscribed - numbered 129 - dated July 1848 - pen and brown in - watercolour on grey paper - 6 x 10in.
(Sotheby's)   **$540   £300**

EDWARD LEAR - Pentelicus From Varnava - inscribed with colour and other notes and dated June 16, 1848 - pencil, pen and brown ink and watercolour - 10¼ x 18in.
(Christie's)   **$990 £550**

EDWARD LEAR - Corfu Seen From The Village Of Ascension - inscribed, numbered and dated 1855 and 1856 - pen and brown ink and watercolour - 4½ x 7in.
(Sotheby's)   **$1,260   £700**

CHARLES LEAVER - Winter Landscape, Easton, Wiltshire - inscribed and dated 1867 on the reverse - 19¼ x 29½in.
(Sotheby Bearne) **$1,443 £740**

NOEL HARRY LEAVER - A Flower Stall Outside A Mosque - signed - watercolour - 10½ x 14in.
(Christie's) **$72 £40**

MILDRED MAI LEDGER - 'I A Princess King Descended' - signed - inscribed and dated 1912 - heightened with bodycolour - circular 18in. diameter.
(Sotheby's Belgravia) **$135 £75**

F. R. LEE - An Artist Painting A Girl By A Stream - bears signature - on board - 17¼ x 21¾in.
(Sotheby's Belgravia) **$99 £55**

FREDERICK RICHARD LEE - The Valley Mill - signed and dated 1862 and inscribed on an old label on the reverse - 23½ x 20½in.
(Christie's) **$2,925 £1,500**

JOHN LEECH - A Life Study Of Tom Hood - signed - inscribed 'Newmarket' - 6¾ x 5in.
(Sotheby's Belgravia) **$58 £32**

LEE-HENG - Portrait Of A European Woman, standing full length, wearing a black dress resting her arm on a chair - a stamp, prior to relining, reads 'Lee-Heng, Painter, Hong Kong' - on reverse - 23½ x 18in.
(Sotheby's, Hong Kong) **$353 £196**

ALEXIS DE LEEUW - Winter Landscape
with figures around a logging cart drawn
by four horses - signed - 29 x 49in.
(Sotheby Bearne)   **$3,315 £1,700**

CHARLES HENRI JOSEPH LEICKERT -
A Frozen River Landscape With Figures On
The Ice, and a village - signed and dated -
38 x 54in.
(Christie's)   **$28,800 £16,000**

A. LEGGATT - A Young Fishergirl -
43½ x 33½in.
(Sotheby's Belgravia)   **$540 £300**

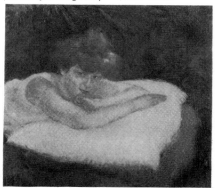

LOUIS LEGRAND - On The Pillow -
77 x 65cm.
(Auktionshaus am Neumarkt)
                $9,100 £4,972

LORD LEIGHTON - Sun-Gleams (The
Arab Hall) - 32¾ x 15¾in.
(Christie's)   **$7,800 £4,000**

LORD LEIGHTON - The Fair Persian - unfinished - 26 x 19¾in.
(Christie's) **$1,440 £800**

ADRIAEN DE LELIE - A Peasant With A Stick - signed - pen and brown ink, brown wash, watermark a Fleur-de-Lys - 27.9 x 18.3cm.
(Christie's) **$45 £25**

SIR PETER LELY, Attributed to - Portrait Of Mary Harvy, Lady Dering, seated, three-quarter length, in an orange dress, and purple shawl with red lining, by a vase of flowers on a plinth - inscribed - 50 x 40in.
(Christie's N. York) **$1,100 £601**

LEMAIRE - Domestic Fowl in landscapes - oil - 12 x 16in.
(G. A. Key) **$396 £220 Pair**

SIR PETER LELY - Portrait Of Henry Marten, half length, wearing a dark coat and cap - inscribed "now" by a later hand - 28¾ x 24in.
(Christie's) **$4,320 £2,400**

JEAN LEMAIRE, Attributed to - A Capriccio Of Classical Ruins, with a shepherd piping to his flock and a sleeping figure in the foreground - 30¼ x 29in.
(Christie's N. York) **$935 £511**

LEMOYNE

LEMOYNE - Boreas And Oriethyia - pen and grey ink, grey wash on blue paper - 27.4 x 41.4cm.
(Christie's)   **$135**   **£75**

LEMOYNE - Diana And Actaeon - 27½ x 48½in.
(Christie's)   **$1,440 £800**

LEMOYNE - Lot And His Daughters - red chalk - 20.2 x 27.2cm.
(Christie's)   **$162**   **£90**

LORENZO LEONBRUNO DA MANTOVA - The Nativity - signed Leobrun . Man - on panel - 17½ x 14¼in.
(Christie's)   **$61,200 £34,000**

CHARLES LESLIE - 'Devoke Water, Cumberland' - signed and dated 1876 - oil - on canvas - 12 x 24in.
(Walker, Barnett & Hill)
     $423 £235

CHARLES ROBERT LESLIE - The Reading Of The Will. a scene from Smollett's 'Roderick Random' - 39 x 56¼in.
(Christie's)   **$7,410 £3,800**

G. LESLIE - The Evening's Catch; Bringing Down The Sails - signed - 15½ x 23½in.
(Sotheby's Belgravia)   **$414**   **£230 Pair**

P. LESLIE - Haymaking By A River - signed - 29½ x 49½in.
(Sotheby's Belgravia)   **$684**   **£380**

ADOLPHE ALEXANDRE LESREL - The Rehearsal - signed and dated 1894 - on panel - 22 x 17¼in.
(Christie's)   **$6,300**   **£3,500**

A. A. LESREL - A Rare Vintage - signed and dated 1907 - oil - on panel - 13½ x 9½in.
(Swetenham's)   **$5,510 £2,900**

ADOLPHE ALEXANDRE LESREL - A Musical Trio - signed and dated 1912 - on panel - 22½ x 18¼in.
(Christie's)   **$5,400   £3,000**

ADOLPHE ALEXANDRE LESREL - The Gift Bearers - signed and dated 1906 - on panel - 23 x 18¼in.
(Christie's)   **$4,680   £2,600**

ADOLPHE ALEXANDRE LESREL - The Connoisseurs - signed and dated 1901 - on panel - 22¼ x 18¼in.
(Christie's)   **$8,100   £4,500**

A. A. LESREL - The Singing Cavalier - signed - oil - on panel - 33½ x 25½in.
(Swetenham's)   **$4,560 £2,400**

CHARLES JAMES LEWIS - Near Medmenham-On-Thames - signed and dated 1870 - 19½ x 29¾in.
(Christie's) $2,340 £1,200

VICTOR HENRY LESUR - A Man Smoking By A Window - signed - on panel - 13¾ x 9¾in.
(Christie's) $1,260 £700

HENRI LEVEQUE - A Group Of Peasants near a building - signed - pencil and watercolour - 23.5 x 32.0cm.
(Christie's) $288 £160

FREDERICK CHRISTIAN LEWIS - Northwick Park, Gloucestershire - signed and inscribed - on blue paper - 9½ x 12½in.
(Sotheby's) $540 £300

J. LEWIS - River Scenes with town in background - signed - oil - on canvas - 15½ x 24in.
(David Symonds) $405 £220 Pair

MAURICE LEVIS - 'Bords de la Marne'; and 'Un Moulin sur L'Indre' - signed - on panel - 5¼ x 6¾in.
(Sotheby Bearne) $2,160 £1,200

C. J. LEWIS - Evening On The Thames - well wooded river landscape with sailing barges on the water, a windmill on the near bank - signed and dated 1887 - 16 x 25½in.
(H. Spencer & Sons) $360 £200

JOHN FREDERICK LEWIS - Sir Edwin Landseer, in the act of angling - signed and inscribed - 19¼ x 25½in.
(Sotheby's) $14,760 £8,200

JOHN FREDERICK LEWIS - Peasants Of The Italian Tyrol At Their Devotions - signed and dated 1829 - heightened with white - 19 x 24½in.
(Sotheby's)   **$1,170 £650**

JOHN FREDERICK LEWIS - Head Of An Old Man - watercolour and body-colour · 11¾ x 9in.
(Christie's)   **$936 £520**

JOHN FREDERICK LEWIS - The Mosque Door, Brussa - signed - watercolour heightened with white - 10¼ x 14½in.
(Christie's)   **$2,160 £1,200**

JOHN FREDERICK LEWIS - An Old Woman Shelling Peas - signed and dated 1830 - heightened with white - 5 x 6in.
(Sotheby's)   **$108 £60**
L LEWIS - River Scene With Cattle Crossing - watercolour - 8 x 12in.
(G. A. Key)   **$58 £32**

SOL LEWITT - 7-Part- Piece - white baked steel - 41 x 41 x 11¾in.
(Christie's)   **$4,941 £2,700**

ROY LICHTENSTEIN - Hot Dog - signed and dated '64 on the reverse - enamel on steel - 24 x 48¼in.
(Sotheby's)   **$3,843 £2,100**

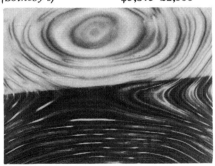

ROY LICHTENSTEIN - Kinetic Seascape No. 10 - signed and dated '66 on the reverse - rowlux, vinyl and motor - 17¾ x 21½in.
(Christie's)   **$2,745 £1,500**

LICINIO

LICINIO - Portrait Of A Young Woman, half length, turned to the right, holding a letter in her right hand - black and red chalk - 22.3 x 19.0cm.
(Christie's) $234 £130

CHARLES SILLEM LIDDERDALE - Portrait Of A Young Girl wearing a white bonnet and a brown cape - signed with monogram and dated (18)82 - oval - 26 x 21½in.
(Sotheby Bearne) $540 £300

CHARLES SILLEM LIDDERDALE - Portrait Of A Country Girl, half length - signed with monogram - heightened with bodycolour - 13 x 10½in.
(Sotheby's Belgravia) $117 £65

JOSEPH LIES - A Marriage Of Convenience - signed and dated 1843 - oil - on panel - 33½ x 40½in.
(Swetenham's) $5,700 £3,000

THE MASTER OF LIESBORN - The Road To Calvary - canvas - on panel - 63½ x 35½in.
(Christie's) $23,660 £13,000

ANDREA LILIO - Christ Seated, Crowned With Thorns - red chalk, squared in black chalk - 32.7 x 13.7cm.
(Christie's) **$135 £75**

BERNDT LINDHOLM - Landscape - signed and dated 1881 - 26 x 40cm.
(Goteborgs Auktionsverk) **$6,686 £3,714**

THOMAS LINDSAY - The Wilds Of Caernarvonshire - signed and inscribed - 13¼ x 24¼in.
(Sotheby's) **$180 £100**

NORMAN ALFRED WILLIAMS LINDSAY - "Self Portrait" - inscribed - 1928 - pencil - 22 x 13cm.
(Australian Art Auctions) **$760 £422**

NORMAN ALFRED WILLIAMS LINDSAY - "Benevolence" - coloured litho - 38 x 29cm.
(Australian Art Auctions) **$49 £27**

NORMAN ALFRED WILLIAMS LINDSAY - "Madam Innocence" - 1928 - watercolour - 35 x 28cm.
(Australian Art Auctions) **$2,059 £1,144**

J. LINNELL - Sunset with sheep and cattle in foreground - signed - oil - on canvas - 27½ x 36in.
(Swetenham's) **$2,280 £1,200**

JAMES THOMAS LINNELL - A Sketch On The Thames Near Erith - inscribed on the reverse - on board - 6¾ x 9¼in.
(Sotheby's Belgravia) **$216 £120**

JOHN LINNELL, SEN - The Proud
Rooster - signed and dated 1846 - on
panel - 21 x 27in.
(Christie's) **$189 £105**

JOHN LINNELL, SEN - Portrait Of An
Elderly Gentleman, with a landscape seen
through an open window beyond - signed
and dated 1815 - on panel - 9¾ x 7in.
(Sotheby's) **$1,182 £660**

LINTON - A Mountain River Landscape
with a shepherd and sheep near a bridge
in the foreground - 40½ x 58¼in.
(Sotheby's) **$864 £480**

WILLIAM LINTON - Anglers By A
Stream, temple in the background - oil -
21 x 17in.
(Richard Baker & Baker) **$342 £190**

LIOTARD - Portrait Of Jean-Jacques
Rousseau - inscribed 'Rembrandt 1644' -
black chalk, grey wash - 29.2 x 23.3cm.
(Christie's) **$72 £40**

JOHANN LISS - A Bacchanalian Feast - on
panel - 13½ x 10¾in.
(Christie's) **$27,000 £15,000**

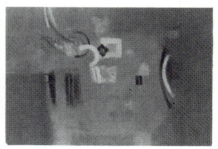

WILLIAM LITTLEJOHN - Still Life And
Harbour - signed with initials - 17 x
23¼in.
(Sotheby's Belgravia) **$180 £100**

EDWARD LITTLEWOOD - River Scene
At Hellesdon, Norwich - oil - oval -
10 x 8in.
(G. A. Key) **$54 £30**

EDWARD LITTLEWOOD - Wooded
Landscape With Figures On Path -
signed and dated 1883 - oil - 37 x 32in.
(G. A. Key) **$414 £230**

HENRY LIVERSEEGE - Study Of Banditi - signed and dated 1826 - oil - on canvas - 31 x 26cm.
(King & Chasemore)   **$98 £50**

STUART LLOYD - Riverscape At Fishbourne, nr. Chichester - signed and dated 1900 - watercolour - 7¾ x 23¾in.
(Brown & Merry)   **$68 £38**

JOHN HODGSON LOBLEY - On The Garden Seat - signed and dated 1911 - 35½ x 27½in.
(Sotheby's Belgravia)   **$360 £200**

JAMES LOBLEY - Little Nell Leaving The Church (The Old Curiosity Shop) - signed and dated 1867 - 53 x 29½in.
(Christie's)   **$54 £30**

ANDREA LOCATELLI - Cephalus And Procris - 75 x 43in.
(Christie's)   **$7,280 £4,000**

LOCATELLI

ANDREA LOCATELLI - Italianate Landscapes With Centaurs Piping To Goats And A Nymph - 30 x 7½in.
(Christie's) **$2,520 £1,400 Pair**

ANDREA LOCATELLI, School of - Peasants Drinking, In A Landscape - 19 x 14in.
(Christie's N. York) **$352 £192**

JOHN LOCHHEAD - By The Ford - signed - 15½ x 9½in.
(Sotheby's Belgravia) **$468 £260**

EDWARD HAWKE LOCKER - 'Rougemont Castle, Exeter' - signed - watercolour - 7 x 10in.
(Hussey's) **$90 £50**

JAMES LODER - A Bay And A Grey Carriage Horse Outside A Stable - signed - inscribed and dated 1834 - 30 x 44in.
(King & Chasemore) **$1,350 £750**

JAMES LODER OF BATH - Two Gentlemen With A Dog And Two Hunters In A Parkland - 21¼ x 30¼in.
(Lawrence) **$1,080 £600**

GEORGE EDWARD LODGE - Common Pochard - signed - heightened with bodycolour - 8½ x 11in.
(Sotheby's Belgravia) **$1,368 £760**

GEORGE EDWARD LODGE - Peregrine Falcons Weathering - signed - on board - 15½ x 23¼in.
(Sotheby's Belgravia) **$1,170 £650**

GEORGE EDWARD LODGE - Citril
Finch, Parrot, Crossbill, Hornemann's
Redpoll - signed - heightened with
bodycolour - 11½ x 8¾in.
(Sotheby's Belgravia) **$1,044 £580**

GEORGE EDWARD LODGE - Spoon-
bill - signed - heightened with bodycolour - 10¾ x 8¼in.
(Sotheby's Belgravia) **$900 £500**

GEORGE EDWARD LODGE - Woodlark -
signed - heightened with bodycolour -
10¾ x 8½in.
(Sotheby's Belgravia) **$540 £300**

WILLIAM LOGSDAIL - The Gates Of
The Khalif - signed and dated '87 - 43½
x 31½in.
(Christie's) **$15,300 £8,500**

LOMBARD - A Pope Overcoming
Aryan Heresy - red chalk, pen and
black ink, grey wash - 24.6 x 34.5cm.
(Christie's) **$117 £65**

EDWIN LONG - The Spanish Betrothal -
signed with monogram and dated
Burgos 1860 - 46 x 37½in.
(Christie's) **$1,530 £850**

LONGHI

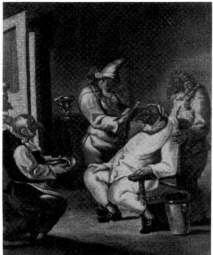

PIETRO LONGHI, School of - Scenes
With Figures From The Commedia
Dell 'Arte, The Barber's Shop; The
Artist's Studio; and The Drawing
Lesson - 18¾ x 13¾in.
(Christie's N. York) **$3,080 £1,683 Three**

LONGSTAFFE - A Woodland Stream -
36 x 28in.
(Sotheby's Belgravia) **$68 £38**

EDGAR LONGSTAFFE - Glencoe,
Argyllshire; White Cliff Bay, Isle Of
Wight - signed with monograms -
gouache - 7½ x 11½in.
(Sotheby's Belgravia) **$234 £130 Pair**

WILLIAM LONGSTAFF - An English
Village - signed - oil - on canvas - 13¾
x 18in.
(Sotheby's) **$425 £220**

C. VAN LOO - Diana, The Huntress in
an extensive landscape - 30 x 40in.
(Christie's) **$1,080 £600**

JOHN ARTHUR LOMAX - The Victim -
signed - on panel - 12 x 17½in.
(Christie's) **$3,060 £1,700**

JAN LOOTEN - A Wooded Landscape
With Travellers - traces of initials - 18 x
22½in.
(Lawrence) **$18,900 £10,500**

JAN LOOTEN - A Wooded Landscape
With Sportsmen By A Pond - 41 x 34½in.
(Christie's) **$6,300 £3,500**

W. LORING - A View Of Hong Kong, with a junk and prison ship offshore; A Junk Off The Coast - both signed - 8¾ x 17½in.
(Sotheby's, Hong Kong) **$144 £80 Pair**

CLAUDE LORRAIN, After - A Wooded River Landscape, with peasants driving cattle, and a ruined aqueduct in the distance - 35½ x 47½in.
(Christie's N. York) **$462 £252**

GABRIEL LORY - Isola Bella (recto) - signed - pencil and brown wash; A Mountain Landscape (verso) - water-colour - 19.4 x 28.7cm.
(Christie's) **$54 £30**

LORENZO LOTTO - The Madonna And Child with a Donor and his wife, a coastal landscape beyond - 33¾ x 45½in.
(Christie's) **$400,400 £220,000**

MORRIS LOUIS - Beta Tau - acrylic on canvas - 102 x 192in.
(Christie's N. York) **$93,500 £51,944**

THOMAS LOUND - Sunlit Landscape with figures conversing by a cottage gate - signed with initials - oil - on panel - 10 x 14in.
(Bonham's) **$2,970 £1,650**

LOUTHERBOURG

LOUND - River Scene At Lakenham With Man Fishing - watercolour - 13 x 16in.
(G. A. Key) **$40 £22**

DE LOUTHERBOURG - Study Of Trees - pencil and brown wash - 39.4 x 32.8cm.
(Christie's) **$58 £32**

PHILIP JAMES DE LOUTHERBOURG - A Wooded River Landscape with peasants in a cart on a path and a cottage beyond - signed - 14½ x 20¼ in.
(Christie's) **$4,320 £2,400**

PHILIP JAMES DE LOUTHERBOURG - A Chief Of New Zealand; A Chief Warrior, New Zealand; and A Woman, New Zealand - pencil, pen and black ink, watercolour - 11¾ x 7in.
(Sotheby's) **$1,930 £1,000 Three**

LOUTHERBOURG

PHILIP JAMES DE LOUTHERBOURG - A Warrior Defying A Witch With A Group Of Captives - the mount inscribed 'Loutherbourg' - pencil - 21.3 x 30.1cm.
(Christie's) **$45 £25**

JOHN S. LOXTON - Old Stock Road, Flowerdale,.N.E. Victoria - signed and inscribed on the reverse - watercolour - 13¼ x 16½in.
(Sotheby's) **$540 £280**

LOWES LUARD - A Mosque Graveyard - signed - watercolour - 15½ x 9½in.
(Christie's) **$90 £50**

A. L. LUCAS - New Forest Woodland Scene with wood gatherer and child - signed and dated 1877 - 17½ x 23in.
(Elliott & Green) **$540 £300**

H. F. LUCAS LUCAS - Setters, Daisy, Dasher, Prince and Rose - signed - inscribed and dated 1898 on the reverse - 17½ x 25¼in.
(Sotheby's Belgravia) **$360 £200**

MAX LUDBY - The Evening Walk - watercolour - 15 x 21in.
(G. A. Key) **$54 £30**

A. LUĪNI - Studies Of An Arm, An Ecorche Arm And Visionary Heads - pen and brown ink, brown wash - 20.7 x 22.5cm.
(Christie's) **$234 £130**

WILLIAM LUKER - Cattle And Goats by the seashore - signed and dated 1855 - 23½ x 35½in.
(Christie's) **$1,260 £700**

GERRIT LUNDENS - A Crowd Watching a Troupe With A Performing Bear At The Heligewegspoort, Amsterdam - signed - 32½ x 33½in.
(Christie's) **$7,560 £4,200**

G. LUNDENS - Revellers At A Blacksmith's - 26 x 21½in.
(Christie's) **$1,170 £650**

THOMAS LUNY - Moonlit Coastal Scene with shipping in a calm sea and smugglers on the beach - signed and indistinctly dated - 19¾ x 26¾in.
(Sotheby Bearne) **$900 £500**

THOMAS LUNY - The Battle Of The Saints - signed and dated 1782 - 36½ x 59¼in.
(Sotheby's) **$3,240 £1,800**

T. LUNY - Figures Landing On The Shore From A Small Boat - inscribed and dated 1807 - 33½ x 47in.
(Sotheby's)   **$900**   **£500**

JAN LUYKEN - The Interior Of A Church With Iconoclasts Displacing Crucifixes And Statues - pen and brown ink - 10.7 x 15.3cm.
(Christie's)   **$117 £65**

ANTONIE DE LUST - A Still Life Of Roses, Tulips And Honeysuckle in an urn on a stone ledge - 23 x 18½in.
(Christie's)   **$4,320**   **£2,400**

R. LYNDE - Sweet And Twenty - signed - 23¼ x 19¼in.
(Sotheby's Belgravia)   **$522 £290**

HENRY J. LYON - Village Scene with church and cottages - watercolour - 7 x 11in.
(G. A. Key)   **$22 £12**

J. HOWARD LYON - Near Callander; The Heart Of Lubnaig - signed - 19½ x 29½in.
(Sotheby's Belgravia)   **$432 £240 Pair**

JOHN HOWARD LYON - Near Strathur, Winter - signed - 23½ x 35½in.
(Sotheby's Belgravia)   **$324 £180**

ANTONIE DE LUST - A Still Life Of Roses And Tulips in an urn on a stone ledge - 23 x 18½in.
(Christie's)   **$5,400**   **£3,000**

BENEDETTO LUTI - A Male Nude, a tree behind - red chalk - 38.8 x 27.8cm.
(Christie's)   **$144**   **£80**

ELIZABETH LYTTELTON - A Discontented Gentlewoman - signed and dated 1755 - watercolour, on vellum - 8¾ x 7in.
(Sotheby's)   **$432 £240**

M

HAMILTON MACALLUM - The Tidal Dip Of Heligoland - signed and dated 1889 - 33¼ x 65½in.
(Christie's) **$2,730 £1,400**

ROBERT WALKER MACBETH - Roof Studies, Harrogate - signed with initials - inscribed and dated May 1894 - 5½ x 3½in.
(Sotheby's Belgravia) **$9 £5**

A. MacDONALD - St. Monance, Fife - signed - 19½ x 23½in.
(Sotheby's Belgravia) **$216 £120**

JOHN BLAKE MacDONALD - St. Monance - signed - 47 x 76in.
(Sotheby's Belgravia) **$2,700 £1,500**

McNEIL MACLEAY - A Scene On Loch Ard, Ben Lomond In The Distance - signed and dated 1870 - on paper - 8½ x 15½in.
(Sotheby's Belgravia) **$540 £300**

ROBERT RUSSELL MacNEE - A Pastoral - signed - inscribed - 7½ x 13½in.
(Sotheby's Belgravia) **$360 £200**

PERCY MACQUOID - Picking Flowers By A River - signed - 9¼ x 13½in.
(Sotheby's Belgravia) **$324 £180**

MacWHIRTER - Mending Nets On The Edge Of A Loch - bears monogram - 27½ x 35½in.
(Sotheby's Belgravia) **$76 £42**

N. MAES - Portrait Of A Lady, half length, wearing a dark cloak and cap - 28½ x 23in.
(Christie's) **$864 £480**

NICOLAES MAES - Portrait Of A Nobleman, small half length, wearing a brown coat - signed - canvas - on panel - oval - 15¾ x 11½in.
(Christie's) **$1,440 £800**

NICOLAES MAES - Portrait Of A Nobleman, small half length, wearing a yellow jacket and red cloak - oval - 17½ x 12½in.
(Christie's) **$990 £550**

MAGGIOTTO - A Laundress - inscribed - black chalk, pen and brown ink, grey wash - 38.4 x 27.4cm.
(Christie's) **$108 £60**

MAGGS - A Coach And Four - 10½ x 14¼in.
(Sotheby's Belgravia) **$162 £90**

JOHN CHARLES MAGGS - The Exeter to London Mail Coach encountering a fox hunt - signed - oil - on canvas - 26½ x 13½in.
(Gribble, Booth & Taylor) **$1,530 £850**

JOHN CHARLES MAGGS - The Oxford To London Coach with a hunt in full cry beyond - signed and dated 1878 - 13½ x 26½in.
(Christie's) **$2,730 £1,400**

JOHN CHARLES MAGGS - The Oxford To London Coach outside an inn, in a blizzard - signed and dated 1878 - 13½ x 26½in.
(Christie's) **$3,120 £1,600**

A. MAGNASCO - A Wooded Italianate
Landscape with peasants washing
clothes - 22½ x 27¼in.
(Christie's)   **$5,040 £2,800**

ALESSANDRO MAGNASCO - A Wooded
Italianate Landscape With A Fisherman -
oval - 17 x 13½in.
(Christie's)   **$3,420 £1,900**

HENRY MAIDMENT - On The River
Stort, Near Grove Ferry, A View Near
Wheathampstead, Hertfordshire -
signed with monogram and dated 1903 -
11½ x 23½in.
(Sotheby's Belgravia)   **$756 £420 Pair**

HENRY MAIDMENT - Crossing A
Bridge; A Cart Track - signed with mono-
gram and dated - 20¼ x 16¼in.
(Sotheby's Belgravia) **$1,224 £680 Pair**
RAFFAELO MAINELLA - Venetian
Scenes - signed - watercolour - 13 x 5in.
(Hussey's)   **$423 £235 Pair**

PAOLO DE MAIO - Benjamin And His
Brothers Before Joseph - 56 x 69½in.
(Christie's)   **$6,840 £3,800**

WILLIAM MALBON - A Bay Hunter
With Dogs In A Landscape - signed -
inscribed 'Mansf.' and dated 1848 -
22¾ x 28¾in.
(Sotheby's Belgravia)   **$648 £360**

KAREL VAN MANDER, Circle of - An Elegant Couple in a landscape on the outskirts of a town - on panel - 14 x 22½ in.
(Christie's N. York) **$880 £481**

WILLIAM HENRY MANDER - On The Whion, Dolgelley, North Wales - signed and dated '09 - signed, inscribed and dated on the reverse - 19½ x 29½in.
(Christie's) **$2,520 £1,400**

JAN MANDIJN - The Temptation Of St. Anthony - on panel - 21¼ x 15in.
(Sotheby's) **$16,650 £9,000**

ALFRED MANESSIER - Port du Cortoy au Petit Jour - signed and dated '49 - signed and titled on the stretcher - oil - on canvas - 39½ x 32in.
(Sotheby's) **$9,516 £5,200**

S. J. MANN - Extensive Landscape With Figures Conversing, cattle etc. - oil - 24 x 42in.
(G. A. Key) **$90 £50**

JOSEF MANSFELD - Still Life with a roemer, ewer, coffee pot etc., on a table with a copy of a newspaper - signed and dated 1887 - oil - on panel - 12 x 10in.
(Graves, Son & Pilcher) **$2,340 £1,300**

MORIZ MANSFELD - Still Life with a
roemer, ewer, coffee pot etc., on a table
and with a newspaper - signed and dated
1886 - oil - on panel - 10 x 6in.
(Graves, Son & Pilcher) **$1,530 £850**

CARL WILHELM MANTEL - An Extensive
View Of Tivoli - signed and dated 1855 -
on panel - 13½ x 22½in.
(Christie's) **$360 £200**

MARATTA - Portrait Of A Youth (recto);
The Virgin And Child With Saints (verso)
- inscribed - black chalk - 17.2 x 13.1cm.
(Christie's) **$76 £42**

CARLO MARATTA, Circle of - The
Adoration Of The Shepherds.
(Christie's N. York) **$660 £360**

C. MARATTI - The Adoration Of The
Shepherds - oval - 35½ x 32in.
(Christie's) **$1,170 £650**

SCHOOL OF THE MARCHES, circa 1420 -
The Madonna Of Humility - on gold ground
panel - shaped top - 21¾ x 16¼in.
(Christie's) **$6,300 £3,500**

DE MARCHIS - A View Near Rome -
inscribed - a study of classical fragments
on the reverse - red chalk, pink wash -
26.6 x 37.2cm.
(Christie's) **$72 £40**

BRICE MARDEN - Untitled - signed and
dated '72 - black ink - 11¾ x 8in.
(Christie's) **$586 £320**

POMPEO MARIANI - Cairo: A Man
With A Camel - signed, inscribed and
dated 1881 - on panel - 7½ x 8¼in.
(Christie's) **$468 £260**

MARIESCHI - The Salute, Venice -
pen and brown ink and watercolour -
21.0 x 32.3cm.
(Christie's) **$108 £60**

MARLOW - A Country House In An
Extensive Park, deer and a carriage in the
foreground - 16 x 24½in.
(Sotheby's) **$468 £260**

WILLIAM MARLOW - A View Of The Adelphi From The River Thames, with the York Water Gate - 41½ x 65in.
(Christie's)   **$17,100 £9,500**

MARMION - The Mass Of Saint Gregory - on panel - 18 x 11in.
(Christie's)   **$1,800 £1,000**

JEAN-LOUIS DE MARNE - A Wooded River Landscape with figures and animals in the foreground and a church beyond - 12½ x 16in.
(Christie's)   **$2,160 £1,200**

P. MARNY - Mayenne, Brittany, with a view of the river bridge - signed and inscribed - watercolour - 16½ x 26½in.
(Warner, Sheppard & Wade)
    $588 £300

P. MARNY - Westminster From The River - signed - watercolour - 3¾ x 5½in.
(Warner, Sheppard & Wade)
    $108 £55

PAUL MARNY - Continental Town Scene - signed and indistinctly inscribed - watercolour heightened with white - 12½ x 18½in.
(Christie's S. Kensington)   **$216 £120**

LUDWIG MAROLD - In A Bazaar - signed with initials - watercolour heightened with white - 39.8 x 30.0cm.
(Christie's)   **$180 £100**

ANTON VON MARON - A Bacchante - signed and dated Roma 1765 - shaped top - 28¾ x 24in.
(Christie's)   **$1,260 £700**

J. MARSH - 'Dutch Canal'; and 'Greenwich Reach' - signed - watercolours - 9¾ x 14½in.
(Brown & Merry)   **$117 £65 Pair**

HERBERT MENZIES MARSHALL - On The Thames - signed and dated 1901 - 12 x 20in.
(Sotheby's Belgravia)   **$198 £110**

MARSHALL

JOHN MILLER MARSHALL - An Old Roman Bridge In Dunster Castle Grounds, Somerset - signed - on board - 10¼ x 13in.
(Sotheby's Belgravia) **$25 £14**

ANDREAS MARTIN - A Winter Landscape with peasants on a path outside a town - signed - on panel - 8 x 10½in.
(Christie's) **$14,560 £8,000**

FRANK P. MARTIN - A Village Street - signed - 19¾ x 23½in.
(Sotheby's Belgravia) **$90 £50**

HENRY MARTIN - 'A Distant Sail' - signed and inscribed Penzance - 26½ x 30in.
(Christie's) **$40 £22**

HENRY MARTIN - A Village Street, Cornwall - signed - on panel - 5 x 8¾in.
(Sotheby's Belgravia) **$288 £160**

SILVESTER MARTIN - The North Warwickshire Foxhounds meeting outside the Creswolde Arms, Knowle - signed and dated 1880 - oil - on canvas - 11½ x 19½in.
(Phillips, Solihull) **$510 £260**

J. MARTIN - Mountainous Landscape with two figures in the foreground - 24½ x 29½in.
(Sotheby Bearne) **$378 £210**

GERTRUDE MARTINEAU - Kenrara Marsh And Craigillachie Hill, Aviemore - signed and dated September 1895 - heightened with bodycolour - 15 x 22in.
(Sotheby's Belgravia) **$72 £40**

MASKELL - A Windmill By A River - 19¼ x 23in.
(Sotheby's Belgravia) **$99 £55**

FRANK A. MASON - An Estuary Scene with shipping - signed and dated 1899 - watercolour - 5 x 14½in.
(Warner, Sheppard & Wade) **$235 £120**

FRANK MASON - Saint Cecilia - signed and dated '89 - 9 x 13½in.
(Christie's) **$1,365 £700**

FRANK H. MASON - Yachting On The Clyde - 49 x 75cm.
(Edmiston's) **$324 £180**

P. MASSIUS - The Pool Of Bethesda - signed - 46½ x 34½in.
(Christie's N. York) **$605 £330**

JAN MASSYS - Susannah And The
Elders - signed and dated 1556 - on
panel - 50¾ x 43¼in.
(Sotheby's) **$59,200 £32,000**

WILLIAM GODFREY RAYSON
MASTERS - Two Chinese Figures -
inscribed 'Hong Kong' and dated '59 -
watercolour - 4½ x 6½in.
(Sotheby's, Hong Kong) **$104 £58**

THE MASTER OF THE FEMALE HALF
LENGTHS, Circle of - Saint Hubert - on
panel - 17 x 8in.
(Christie's) **$6,300 £3,500**

A. MASUCCI - An Angel Holding A
Vessel - red and white chalk on blue
paper - 20.0 x 15.0cm.
(Christie's) **$81 £45**

THE MASTER OF THE FEMALE HALF
LENGTHS - The Madonna And Child -
on panel - 15 x 11in.
(Christie's) **$3,640 £2,000**

FORTUNINO MATANIA - The State
Coach Outside Westminster Abbey,
The Coronation 1953 - signed - 14 x
23½in.
(Sotheby's Belgravia) **$270 £150**

MATHIEU

GEORGES MATHIEU - Sans Titre - signed and dated '52 - oil - on canvas - 38 x 77¼in.
(Sotheby's) $10,980 £6,000

Q. MATSYS - Saint Jerome In His Study - on panel - 24 x 20in.
(Christie's) $3,600 £2,000

PAOLO DE MATTEIS - An Allegory Of The Consequences Of The Peace Of Utrecht with a self-portrait of the artist - bears indistinct Coypel signature and the date 1698 - 30 x 40in.
(Christie's) $12,740 £7,000

JAMES MATTHEWS - At Bury, Sussex - signed and inscribed - 13½ x 20½in.
(Sotheby's Belgravia) $108 £60

J. MAURICE - Waterfall Scene In The Highlands At Evening Time - oil - 16 x 24in.
(G. A. Key) $18 £10

HENRY MAWDSLEY - The Cornfield - 11½ x 17½in.
(Sotheby's Belgravia) $29 £16

WALTER WILLIAM MAY - On The Coast - signed - heightened with body-colour - 4½ x 6¾in.
(Sotheby's Belgravia) $144 £80

W. E. MAYES - Round Mill, nr. Acle - watercolour - 10 x 17in.
(G. A. Key) $79 £44

BEDOLI MAZZOLA - The Annunciation - pen and wash drawing - 21 x 33.5cm.
(Christian Rosset) $671 £373

HAMILTON McALLUM - "The Lobster Pots" - signed and dated 1883 - oil - 18¼ x 30in.
(Richard Baker & Baker) $405 £225

W. McALPINE - Wrecks Off The Coast - 30 x 50in.
(Sotheby's Belgravia) $180 £100

WILLIAM McALPINE - On The Coast Near Naples - indistinctly inscribed on the stretcher - 17½ x 31½in.
(Sotheby's Belgravia) $540 £300

JAMES J. McAULIFFE - Trotting Horses In A New York Park - signed and dated New York 1880 - oil - on canvas - 26 x 36in.
(Bonham's) $2,880 £1,600

HORATIO McCULLOCH - A Summer Day In Cadzow - oil - 30 x 15in.
(Thomas Love & Sons Ltd.) $432 £240

HORATIO McCULLOCH - An Extensive Scottish Landscape - signed - 15¾ x 23½in.
(Sotheby's Belgravia) $810 £450

JOHN McGHIE - 'Bathers' - signed - 27½ x 23½in.
(Sotheby Bearne) $900 £500

ROBERT McGREGOR - Dutch Girls On
The Seashore - 9½ x 13½in.
(Sotheby's Belgravia)   **$396 £220**

JOHN McGHIE - Waiting For The
Boats - signed - 23½ x 17½in.
(Sotheby's Belgravia)   **$684 £380**

JOHN McGHIE - Harbour Scene With
Fisher Folk - 40 x 48cm.
(Edmiston's)   **$648 £360**

ROBERT McGREGOR - The Young
Milkmaid - signed - 27 x 16in.
(Sotheby's Belgravia)   **$1,080 £600**

JESSIE MacGREGOR - 'Through The
Brambles And The Bracken,' a portrait
of Nora, daughter of W. B. Turner -
signed - 71 x 47½in.
(Sotheby Bearne)   **$504 £280**

ROBERT McGREGOR - Single Blessed-
ness - signed - inscribed on the reverse -
19½ x 29½in.
(Sotheby's Belgravia)   **$2,700 £1,500**

McGREGOR

WILLIAM YORK McGREGOR - Lucille - signed - canvas laid on board - 15¾ x 10¼in.
(Sotheby's Belgravia) $288 £160

ROBERT RONALD McIAN - The Omen - signed and dated 1852 - 39 x 49¼in.
(Sotheby's Belgravia) $1,260 £700

R. W. McINTOSH - Woodland Scene with figure in foreground - oil - 23½ x 41½in.
(J. Entwistle & Co.) $234 £130

K. F. McINTYRE - Passing Showers, Whitby Moor - oil - 12 x 20in.
(G. A. Key) $101 £56

W. D. McKAY - The Teigne At Haddinton with a view of Nungate Bridge - signed with initials - oil - on canvas - 12 x 16in.
(Warner, Sheppard & Wade)
$588 £300

DANIEL McLAURIN - Sheep On A Wooded Path - signed and dated '10 - 20 x 24in.
(Sotheby's Belgravia) $40 £22

HAMILTON McMILLAN - The Glennan Burn, Helensburgh - signed with monogram - 11¾ x 17½in.
(Sotheby's Belgravia) $234 £130

EUGENE J. McSWINEY - Stoke Poges Church - signed - 9¼ x 15½in.
(Sotheby's Belgravia) $81 £45

WILLIAM McTAGGART - The Blackberry Pickers - signed - 27 x 39in.
(Christie's) $2,340 £1,300

J. McWHIRTER - A Beach Scene with a thatched cottage - oil - on board - 5½ x 8in.
(Warner, Sheppard & Wade)
$637 £320

ARTHUR MEADOWS - Rouen from the River Seine - signed and dated 1889 - signed, inscribed and dated on the reverse - 11½ x 17½in.
(Christie's) $2,700 £1,500

ARTHUR MEADOWS - Amalfi In The Gulf Of Salerno - signed and dated '92 - on panel - 10 x 12in.
(Christie's) **$1,260 £700**

ARTHUR JOSEPH MEADOWS - Orleans On The Loire - signed and dated 1870 - 13½ x 23¼in.
(Christie's) **$72 £40**

EDWIN L. MEADOWS - The Village, Great Hormead, Hertfordshire - signed and dated 1864 - 16 x 28½in.
(Christie's) **$1,710 £950**

GORDON ARTHUR MEADOWS - The Baccino Di San Marco, Venice, From The Steps Of Santa Maria Della Salute - signed - signed and inscribed on the reverse - 11½ x 17½in.
(Christie's) **$1,170 £650**

JAMES EDWIN MEADOWS - Country Landscape with a cottage and a group of children in the foreground - signed and dated 1878 - 23½ x 41½in.
(Sotheby Bearne) **$4,095 £2,100**

J. E. MEADOWS - Woodland Landscapes With Figures - oil - 12 x 16in.
(G. A. Key) **$864 £480 Pair**

JAMES MEADOWS - Fishing Smacks Offshore In A Choppy Sea - signed - 23½ x 42in.
(Christie's) **$1,350 £750**

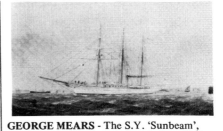

GEORGE MEARS - The S.Y. 'Sunbeam', coming out of harbour - signed - inscribed - indistinctly dated - 14¼ x 23¼in.
(Sotheby's Belgravia) **$612 £340**

MEARS - The 'Frederick' Off The Coast - indistinctly inscribed - 17¼ x 24in.
(Sotheby's Belgravia) **$72 £40**

HENRY MEEGAN - A Moonlit Harbour - signed - 9½ x 13½in.
(Sotheby's Belgravia) **$153 £85**

BAREND VAN DER MEER - A Basket Of Grapes, a bowl of raspberries, a melon, peaches, a bottle of wine and a cockatoo on a stone ledge - signed - 34 x 49½in.
(Christie's) **$6,916 £3,800**

JAN MEERHOUD - A Wooded River Landscape with a village - signed - on panel - 11 x 14½in.
(Christie's) **$6,916 £3,800**

JOHANN JAKOB MEIER - Figures In A Garden, a lake beyond - signed - watercolour - 21.2 x 28.2cm.
(Christie's)   **$468   £260**

MEISSONIER - A Prussian Soldier Smoking; and A French Soldier On Guard - both on panel - 8½ x 5in.
(Christie's)   **$198   £110 Two**

MEISSONIER - Design For A Candlestick With A Seated Female Figure Supporting A Palm; and Design For An Altar-Piece - pen and brown ink, grey wash; and black chalk, pen and brown ink - 52.7 x 28.8cm. and 46.3 x 30.4cm.
(Christie's)   **$72   £40 Two**

JEAN LOUIS ERNEST MEISSONIER - The Confidence, two men talking at table - bears signature and dated 1865 - a sketch - pen, ink and oil - 13½ x 16¼in.
(Christie's)   **$504   £280**

JEAN LOUIS ERNEST MEISSONIER - Head Of A Bearded Man, said to be the artist's brother - signed with monogram - on panel - 8 x 5¾in.
(Christie's)   **$360   £200**

JEAN LOUIS ERNEST MEISSONIER - Off Guard - signed and dated 1873 - black chalk watercolour heightened with white - 34.5 x 24.0cm.
(Christie's)   **$1,710   £950**

ANTON MELBY - A Naval Engagement In The American Civil War - signed and dated 1862 - oil - on canvas .
(Sotheby's)   **$5,404 £2,800**

THOMAS MELLISH - The Thames At Greenwich, with the 'Royal Caroline' and a fishing boat in the foreground - 24¾ x 42½in.
(Christie's)   **$11,700 £6,500**

WILLIAM MELLOR - Near Barnard Castle; and North Wales - signed and inscribed - oil - on canvas - oval - 24 x 20in.
(Bonham's)   **$1,260 £700 Pair**

WILLIAM MELLOR - On The River Greta, Near Barnard Castle - signed, and signed and inscribed on the reverse - 29½ x 49½in.
(Christie's)   **$1,072 £550**

WILLIAM MELLOR - "On The Derwent" and "Ullswater" - oil - 17¼ x 11½in.
(Dacre, Son & Hartley) **$1,980 £1,100 Pair**
WILLIAM MELLOR - "High Force, Teesdale" - signed - canvas - 23½ x 35½in.
(Morphets of Harrogate)
                              $738 £410
WILLIAM MELLOR - "High Force", Teesdale, waterfall scene with two figures on rocks below - signed - oil - 24 x 36in.
(Richard Baker & Baker) **$414 £230**

WILLIAM MELLOR - 'View On The Tees', Rokeby, near Barnard Castle - signed and inscribed - oil - on canvas - 36 x 28in.
(Walker, Barnett & Hill)
                              $360 £200
A. MELVILLE - Horse Drawn Timber Drag - oil - 11 x 18in.
(G. A. Key)   **$108   £60**

ARTHUR MELVILLE - Homewards - signed and dated 1880 - 25 x 37¾in.
(Sotheby's Belgravia)   **$990 £550**

MELVILLE

ARTHUR MELVILLE - The Net Mender - watercolour - 33 x 24cm.
(Edmiston's) **$396 £220**

HARDEN SIDNEY MELVILLE - Carting Lumber - signed - 12 x 17¾in.
(Sotheby's Belgravia) **$162 £90**

F. DE MENESES Y OSSORIO - The Madonna And Child Appearing To Saint Bernard - arched top - 32½ x 16½in.
(Christie's) **$1,350 £750**

ANTON RAFAEL MENGS - Portrait Of William Fermor - signed and inscribed - oil - on canvas - 60 x 45cm.
(King & Chasemore) **$6,468 £3,300**

I. MENNIE - Country River Scenes - oil - 8 x 5¾in.
(J. Entwistle & Co.) **$181 £95 Pair**

P. MERCIER - A Fete Champetre - 34 x 40½in.
(Christie's) **$2,184 £1,200**

PHILIP MERCIER - Portraits Of Two Girls, standing, full length, one building a house of cards - 60½ x 46½in.
(Christie's) **$4,320 £2,400**

298

JACOB MERTENS - A Still Life Of Baskets Of Grapes, Peaches, Lemons and other fruit on a bank, a formal landscape beyond - 34 x 43in.
(Christie's)   **$7,560 £4,200**

GEZA MESZOLY - Entitled "Alkonyar" - peasants with donkey and cart in lane - oil - 5 x 8in.
(G. A. Key)   **$684 £380**

G. METSU - A Fruit Seller - a young woman holding a bunch of grapes at a window with a vine to the side, more grapes and other fruit in a shallow bucket on a ledge before her - on panel - 8½ x 6¾in.
(Sotheby's)   **$4,625 £2,500**

METZIER - Wooded Landscape with figure by log gathering flowers - oil - 16 x 25in.
(G. A. Key)   **$61 £34**

MEXICAN SCHOOL, 17th century - Adoration Of The Virgin - oil - on canvas - 83 x 59cm.
(Christian Rosset)   **$599 £333**

H. DE MEYER - Numerous Figures At A Village Fair - on panel - 17½ x 23¾in.
(Christie's)   **$2,160 £1,200**

MEYERINGH - A Landscape With Trees - pen and grey ink, grey wash - 12.7 x 15.3cm.
(Christie's)   **$32 £18**

MEYVOGEL - Venus And Cupid - signed and dated 1633 - brown wash heightened with white - 8.4 x 11.9cm.
(Christie's)   **$117 £65**

THEOBALD MICHAU, Circle of - An Extensive Landscape, with cottages by trees near a lake, and figures in the foreground - on copper - 6¾ x 9in.
(Christie's N. York)   **$880 £481**

THEOBALD MICHAU - A Wooded Landscape with peasants on a path and a village beyond - on panel - 9 x 11½in.
(Christie's)   **$5,760 £3,200**

T. MICHAU - A Wooded River Landscape with figures on a path; and A Wooded River Landscape with horsemen, and dogs on a path - both on panel - 10½ x 14½in.
(Christie's) **$5,760 £3,200 Pair**

THEOBALD MICHAU, School of - An Extensive Wooded Landscape, with travellers on a road above a valley; and A Wooded Landscape, with travellers by a cottage on a lake - on panel - 10¾ x 14in.
(Christie's N. York) **$3,080 £1,683 Pair**

T. MICHAU - A Winter Landscape with figures by a cottage - on panel - 9 x 14in.
(Christie's) **$1,170 £650**

MICHELANGELO - A Nude And A Man Dressing: fragment from the battle of Cascina - black chalk - 37.5 x 24.1cm.
(Christie's) **$162 £90**

W. H. MIDWOOD - Learning To Play The Flute - signed - 9¾ x 7¾in.
(Sotheby's Belgravia) **$252 £140**

PIERRE MIGNARD, Circle of - Portrait Of A Lady, half length, in a brown dress - 21½ x 18¼in.
(Christie's N. York) **$330 £180**

MIGNARD SCHOOL - Novice - oil - on canvas - 47 x 34cm.
(Christian Rosset) **$193 £107**

MIGNON - Fruit And A Roemer On A
Stone Slab in a landscape - 22½ x 31¼in.
(Christie's) **$756 £420**

A. MIGNON - Flowers In A Vase -
inscribed - 28¾ x 24in.
(Sotheby's) **$14,800 £8,000**

ABRAHAM MIGNON - Grapes, Peaches,
A Melon, Chestnuts, And Insects On A
Stone Ledge - 22 x 18in.
(Christie's) **$29,120 £16,000**

M. R. MILBANKE - Portrait Of A Young
Girl, member of the Scottish family of
Dunbars .
(G. A. Key) **$38 £21**

F. MILES - Shiplake On Thames -
signed - inscribed on the reverse -
19¾ x 29½in.
(Sotheby's Belgravia) **$360 £200**

T. R. MILES - Channel Pilots - 59 x
104cm.
(Edmiston's) **$918 £510**

THOMAS ROSE MILES - 'Outward Bound';
and 'Outward Bound From Lowestoft' -
signed and fully inscribed on the reverse -
29¼ x 24¼in.
(Sotheby Bearne) **$1,326 £680 Pair**

THOMAS ROSE MILES - Solitude,
Mackdara's Isle - signed - inscribed on
the reverse - 24 x 42in.
(Sotheby's Belgravia) **$144 £80**

301

MILLAIS

MILLAIS, After - The Huguenot - 26 x 16in.
(Sotheby's Belgravia) **$22 £12**

SIR J. E. MILLAIS, After - The Order Of Release - arched top - 40½ x 30¼in.
(Sotheby's Belgravia) **$216 £120**

SIR JOHN EVERETT MILLAIS - A Study For 'The Eve Of Saint Agnes' - a sketch - on paper - shaped top - 36 x 19in.
(Christie's) **$4,680 £2,600**

SIR JOHN EVERETT MILLAIS - 'The Crown Of Love' - signed with monogram and dated 1875 - 50¼ x 34¼in.
(Christie's) **$3,960 £2,200**

JOHN GUILLE MILLAIS - Game Pie - signed and dated 1901 - grey and white bodycolour - 11¼ x 9in.
(Sotheby's Belgravia) **$450 £250**

JAMES H. C. MILLAR - Shipping, Moonlight - signed - 9¾ x 19¾in.
(Sotheby's Belgravia) $108 £60

MILLET - An Extensive Italian Landscape - pen and brown ink, brown wash - 32.5 x 39.7cm.
(Christie's) $108   £60

CARL MILLNER - An Alpine Landscape With Figure And A Horse Drawn Cart by a watermill with mountains in the background - signed and dated 1872 - on canvas - 54½ x 72in.
(King & Chasemore) $3,780 £2,100

JEAN FRANCOIS MILLET - Two Nude Figures - signed - charcoal on grey paper - 4½ x 6in.
(Richard A. Bourne Co. Inc.)
$1,200 £667

WILLIAM EDWARD MILLNER - Good News - signed with initials - dated - on board - 14 x 10in.
(Sotheby's Belgravia) $234   £130

R. W. MILLIKEN - Pheasants In Winter - signed - heightened with bodycolour - 14¼ x 19in.
(Sotheby's Belgravia) $270 £150

W. MILLINGTON - By A Wooded River, Evening - indistinctly signed - arched top - 23 x 19¾in.
(Sotheby's Belgravia) $198 £110

EDWARD MILLS - Temples Of Phaelae - signed and dated 1889 - oil - on board - 19 x 30cm.
(King & Chasemore) $127 £65

L. M. MILLS - A Trompe L'Oeil, with a photograph of Queen Victoria and a copy of the 'Yorkshire Post' - signed and dated - 20 x 16in.
(Sotheby's Belgravia) $216 £120

W. F. MILLS - Seascape With Sailing Ships and Figures - signed and dated 1883 - oil - 30 x 50in.
(Richard Baker & Baker) $450 £250

JOHN MacLAUCHLAN MILNE - Still Life Of Flowers - signed and dated '31 - 28 x 20¾in.
(Sotheby's Belgravia) $468 £260

JOHN MacLAUCHLAN MILNE - High Corrie, Arran - signed and dated '41 - on board - 14¼ x 17¼in.
(Sotheby's Belgravia) $612 £340

JOHN MacLAUCHLAN MILNE - Figures In A Rocky Cove - signed - 19¾ x 22½in.
(Sotheby's Belgravia) $360 £200

JOHN MacLAUCHLAN MILNE - By A Scottish Loch - signed - 19 x 23in.
(Sotheby's Belgravia) $774 £430

J. MacLAUCHLAN MILNE - Beach Scene With Figures And Boats, mountains in the background - 50 x 60cm.
(Edmiston's) $576 £320

J. MacLAUCHLAN MILNE - White
Cottages - 48 x 58cm.
(Edmiston's) **$342 £190**

WILLIAM WATT MILNE - In The
Orchard, France - signed - 19¼ x
23¼in.
(Sotheby's Belgravia) **$630 £350**

TOMMASO MINARDI - Saint George
Killing The Dragon - signed and dated
1818 - pencil, pen and brown ink, brown
wash heightened with white on buff
paper - 37.0 x 30.6cm.
(Christie's) **$99 £55**

BERNARDO MINOZZI - A View Near
An Italian Town with figures and a
horseman - brown and grey-brown wash
heightened with white on light brown
paper - 34.4 x 50.0cm.
(Christie's) **$180 £100**

FLAMINIO MINOZZI - Alternative Projects For A Trompe L'Oeil Ceiling - red
chalk, pen and brown ink, brown wash -
14.5 x 20.4cm.
(Christie's) **$90 £50**

A. MIROU - Landscape With Travellers -
on panel - 22¾ x 32in.
(Sotheby's) **$6,660 £3,600**

ANTOINE MIROU - Travellers In A
Wooded Landscape - indistinctly inscribed
and dated - on panel - 17¾ x 22¾in.
(Christie's) **$3,420 £1,900**

IL MAESTRO DELLA MISERICORDIA -
The Crucifixion - on the reverse, a bust
of an angel in a quatrefoil design - a fragment - on gold ground panel - 16¾ x
10¼in.
(Christie's) **$12,600 £7,000**

JOAN MITCHELL - L'Ecole Buisson-
niere - 39½ x 31½in.
(Christie's N. York) **$8,800 £4,889**

JOHN CAMPBELL MITCHELL - A
Perthshire Upland - signed - inscribed
and dated 1917 on the reverse - on
panel - 11¾ x 13½in.
(Sotheby's Belgravia)   **$270 £150**

THOMAS MITCHELL - A British Man-Of-
War And Other Shipping Off The Coast in
calm waters - signed and dated 1778 - on
panel - 14 x 20¾in.
(Sotheby's)   **$2,520 £1,400**

WILLIAM MITCHELL - Coming Out
Of Harbour - signed twice with monogram - heightened with bodycolour -
15½ x 27in.
(Sotheby's Belgravia) **$36 £20**

VINCENZO DE MITA - An Allegory
Of Victory: design for a ceiling - signed
and dated 1767 - black chalk, pen and
brown ink, grey wash - 30.8 x 19.4cm.
(Christie's)   **$32 £18**

MITO - The Dice Players; and Merrymaking In The Guard Room - both
signed - 19½ x 29½in.
(Christie's)   **$1,980 £1,100 Pair**

LOUISE MOILLON - Peaches And Grapes In
A Bowl On A Ledge - signed and dated 1634
- on panel - 19 x 25in.
(Christie's)   **$162,000 £90,000**

PIER FRANCESCO MOLA, Manner of -
A Shepherd Piping By A Tree, with a
shepherdess, cattle and sheep nearby -
25¼ x 20in.
(Christie's N. York)   **$308 £168**

PIER FRANCESCO MOLA, School of -
Abraham Entertaining The Angels - 34
x 45½in.
(Christie's N. York)   **$528 £288**

JOHN HENRY MOLE - A Farmstead By
A Stream - pencil and watercolour - 12½ x
19½in.
(Sotheby's)   **$270 £150**

KLAES MOLENAER - An Extensive Landscape with a bleaching ground and windmills
beyond - signed and dated 1652 - on panel -
17¾ x 24½in.
(Christie's)   **$16,380 £9,000**

KLAES MOLENAER - A Winter Landscape with figures and a horse on a frozen waterway by a cottage - signed - on panel - 14¼ x 13¼in.
(Christie's) **$6,840 £3,800**

KLAES MOLENAER - A Wooded Landscape with figures on a path and a fisherman by a pond - signed - on panel - 12½ x 18in.
(Christie's) **$5,400 £3,000**

KLAES MOLENAER - A Dune Landscape with peasants - bears initials - on panel - 14 x 12in.
(Christie's) **$2,520 £1,400**

KLAES MOLENAER, School of - A River Landscape with a windmill near a village, and fishermen - bears S. Ruysdael signature - 33 x 43¾ in.
(Christie's N. York) **$1,320 £721**

PIETER DE MOLIJN - An Extensive Landscape - inscribed with the artist's name and a date, 1637 - on panel - 15¾ x 24in.
(Sotheby's) **$12,025 £6,500**

MOLTINI - Figures On A Continental Lake, Evening - 12¼ x 16¾in.
(Sotheby's Belgravia) **$72 £40**

HENDRICK MOMMERS, Circle of - An Italianate Landscape, with travellers near a fountain by ruins - indistinctly signed - on panel - 20¼ x 32¼in.
(Christie's N. York) **$2,860 £1,562**

JOOS DE MOMPER, THE YOUNGER - An Extensive Mountainous Landscape with travellers on a path and a hill town beyond - on panel - 28½ x 41in.
(Christie's) **$23,660 £13,000**

PETER MONAMY - The Evening Gun -
26¾ x 35¼in.
(Sotheby's)   **$2,700 £1,500**

PAOLO MONALDI - Horsemen Resting
Among Classical Ruins with a fortune-teller
and a musician - 24¾ x 28¼in.
(Christie's)   **$8,100 £4,500**

P. MONAMY - A British Man-O'-War
Firing On The Enemy and sending out
boarding parties - oil - on canvas - 23 x
32in.
(Bonham's)   **$2,340 £1,300**
P. MONAMY - British Men of War - oil
- on canvas - 24½ x 43in.
(Brackett's)   **$1,720 £940**

PETER MONAMY - The Evening Gun, British
men-of-war and smaller boats at anchor in a
calm sea - signed - 39¼ x 24½in.
(Sotheby's)   **$3,600 £2,000**

PETER MONAMY - A Ketch-Rigged
Yacht and other shipping offshore in a
choppy sea - bears Brooking signature -
25 x 30 in.
(Christie's)   **$4,680 £2,600**

PETER MONAMY - A Fleet Of East India-
Men Gathering Off The Coast, possibly by
Plymouth - 30½ x 52in.
(Sotheby's)   **$5,580 £3,100**

MONCALVO - The Madonna With The Child And Holding Her Girdle Appearing To Saint Thomas And A Cleric Holding A Heart, A Papal Tiara Below - black chalk, pen and brown ink, brown wash, the tiara crossed through in red chalk - 15.1 x 10.0cm.
(Christie's) $54 £30

HENRY MONNIER - Count D'Orsay - signed and dated 1838 - pen and ink and watercolour heightened - oval - 16.7 x 11.1cm.
(Christie's) $99 £55

HENRY MONNIER - 'Vous M'Appelez? Oh Non, Allez!...' - inscribed - pen and brown ink and watercolour heightened with white - 13.4 x 10.2cm.
(Christie's) $45 £25

PHILIPPE MONNIER - Miniature Portrait Of A Young Girl - 4in. diameter.
(Christie's S. Kensington) $126 £70

JEAN-BAPTISTE MONNOYER - Tulips, Irises, Convolvuli, Sunflowers, Honeysuckle and other flowers in a basket on a ledge - 39 x 51¼in.
(Christie's) $23,660 £13,000

JEAN-BAPTISTE MONNOYER - A Basket Of Flowers On A Table - 19½ x 23¾in.
(Christie's) $4,680 £2,600

MONNOYER - Still Life Of Mixed Flowers in a two-handled urn standing on a stone plinth - oil - on canvas - 30 x 19½in.
(Neales of Nottingham) $444 £230

MONTI - Mediterranean Fishing Village - signed - oil - on canvas - 49.5 x 70cm.
(Australian Art Auctions) $27 £15

CAREL DE MOOR, Circle of - Portrait Of A Gentleman, seated, three-quarter length, in a dark embroidered robe with lace cuffs and collar, leaning on a table - 44 x 34in.
(Christie's N. York) $715 £391

CLAUDE T. S. MOORE - Hospital Ships Lying Off Greenwich, a scene at sunset - signed and dated '95 - signed and dated on the reverse - bearing artist's label with address - oil - on canvas - 12½ x 18½in.
(Neales of Nottingham) **$811 £420**

EDWARD MOORE - Coastal Scene with cliffs and rocks - signed - 17½ x 35in.
(Elliott & Green) **$360 £200**

H. MOORE - Victorian landscapes with fishing smacks on river - oil - on canvas - 15½ x 7½in.
(The Nottingham Auction Mart) **$347 £180 Pair**

LESLIE L. H. MOORE - View Of Happisburgh Church along the cliff-top - watercolour - 14 x 22in.
(G. A. Key) **$61 £34**

THOMAS COOPER MOORE - A Fleet Off The Coast, Sunset - signed - indistinctly inscribed - dated 1861 - 8¾ x 12½in.
(Sotheby's Belgravia) **$234 £130**

FRANS MOORMANS - A Summer Evening On The Terrace - signed and dated Paris, 1887 - on panel - 5½ x 8in.
(Christie's) **$756 £420**

THOMAS MORAN - Venice At Dawn - signed and dated 1884 - oil - on canvas - 15 x 25¾in.
(Sotheby's) **$16,405 £8,500**

JACOB MORE - The Monument Of The Curati At Lake Albana; and The Falls At Tivoli - both signed and one inscribed Rome 1787 - 20½ x 28¼in. and 20 x 27¾in.
(Sotheby's) **$432 £240 Two**

JACOB MORE, (After Claude) - An Italianate River Landscape with classical figures by a waterfall - 19 x 23¼in.
(Christie's) **$2,340 £1,300**

PAULUS MOREELSE - Portrait Of A Gentleman, full length, standing by a table in an interior - bears inscription - 77½ x 49½in.
(Christie's) **$9,000 £5,000**

G. MORELAND - Landscape with rustic figures - oil - on panel - 7½ x 6½in.
(The Nottingham Auction Mart)
$145 £75

A. MORIANI - Study Of A Peasant - signed, watercolour - 37.5 x 24.0cm.
(Christie's) **$36 £20**

D. MORIER - An Equestrian Portrait Of Frederick The Great, a battle scene beyond - 50 x 40in.
(Sotheby's) **$1,440 £800**

G. MORLAND - Nine Miles From London: Travellers with a donkey in a snow covered landscape - 12¼ x 15in.
(Sotheby's) **$936 £520**

GEORGE MORLAND - Portrait Of A Soldier, half length, wearing uniform - bears initials - inscribed on the reverse - on panel - 11¼ x 7½in.
(Sotheby's) **$540 £300**

G. B. MORONI - Portrait Of A Nobleman, full length, wearing dark doublet and hose, holding a pair of gloves, leaning on a draped table - bears inscription - 79½ x 50in.
(Christie's) **$5,040 £2,800**

C. MORRIS - Stream And Mill Scene - signed - oil - on canvas - 13½ x 17½in.
(Swetenham's) **$95 £50**

CHARLES MORRIS - Landscapes And A Moonlight Scene - all signed - on board - 4¾ x 6¾in.
(Sotheby's Belgravia) **$171 £95 Three**

GARMAN MORRIS - A Misty Morning Off Scarborough - signed and inscribed - 7 x 20½in.
(Sotheby's Belgravia) **$27 £15**

J. MORRIS - Highland Cattle With Gillie In Landscape - oil - 20 x 30in.
(G. A. Key) **$162 £90**

JOHN MORRIS - Highland Cattle Watering - signed - 36 x 27¼in.
(Sotheby's Belgravia) **$81 £45**

J. D. MORRIS - A Wooded River - signed - 11½ x 23½in.
(Sotheby's Belgravia) **$135 £75**

JOHN W MORRIS - Guarding The Flock - signed and dated '89 - 19½ x 29½.
(Sotheby's Belgravia)   **$216 £120**

JOHN W. MORRIS - Sheep On A Moor - signed and dated '87 - 19½ x 29½in.
(Sotheby's Belgravia)   **$108 £60**

PHILIP RICHARD MORRIS - Pleasant Dreams - signed and dated 1856 - 27½ x 35½in.
(Christie's)   **$1,072 £550**

PHILIP RICHARD MORRIS - Jack's Yarn - signed and dated 1892 - signed and inscribed on the reverse - 27¾ x 35¾in.
(Christie's)   **$90 £50**

WILLIAM BRIGHT MORRIS - Rabbiting - signed - 29½ x 49½in.
(Christie's)   **$1,080 £600**

G. MORTIMER - The Horse Fair - men and horses with distant view of village - oil - 9 x 14in.
(G. A. Key)   **$126 £70**

JOHN HAMILTON MORTIMER - Sir John Falstaff - pencil and coloured chalks - oval - 13¼ x 10in.
(Sotheby's)   **$1,080   £600**

THOMAS CORSAN MORTON - A Mountain Pass - signed - inscribed 'Glasgow' and dated 1897 on the reverse - 27½ x 35½in.
(Sotheby's Belgravia)   **$216 £120**

ROBERT S. MOSELEY - The Rat Catcher, He caught rats; The Rat Catcher's Daughter, She sold sprats - signed with monogram and dated - inscribed on the reverse - on board - 5 x 3in.
(Sotheby's Belgravia) **$117   £65 Pair**

MOSSMAN - Edinburgh Street Scenes - both inscribed on the reverse - on board - 4¾ x 3¾in.
(Sotheby's Belgravia)   **$198 £110 Pair**

GEORGE WILLIAM MOTE - A Woody Landscape with a stonebreaker - signed and dated 1868 - signed on an old label on the reverse - 14½ x 19½in.
(Christie's)   **$3,900 £2,000**

GEORGE WILLIAM MOTE - An Extensive Wooded Landscape Near Barnet, Hertfordshire, with children on a path by a pond and a windmill beyond - signed, inscribed and dated 1859 - 31½ x 49¾in.
(Christie's)   **$3,420 £1,900**

D. MOTTEN - A Lochside Castle, signed - on board - 23½ x 35¼in.
(Sotheby's Belgravia)   **$50 £28**

CHARLES SIM MOTTRAM - Over The Rocks - signed and dated - inscribed on the reverse - heightened with white - 13½ x 20½in.
(Sotheby's Belgravia)   **$108 £60**

MOUCHERON - An Italian River Landscape With A Monument - pen and brown ink, grey wash - 14.5 x 19.3cm.
(Christie's)   **$99 £55**

ISAAC DE MOUCHERON - An Extensive Well-wooded Landscape, a stag hunt in the foreground - 24 x 30½in.
(H. Spencer & Sons)   **$1,080 £600**

FREDERICK DE MOUCHERON, School of - A Rocky Italianate Landscape, with travellers on a road, and a bridge in the distance - bears signature 'Daubiny' - 34 x 44in.
(Christie's N. York)   **$1,100 £601**

PIEDRO DE MOYA - Joseph With The Infant Saviour - oil - on canvas - 60 x 42cm.
(King & Chasemore)   **$1,568 £800**

LEOPOLD CARL MULLER - Food For The Blind Beggar - signed and dated 1879 - 27 x 43in.
(Christie's)   **$7,200 £4,000**

MULLER

ROBERT A. MULLER - Portrait Of A
Gentleman - signed - oil - 14 x 12in.
(Hussey's) **$126 £70**

W. MULLER - "Market Square, Cairo" -
signed - oil - on panel - 17 x 21cm.
(Australian Art Auctions) **$7 £4**

W. MULLER - A Rustic Cottage with cattle
in a wooded glade - indistinctly signed - on
panel - 7½ x 11½in.
(Sotheby's) **$396 £220**

WILLIAM JAMES MULLER - The
Sphinx - signed and indistinctly dated -
28½ x 52in.
(Christie's) **$2,535 £1,300**

WILLIAM JAMES MULLER - The Rialto,
Venice - heightened with white, gum
arabic - 12 x 18½ in.
(Sotheby's) **$2,880 £1,600**

WILLIAM JAMES MULLER - A Ruined
Abbey by a River in Yorkshire - signed
and dated 1833 - 10 x 14 in.
(Sotheby's) **$396 £220**

WILLIAM JAMES MULLER - Arabs In
A Courtyard - signed and dated 1839 -
pencil and wash - 8¼ x 11in.
(Christie's) **$54 £30**

WILLIAM JAMES MULLER - A Rocky
River Landscape with a waterfall - signed
and dated 1837 - 25¼ x 22¼in.
(Christie's) **$684 £380**

W. J. MULLER - A View Of Gizeh,
With The Sphinx And The Pyramids
Beyond - bears signature and dated
1841 - 25 x 41in.
(Christie's) **$342 £190**

AUGUSTUS E. MULREADY - 'Favourable
Critics' - signed, and signed, inscribed and
dated 1892 on the reverse - on board - 6¾
x 9¾in.
(Christie's) **$1,170 £600**

J. MUNDELL - A Summer River Landscape - signed - 9¼ x 17½in.
(Sotheby's Belgravia) **$234 £130**

PAUL SANDBY MUNN - The Langdale
Pikes from near Side House, Westmorland
signed and dated 1805 - 16½ x 24¾ in.
(Sotheby's) **$576 £320**

ROBERT MUNRO - Lamlash Bay, Arran -
signed and dated 1884 - 21¼ x 35½in.
(Sotheby's Belgravia) **$432 £240**

FRANCESCO DE MURA - Santa Rosa -
on copper - oval - 10 x 8in.
(Christie's N. York) **$1,100 £601**

DOMENICO MARIA MURATORI - The
Entry Into Naples Of Don Juan Jose Of
Austria accompanied by the Archbishop
of Naples, Ascanio Filomarino - 112½ x
133½in.
(Christie's) **$6,370 £3,500**

MURILLO - An Allegory Of The Immacu-
late Conception - bears monogram - black
chalk, grey wash - 24.3 x 19.0cm.
(Christie's) **$36 £20**

BARTOLOME ESTEBAN MURILLO -
Portrait Of The Artist, half length, wearing
a black costume with slashed sleeves and
golilla - in a simulated stone cartouche -
30 x 25in.
(Christie's) **$43,200 £24,000**

EDWARD MURPHY - Merchants' Flags
In Hobart Town, vignettes of Flags and
Ships that appeared in the harbour at
Hobart - signed, inscribed and dated 1855
- watercolour - 24 x 34¾in.
(Sotheby's) **$965 £500**

H. C. MURPHY - Wagons Roll - signed -
oil - on canvas - 36¼ x 16¼in.
(Sotheby's) **$463 £240**

MURRAY

SIR DAVID MURRAY - 'A Whisper Of Winter' - The Trossachs - signed and indistinctly dated 1912 - inscribed on the reverse - 47½ x 71½in.
(Christie's)   **$468 £260**

SIR DAVID MURRAY - Bickerley Common, Ringwood, Hampshire - signed and dated '92 - indistinctly inscribed on the stretcher - 11½ x 17½in.
(Sotheby's Belgravia)   **$900 £500**

H. MURRAY - First Scent; Taking A Walk; Problems At The Water; The Kill - all signed - two heightened with white - 6¾ x 9¾in.
(Sotheby's Belgravia)   **$550 £300 Four**

FRANCIS MUSCHAMP - A Girl On The Edge Of A Loch - signed and dated 1871 - 12 x 24in.
(Sotheby's Belgravia) **$153 £85**

S. MUSCHAMP - Lake Scene With Female Figure At Lakeside - signed and dated 1867 - oil - 12 x 24in.
(Richard Baker & Baker) **$180 £100**

SYDNEY MUSCHAMP - Imogen, Cymbeline, Act II, Scene 2, Shakespeare - arched top - 16½ x 25¼in.
(Sotheby's Belgravia)   **$81 £45**

EWERT LOUIS VAN MUYDEN - Homme Avec Lance A Cheval - signed - pen and black ink over pencil on tracing paper - 28 x 22cm.
(Christie's)   **$18 £10**

GIROLAMO MUZIANO - St. Jerome - on panel - 6¾ x 5¾in.
(Sotheby's)   **$13,875 £750**

MARTIN VAN MYTENS, THE YOUNGER - Portrait Of A Young Man, bust length, wearing grey cloak and turban - 28 x 22½in.
(Christie's)   **$1,800 £1,000**

J. G. NAISH - "The Leap Ashore", depicting three men in an open boat returning from lobster fishing, with figures and cottage on headland path - signed and dated 1884 - oil - 24 x 48in.
(Richard Baker & Baker) $585 £325

MAITHYS NAIVEU - The Holy Family In An Embrasure with fruit and flowers above - bears signature and dated 1710 - on panel - arched top - 13 x 9½in.
(Christie's) $2,700 £1,500

NAMCHEONG - The Wampoa Pagoda - both bear the artist's stamp on reverse - oval - 19¼ x 14¼in.
(Sotheby's, Hong Kong) $311 £173 **Pair**

FILIPPO NAPOLITANO - Sportsmen With Their Horses And Dogs - 10¼ x 16½in.
(Christie's) $11,700 £6,500

NASH - The Quadrangle Outside Eton College Chapel; A House At Eton - both on board - 8 x 13in.
(Sotheby's Belgravia) $99 £55 **Pair**

JOSEPH NASH - Old Refectory, Rouen Cathedral - heightened with white - 14¼ x 10 in.
(Sotheby's) $144 £80

ALEXANDER NASMYTH - A View Of Culzean Castle From The North - 27 x 35in.
(Christie's) $2,700 £1,500

ALEXANDER NASMYTH - A View Of Edinburgh From The Dean Village - 26 x 35in.
(Christie's) $1,800 £1,000

ALEXANDER NASMYTH - An Italian Landscape - 23½ x 17½in.
(Sotheby's Belgravia)   **$2,340 £1,300**

ANNE GIBSON NASMYTH - Panoramic View Of Edinburgh And The Firth Of Forth - 20½ x 21¾in.
(Sotheby's Belgravia)   **$5,220 £2,900**

CHARLOTTE NASMYTH - Returning Home - inscribed - 11½ x 15½in.
(Sotheby's Belgravia)   **$1,620 £900**

CHARLOTTE NASMYTH - A Wooded Landscape With Travellers On A Path - signed and dated 1813 - 27 x 35in.
(Christie's)   **$2,160 £1,200**

MARGARET NASMYTH - An Old Country House - on panel - 8½ x 12in.
(Sotheby's Belgravia)   **$2,700 £1,500**

MARGARET NASMYTH - Above A Highland Loch - signed with initials and dated 1836 - 17½ x 23¾in.
(Sotheby's Belgravia)   **$5,040 £2,800**

PATRICK NASMYTH - A Wooded Landscape with figures in a farmyard - signed and dated 1817 - on panel - 14½ x 18½in.
(Christie's)   **$306 £170**

PATRICK NASMYTH - A Wooded River
Landscape with figures and a horse by a
cottage - signed and dated 1826 - on panel
- 13 x 17in.
(Christie's)   **$1,755 £900**

PATRICK NASMYTH - Peasants On A
Path near Woburn - signed and dated
1824 - 27 x 37½in.
(Christie's)   **$12,600 £7,000**

PATRICK NASMYTH - A River Estuary
with barges and figures at a quay - signed
and dated 1841 - 10¼ x 12¼in.
(Sotheby's)   **$1,044 £580**

PIETER NASON - Portrait Of A Lady,
seated three-quarter length, wearing
black dress with white lace collar and
cuffs holding a lemon, a garden and
river landscape beyond - signed and
dated 1655 - 44½ x 35½in.
(Christie's)   **$2,700 £1,500**

JOHN CLAUDE NATTES - A Wooded
Landscape with a figure approaching
a bridge and a town in the mountains
beyond - signed, inscribed and dated
1816 on the reverse - heightened with
bodycolour - 6 x 8¾in.
(Sotheby's)   **$108 £60**

J. M. NATTIER - Portrait Of A Lady,
bust length, wearing blue drapery -
oval - 23 x 19in.
(Christie's)   **$1,530 £850**

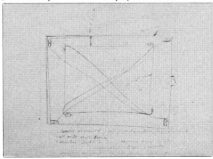

BRUCE NAUMAN - Four Corner Piece -
signed, inscribed and dated '71 - pencil -
19¾ x 26in.
(Christie's)   **$3,660 £2,000**

BRUCE NAUMAN - Spilling Coffee
Because The Cup Was Too Hot -
signed and dated 1966 - pencil and
coloured chalk - 24¾ x 37¾in.
(Christie's) **$2,745 £1,500**

EDWARD NEALE - Grouse Sheltering -
signed and dated 1896 - 29¼ x 35½in.
(Sotheby's Belgravia) **$2,700 £1,500**

GEORGE HALL NEALE - Sorrows
Crowning Sorrow Is Remembering Happy
Days - signed and dated - 21 x 25in.
(Sotheby's Belgravia) **$162 £90**

NEAPOLITAN SCHOOL, 18th century -
The Madonna Of Loreto - on panel -
16 x 20¼in.
(Christie's N. York) **$176 £96**

NEAPOLITAN SCHOOL - Golfo
Di Baia; Isola D'Ischia; Isola Di Capri;
and Grotta Azzurra - dated 1850 - bodycolour - 35.5 x 50.0cm.
(Christie's) **$810 £450 Four**

NEAPOLITAN SCHOOL, Early 18th
century - The Turks Invading Austria;
and A Fleet Bombarding A North
African Town, with soldiers attacking
the ramparts - both inscribed - 32½ x
42¼in.
(Christie's N. York) **$2,310 £1,262 Pair**

PIETER NEEFFS, THE ELDER and
FRANS FRANCKEN II - The Interior
Of A Cathedral With Double Aisles -
seen from the West end: a tablet on
a column in the right foreground is
inscribed - on panel - 14½ x 22¼in.
(Sotheby's) **$12,025 £6,500**

PEETER NEEFFS III - The Interior Of A Church with numerous figures - signed with initials and dated 1658 - on copper - oval - 4¼ x 5½in.
(Christie's) $2,700 £1,500

PEETER NEEFFS II - The Interior Of A Cathedral - signed and dated 1623 - on panel - 5½ x 7½in.
(Christie's) $3,960 £2,200

PIETER NEEFFS, THE YOUNGER - A Prison, with Saint Peter in prayer, and soldiers playing dice - 21 x 28¾in.
(Christie's N. York) $1,540 £841

PEETER NEEFFS, THE ELDER and FRANS FRANCKEN, THE YOUNGER - The Interior Of A Church with services taking place - dated 1616 - on panel - 14 x 22¼in.
(Christie's) $7,560 £4,200

A. VAN DER NEER - A Moonlight Wooded River Landscape with fishermen - bears monograms - 13 x 15½in.
(Christie's) $1,440 £800

AERT VAN DER NEER - A Moonlit River with barges and a windmill - signed with monogram - on panel - 17½ x 24¼in.
(Christie's) $12,600 £7,000

AERT VAN DER NEER - A Wooded River Landscape With A Ferry And A Town Beyond - on panel - 23½ x 32½in.
(Christie's) $12,600 £7,000

J. NEIMAN, JUN - Italianate River Landscape with evening sunlight, classical ruins and pavilion, a boat and figure in the foreground - signed - oil - on canvas - 30 x 50in.
(Neales of Nottingham) $186 £100

WILLIAM J. NELSON - Study Of A Moroccan, head and shoulders - 15¼ x 11½in.
(Sotheby's Belgravia) $4 £2

NERONE - Head Of A Youth With Long Hair - pen and brown ink - circular - 11.0cm. diameter.
(Christie's) $117 £65

JOHN NESBITT - A Beach Scene - signed and dated 1891 - watercolour - 13½ x 20in.
(Warner, Sheppard & Wade) $69 £35

CASPAR NETSCHER, Manner of - A Concert - bears signature - on panel - 22 x 18in.
(Christie's N. York) $1,650 £902

321

NEUGEBAUER

JOSEPH NEUGEBAUER - A Rabbit, And An Upturned Basket Of Grapes With Peaches, Plums And A Pear by a pedestal - signed and dated 1848 - canvas laid down on board - 18¼ x 26in.
(Christie's) $612 £340

ALFRED BRUNEL DE NEUVILLE - Cat Watching Three Kittens playing with a ball of wool - signed - 28 x 15in.
(Phillips, Solihull) $3,240 £1,800 Pair

LOUIS NEVILLE - Fishing Boats Off The South Coast - watercolour - 4 x 9in.
(G. A. Key) $8 £4

DAVID NEWHOUSE - Seashore Scenes with boats and figures - watercolour - 6 x 9in.
(G. A. Key) $29 £16

ALGERNON CECIL NEWTON - Path Through The Wood - signed with monogram and dated '43 - oil - on canvas - 21¾ x 29¾in.
(Geering & Colyer) $1,258 £680

PHYLLIS K. NEWTON - Peonies In A Vase - watercolour - 17 x 16in.
(G. A. Key) $27 £15

P. DE NEYN - A Woody Landscape with travellers by an inn - on panel - 15 x 26in.
(Christie's) $4,680 £2,600

RICHARD HENRY NIBBS - Sunset Over An Estuary - signed - 15 x 30in.
(Sotheby's Belgravia) $144 £80

ANDREW NICHOLL - By The Banks Of A River - signed - heightened with body-colour - 12 x 18in.
(Sotheby's Belgravia) $126 £70

FRANCIS NICHOLSON - A Wooded River Landscape with a mill in the middle and a bridge in the distance - 10½ x 15in.
(Sotheby's) $198 £110

FRANCIS NICHOLSON - A Mountainous Torrent - signed - 26¼ x 19½in.
(Sotheby's) $216 £120

FRANCIS NICHOLSON - Scarborough - etched outline and watercolour - 11¾ x 16½in.
(Christie's) $504 £280

FRANCIS NICHOLSON - A Watermill On A River, barns in the background - 10 x 14½in.
(Sotheby's) $126 £70

ERSKINE NICOL - As The Old Cock Crows, The Young One Learns - signed - on panel - 28 x 24cm.
(Edmiston's) $810 £450

ERSKINE NICOL - The Donkey Race -
24 x 29in.
(Christie's) **$2,340 £1,300**

E. NICOL - "Common Pleas" - signed
- oil - 12½ x 10in.
(Warner, Sheppard & Wade) **$980 £500**

J. WATSON NICOL - A Cavalier hiding
a letter in a bouquet - signed - oil - 7½
x 9½in.
(Warner, Sheppard & Wade) **$862 £440**

ERSKINE NICOL - Lonely Thoughts -
signed - inscribed and dated '57 -
heightened with bodycolour - 10 x
7½in.
(Sotheby's Belgravia) **$216 £120**

VICTOR JEAN NICOLLE - An Extensive View Of Rome - pen and brown ink,
grey and yellowish-brown wash on light
blue paper - 29.2 x 43.3cm.
(Christie's) **$378 £210**

NIEMANN - Figures In A Landscape -
bears signature - 13½ x 17in.
(Sotheby's Belgravia) **$90 £50**

ERSKINE NICOL - Changing Weather -
signed and dated '62 - heightened with
bodycolour - 12 x 8¼in.
(Sotheby's Belgravia) **$306 £170**

EDMUND JOHN NIEMANN - An Extensive Wooded River Landscape, with
figures in the foreground and a village
beyond - signed - 29½ x 49¾in.
(Christie's) **$741 £380**

EDMUND JOHN NIEMANN - Cader Idris - signed - inscribed and dated '66 - 24 x 41½in.
(Sotheby's Belgravia)   **$396 £220**

EDMUND JOHN NIEMANN, SEN - The Interior Of Saint Gudule, Brussels - signed, inscribed and dated '65 - on board - 15 x 10½in.
(Christie's)   **$540 £300**

A. NIKOLSKY - "Autumn Berries" - signed and dated 1957 - oil - on canvas - 24 x 27in.
(Walker, Barnett & Hill) **$288 £160**

POLLOCK J. NISBET - An Arab Street Scene - signed - 30 x 22½in.
(Christie's)   **$1,530 £850**

POLLOCK SINCLAIR NISBET - Cattle Watering, A Summer's Day - signed - on board - 9½ x 14¾in.
(Sotheby's Belgravia)   **$108 £60**

ROBERT BUCHAN NISBET - An October Day Near Crieff - signed - on board - 10¼ x 13¼in.
(Sotheby's Belgravia)   **$234 £130**

GIUSEPPE DE NITTIS - La Place Des Pyramides, Paris - signed - on panel - 12½ x 9¼in.
(Christie's)   **$2,340 £1,300**

JOHN NIXON - Cuckfield, Sussex - inscribed - pen and black ink and watercolour - 5½ x 8½in.
(Sotheby's)   **$144 £80**

JOHN NIXON - 'Ladies Of The Town' being charged in the Watch House, Fleet Market - signed with initials - inscribed on the reverse - pen and brown and grey ink, grey wash - 4¼ x 7in.
(Sotheby's)   **$252 £140**

JAMES NOBLE - Still Life Of Spring Flowers, in a vase on a plinth - signed - 20 x 22in.
(Sotheby's Belgravia)   **$1,170 £650**

JOHN SERGEANT NOBLE - The Day's
Bag - signed - 13¾ x 17¾in.
(Sotheby's Belgravia)   **$1,620 £900**

ROBERT NOBLE - A Farm By A River -
signed - 11¾ x 19¾in.
(Sotheby's Belgravia)   **$720 £400**

GIUSEPPE NOGARI - Portrait Of A
Bearded Man, half length, wearing a brown
coat - 22½ x 17in.
(Christie's)   **$3,640 £2,000**

P. R. NOGARI - The Taking Of Christ -
inscribed - pen and brown ink, grey
wash - 19.5 x 28.5cm.
(Christie's)   **$432 £240**

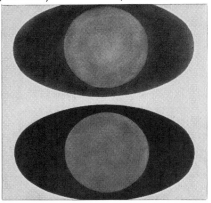

KENNETH NOLAND - Red and
Purple Octuple - signed, inscribed
and dated 1962 on the reverse -
22 x 22 in.
*(Christie's N. York)***$8,250 £4,383**

KENNETH NOLAND - Cite - signed,
inscribed and dated 1964 on the reverse -
acrylic on canvas - 45 x 45in.
(Christie's N. York)   **$22,000 £12,222**

EMIL NOLDE - Schiffe Auf Der Elbe -
22 x 32cm.
(Auktionshaus am Neumarkt)
$9,606 £5,249

JOSEPH NOLLEKINS, Manner of -
Children Playing With A Hobby Horse
On A Terrace - 42 x 51½in.
(Christie's N. York)   **$330 £180**

P. NOLPE - A River Landscape With
Fishermen - 16¼ x 22in.
(Christie's)   **$504 £280**

JOANNES VAN NOORT - The Triumph Of
David - indistinctly signed - 53¼ x 69½in.
(Christie's)   **$6,840 £3,800**

NORBURY

EDWIN A. NORBURY - Beached
Fishing Boats - signed - 18½ x 11¼in.
(Sotheby's Belgravia) **$54 £30**
C. NORDMANN - Poppies - 59 x 76cm.
(Edmiston's) **$180 £100**
PARSONS NORMAN - Paddle Steamer
Towing Boat Out Of Harbour - water-
colour - 13 x 9in.
(G. A. Key) **$40 £22**

NORTH AMERICAN SCHOOL, 19th
century - The S.S. Shatemuc - inscribed -
oil - on canvas - 23½ x 35¼in.
(Sotheby's) **$810 £420**

NORTH ITALIAN SCHOOL, 16th
century - "The Deposition In The Tomb" -
oil - on panel - 22 x 24in.
(Graves, Son & Pilcher) **$2,700 £1,500**

**JEAN JULES ANTOINE LECOMTE
DE NOUY** - The Guard Of The Seraglio,
Egypt - signed and dated 1876 - 29 x 47in.
(Christie's) **$57,600 £32,000**

NOVELLI - Head Of A Youth - pen
and black ink - 22.7 x 19.0cm.
(Christie's) **$27 £15**

F. A. NOYES - Country Children With
Their Pet Lamb - signed and dated 1879 -
23½ x 19½in.
(Sotheby's Belgravia) **$198 £110**

NUZZI - Carnations And Peonies And
Other Flowers In A Silver Ewer with
fruit and an earthenware jug nearby -
28½ x 18¾in.
(Christie's) **$2,160 £1,200**

GERARD VAN NYMEGEN - A
Wooded Landscape with figures and cattle
by a gateway - signed and dated 1784 - on
panel - 13 x 15½in.
(Christie's) **$1,980 £1,100**

GERARD VAN NYMEGEN - A
Wooded Landscape with figures and
cattle by a bridge - on panel - 13 x
15½in.
(Christie's) **$1,080 £600**

JOHN WRIGHT OAKES - A Cornfield - on board - 7½ x 17in.
(Sotheby's Belgravia)   **$160 £90**

JOHN WRIGHT OAKES - Between The Showers - signed - inscribed - 22 x 36in.
(Sotheby's Belgravia)   **$250 £130**

LUDWIG OBERSTEINER - First Aid - signed and dated - on panel - 19½ x 15½in.
(Sotheby's)   **$1,710 £950**

OBERMAN - Roses, Daffodils And A Tulip in a pitcher with a dead bird in a niche - 16 x 12½in.
(Christie's)   **$576 £320**

JAMES ARTHUR O'CONNOR - Queen Eleanors Cross - on panel - 8¼ x 10in.
(Sotheby's)   **$630 £350**

JAMES ARTHUR O'CONNOR - A Wooded River Landscape - signed and dated 1809 - 20½ x 30¼in.
(Christie's)   **$1,170 £650**

JOHN O'CONNOR - The Market Place, Verona - signed and dated 1887 - 29¼ x 50in.
(Christie's)   **$2,340 £1,300**

RODERIC O'CONOR - The Orchard - stamped on reverse - on board - 15 x 18in.
(Christie's)   **$1,710 £950**

RODERIC O'CONOR - Still Life With Flowers in a vase - stamped on the back of canvas - 36¼ x 28¾in.
(Christie's)   **$5,400 £3,000**

F. OCTAVIEN - A Wooded Landscape with a hunting party at rest in a clearing in the foreground - 23 x 19in.
(Christie's)   **$1,440 £800**

TEN OEVER - A River Landscape At Sunset - on panel - 12½ x 15¼in.
(Sotheby's)   **$288 £160**

JOHN EDWIN OLDFIELD - A Landscape In The Lake District - watercolour - 6¾ x 10½in.
(Christie's)   **$27 £15**

OLIS - A Woman At Her Toilette, A Gentleman Beside Her, a map hanging on the wall behind - on panel - 13½ x 10½in.
(Sotheby's)   **$684 £380**

JULES OLITSKI - Questa Pink - signed, inscribed and dated '68 on the reverse - 38 x 123in.
(Christie's N. York)   **$11,000 £6,111**

JULES OLITSKI - Lament Of Absalom 8 - signed, inscribed and dated 1973 on the reverse - water base acrylic on canvas - 77 x 55in.
(Christie's N. York)   **$6,600 £3,667**

ISAAC OLIVER - Madonna and Child - pen and brown ink, blue wash on blue-grey paper - 7 x 5¼ in.
(Sotheby's)   **$5,400 £3,000**

PETER OLIVER - The Holy Family, after Correggio - pen and brown ink, grey wash heightened with white - 8.1 x 6.4cm.
(Christie's)   **$270 £150**

W. OLIVER - A Portrait Of A Young Lady With Poppies And Wheat-Ears In Her Hair, wearing an amber dress with black trimming and holding a posy of flowers, half length - signed - 17½ x 13½in.
(H. Spencer & Sons)   **$1,116 £620**

WILLIAM OLIVER - A Backwater, Venice - 14 x 12in.
(Sotheby's Belgravia)   **$783 £440**

WILLIAM OLIVER - The Convent Of The Angels; and A Spanish Monastery - inscribed - 9½ x 14½in. and 9¾ x 13½in.
(Sotheby's)   **$99 £55 Pair**

P. D. OLIVERO - A Southern Market Place, numerous figures before the walls of a town, mountains beyond - 63 x 90in.
(Sotheby's)   **$7,200 £4,000**

JULIUS OLSSON - Breakers, Evening -
signed - 17 x 23in.
(Sotheby's Belgravia) **$267 £150**

OMMEGANCK - Cattle And Sheep By
A Cottage in a wooded landscape - on
panel - 14 x 12in.
(Sotheby's) **$618 £320**

OMMEGANCK - Bringing In The Fishing
Lines - on panel - 5¾ x 7in.
(Sotheby's) **$90 £50**

DANIEL O'NEILL - Interior With
Figure; girl reading - signed - on board -
17¼ x 13¼in.
(Christie's) **$900 £500**

GEORGE BERNARD O'NEILL - New
Year's Day - signed and dated 1889 - oil -
on canvas - 30½ x 24½in.
(Gribble, Booth & Taylor)
$10,440 £5,800

GEORGE BERNARD O'NEILL -
Grandfather's Visit - signed and dated
1854 on the reverse - 20½ x 15¼in.
(Christie's) **$360 £200**

G. B. O'NEIL - A Woodland Glade,
young boy and girl seated on a grassy
bank examining a bird's nest - verso
inscribed - oil - on board - 7½ x 6½in.
(Neales of Nottingham) **$425 £220**

A. ONSLOW - H.R.H. The Prince Of Wales'
Yacht 'Hildegarde', 205 tons, racing in a
gale of wind - signed and dated 1892 - on
board - 8½ x 13in.
(Sotheby's Belgravia) **$252 £140**

A. W. ONSLOW - H.M.S. 'Powerful' -
signed with monogram and inscribed -
9¼ x 13½in.
(Sotheby's Belgravia) **$55 £30**

ISAAC VAN OOSTEN - A Wooded River Landscape with horses and cattle watering, peasants on a path and a cottage beyond - on panel - 11 x 17in.
(Christie's) **$23,660 £13,000**

OPIE - A Boy Leaning On A Table - 16¼ x 13¾in.
(Sotheby's) **$108 £60**

OPIE - Portrait Of A Lady Wearing A Mop Cap - on board - 29¾ x 25in.
(Sotheby's) **$72 £40**

CHARLES M. Q. ORCHARDSON - The Lock Gates, Rye - signed - on panel - 10¾ x 15in.
(Sotheby's) **$116 £60**

BRYAN ORGAN - Bullfight - signed and dated 1962 - gouache - 34 x 48¼in.
(Sotheby's) **$173 £90**

UMBERTO ORGANIA - Near The Rialto, Venice - signed - 7¼ x 12in.
(Sotheby's) **$76 £40**

VAN ORLEY - The Judgment Of Solomon - on panel - 24½ x 21½in.
(Christie's) **$1,080 £600**

RICHARD VAN ORLEY, Attributed To - The Presentation - inscribed with monogram on the reverse - black chalk, pen and brown ink, brown wash - 35 x 25.3cm.
(Christie's) **$63 £35**

J. ORLOFF - Horse drawn sleighs in snow covered landscapes - signed - on panel - 6¼ x 12½in.
(Sotheby's) **$468 £260 Pair**

ALEXANDER ORLOWSKI - Portrait Of A Young Officer In Highland Dress, a landscape with a castle behind - signed and dated 1825 - bodycolour - 43.0 x 33.6cm.
(Christie's) **$2,520 £1,400**

WILLIAM ORME - West Ham Church, Essex - signed - inscribed and dated 1802 on the reverse - 10¾ x 15½in.
(Sotheby's) **$162 £90**

SIR WILLIAM ORPEN - Monsieur Eleuth-erios Venezelos - signed and dated 1919 - 36 x 28in.
(Christie's) **$3,060 £1,700**

SIR WILLIAM ORPEN - Prince Kimimon-chi Saionzi - signed - 30 x 25in.
(Christie's)   **$990 £550**

PEDRO ORRENTE - Joseph Abandoned By His Brethren - 43 x 56in.
(Christie's)   **$4,732 £2,600**

JAMES ORROCK - On The Border Of Lochar Moss - signed and dated 1881 - heightened with bodycolour - 29 x 34in.
(Sotheby's Belgravia)   **$180 £100**

JAMES ORROCK - Mackerel Fishing, Hastings - signed, inscribed and dated 1903 - 6¾ x 13½in.
(Sotheby's Belgravia)   **$164 £85**

JAMES ORROCK - Deer In The Park At Arundel - inscribed and dated 1902 - pencil, black chalk and watercolour heightened with white - 5½ x 8½in.
(Christie's)   **$370 £190**

JAMES ORROCK - Sheep In A Field At Bewcastle, Cumberland - signed and inscribed - pen and black ink, pencil and watercolour heightened with white - 10 x 13½in.
(Christie's)   **$195 £100**

LELIO ORSI, Circle of - Design for the decoration of a pediment with a central cartouche: Vulcan snaring Mars and Venus in his net, watched by the other Gods - inscribed - black chalk, pen and brown ink, brown wash heightened with white, on light brown paper - 14.4 x 31,2cm.
(Christie's)   **$396 £220**

FRANCOIS AUGUSTE ORTMANS - A View On The Seine with horse-drawn barges - signed and inscribed on the reverse - on panel - 4¾ x 8¼in.
(Christie's)   **$720 £400**

GEORG JAKOB JOHAN VAN OS - A Vase Of Roses, Tulips, Irises And Other Flowers - signed on the reverse - water-colour - 46.5 x 37.8cm.
(Christie's)   **$1,980 £1,100**

JAN VAN OS - A River Estuary With Shipping, and cattle and a horseman near cottages - signed - 20 x 24¼in.
(Christie's New York) **$39,600 £20,518**

GIORGINS JACOBUS JOHANNES VAN OS - Grapes, Peaches, A Melon And Other Fruit, and insects in a landscape - signed - 29½ x 23½in.
(Christie's) **$8,100 £4,500**

J. VAN OS - An Extensive River Landscape with sailing barges and a town beyond - on panel - 13¾ x 16½in.
(Christie's) **$1,170 £650**

JAN VAN OS - A Dutch State Barge firing a salute, with other shipping becalmed in an estuary - signed - 20 x 24½in.
(Christie's New York) **$38,500 £19,948**

JAN VAN OS - Roses, Poppies, And Other Flowers In A Sculptured Vase With grapes, plums, peaches, a pineapple and a bird's nest on a stone ledge in a wooded landscape - signed - on panel - 34¼ x 26¾in.
(Christie's) **$36,000 £20,000**

JAN VAN OS - A Coastal Landscape With Travellers On A Path and sailing vessels offshore - signed with initials and dated 1796 - 23½ x 30in.
(Christie's) **$27,000 £15,000**

OSBORNE - The Street Seller - on board
- 24 x 19in.
(Sotheby's Belgravia)   **$18 £10**

W. OSBORNE, After Young Hunter -
The Enchanted Garden - signed and
inscribed - 20½ x 35½in.
(Christie's)   **$630 £350**

OSTADE - The Interior Of A Cottage,
to the right peasants sitting round a
barrel drinking and reading, others
beyond beside a fire - on panel - 14 x
13in.
(Christie's)   **$5,400 £3,000**

ISAAC VAN OSTADE - A Wooded Landscape with a milkmaid, cows and a horse -
bears signature - on panel - 15 x 20½in.
(Christie's)   **$10,010 £5,500**

ADRIAEN VAN OSTADE - The Schoolroom
- signed and dated 1636 - on panel - 16 x
20½in.
(Christie's)   **$43,200 £24,000**

OSTADE - A Man With A Horn, beneath
an arched doorway, a small boy to the
left - on panel - 10¼ x 8¼in.
(Sotheby's)   **$576 £320**

ANDERS OSTERLIND - The Parc - 80 x
100cm.
(Auktionshaus am Neumarkt)
$3,539 £1,934

ISAAC VAN OSTADE - A Wooded Landscape with travellers outside a cottage -
indistinctly signed and dated 1646 - on
panel - 28¾ x 34¾in.
(Christie's)   **$54,600 £30,000**

GEORG OSTERWALD - Lake Nemi -
signed and inscribed - pencil and
watercolour - 49 x 71.4cm.
(Christie's)   **$288 £160**

C. W. OSWALD - A View In North Wales -
signed and inscribed - 15½ x 11½in.
(Sotheby's Belgravia)   **$116 £65**

OSWALD

C. W. OSWALD - Highland Cattle And Landscape - oil - 19 x 29in.
(G. A. Key) **$216 £120**

WILLIAM OTTLEY - Lamentation - signed, inscribed and dated 1793 - 10¾ x 10¾in.
(Sotheby's) **$18 £10**

ROLAND OUDOT - Route de Provence - signed - oil - on canvas - 28¼ x 35¾in.
(Sotheby's) **$1,110 £620**

J. B. OUDRY - A Wolf - black chalk, grey and pink wash - 25.5 x 26.0cm.
(Christie's) **$117 £65**

PIERRE OUTIN - At The Balcony · signed on buff paper - pencil - 11 x 10in.
(Sotheby's) **$85 £45**

GRAHAM OVENDEN - A Girl With A Doll - signed - pencil - 18 x 13in.
(Sotheby's) **$386 £200**

JOEL OWEN - Highland Cattle Watering - signed - 9½ x 13½in.
(Sotheby's Belgravia) **$98 £55 Pair**

JOEL OWEN - Landscape With Cottage, Figures In Lane And Domestic Fowl - oil - 16 x 24in.
(G. A. Key) **$126 £70**

S. OWEN - A Fishing Boat and other vessels in the open sea - watercolour heightened with white - 10¼ x 16¼in.
(Christie's) **$90 £50**

SAMUEL OWEN - Boats in a Rough Sea near a Castle - 8¾ x 13¼ in.
(Sotheby's) **$360 £200**

W. OWEN - Portrait Of A Lady, half length, wearing a white dress - 29½ x 24½in.
(Christie's) **$360 £200**

DAVID OXTOBY - Elvis Presley - The Young King - signed - titled and dated '75 - coloured crayons - on paper - 10¼ x 6¾in.
(Sotheby's) **$1,372 £750**

NICOLAS MARIE OZANNE - Views Of Seine At Paris: the Ile de la Cite and the Louvre from the Pont Neuf; and the City from the Arsenal - black chalk, grey wash - 22.2 x 40.4cm.
(Christie's) **$1,170 £650 Two**

PAGGI - The Death Of Adonis - pen and brown ink - 27.1 x 19.8cm.
(Christie's) $45 £25

GEORGE PAICE - Sultan - signed - inscribed and dated - 13½ x 17½in.
(Sotheby's Belgravia) $54 £30

ANTHONIE PALAMEDESZ - A Merry Company In An Interior - indistinctly inscribed - on panel - 19 x 26in.
(Christie's N. York) $3,850 £2,104

GIUSEPPE PALIZZI - Three Donkeys - 14¾ x 18¼in.
(Christie's) $1,980 £1,100

G. PALIZZI - A Boating Party - 10¼ x 18¾in.
(Christie's) $1,080 £600

J. PALMA IL GIOVANE - The Flagellation - 73 x 47½in.
(Christie's) $1,710 £950

JACOPO PALMA, called Palma Il Giovane - The Pieta - signed - 64 x 43in.
(Christie's) $5,460 £3,000

PALMIERI - A Bust Of A Youth By A Plinth - pen and brown ink - 25.7 x 18.2cm.
(Christie's) $72 £40

PANNINI - The Nine Muses - oil - on canvas - 39¾ x 48in.
(Geering & Colyer) $1,757 £950

PANNINI

PANNINI - A Capriccio Of Roman Ruins - grey wash - 35.2 x 52.0cm.
(Christie's) **$162 £90**

G. PANNINI - A Capriccio Of The Colosseum And The Arch Of Constantine with figures in the foreground near a porphyry sarcophagus - 37½ x 39½in.
(Christie's) **$8,736 £4,800**

G. P. PANNINI - Classical Ruins with soldiers by a statue - 43 x 53in.
(Christie's) **$5,460 £3,000**

GIOVANNI PAULO PANNINI - The Interior Of Saint Peter's, Rome, with numerous figures - 57½ x 86½in.
(Christie's) **$436,800 £240,000**

G. P. PANNINI - A Capriccio With A Curving Colonnade - pen and brown ink, grey wash - 22.4 x 16.2cm.
(Christie's) **$90 £50**

PAOLETTI - Gondolas On The Bacino, Venice - signed - watercolour heightened with white - 42.5 x 17.1cm.
(Christie's) **$81 £45**

DOMINIQUE LOUIS FERREOL PAPETY - A Peasant Family - signed - watercolour heightened with white - 23.0 x 30.5cm.
(Christie's) **$504 £280**

JOHN PARDOE - A Gentleman, His Brown Hunter And Spaniel In A Street - 25 x 30in.
(Christie's) **$288 £160**

JAMES STUART PARK - Pansies - signed - 16 x 15¼in.
(Sotheby's Belgravia) **$324 £180**

JAMES STUART PARK - Red And White Roses - signed oval - 22¾ x 35in.
(Sotheby's Belgravia) **$576 £320**

J. STUART PARK - Red and White Roses - oval - 75 x 57cm.
(Edmiston's) **$414 £230**

J. STUART PARK - White And Pink Roses - oval - 58 x 48cm.
(Edmiston's) **$414 £230**

HENRY H. PARKER - A Rural River
Landscape - on canvas - 14 x 22in.
(King & Chasemore) **$1,440 £800**

HENRY H. PARKER - A Woody River
Landscape with a man in a punt cutting
reeds - signed - 23½ x 41½in.
(Christie's) **$1,852 £950**

HENRY H. PARKER - The River Llugwy,
Near Trefriw, North Wales - signed and
signed and inscribed on the reverse - 17½
x 39½in.
(Christie's) **$5,070 £2,600**

HENRY H. PARKER - Cattle In A
Wooded River Landscape - signed - 23
x 41in.
(Christie's) **$2,880 £1,600**

HENRY H. PARKER - A River Scene At
Elstead; Dunsfold, Near Cranleigh,
Surrey - signed - heightened with white -
14¼ x 21in.
(Sotheby's Belgravia) **$612 £340 Pair**

HENRY H. PARKER - A Wooded
River Landscape with cattle -
signed - 9½ x 13½in.
(Christie's) **$234 £130**

H. P. PARKER - Learning To Count -
17½ x 14¼in.
(Sotheby's Belgravia) **$504 £280**

HENRY PERLEE PARKER - "The
Opiate", interior scene with a woman
reading a book beside a girl sleeping
in a chair - on oak panel - 22 x 18in.
(Morphets of Harrogate) **$522 £290**

P. PARLE - The Oyster Seller - signed
and dated Dec. 18 - 28½ x 24in.
(Christie's) **$720 £400**

PARMIGIANINO

JOSEPH FRANCOIS PARROCEL -
The Baptist Preaching - inscribed -
black chalk, pen and grey ink,
grey wash - 18.2 x 24.8cm.
(Christie's) **$180 £100**

P. PARROCEL - A Horseman Issuing
Instructions And Soldiers Marching -
black chalks - 17.5 x 23.4cm.
(Christie's) **$68 £38**

FRANCESCO MAZZOLA BEDOLI,
called IL PARMIGIANINO - Portrait Of A
Collector, half length, seated in a window
embrasure; behind his right shoulder is a
marble relief of Venus, Cupid and Mars -
on panel - 35 x 25¼in.
(Christie's) **$1,170,000 £650,000**

PARRINI - Venice - signed - bodycolour
- 18.3 x 39.4cm.
(Christie's) **$50 £28**

EDMOND THOMAS PARRIS - 'Petruccio's
Courtship' - signed and dated 1864 - mill
board - 11½ x 13½in.
(Sotheby Bearne) **$468 £240**

C. PARROCEL - A Mounted Trumpeter -
the mount inscribed 'Parocel' - pen and
brown ink, brown wash - 21.9 x 16.4cm.
(Christie's) **$144 £80**

PHILIPPE PARROT - Moorish Women -
signed - on panel - 22 x 12in.
(Christie's) **$1,980 £1,100**

WILLIAM PARS - Harlech Castle In
Merioneth - inscribed - watercolour -
10½ x 14¾in.
(Christie's)   **$396 £220**

ALFRED WILDE PARSONS - Coastal
Scene with a castle on the cliffs and
numerous small vessels around the hulk
of a wrecked ship - signed and dated 1881
- 29½ x 49¼in.
(Sotheby Bearne)   **$1,014 £520**

ALFRED PARSONS - Allotments -
signed - 55½ x 71½in.
(Christie's)   **$90 £50**

ARTHUR WILDE PARSONS - Breakers
- signed and dated 1900 - 25½ x 41¼in.
(Sotheby's Belgravia)   **$45 £25**

LORENZO PASINELLI - Saint Catherine -
38½ x 28½in.
(Christie's)   **$2,002 £1,100**

ALBERTO PASINI - The Retreat -
signed and dated 1884 - 31½ x 47in.
(Christie's)   **$27,000 £15,000**

VICTOR PASMORE - Brush Drawing, 1964
signed with initials - pen, brush, black ink
and grey wash - 20 x 15¼in.
(Christie's)   **$512 £280**

ROBERT D. PASQUOLL - On The Clyde -
signed - 20 x 30in.
(Christie's S. Kensington) **$288 £160**

PASSE

C. VAN DER PASSE - A Warrior's Farewell - black chalk, pen and brown ink - 18.1 x 25.8cm.
(Christie's) **$21 £12**

CHARLES H. PASSEY - A Lane, Dorking, Surrey - signed - inscribed on the reverse - 23¼ x 19¼in.
(Sotheby's Belgravia) **$216 £120**

CHARLES H. PASSEY - Harvest Time - Cuffley - signed - canvas laid on board - 15½ x 43½in.
(Sotheby's Belgravia) **$144 £80**

LUDWIG PASSINI - The Confessional - signed and dated Rome 1863 - watercolour - 24.3 x 34.4cm.
(Christie's) **$234 £130**

PIERRE PATEL, THE YOUNGER - An Extensive Wooded Landscape, with travellers on a road and a river valley in the distance - signed and dated 1691 - on panel - 10¾ x 14¼in.
(Christie's N. York) **$4,620 £2,524**

DONALD A. PATON - The Trossachs Near Loch Venacher; Misty Evening Near Loch Moy - both signed - circular - diameter 11½in.
(Sotheby's Belgravia) **$50 £28 Pair**

SIR J. N. PATON - After The Chase - indistinctly dated - arched top - heightened with bodycolour - 6¾ x 8½in.
(Sotheby's Belgravia) **$342 £190**

RICHARD PATON, Attributed to - Dutch And British Men-O'-War At Sea - 31½ x 42in.
(Christie's N. York) **$935 £511**

EMILY M. PATTERSON - The Windmill On The Maas - watercolour - 11 x 15in.
(G. A. Key) **$45 £25**

DU PATY - French Artillery in action - signed - oil - on panel - 7½ x 9in.
(Warner, Sheppard & Wade) **$1,225 £625**

JOHN PAUL - A View Of Westminster Bridge From The River Thames - 28¾ x 46¼in.
(Christie's) **$270 £150**

JOHN PAUL - A View Of Chelsea Reach, including boats on the River Thames and figures and coaches by the riverside - signed - 29½ x 49¼in.
(Sotheby's) **$1,980 £1,100**

JOSEPH PAUL - An East Anglian Landscape - on panel - 12¾ x 16¾in.
(Sotheby's Belgravia) **$288 £160**

JOSEPH PAUL - Backwater On The Wensum with figure in boat and cottage in background - oil - 12 x 10in.
(G. A. Key) **$169 £94**

A. PAULIS - Portrait Of A Gentleman, small full length, in a dark blue coat and grey trousers, with a lady, seated, small full length in a white dress, in a landscape - indistinctly signed and dated 1819 - indistinctly inscribed on the reverse - 18½ x 15in.
(Christie's N. York) **$550 £300**

EUGENE PAVY - A Market Scene In Cairo - signed and dated 1885 - 27 x 38½in.
(Christie's) **$2,700 £1,500**

EUGENE PAVY - In The Bazaar - signed and dated 1863 - on panel - 15½ x 11½in.
(Christie's) **$1,080 £600**

EUGENE PAVY - The Snake Charmer - signed and dated 1886 - on panel - 14 x 22½in.
(Christie's) **$2,340 £1,300**

EUGENE PAVY - The Sentry - signed - on board - 27 x 12½in.
(Christie's) **$5,400 £3,000**

PHILIPPE PAVY - The Water Carrier - signed and dated Alger 1882 - 18½ x 28in.
(Christie's) **$2,160 £1,200**

PAVY

PHILIPPE PAVY - Figures Sitting In A
Courtyard - signed and dated 1887 - on
panel - 10¾ x 8½in.
(Christie's) **$2,160 £1,200**

PHILIPPE PAVY - Chess Players - Cairo -
signed and dated '90 - on panel - 15½ x
19in.
(Christie's) **$3,060 £1,700**

DAVID PAYNE - In Sutton Park, a summer sunlit wooded landscape with cattle at
pasture, the foreground with young girl
feeding a calf, an old lady and her grand-
daughter seated on a bench - signed -
inscribed on the reverse - oil - on canvas -
21½ x 15½in.
(Neales of Nottingham) **$1,621 £840**

WILLIAM PAYNE - The Surveyor -
12½ x 9¾in.
(Sotheby's) **$198 £110**

WILLIAM PAYNE - Devonport Barracks
- pen and black ink, and watercolour -
11 x 17in.
(Sotheby's) **$396 £220**

WILLIAM PAYNE - A Romantic
Landscape with a figure crossing a
rustic bridge - 5¾ x 8½in.
(Sotheby's) **$108 £60**

CORNELIUS PEARSON - Cattle By A
Lake - signed and dated 1861 - heightened
with bodycolour - 12 x 20in.
(Sotheby's Belgravia) **$68 £38**

R. PEARSON - Coastal Scene And
Rural Landscape - signed - on canvas -
7½ x 11½in.
(Morphets of Harrogate) **$207 £115 Pair**

W. H. PEARSON - Evening At Lime-
house - signed with initials and inscribed -
heightened with white - 14¼ x 21½in.
(Sotheby's Belgravia) **$81 £45**

CARL HENNING PEDERSEN - The
Lucky Red Bird - signed, inscribed
'New York' and dated 1974 - water-
colour - 30¼ x 22in.
(Christie's N. York) **$1,980 £1,100**

PEEL - A Showery Day, Kenilworth -
17 x 25½in.
(Sotheby's Belgravia) **$63 £35**

JAMES PEEL - A View Of Derwentwater
with a herdsman and cattle - bears
Creswick signature and dated 1860 - 19½
x 29½in.
(Christie's) **$288 £160**

JAMES PEEL - On Sapey Brook, Here-
fordshire - signed and dated 1868 -
signed, inscribed and dated on a label
on the reverse - 13 x 21in.
(Christie's) **$990 £550**

GILLIS PEETERS - Peasants And Travellers On A Path in a woody landscape -
indistinctly signed - on panel - 18¼ x 24in.
(Christie's) **$5,460 £3,000**

GILLIS PEETERS - An Extensive Wooded
Valley with a goatherd - bears monogram -
on panel - 11 x 17½in.
(Christie's) **$9,000 £5,000**

T. K. PELHAM - A Man And Woman In
Gipsy Type Attire With Mules, resting
on a mountain path, entitled "A Rest By
The Way" - oil - 24 x 19½in.
(Richard Baker & Baker) **$234 £130**

HONORE PELLEGRIN - 'Cadmus Of
Boston. George Brown', a full rigged
ship sailing from the Port Of Marseilles -
signed and dated 1829 - watercolour -
17½ x 23½in.
(Richard A. Bourne Co. Inc.) **$5,200 £2,888**

GIOVANNI ANTONIO PELLEGRINI -
The Marriage At Cana - 24 x 34½in.
(Christie's) **$20,020 £11,000**

GIOVANNI ANTONIO PELLEGRINI -
The Continence Of Scipio - 51¼ x 41½in.
(Christie's) **$6,840 £3,800**

FRANCESCO PELUSO - Interiors
With Italian Peasants Courting - one
signed - 15 x 10in.
(Christie's) **$720 £400 Pair**

PENLEY

AARON PENLEY - Llyn Y Cwm Fynnon - signed, extensively inscribed on the reverse and dated 1866 - 14½ x 29½in.
(Sotheby's)   **$144   £80**

HARRY PENNELL - A Cornfield At Hackfield - signed - 13¾ x 20½in.
(Sotheby's Belgravia)   **$126   £70**

JOHANNES PENNIS - A River Landscape - signed - on panel - 14¼ x 19¼in.
(Sotheby's)   **$3,330 £1,800**

SAMUEL JOHN PEPLOE - Ile De Brehat, Brittany - signed - on board - 12½ x 15½in.
(Sotheby's Belgravia)   **$3,420 £1,900**

SAMUEL JOHN PEPLOE - A Reclining Girl Reading - signed - coloured chalks - on buff paper - 14½ x 18¾in.
(Sotheby's Belgravia)   **$864   £480**

SAMUEL JOHN PEPLOE - Royan - signed - on board - 10½ x 13½in.
(Sotheby's Belgravia)   **$2,700 £1,500**

PERCY - "The Strid, Bolton Wood, Yorkshire" - oil - 15½ x 25in.
(Warner, Sheppard & Wade)
                              $627   £320

H. PERCIVAL - The 'Glenlora' In Full Sail - inscribed - watercolour, heightened with white - 17¼ x 25¾in.
(Sotheby's Belgravia) **$216   £120**

SIDNEY RICHARD PERCY - A Heath Scene Near Leatherhead, Surrey - signed and dated 1849 - 15½ x 23½in.
(Christie's)   **$3,705 £1,900**

SIDNEY RICHARD PERCY - Llyn Dinas, North Wales - signed and dated 1872 - 23½ x 39¼in.
(Christie's)   **$1,440 £800**

SIDNEY RICHARD PERCY - Llanberis, North Wales - signed and dated 1871 - 23¼ x 39¼in.
(Christie's) $5,400 £3,000

WILLIAM PERRY - Courting Couples By A Well And By A Stile - both signed and dated '57 - 25¼ x 19¼in.
(Sotheby's Belgravia) $658 £350 **Pair**

PERUGINO, School of - The Madonna And Child, with seraphs, set in a landscape - on panel - 17 x 12in.
(Christie's) $4,732 £2,600

CHARLES EDWARD PERUGINI - At The Well - signed with monogram - 52½ x 28in.
(Christie's) $2,535 £1,300

SIMONE CANTARINI, called IL PESARESE - Portrait Of An Elderly Gentleman, bust length, wearing black costume - oval - 27 x 20in.
(Christie's) $7,560   £4,200

345

ANTOINE PESNE - Portrait Of A Gentleman, half length, wearing a brown coat with white cravat - 32½ x 25in.
(Christie's) **$2,160** **£1,200**

E. PETERINI - A View Of Venice From The Grand Canal - signed - oil - on board - 7 x 11¾in.
(Buckell & Ballard) **$90 £50**

BONAVENTURA PETERS - A Galley - black chalk - 16.8 x 28.3cm.
(Christie's) **$126** **£70**

ABRAHAM PETHER - An Extensive Moonlit River Landscape with numerous cottages and windmill - signed - oil - on canvas - 24 x 29in.
(Bonham's) **$1,564 £850**

ABRAHAM PETHER - An Extensive Wooded Landscape at sunset with figures in the foreground and a town beyond - signed and dated 1811 - on panel - 9 x 12in.
(Christie's) **$54 £30**

HENRY PETHER - A View On The River Thames, with Lambeth Palace in the foreground and the Houses of Parliament, under construction, beyond - 23¼ x 35¼in.
(Christie's) **$8,640 £4,800**

HENRY PETHER - A Moonlit View Of The Grand Canal, Venice, with Santa Maria Della Salute - signed - 23½ x 35½in.
(Christie's) **$54 £30**

SEBASTIAN PETHER - An Italianate River Landscape at sunset - signed with initials and dated 1839 - 13 x 16½in.
(Christie's) **$1,620 £900**

SEBASTIAN PETHER - A Moonlight Harbour Scene, with figure and vessels and a town beyond - signed and dated 1819 - 27¼ x 35¼in.
(Christie's) **$45 £25**

AUGUST VON PETTENKOFEN -
Portrait Of A Girl, bust length - oval -
21 x 17in.
(Christie's) **$1,260** **£700**

PETTIT - Men In Punt On River With
Castle background - oil - 18 x 24in.
(G. A. Key) **$54** **£30**

EDWIN ALFRED PETTITT - Bowness
Knott and Pillar Mountain, Emmerdale
- signed and dated 1877 - 20 x 34in.
(Christie's S. Kensington) **$468** **£260**

JOSEPH PAUL PETTITT - On The
River Neckar, Germany, with a view of
Heidelberg - signed and dated 1847 -
signed, inscribed and dated on the reverse
- 36 x 52in.
(Christie's) **$2,160** **£1,200**

JOSEPH PAUL PETTITT - An Alpine
Landscape with peasants, cattle and goats
in the foreground, a town and castle on a
cliff beyond - signed and dated '68 - 22½
x 35in.
(Christie's) **$1,755** **£900**

JOSEPH PAUL PETTITT - A Winter Landscape with a Continental town on a river
and figures on a path in the foreground -
signed and dated 1868 - 47¾ x 72in.
(Christie's) **$1,710** **£950**

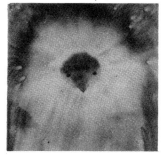

HENRI PFEIFFER - Oiseau - mono-
grammed and dated '30 - watercolour on
blotting paper - 47.5 x 31cm.
(Christian Rosset) **$256** **£140**

JOHN PHILLIP - Hidalgo - 35½ x
27½in.
(Sotheby's Belgravia) **$720** **£400**

347

PHILLIPS

CHARLES PHILLIPS - Portrait Of Sir
Peter And Lady Denis, small full length,
in a coastal landscape with a man-o'-war
beyond - 21½ x 24½in.
(Christie's) **$3,240 £1,800**

F. A. PHILLIPS - Playing With The
Doll - signed and dated 1890 - on
board - 8 x 9½in.
(Christie's) **$54 £30**

PETER PHILLIPS - "You never can tell" -
signed - dated '63 - charcoal - on paper -
24¾ x 20¼in.
(Sotheby's) **$439 £240**

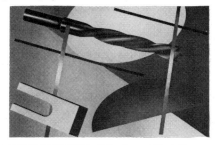

PETER PHILLIPS - Selectomat Variation
No 11 - signed, inscribed and dated '73-'74
on the reverse - acrylic - 35¾ x 52in.
(Christie's) **$2,745 £1,500**

PIAZZETTA - Head Of A Girl Looking
Up To The Left - black and white
chalk on grey paper - 32.8 x 28.9cm.
(Christie's) **$153 £85**

PICART - A Greek Horseman With A
Standard - grey wash - 27.4 x 18.7cm.
(Christie's) **$54 £30**

B. PICART - Sheets Of Studies Of Figures
And Heads - pen and brown ink - 9.1 x
13.7cm.
(Christie's) **$198 £110 Four**

B. PICART - The Sleeping Gladiator -
black chalk, watermark - 31.0 x 23.2cm.
(Christie's) **$58 £32**

BERNARD PICART - Rebecca And
Eliezer At The Well - inscribed 'Picard'
on the reverse - pen and grey ink, grey
wash - 21.9 x 15.2cm.
(Christie's) **$117 £65**

C. E. PICAULT - Rural Rock-Strewn
And Wooded Scene With Pond - signed -
oil - 9 x 12in.
(Richard Baker & Baker) **$198 £110**

FREDERICK RICHARD PICKERSGILL
- The Faerie Queen - inscribed on the
mount - pen and sepia ink - 9¼ x 18½in.
(Sotheby's Belgravia) **$14 £8**

HENRY WILLIAM PICKERSGILL -
Portrait Of A Girl Holding A Dove -
29½ x 24½in.
(Sotheby Bearne) **$244 £125**

GUSTAVE LOUIS MARIE PIERON -
A Woodland Landscape With A Shepherd
And Sheep, a faggot gatherer and other
figures - signed - dated 1860 - 23¾ x 32¼in.
(Lawrence) **$1,530 £850**

S. PIGNONI - Saint Rosalie - 31 x 52½in.
(Christie's)   **$4,004 £2,200**

SIMONE PIGNONI - Saint Scholastica -
33½ x 28in.
(Christie's)   **$3,600 £2,000**

WILLIAM CHARLES PIGUENIT - Boys
In Boats By A River - signed - oil - on
board - 5 x 10in.
(Sotheby's)   **$733 £380**

WILLIAM CHARLES PIGUENIT -
Fishermen Hauling In A Net At The
Bend In A River - signed - oil - on
board - 5 x 9¾in.
(Sotheby's)   **$926 £480**

RODOLPHE PIGUET - An Interior With
Porcelain On A Draped Table - signed - 9½ x
12½in.
(Christie's)   **$1,350   £750**

HENRY PILLEAU - The Great Temple
Of Kernae, Thebes - signed with monogram - signed and inscribed on an old
label on the reverse - 24½ x 16½in.
(Christie's)   **$270 £150**

J. B. PILLEMENT - A Rocky Coastal
Landscape with sailing ships in a storm -
18 x 28in.
(Christie's)   **$2,880 £1,600**

J. B. PILLEMENT - Decorative Panels
In The Chinese Taste - pencil on tracing
paper - 30.3 x 20.8cm.
(Christie's)   **$306   £170 Pair**

JEAN PILLEMENT - A Wooded River
Landscape with figures and a water-mill
beyond - signed and dated 1748 - 7¾ x 11½in.
(Christie's)   **$9,000 £5,000**

GEORGE PINE - Eton College And The
Chapel seen from the bridge - signed and
dated 1851 - 8¾ x 12¼in.
(Sotheby's)   **$1,350   £750**

GEORGE JOHN PINWELL - The
Tryst - signed with monogram - 5¾
x 6¼in.
(Christie's)   **$234 £130**

DOMENICO PIOLA - The Education Of
The Virgin - pen and wash drawing - 15
x 21cm.
(Christian Rosset)   **$864 £480**

ADOLPHE PIOT - 'Thoughts': study of a
lady, bust length - signed - 18 x 14½in.
(Christie's)   **$1,080 £600**

JOHN PIPER - Halifax - signed and dated
'63 - gouache - 24 x 33cm.
(King & Chasemore)   **$510 £260**

HENRI PITCHER - A Found Treasure -
signed and dated 1901 - 11½ x 9½in.
(Sotheby's Belgravia)   **$144 £80**

WILLIAM PITT - Near Cheddar, Somerset,
mountainous summer river landscapes with
figures and thatched cottages - both signed
and dated 1867 - oil - on board - 7½ x
9¾in.
(Neales of Nottingham) **$598 £310 Pair**

WILLIAM PITT - Old Farm Yard At Beer,
Near Calyton, Devon - signed with monogram and dated 1860 - signed, inscribed
and dated 1860 on the reverse - 10½ x
17¼in.
(Christie's)   **$780 £400**

PITTONI - An Angel With A Lute - red
chalk - 25.8 x 35.2cm.
(Christie's)   **$126 £70**

GIOVANNI BATTISTA PITTONI -
Alexander's Triumphal Entry Into
Babylon - 24 x 31in.
(Christie's)   **$18,000 £10,000**

ANDRE PLANSON - Nude - signed -
watercolour - 63 x 48cm.
(Christian Rosset)   **$393 £215**

ANTOINE EMILE PLASSAN - Sugar For
Her Favourite - signed and dated - on
panel - 13 x 11½in.
(Christie's)   **$3,240   £1,800**

JAMES CHARLES PLAYFAIR - A
London Flower Seller - signed and
dated - heightened with bodycolour -
13 x 9½in.
(Sotheby's Belgravia)   **$153   £85**

N. POCOCK - 'The Wreck Of The Magni-
ficent' - watercolour - 26½ x 18in.
(Dacre, Son & Hartley) **$270 £140**

E. VAN DER POEL - A Coastal
Landscape with shipping and fisherfolk
- on panel - 11¼ x 18¼in.
(Christie's)   **$2,880 £1,600**

E. VAN DER POEL - A Village With
Travellers By An Inn - bears initials
CWZ and dated 1663 - on panel -
17¾ x 25in.
(Christie's)   **$5,760 £3,200**

POELENBURGH

CORNELIS POELENBURGH, Attributed to - The Child On The Red Cloth - oil - on panel - 11 x 13.5cm.
(Christian Rosset) $239 £133

C. VAN POELENBURGH - The Rest On The Flight Into Egypt - oil - on canvas - 9¼ x 12¾in.
(Bonham's) $1,800 £1,000

CORNELIS VAN POELENBURGH, Attributed to - Elijah The Prophet - oil - on copper - 23 x 31cm.
(Christian Rosset) $527 £293

SERGE POLIAKOFF - Composition Orange - signed - gouache - 24 x 18in.
(Sotheby's) $3,477 £1,900

SERGE POLIAKOFF - Bleu Rouge Noir - signed - 38½ x 51in.
(Christie's) $16,470 £9,000

SERGE POLIAKOFF - Composition Bleue Grise - signed - oil - on canvas - 32 x 25½in.
(Sotheby's) $9,150 £5,000

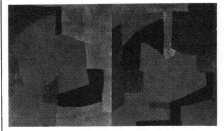

SERGE POLIAKOFF - Double Composition Abstraite - signed twice - gouache - 25¼ x 38½in.
(Sotheby's) $5,856 £3,200

POLIDORO - The Execution Of A Saint With Roman Soldiers Looking On - pen and brown ink - 21.4 x 32.6cm.
(Christie's) $90 £50

JAMES POLLARD - A Royal Mail Coach on a flooded road in a river valley - 20 x 29¼in.
(Christie's) $32,400 £18,000

JAMES POLLARD - Stakes And Trotters
- signed and dated 1851 - 8¼ x 11¼in.
(Christie's)   **$900 £500**

ALFRED POLLENTINE - A View Of
Constantinople, with shipping - signed
and dated '78 - 29½ x 49½in.
(Christie's)   **$36 £20**

ALFRED POLLENTINE - The Grand
Canal; and The Ducal Palace, Venice -
both signed and dated '84 - 15½ x
23½in.
(Christie's)   **$1,440 £800 Pair**

ALBERT POLLITT - Delamere Forest -
watercolour - 13 x 7in.
(Andrew Hilditch & Son)
    $27 £15

JACKSON POLLOCK - Untitled 1951 -
43 x 51.5cm.
(Auktionshaus am Neumarkt)
    $27,803 £15,193

POMERANCIO - Charity - pen and
grey ink, grey wash - 19.7 x 14.4cm.
(Christie's)   **$54 £30**

SERGE PONOMAREW - White water-
lilies - signed - oil - on panel - 33 x 46cm.
(Christian Rosset)   **$393 £215**

JAMES POOLE - Above A Highland
Loch - signed - 27¼ x 41¼in.
(Sotheby's Belgravia)   **$720 £400**

JAMES POOLE - A Wooded River Landscape - signed - 19 x 29½in.
(Christie's)   **$720 £400**

LARRY POONS - Untitled - acrylic on
canvas - 96 x 74½in.
(Christie's N. York)   **$7,150 £3,972**

POONS

LARRY POONS - Untitled P26 - signed and dated 1974 on the reverse - 77½ x 61in.
(Christie's N. York)   **$6,600 £3,667**

W. L POPE - Faith, Hope And Charity; The Arts; The Feast - one signed and inscribed - two 16 x 55in. and one 16½ x 44in.
(Sotheby's Belgravia)   **$216 £120 Three**

FERDINANDO PORTA - Portrait Of A Prelate, half length, in an interior - black chalk, brown wash - 25.2 x 18.8cm.
(Christie's)   **$36 £20**

C. PORTELLI - The Holy Family With The Infant Saint John The Baptist - on panel - 41 x 29½in.
(Christie's)   **$2,160 £1,200**

GERARD PORTIELJE - The Pedlar - signed - on panel - 5 x 7½in.
(Christie's)   **$4,140 £2,300**

GERARD PORTIELJE - The Attorney - signed and inscribed 'Autwerpen' - 16½ x 20½in.
(Christie's)   **$16,200 £9,000**

FRANS JANSZ. POST - The Ruins Of The Basilica Of San Salvador At Olinda with an extensive Brazilian landscape beyond - signed - on panel - 21 x 27in.
(Christie's)   **$118,300 £65,000**

FRANS JANSZ. POST - Panoramic View Of Olinda, in the distance, the harbour and the two white towers of the residence of Prince Maurice of Nassau, Governor of Brazil - signed and dated 1665 - 31½ x 43¼in.
(Christie's)   **$180,000 £100,000**

LASLETT J. POTT - A Toast Henry VIII And Ann Boleyn - signed - oil - on canvas - 44½ x 35in.
(Swetenham's) **$1,710 £900**

LASLETT JOHN POTT - "Catherine Douglas Barring The Door With Her Arm Against The Assassins Of James I Of Scotland in the Monastery of the Black Friars, Perth, 1437" - signed and dated 1879 - 37¼ x 59¼in.
(Sotheby Bearne) **$1,800 £1,000**

BEATRIX POTTER - Study Of Berries - watercolour - 10 x 8in.
(G. A. Key) **$76 £42**

SYDNEY POTTER - The Haymaker - signed - inscribed on the reverse - 45 x 33½in.
(Sotheby's Belgravia) **$810 £450**

POURBUS - Portrait Head Of A Woman In A Fur Cape - black chalk - 10.5 x 8.8cm.
(Christie's) **$153 £85**

C. M. POWELL - A Dutch River Scene, a ferry boat and barges in the foreground - signed - 11 x 16½in.
(Sotheby's) **$4,140 £2,300**

C. M. POWELL - British Men-Of-War And Other Shipping Off The Coast in choppy seas - signed and dated 1820 - 52½ x 72in.
(Sotheby's) **$6,480 £3,600**

C. M. POWELL - A British Man-Of-War And Other Shipping In Choppy Seas - signed - on panel - 7½ x 10½in.
(Sotheby's) **$1,350 £750**

C. M. POWELL - A 'botter' And Other Shipping On The Ijselmeer - 24 x 36in.
(Lawrence) **$2,430 £1,350**

SIR EDWARD JOHN POYNTER - A
Little Mishap - signed with monogram
and dated 1912 - in original classical
frame - 49½ x 39½in.
(Christie's)   **$7,560 £4,200**

SIR EDWARD JOHN POYNTER -
A Study For 'The Ides Of March' -
signed with monogram and dated
1881 - 16 x 11in.
(Christie's)   **$126 £70**

**LODEWYK TOEPUT, IL
POZZOSERRATO** - An Allegory Of
Summer: a lady in a wooded landscape
with baskets of fruit and vegetables, and
figures harvesting beyond - 73¼ x 46½in.
(Christie's)   **$6,916 £3,800**

ATTILIO PRATELLA - Crab Catchers,
Corsica, harbour scene with fishing
boats and figures, buildings beyond -
signed - panel - 8¼ x 13½in.
(H. Spencer & Sons)   **$2,430 £1,350**

JONATHAN PRATT - Feeding Pet
Rabbits - signed with initials and dated
1867 - heightened with white - 12¼ x
10in.
(Sotheby's Belgravia) **$396   £220**

**THE MASTER OF THE ASHMOLEAN
PREDELLA** - The Madonna And Child
Enthroned, between the Baptist, Saint Peter,
Saint Lawrence, Saint Zenobius, Saint
Catherine, Saint Lucy, Saint Anthony Abbot
and Saint Eustace - on gold ground panel -
arched top - 28¾ x 16¼in.
(Christie's)   **$27,000 £15,000**

PRINSEP

J. PRESTON - Still Lifes Of Roses And Fruit - signed - 12 x 24in.
(Sotheby's Belgravia) **$270 £150 Pair**

AMADEO COUNT PREZIOSI - Constantinople - signed and dated 1865 - pencil and watercolour heightened with white and gold - 27.6 x 41.4cm.
(Christie's) **$252 £140**

EDWARD PRICE - Norwegian River Scene with waterfalls - inscribed on the reverse - mill board - 23 x 18in.
(Sotheby Bearne) **$99 £55**

ALOIS PRIECHENFRIED - The Chess Players - 20 x 16in.
(Christie's) **$1,260 £700**

PRIMATICCIO, After - Moses Striking The Rock - traces of a ruled margin at the top and the two sides - on panel - 9 x 6¾in.
(Christie's) **$1,980 £1,100**

PRIMATICCIO - Parnassus - pen and brown ink brown wash heightened with white - 26.2 x 26.2cm.
(Christie's) **$252 £140**

E. R. PRINSEP - A Mountain Lake View - signed and dated 1836 - watercolour - 8¾ x 12½ in.
(Sotheby's, Hong Kong) **$207 £115**

VALENTINE CAMERON PRINSEP - The Harvest Of Spring - signed and inscribed on an old label on the reverse - 34 x 38½in.
(Christie's) **$6,120 £3,400**

WILLIAM PRINSEP - A Street Scene, Canton, a tea shop to the left, a meat shop to the right - inscribed - watercolour - 12¾ x 9 in.
(Sotheby's, Hong Kong) **$1,454 £808**

357

WILLIAM PRINSEP - A Street behind the factories, Canton - signed and dated 1839 - waterco.our - 9¼ x 11¼in.
(Sotheby's, Hong Kong) **$702 £390**

EDWARD PRITCHETT - An Extensive View Of Venice From The Bacino Di San Marco - signed and dated 1857 - 25¾ x 43½in.
(Christie's) **$17,550 £9,000**

EDWARD PRITCHETT - The Piazzetta, Venice - bears David Roberts signature and the date 1846 - 20½ x 16½in.
(Christie's) **$3,510 £1,800**

EDWARD PRITCHETT - The Fish Market At Calais - 13½ x 17½in.
(Christie's) **$780 £400**

M. PROCTOR - 'Coastal Scenes' - signed and dated - oil - on board - 10 x 14in.
(Lalonde Bros. & Parham) **$82 £45 Pair**

CORNELIS PRONCK - The Castle At Abcoude - inscribed - pen and grey ink - 6.8 x 8.8cm.
(Christie's) **$54 £30**

S. PROUT - "Italian Piazza With Cathedral And Figures" - signed - on card - 12¼ x 18¼in.
(Walker, Barnett & Hill) **$126 £70**

SAMUEL PROUT - Rouen - pencil and watercolour, heightened with body-colour on buff paper - 14 x 9¾in.
(Sotheby's) **$432 £240**

SAMUEL PROUT - A Capriccio View Of The Market Place At Wurzburg - signed - pen and brown and blue ink and watercolour heightened with white - 17 x 11¾in.
(Christie's) **$3,420 £1,900**

SAMUEL PROUT - "Venetian Waterfront" - watercolour - 8 x 5in.
(Andrew Hilditch & Son) **$90 £50**

SAMUEL PROUT - Old House By The River, Strasbourg - heightened with white - 10½ x 8in.
(Sotheby's) **$432 £240**

ALFRED PROVIS - A Kitchen Interior With A Girl Seated By A Hearth Peeling Turnips - signed and dated 1872 - oil - on panel - 9 x 11½in.
(Bonham's) **$1,980 £1,100**

ALFRED PROVIS - A Kitchen Interior - on panel - 11¾ x 16in.
(Christie's) **$432 £240**

PRUD'HON - A Putto With A Dragon - black chalk on grey-blue paper - 22.0 x 27.6cm.
(Christie's) **$144 £80**

THOMAS PRYTHERCH - The Vernon Tombs In Tong Church, Salop - signed and dated 1903 - heightened with bodycolour - 16¼ x 14¼in.
(Sotheby's Belgravia) **$45 £25**

J. PUDDAY - Street Scene With Bridge - oil - 16 x 22in.
(G. A. Key) **$18 £10**

AUGUSTUS CHARLES DE PUGIN - View Of Greenwich Hospital from the West India West Docks, Blackwall, taken at sunset - signed, inscribed and dated July 1803 on the reverse - pencil and grey wash - 6¼ x 13in.
(Christie's) **$117 £65**

AUGUSTUS WELBY PUGIN - Queen Elizabeth Receiving The Bishops In The Dining Hall, Hampton Court Palace - pen and ink and watercolour, heightened with white - 10½ x 11¾in.
(Sotheby's) **$288 £160**

PURCHASE

ALFRED PURCHASE - Lands End And
Scilly - heightened with bodycolour -
10½ x 14½in.
(Sotheby's Belgravia)   **$14   £8**

PIETER DE PUTTER - A Still Life Of
Freshwater Fish - signed in monogram -
32½ x 38¾in.
(Sotheby's)   **$8,140 £4,400**

ADAM PYNACKER - A Mountainous Coastal
Landscape, with figures and cattle - on panel -
23¾ x 35¾in.
(Christie's)   **$68,400   £38,000**

GEORGE PYNE - Magdalen Bridge, Oxford
looking from the East towards Magdalen
College and the High - signed and dated
1850 - 8½ x 12¼ in.
(Sotheby's)   **$1,170 £650**

J. B. PYNE - 'Raveno On The Lago
Maggiore' - signed and dated 1864 - oil ·
32½ x 23½in.
(Dacre, Son & Hartley) **$2,316 £1,200**

J. B. PYNE - A Venetian Canal Scene
with shipping and figures - a tondo -
10¼in. diameter.
(Warner, Sheppard & Wade) **$627 £320**

J. B. PYNE - A Continental Lake Scene -
watercolour - 15 x 14in.
(Andrew Hilditch & Son) **$135 £75**

J. B. PYNE - A Classical Landscape -
signed - on board - 10½ x 14in.
(Sotheby's Belgravia)   **$200 £110**

JAMES BAKER PYNE - Figures By A
Watermill In The Alps - signed and dated
1865 and numbered 635 - 22½ x 32½in.
(Christie's)   **$1,950 £1,000**

360

LAM QUA - A Fish Seller and other figures by a river - inscribed on the reverse - 8¾ x 7½in.
(Christie's) **$576 £320**

LAM QUA - An Old Man And A Boy In A Landscape - inscribed on the reverse - 6 x 4¾in.
(Christie's) **$810 £450**

MARTIN FERDINAND QUADAL - A Spaniel Flushing A Mallard - signed and dated 1788 - 25½ x 30in.
(Christie's) **$780 £400**

QUELLINUS - The Virgin And Child - pen and brown ink, brown wash - 31.2 x 17.7cm.
(Christie's) **$45 £25**

QUELLINUS - The Penitent Magdalen - 32 x 43¼in.
(Christie's) **$624 £320**

E. QUELLINUS - The Holy Family On A Terrace with a landscape beyond - 33 x 47½in.
(Christie's) **$1,116 £600**

J. E. QUELLINUS - The Release Of Saint Peter - 25 x 19in.
(Christie's) **$360 £200**

ERASMUS QUELLINUS, Circle of - Saint Jerome Succoured By The Angels - 11¾ x 15¼in.
(Christie's N. York) **$440 £240**

CECIL WATSON QUINNELL - The Season's Greetings - signed and dated 1907 and 1908 - 13½ x 9½in.
(Sotheby's Belgravia) **$188 £100 Pair**

LOUIS QUILICI - Scene Rural - signed - oil - on canvas - 20¾ x 31in.
(Sotheby's) **$107 £60**

ALPHONSE QUIZET - Les Jardins et le Moulin de la Galette, Montmartre - signed - on board - 27 x 25cm.
(Christie's) **$589 £320**

R

ABRAHAM RADEMAKER - Restes De
La Maison De Hyde, Derriere Leyerdorp -
inscribed on the reverse and on the mount
- pen and brown ink, brown wash - 9.7 x
15.7cm.
(Christie's)   **$144**   **£80**

SIR HENRY RAEBURN - Portrait Of
Lady Campbell, seated three-quarter
length, wearing a white dress, in a landscape - 28½ x 24in.
(Christie's)   **$3,060**   **£1,700**

SIR HENRY RAEBURN - Portrait Of
Captain James Drummond, half length,
wearing dark uniform and gold epaulettes
- 29½ x 24½in.
(Christie's)   **$1,800**   **£1,000**

SIR HENRY RAEBURN - Portrait Of
The Reverend Dr Thomas Fleming, half
length - 29½ x 24½in.
(Sotheby's Belgravia)   **$450**   **£250**

SIR HENRY RAEBURN - A Portrait Of
Lady Nasmyth, in a white dress and brown
shawl, seated at a table, holding a book -
35¼ x 25¼in.
(Christie's)   **$1,800**   **£1,000**

VICTOR NOBLE RAINBIRD - Rouen;
Coming Out Of Church - both signed -
one inscribed - 10 x 6¾in.
(Sotheby's Belgravia)   **$47**   **£26 Pair**

AUGUSTE RAFFET - Military Scene -
signed - sepia - 19.5 x 13cm.
(Christian Rosset)   **$265**   **£148**

ARNULF RAINER - Ohne Title - signed
and dated '60-61 on the reverse - 19¾ x
27½in.
(Christie's)   **$2,379**   **£1,300**

ARNULF RAINER - Berg Karmel - signed, inscribed with title and dated 1962/63 on the reverse - oil and chalk on canvas - 26 x 20in.
(Christie's) $2,562 £1,400

THEODORE JACQUES RALLI - Repos Au Bain - signed and dated '88 and signed and inscribed on an old label on the reverse - 18 x 15in.
(Christie's) $6,840 £3,800

THEODORE JACQUES RALLI - Lighting The Hookah - signed and dated '79 - 15½ x 12in.
(Christie's) $4,680 £2,600

THEODORE JACQUES RALLI - Boa Charmer In A Harem In Cairo - signed and dated 1882 - 25½ x 36½in.
(Christie's) $5,400 £3,000

A. RAMSAY - Portrait Of A Gentleman, half length, wearing a brown jacket, a white waistcoat embroidered with gold and a white stock; Portrait Of A Lady, half length, wearing a blue dress trimmed with white lace and decorated with pearls - both in painted ovals - 29¼ x 24¼in.
(Sotheby's) $900 £500 Pair

ALLAN RAMSAY - Portrait Of A Gentleman, standing three-quarter length, wearing a buff coat and red breeches, with flute music on a pedestal beside him - signed and dated 1741 - 49½ x 38in.
(Christie's) $3,960 £2,200

ALLAN RAMSAY - Portrait Of A Lady, half length, wearing a white dress, grey ermine lined cloak and white bonnet - 29¼ x 24¼in.
(Christie's) $756 £420

ALLAN RAMSAY - Portrait Of A Lady, half length, in a blue dress and mop cap - signed and dated 1749 - in a painted oval - 29¼ x 24¼in.
(Christie's)   **$8,640 £4,800**

ALLAN RAMSAY - Portrait Of Colonel James Dallas, half length, wearing a grey coat - signed and dated 1740 - in a painted oval - 29½ x 24½in.
(Christie's)   **$1,260 £700**

ALLAN RAMSAY - Portrait Of A Scholar, half length, holding a book, wearing a brown jacket and black gown - 30¼ x 25¾in.
(Christie's)   **$1,080 £600**

ALLAN RAMSAY - Portrait Of Lady Caroline Peachey, half length, wearing a white dress and blue shawl - 29½ x 24½in.
(Christie's)   **$900 £500**

JAMES RAMSAY - Reliving Old Battles Over A Glass Of Ale - signed and dated 1848 - 29½ x 24½in.
(Sotheby's)   **$810 £450**

J. RAOUX - Study Of A Lady Wearing A Flower-Trimmed Dress, Hooded Cloak, and holding a handmirror, a female servant stands behind - 20 x 17in.
(H. Spencer & Sons)   **$396 £220**

RAPPINI - The Rialto, Venice - signed - watercolour heightened with white - 34.0 x 23.8cm.
(Christie's)   **$81 £45**

R. RAPPINI - On The Nile - signed - heightened with bodycolour - 10½ x 14¾in.
(Sotheby's Belgravia)   **$22 £12 Pair**

HEINRICH RASCH - Spring Time, Bavaria - signed - inscribed and dated Munchen Mursch '78 - 14 x 27½in.
(Christie's)   **$3,960 £2,200**

HAROLD S. RATHBONE - Portrait Of Gabriel - signed with monogram - dated 1910 - heightened with bodycolour - 11¼ x 9½in.
(Sotheby's Belgravia)   **$25 £14**

G. D. RAWLINSON - Hunting Scenes - signed - 28 x 19½ in.
(Phillips, Solihull)   **$1,757 £950 pair**

HAROLD S. RATHBONE - Portrait Of Miss Evelyn Cunningham - signed with monogram - dated 1900 - coloured chalk - 24 x 19¾in.
(Sotheby's Belgravia)   **$324 £180**

HAROLD S. RATHBONE - Summer - inscribed - heightened with bodycolour - 9½ x 13½in.
(Sotheby's Belgravia)   **$252 £140**

GIUSEPPE RECCO - A Basket Of Lobsters And Fish On A Stone Ledge - indistinctly signed - 38 x 28¾in.
(Christie's)   **$9,900 £5,500**

JULES RAVEL - Marie De Medici And The Fortune Teller - signed and dated 1863 - 25 x 20in.
(Christie's)   **$1,530   £850**

ARTHUR W. REDGATE - A Woodland Glade - signed - inscribed on the reverse - 19¾ x 16¾in.
(Sotheby's Belgravia)   **$432 £240**

RICHARD REDGRAVE - The Haunt Of The Moorhen - signed and dated 1846 - signed and inscribed on an old label on the reverse - on panel - 7¾ x 11¾in.
(Christie's) **$135 £75**

E. K. REDMORE - A Busy Shipping Lane with fishing boats - signed - oil - on board - oval - 6 x 8in.
(Neales of Nottingham) **$289 £150**

HENRY REDMORE - Studies Of Men-O'-War and other shipping in rough and calm seas - signed and dated 1854 - canvas - on panel - oval - 9¾ x 13¼in.
(Sotheby Bearne) **$720 £400**

HENRY REDMORE - The Men-of-War becalmed in estuary - signed and dated 1856.
(Dee & Atkinson) **$4,320 £2,400**

H. T. REDWAY - Still Life Of Fruit On A Ledge - signed and dated 1903 - 17¾ x 22in.
(Sotheby's Belgravia) **$18 £10**

JOHN ROBERTSON REID - A Great Grandmother, Zandvoort, Holland - signed and dated 1876 - inscribed on the reverse - 23½ x 19¾in.
(Sotheby's Belgravia) **$180 £100**

REINAGLE - The Prior Family gathered in an interior by a garden door - 25 x 34½in.
(Sotheby's) **$1,080 £600**

PHILIP REINAGLE - Lord Middleton Out Grouse Shooting, his three pointers at work - signed and dated 1792 - 45 x 67in.
(Sotheby's) **$9,900 £5,500**

R. R. REINAGLE - A Gentleman Out Shooting With His Dogs - 32 x 43in.
(Sotheby's) **$2,880 £1,600**

RAMSAY RICHARD REINAGLE - Portrait Of James Whiting Yorke The Elder, Lieutenant-Colonel Of The Royal Supplementary Lincolnshire Militia, half length, wearing a dark coat and white cravat - signed and dated 1801 - 29½ x 24¼in.
(Sotheby's) **$900 £500**

RAMSAY RICHARD REINAGLE - A View Of Monte Finestra from the great road leading into the town of La Cava, Kingdom of Naples - signed - inscribed on the reverse - dated 1807 - 18½ x 23¾in.
(Sotheby's)   **$252   £140**

REMBRANDT, Manner of - A Bearded Oriental, half length - on panel - 17½ x 12½in.
(Christie's N. York)   **$1,100   £601**

JEAN CHARLES JOSEPH REMOND - An Extensive Italianate Landscape With A Huntsman And His Dog - signed and dated 1838 - 22½ x 31½in.
(Christie's)   **$576   £320**

GUIDO RENI - Moses And Pharoah's Crown - 53 x 68in.
(Christie's)   **$136,500   £75,000**

M. VAN REYMERSWAEL - Saint Jerome In His Study - on panel - 28 x 38in.
(Christie's)   **$3,240   £1,800**

REYNOLDS - Portrait Of The Artist wearing a wide brimmed hat, and a red cloak, a scroll in his left hand - 31 x 24in.
(Sotheby's)   **$270   £150**

SIR JOSHUA REYNOLDS, Attributed to - A Shipwreck Off A Rocky Coast - 21½ x 40in.
(Christie's N. York)   **$2,420   £1,322**

SIR JOSHUA REYNOLDS - Dolores - 29½ x 24½in.
(Sotheby's)   **$11,160   £6,200**

367

SIR JOSHUA REYNOLDS - Portrait Of Richard Crofts Of West Harling, Norfolk, standing three-quarter length, wearing a red coat and breeches with a striped waistcoat, his left hand resting on a stone pedestal, a wooded landscape beyond - 51 x 45in.
(Sotheby's) $4,500 £2,500

F. A. REZIA - 'Continental Lake Scene' - signed - oil - 14 x 24in.
(Hussey's) $432 £240

OLIVER RHYS - Gossip - signed and numbered CVII - 21½ x 29½in.
(Christie's) $504 £280

OLIVER RHYS - On The Terrace - signed and numbered CXIX - 13½ x 17½in.
(Christie's) $342 £190

FRANCISCO RIBALTA, School of - Portrait Of Don Martino De Alala, Archbishop Of Valencia, seated, three-quarter length - inscribed and inscribed with coat of arms - 43½ x 33in.
(Christie's N. York) $550 £300

J. DE RIBERA - Pythagoras, three-quarter length, holding a document and a sandglass - 50½ x 39½in.
(Christie's) $8,640 £4,800

J. DE RIBERA - A Philosopher, three-quarter length in a brown and red cloak, holding a book - 48 x 38in.
(Christie's) $8,100 £4,500

I. RICALL - In The Wine Cellar - signed - 20½ x 27in.
(Sotheby's Belgravia) $198 £110

ATTILIO RICARDI - A Family Reunion - signed - 18½ x 34in.
(Christie's) $2,160 £1,200

RICCI - Designs For Octagonal Ceiling Compartments With Gods And Warriors - pen and brown ink, brown wash, on attached sheets - 37 x 3.25cm.
(Christie's) $180 £100 Two

SEBASTIANO RICCI - The Peasant And The Satyr - 22¼ x 28¼in.
(Christie's) $7,280 £4,000

MARCO RICCI, Circle of - An
Italianate Landscape, with a ruined
arcade, and a river in the distance -
48½ x 35¼in.
(Christie's N. York) **$1,210 £661**

KARL RICHARD - A Horsedrawn Sleigh
- signed - oil - on canvas - 15 x 22in.
(Bonham's) **$3,420 £1,900**

W. RICHARDS - Unloading The Catch, a
quayside scene - signed - oil - on canvas -
15¼ x 23¼in.
(Neales of Nottingham) **$96 £50**

W. RICHARDS - Fisherfolk On A Beach -
signed - indistinctly inscribed - 11½ x
19½in.
(Sotheby's Belgravia) **$117 £65**

W. RICHARDS - River Scene At Loch
Tay - oil - 16 x 24in.
(G. A. Key) **$36 £20**

R. M. RICHARDSON - River Scene With
Bridge And Figure - oil - 13 x 19in.
(G. A. Key) **$50 £28**

THOMAS MILES RICHARDSON, JUN -
The Walls Of Nuremberg - pencil and
watercolour heightened with white - 12
x 17¾in.
(Christie's) **$684 £380**

THOMAS MILES RICHARDSON, JNR -
Balentore, Forfarshire - signed twice with
monogram - inscribed and dated Sept. 1855
- 18¾ x 33½in.
(Sotheby's Belgravia) **$558 £310**

THOMAS MILES RICHARDSON, JNR
- An Italian Coastal Scene - signed and
dated 1858 - heightened with white -
12¾ x 26½in.
(Sotheby's) **$684 £380**

THOMAS MILES RICHARDSON, JNR -
Near the entrance to the Grand Canal,
Venice - signed with initials - pencil,
watercolour heightened with white, on
buff paper - 8¼ x 12¼ in.
(Sotheby's) **$900 £500**

GEORGE RICHMOND - Portrait Of
A Young Officer in uniform of the
9th Foot (Norfolk) - heightened with
white - 19¼ x 12¾in.
(Sotheby's) **$612 £340**

GEORGE RICHMOND - A Woman With Two Children in a hilly landscape - signed and dated 1834 - 15 x 11½in.
(Sotheby's) **$1,116 £620**

A. RICHTER - A View Of The Arch Of Constantine - signed and inscribed - grey and brown wash heightened with white - 17.2 x 26.0cm.
(Christie's) **$117 £65**

JOHANN RICHTER - A Capriccio Mediterranean Harbour Scene - 42 x 48in.
(Christie's) **$4,680 £2,600**

LUDWIG RICHTER - The Flight Of Lot - pencil - 14.4 x 19.5cm.
(Christie's) **$27 £15**

NICOLO RICIOLINI - The Sacrifice Of Elias; and Isaiah And The Angel: projects for demi-lunettes - one apparently signed - both inscribed - pen and brown ink, grey wash - 28.0 x 21.5cm.
(Christie's) **$270 £150 Two**

PHILIP RICKMAN - An Old Stager On The Tops - signed and inscribed - heightened with bodycolour - 9¼ x 7in.
(Sotheby's Belgravia) **$396 £220**

PHILIP H. RIDEOUT - The York To Leeds Coach; In The Snow - one distinctly signed and dated 1906 - 7¼ x 15¼in.
(Sotheby's Belgravia) **$216 £120 Pair**

F. W. RIDLEY - Steamship On A Moonlit Sea - watercolour - 8 x 13in.
(G. A. Key) **$31 £17**

H. RIGAUD - Portrait Of An Officer, Possibly The Duc De Noailles, half length, wearing breast plate and the Order of the Saint-Esprit - 31¼ x 25½in.
(Christie's) **$1,260 £700**

HYACINTHE RIGAUD, Circle of - Portrait of a Marshall of France in armour holding a baton - 46 x 37½ in.
(Christie's N. York) **$990 £541**

J. F. RIGAUD - Portraits Of Two Gentlemen, one seated, half length, the other three-quarter length - indistinctly inscribed - 37 x 28in.
(Christie's) **$1,260 £700**

BRIDGET RILEY - Study For 'Intake' - signed - inscribed with title and drawing instructions and dated '64 - pencil, brush and black wash - 30½ x 22½in.
(Christie's) $1,098 £600

JEAN-PAUL RIOPELLE - Herbeuse - signed and dated '67 - oil - on canvas - 64 x 51in.
(Sotheby's) $11,346 £6,200

JEAN-PAUL RIOPELLE - Le Marronnier - signed and dated '53 - signed and titled on the reverse - oil on canvas - 39½ x 47½in.
(Sotheby's) $9,516 £5,200

PIETER DE RING - A Bowl Of Raspberries, A Pewter Dish With Shellfish, A Glass Of Wine, Grapes, A Lemon And Roses, on a draped table - signed with a ring - on panel - 22½ x 18¼in.
(Christie's) $54,000 £30,000

EDWARD VILLIERS RIPPINGILLE - The Young Trio - signed and dated 1829 - on panel - 16 x 13in.
(Sotheby's) $2,700 £1,500

371

RIVERS

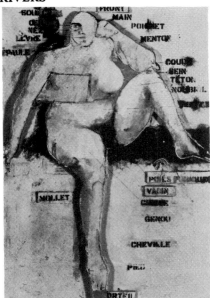

LARRY RIVERS - Parts Of The Body, French - oil on board relief - 12¾ x 8½in.
(Christie's N. York)   **$5,500 £3,055**

BRITON RIVIERE - Interior With Mrs Jolly seated at a window - signed with monogram, verso with label - oil - on canvas - 34½ x 36½in.
(Neales of Nottingham) **$425 £220**

BRITON RIVIERE - Requiescat - signed with monogram and dated 1889 - 25 x 35¾in.
(Christie's)   **$288 £160**

ROBERT - A Youth Climbing Over A Roman Plinth - black chalk and watercolour - 20.0 x 15.4cm.
(Christie's)   **$72 £40**

H ROBERT - Figures In A Roman Ruin - pen and grey ink, grey wash heightened with white - 37.0 x 26.2cm.
(Christie's)   **$252 £140**

HUBERT ROBERT, Manner of - Figures Under An Arch, with a statue of Marcus Aurelius and the temple of Vesta at Tivoli - canvas - on board - 23¼ x 19¼in.
(Christie's N. York)   **$495 £270**

ROBERTS - An Italianate Coastal Landscape, with fishing vessels off-shore - bears signature - 20½ x 28½in.
(Christie's)   **$45 £25**

D. ROBERTS - Shipping On The Nile - 16 x 23in.
(Christie's)   **$540 £300**

DAVID ROBERTS - A View Of Rome showing the Ponte Rotto, the Temple of Vesta and the Church of Santa Maria in Cosmedin, the Palentine hills are seen to the left, the Aventine hills to the right - signed and dated 1863 - 23½ x 41¼in.
(Sotheby's)   **$11,880 £6,600**

DAVID ROBERTS - Pisa - signed and dated 1859 - 35½ x 27in.
(Christie's)   **$6,840 £3,800**

DAVID ROBERTS - A Recollection Of The Desert, On The Approach Of The Simoon - signed and dated 1850 - signed, inscribed and dated on the reverse - on panel - 13¾ x 19¾in.
(Christie's)   **$1,350 £750**

DAVID ROBERTS - Figures By The Forum At Rome in early morning - signed and dated 1868 - 17 x 35¼in.
(Sotheby's)   **$5,400**   **£3,000**

DAVID ROBERTS - A View Of Suez with a rainbow over the Red Sea and Bedouin tribesmen in the foreground - signed and dated 1840 and inscribed - pencil and watercolour heightened with white on buff paper - 12½ x 18¾in.
(Christie's)   **$9,360**   **£5,200**

WILLIAM GOODRIDGE ROBERTS - The Coming Of The Fall On The Saugeen, near Walkereton - signed - oil - on board - 12 x 15in.
(Sotheby's)   **$1,158**   **£600**

CHARLES ROBERTSON - The Beautiful Persian - signed - watercolour heightened with white - 14 x 20½in.
(Christie's)   **$1,350**   **£750**

CHARLES ROBERTSON - Leaving The Mosque - signed with monogram and dated 1881 - 45 x 33in.
(Christie's)   **$7,200**   **£4,000**

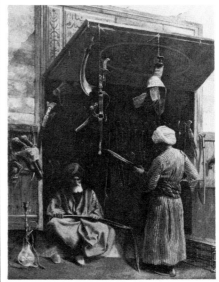

CHARLES ROBERTSON - The Arzu Bazaar, Cairo - signed with monogram - watercolour and bodycolour - 13½ x 9½in.
(Christie's)   **$936**   **£520**

ROBERTSON

DAVID J. ROBERTSON - Haymaking, Evening - signed - heightened with body-colour - 17½ x 22½in.
(Sotheby's Belgravia) **$54 £30**

GEORGE ROBERTSON - Horses Under A Tree during a storm - signed and dated 1777 - pencil and sepia wash heightened with white on buff paper - 10 x 14½in.
(Sotheby's) **$171 £95**

TOM ROBERTSON - A Riverside Village - signed - 12 x 29in.
(Sotheby's Belgravia) **$828 £460**

TOM ROBERTSON - On The Loch At Lochmore - signed - 28 x 36in.
(Sotheby's Belgravia) **$252 £140**

THOMAS SEWELL ROBINS - Fishing Boats in calm water with a town in the distance - signed - 26¼ x 39½in.
(Sotheby Bearne) **$4,875 £2,500**

THOMAS SEWELL ROBINS - Dutch Fisherfolk By The Shore - signed with initials and dated - 7 x 14in.
(Sotheby's) **$630 £350**

THOMAS SEWELL ROBINS - A Continental City with fishing folk in the foreground and a walled city in the distance - signed and dated '76 - heightened with white - 6¾ x 14in.
(Sotheby's) **$720 £400**

THOMAS SEWELL ROBINS - Rowing To The Shore In Choppy Seas - signed with initials - 7¼ x 11in.
(Sotheby's) **$396 £220**

CHARLES ROBINSON - Love's Captive - signed - inscribed on the reverse - pen and ink and wash - 6¾ x 18½in.
(Sotheby's Belgravia) **$468 £260**

T. ROBINSON - Portrait Of A Child - oil - 21 x 17in.
(G. A. Key) **$50 £28**

ALEXANDER ROCHE - Welford Farm - signed - on board - 14½ x 17¼in.
(Sotheby's Belgravia) **$288 £160**

CHARLES ROCHUSSEN - A Dutch Landscape - signed with initials - water-colour - 21.4 x 26.4cm.
(Christie's) **$288 £160**

CHRISTIAN BERNHARD RODE - Elegant Figures Before The Tomb Of Count Algarotti - inscribed in Latin - 47 x 33in.
(Christie's)   **$9,900**   **£5,500**

KARL RODECK - Sunlit Woods - signed - 29¼ x 46½in.
(Christie's)   **$576**   **£320**

E. RODZYNKIEWICZ - Portrait Of An Old Arab; and Portrait Of A Young Girl - signed on mounts - grey wash - 14¾ x 11in.
(Christie's)   **$22 £12 Pair**

CLARENCE ROE - Stags In A Highland Landscape - 35½ x 49½in.
(Christie's)   **$153 £85**

P. H. ROGERS - Country Landscapes, one depicting a cottage with animals and figures, the other with sea in the distance - 13 x 18in.
(Sotheby Bearne)   **$1,755 £900 Pair**

PHILIP HUTCHINS ROGERS - An Extensive Country Landscape with cattle and a reclining figure in the foreground - signed and dated 1813 - 31¼ x 41¼in.
(Sotheby Bearne)   **$648 £360**

R. S. ROGERS - Woody River Landscape with cattle resting and a yacht on river - watercolour - 12 x 19in.
(G. A. Key)   **$7 £4**

ROBERT HENRY ROE - Eagles Fighting - signed and dated '96 - coloured chalks - oval - 14½ x 19in.
(Sotheby's Belgravia)   **$90 £50**

W. ROGERS - Salvaging A Wreck Off The Coast - signed - 15¾ x 23½in.
(Sotheby's Belgravia)   **$63 £35**

R. ROGHMAN - An Italianate Wooded Landscape with peasants and cattle on a path and a castle by a river beyond - 39 x 53in.
(Christie's)   **$3,600 £2,000**

ROGRON - An Arab School In Algiers - signed - 8 x 10½in.
(Christie's)   **$630 £350**

GIOV. ROLA - Interior Scene With Young Girl And Guitar - signed and dated 1874 - oil - on canvas - 25 x 18½in.
(The Manchester Auction Mart.)
                    $1,492 £820

HARRIET JANE NEVILLE ROLFE - Croquet; Fishing - coloured chalks - 11½ x 56½in. each.   **$25 £14 Pair**

C. H. ROLT - A Cottage By A Pond - on board - oval - 25½ x 20in.
(Sotheby's Belgravia)   **$76 £42**

HENRY LEONIDAS ROLFE - Still Life Of Fish On A River Bank - signed - 18½ x 21½in.
(Sotheby's Belgravia)   **$288 £160**

GIULIO ROMANO, Manner of - The Holy Family With Saint Anne And The Infant Saint John The Baptist, in a landscape - on panel - 36 x 28½in.
(Christie's N. York)   **$462 £252**

ADRIAEN ROMBOUTS - Cottage Interior With Figures - signed and dated 1663 - oil - on canvas - 18 x 22in.
(Bonham's)   **$5,336 £2,900**

SALOMON ROMBOUTS - A Village In Winter with figures skating on a frozen river - on panel - 18¼ x 23¼in.
(Christie's)   **$16,200 £9,000**

SALOMON ROMBOUTS - A Wooded
Landscape with travellers on a path -
on panel - 24½ x 20¾in.
(Christie's)   **$3,420 £1,900**

WILLEM ROMEYN - An Italianate
River Landscape with cattle by a ruin -
on panel - 17 x 23in.
(Christie's)   **$2,340 £1,300**

ROMNEY - The Birth Of The Virgin -
pen and brown ink - 33.1 x 20.0cm.
(Christie's)   **$45 £25**

GEORGE ROMNEY, Manner of -
Portrait Of A Lady, seated, half length,
in a white dress, a landscape beyond -
30¼ x 10in.
(Christie's N. York)   **$198 £108**

GEORGE ROMNEY, Attributed to -
Head Study Of Lady Hamilton - 26 x
21½in.
(Christie's N. York)   **$660 £361**

GEORGE ROMNEY - Sketch For Portrait
Of Elizabeth, Viscountess Bulkeley, As
Hebe—in the Collection of Sir Richard
Williams-Bulkeley - pen and sepia ink and
wash - 7 x 3½in.
(Sotheby's)   **$288   £160**

GEORGE ROMNEY - Portrait Of A Lady
Said To Be Mrs. Jordan, three-quarter
length, wearing a white dress with a pink
sash resting her elbow upon her raised
knee, with a brass ewer before her - 51 x
40½in.
(Christie's)   **$9,900 £5,500**

E. RONER - Wooded River Scenes In
The Tyrol - oil - 10 x 8in.
(G. A. Key)   **$126   £70 Pair**

H. RONNER - Two Kittens Playing
With Artist's Materials - oil - on panel -
9½ x 13in.
(Brackett's)   **$1,244 £680**

H. RONNER - Portrait Of A Tabby Cat -
oil - on panel - 8¼ x 6¼in.
(Brackett's)   **$604 £330**

HENRIETTE RONNER-KNIP - Children
Racing In Dog Carts - signed - oil - on
panel - 7½ x 9½in.
(Bonham's)   **$1,440 £800**

CHARLES S. ROODHOUSE - Greenbank,
Broughton In Furness - signed with mono-
gram and dated 1918 - 5¼ x 8¼in.
(Sotheby's Belgravia)   **$14 £8**

CHARLES S. ROODHOUSE - Ancient
Chapel Of The Hastings, Ashby De-La-
Zouche Castle - signed with monogram -
dated 1927 - inscribed on the reverse -
7½ x 11½in.
(Sotheby's Belgravia)   **$29 £16**

THOMAS MATHEWS ROOKE - Rouen,
street scene with Cathedral, timbered
buildings and figures - signed - watercolour - 11¼ x 9½in.
(Buckell & Ballard)   **$513 £285 Pair**

MICHAEL 'ANGELO' ROOKER -
Kenilworth Castle - signed - grey wash -
9 x 11¼in.
(Christie's) $756 £420

MICHAEL 'ANGELO' ROOKER - The
Strand Gate, Winchelsea, Sussex - signed
with monogram - inscribed on the reverse
with title - 9 x 11¼in.
(Sotheby's) $3,960 £2,200

P. P. ROOS - The Annunciation To The
Shepherds - 56 x 87in.
(Christie's) $9,900 £5,500

MARGARETE ROOSENBOOM - Study
Of Roses with a butterfly - signed - on
panel - 10¾ x 15in.
(Sotheby Bearne) $1,657 £850

W. ROPERS - Fishing Smacks Off The
Coast, Evening - signed - indistinctly
inscribed - 15½ x 23½in.
(Sotheby's Belgravia) $153 £85

S. ROSA - An Italianate Wooded Landscape with figures by a river - 44½ x
34¼in.
(Christie's) $1,710 £950

ROSALBA - Diana - pastel - 33.5 x
28.5cm.
(Christie's) $36 £20

HERMAN K. ROSK - Queen Mary
Sailing Through Cowes Regatta - oil -
25 x 50in.
(G. A. Key) $54 £30

ALEXANDER ROSLIN - Portrait Of The
Tsarevitch Paul, Later Tsar Of Russia (1745 -
1801); and Portrait Of The Grand Duchess
Dorothea Sophia, second wife of the
Tsarevitch Paul - painted ovals - 32 x 26½in.
(Christie's) $6,300 £3,500 Pair

JAMES ROSS - Peasants Harvesting -
signed - 14¾ x 20in.
(Christie's) $6,300 £3,500

ROTARI - Study Of A Girl - red and
black chalk - 30.6 x 21.3cm.
(Christie's) $117 £65

MARK ROTHKO - Black On Deep
Purple - signed and dated 1964 on the
reverse - 104½ x 80in.
(Christie's N. York) $110,000 £61,111

ROTTENHAMMER - Head Of John The
Baptist On Silver Charger - oil - 4 x 5in.
(G. A. Key) $76 £42

JOHANN MICHAEL ROTTMAYR,
Circle of - Saint Joseph And The Christ
Child - 25 x 80in.
(Christie's N. York) $154 £84

**JOHANN ROTTENHAMMER and JAN
BRUEGHEL THE ELDER** - The Mystic
Marriage Of St. Catherine - on copper -
17 x 13in.
(Sotheby's) $4,810 £2,600

**GIOVANNI BATTISTA DELLA
ROVERE** - A Saint Casting Out Devils
Near A Walled City - inscribed '1588
uchi in venio' on the reverse - black
chalk, pen and brown ink, brown
wash - 24.2 x 13.2cm.
(Christie's) $198 £110

FRANZ JAKOB ROUSSEAU - Views
Of The Tiergarten, Cleves, with figures -
21¾ x 28in.
(Christie's) $36,400 £20,000 Four

CHARLES ROWBOTHAM - Extensive View Of A Mediterranean Bay with a group of Italian peasants and a donkey in foreground - signed - oil - 21½ x 41½in. *(Graves, Son & Pilcher)* **$540 £300**

THOMAS LEESON ROWBOTHAM - On An Italian Lake - signed - inscribed and dated 1863 - heightened with bodycolour - 10¼ x 33¼in. *(Sotheby's Belgravia)* **$396 £220**

THOMAS CHARLES LEESON ROWBOTHAM, JNR - Pill On The Avon - signed and dated 1849 - pencil and watercolour, heightened with bodycolour - 13¾ x 24¾in. *(Sotheby's)* **$792 £440**

TOM ROWDEN - Dartmoor Ponies - signed - heightened with bodycolour - 15 x 25in. *(Sotheby's Belgravia)* **$135 £75**

J. C. ROWLAND - Portrait Of A Young Girl, full length, wearing a pink gown, trailing a straw bonnet, in a garden landscape - signed and dated on reverse 1841 - 20 x 15in. *(H. Spencer & Sons)* **$288 £160**

WM. ROWLAND - Old Houses At Yarmouth - watercolour - 7 x 10in. *(G. A. Key)* **$36 £20**

THOMAS ROWLANDSON - A Highwayman Pursued - signed - pen and ink and watercolour - 5¼ x 8½in. *(Christie's)* **$1,260 £700**

THOMAS ROWLANDSON - The Stag Hunt, hounds swimming a river, pursuing their quarry - pen and black ink and watercolour - 13¾ x 19½in. *(Sotheby's)* **$9,900 £5,500**

THOMAS ROWLANDSON - Weighing in at the Races - pen and grey ink, watercolour - 7 x 10½ in. *(Sotheby's)* **$5,580 £3,100**

THOMAS ROWLANDSON - The Epicurean - inscribed - pen and sepia ink and watercolour - 10¾ x 8in. *(Sotheby's)* **$540 £300**

THOMAS ROWLANDSON - The New Inn Post House at Cross near Axbridge, Somerset - inscribed - pen with grey and sepia ink, watercolour - 5¾ x 9 in.
(Sotheby's) **$4,860 £2,700**

THOMAS ROWLANDSON - The Brawl - pen and brown ink, watercolour - 5½ x 4¼in.
(Sotheby's) **$630 £350**

THOMAS ROWLANDSON - The Church-yard Debate - pen and brown ink and watercolour - 5½ x 9¼in.
(Christie's) **$1,350 £750**

THOMAS ROWLANDSON - The Lord Of The Manor - pencil, pen and ink and watercolour - 4½ x 7¼in.
(Christie's) **$1,440 £800**

THOMAS ROWLANDSON - Improving The Likeness, an imprisoned artist painting his gaoler - indistinctly inscribed - 5¾ x 8¼in.
(Sotheby's) **$1,530 £850**

THOMAS ROWLANDSON - Sulky - pen and ink and watercolour - 9¼ x 10¼in.
(Sotheby's) **$1,800 £1,000**

H. ROYLE - Landscape With Cattle - oil - 16 x 24in.
(Richard Baker & Baker) **$180 £100**

RUBELLI

ENIDIO DE RUBELLI - The Return From The Well - signed and dated Milano - 9½ x 13½in.
(Christie's)   **$450**   **£250**

SIR P. P. RUBENS - Alexander Crowning Roxana - 81½ x 66½in.
(Christie's)   **$6,300** **£3,500**

SIR PETER PAUL RUBENS, Attributed to - The Crucified Christ, with the Madonna at the foot of the Cross, surrounded by Saints, appearing to St. Francis - on panel - 8 x 6½in.
(Christie's)   **$6,370 £3,500**

RUBENS, Studio Of - A Study Of Two Men On White Horses in a landscape - on panel - 25¼ x 29¾in.
(Christie's)   **$8,100 £4,500**

RUBENS, Studio of - Portrait Of Sir Peter Paul Rubens, half length, wearing black costume and beaver hat - 35 x 26½in.
(Christie's)   **$5,760 £3,200**

RUDESHEIM - Testing The Colour Of The Wine - signed and dated 1851 - oil - on canvas - 22¾ x 20in.
(Richard A. Bourne Co. Inc.) **$700 £389**

LOUIS FELIX DE LA RUE - Soldiers And Other Figures In A Tent - signed on the mount - pen and brown ink, brown wash - 8.5 x 13.4cm.
(Christie's)   **$45** **£25**

G. P. RUGENDAS - Soldiers Removing Corpses - pen and brown and grey ink - 18.6 x 28.7cm.
(Christie's)   **$117** **£65**

JACOB ISAACKSZ. VAN RUISDAEL - An Extensive Wooded Landscape With Shepherds And Sheep By A Barn - 40 x 53in.
(Christie's) **$32,400 £18,000**

JUAN RUIZ - An Extensive View Of The Harbour And City Of Naples - signed - 13 x 42½in.
(Christie's) **$2,700 £1,500**

C. F. RUMP - River Scene With Wherries - oil - 9 x 11in.
(G. A. Key) **$41 £23**

JULIUS FRIEDRICH LUDWIG RUNGE - A Coastal View - signed - on canvas laid on board - 11 x 16½in.
(Christie's) **$162 £90**

J. VAN RUISDAEL - A Wooded Landscape With Figures On A Path - bears initials - on panel - 14¼ x 13½in.
(Christie's) **$7,280 £4,000**

GIUSEPPE RUOPPOLO - A Still Life Of Dead Game, Pomegranates And Grapes in a landscape - 42½ x 39½in.
(Christie's) **$2,700 £1,500**

JACOB VAN RUISDAEL - Fishing-Boats In A Breeze - signed in monogram - 18 x 24¾in.
(Sotheby's) **$33,300 £10,000**

GYRTH RUSSELL - The Quays Of Padstow - signed - 21 x 30in.
(Sotheby's Belgravia) **$162 £90**

JOHN RUSSELL - Portrait Of Lady Ross, nee Amelia Sydenham - signed and dated 1802 - inscribed on the reverse - pastel - 23½ x 17½in.
(Sotheby's) **$900 £500**

RUSTICHINO - A Scene From The Story Of Moses - the backing inscribed - pen and brown ink, brown wash - 17.0 x 33.4cm.
(Christie's) **$72 £40**

SALOMON VAN RUYSDAEL - A View Of An Estuary - signed with initials - on panel - 8 x 12½in.
(Sotheby's) **$70,300 £38,000**

JEAN RUYTEN - View Of Antwerp with a procession - signed and dated Antwerp 1848 - 15 x 19¾in.
(Christie's) **$9,000 £5,000**

HENRY RYELAND - Two Classical Females In Marbled Patio Setting With Birds, entitled "Feathered Pets" - signed - watercolour - 21½ x 15in.
(Richard Baker & Baker) **$171 £95**

M. RYCKAERT - A Coastal Landscape with fisherfolk - on panel - 8¼ x 10½in.
(Christie's) **$3,420 £1,900**

MARTEN RYCKAERT - L'Isola Tiberina, Rome, with fisherfolk in the foreground - on panel - 4½ x 10in.
(Christie's) **$10,010 £5,500**

MARTEN RYCKAERT - A Winter Landscape with peasants skating on a frozen waterway in the foreground and a town beyond - on panel - circular - 6¼in. diameter.
(Christie's) **$21,600 £12,000**

ARTHUR JOHNSTON RYLE - Cromarty Woods - Cromarty Firth - signed - 36 x 54in.
(Sotheby's Belgravia) **$153 £85**

ROBERT RYMAN - Untitled — Painted in 1961 - 74¾ x 74¾in.
(Christie's) **$47,580 £26,000**

J. R. RYOTT - Gentlemen With Their Greyhounds In An Extensive Landscape - signed and dated 1817 - on board - 15¼ x 20½in.
(Sotheby's) **$630 £350**

P. RYSBRAECK - A Wooded River Landscape with peasants, cattle and sheep in the foreground and a house beyond - 39 x 49½in.
(Christie's) **$1,440 £800**

FRANCESCO SABATELLI - A Classical Scene - signed - pencil, pen and brown ink - 168 x 244mm.
(Christie's) **$72 £40**

L. SABATELLI - A Girl; and A Man In A Plumed Hat - pen and brown ink - 198 x 153mm.
(Christie's) **$200 £110**

SACCHI - The Baptism - the mount inscribed 'Crespi' - red chalk, brown wash - 37.0 x 31.5cm.
(Christie's) **$180 £100**

G. SACHARIANI - North Italian Fisherman Leaving His Boat and being met by his wife and family - signed and dated 1847 on verso - 10 x 8in.
(H. Spencer & Sons) **$396 £220**

W. SADLER - A View Of Dublin From Phoenix Park, the Wellington Testimonial to the left and the dome of the Four Courts beyond - on panel - 8 x 11½in.
(Sotheby's) **$540 £300**

WALTER DENDY SADLER - The Collector - signed - 21 x 14¾in.
(Christie's) **$720 £400**

J. C. W. SAFT - A Peasant In A Gateway - signed on the reverse - pen and brown ink and watercolour - 24.4 x 25.0cm.
(Christie's) **$270 £150**

C. SAFTLEVEN - A Sportsman With His Two Children, and peasants merrymaking, in a wooded landscape - on panel - 18 x 24½in.
(Christie's) **$4,680 £2,600**

CORNELIS SAFTLEVEN - Peasants And Livestock Outside A Cottage - signed and dated 1664 - on panel - 15¼ x 21¼in.
(Christie's N. York) **$5,720 £3,126**

CORNELIS SAFTLEVEN - A Parade Of Monsters - signed and dated 1627 - inscribed - on panel - 18½ x 24¼in.
(Christie's) **$8,640 £4,800**

HERMAN SAFTLEVEN - A Rhineland Landscape - on panel - 18 x 23in.
(Sotheby's) **$8,325 £4,500**

HERMAN SAFTLEVEN - A Landscape In The Rhineland - 9¾ x 12in.
(Sotheby's) **$16,650 £9,000**

SALIMBENI

SALIMBENI - Saint Bernard - black
and red chalk - 37.0 x 22.6cm.
(Christie's) $72   £40

SALM - Vessels In Choppy Seas - red
chalk, pen and black ink, grey wash -
17.0 x 23.0cm.
(Christie's) $468   £260 Pair

JOHN SALMON - View Of Foway
Castle - watercolour - 14 x 20in.
(G. A. Key) $144 £80

PAUL SANDBY - A Classical River Landscape with groups of figures - signed and
dated 1760 - 19¼ x 24in.
(Woolley & Wallis) $1,368 £760

PAUL SANDBY - Scottish Mountain
Landscape With Lake And Ferry -
signed and dated 1801 - 25 x 35¾in.
(Sotheby's) $9,360 £5,200

PAUL SANDBY - A Cart Leaving A
Harbour, buildings in the distance - pen and
ink - watercolour - 6 x 9½in.
(Sotheby's) $1,044   £580

PAUL SANDBY - A View Of Chepstow
Castle, from the river - signed and dated
1787 - heightened with bodycolour -
16 x 23in.
(Sotheby's) $1,800   £1,000

FREDERICK SANDYS - Isolde - bears
E.B.J. monogram - on panel - 13½ x
10½in.
(Christie's) $975 £500

THE MASTER OF SAN MINIATO -
The Crucifixion with the Virgin Mary,
Saint John, Mary Magdalene, Saint
Jerome and Saint Francis, in a hilly
landscape - on panel - 30½ x 20in.
(Christie's) $5,760 £3,200

SANQUIRICO - Stage Design: A
Prisoner Interior - pen and grey ink,
grey wash - 27.0 x 40.4cm.
(Christie's) $54   £30

A. SANQUIRICO - The Atrium Of A Palace - pencil, brown wash - 22.9 x 29.7cm.
(Christie's)   **$99**   **£55**

JAMES SANT - The Infant John The Baptist - signed with monogram - 35½ x 27½in.
(Sotheby's Belgravia)   **$432 £240**

RUBENS SANTORO - Arabs By The Riverside - signed - on panel - 12½ x 9¼in.
(Christie's)   **$2,520 £1,400**

RUBENS SANTORO - An Arab Guard - signed - on panel - 7¼ x 4¾in.
(Christie's)   **$1,170 £650**

FRANCIS SARTORIUS - 'Bellario', a bay racehorse with jockey up - signed and inscribed on the reverse - 9½ x 13½in.
(Christie's)   **$3,060 £1,700**

DIRCKSZ VAN SANTVOORT - A Family Group, standing, full length, wearing black costume in a landscape - on panel - 34½ x 47in.
(Christie's)   **$7,560**   **£4,200**

ULPIANO CHECA Y SANZ - Souvenir Of Capri - signed - 12½ x 8½in.
(Christie's)   **$900**   **£500**

JOHN SINGER SARGENT - Portrait Of A Bedouin Chief, half length - 28 x 22in.
(Christie's)   **$27,000 £15,000**

FRANCIS SARTORIUS - 'Chance', a bay racehorse with jockey up; 'Farmer', a chestnut racehorse with jockey up; 'General', a bay racehorse with a groom - two are signed and inscribed on the reverse and one is signed, inscribed, and dated 1766 - 9 x 12½in.
(Christie's) **$7,560 £4,200 Three**

JOHN SINGER SARGENT - A Bedouin - with the artist's studio stamp on the back of the canvas - 20¼ x 16½in.
(Christie's) **$4,320 £2,400**

JACQUES SARRAZIN - An Italian Landscape - inscribed 'Sarazin' on the reverse - black chalk, watermark E C below a crowned letter H on its side - 16.8 x 22.4cm.
(Christie's) **$63 £35**

ARTHUR SART - "Mountain Landscape With Rapids" - signed and dated 1876 - oil - 23 x 19in.
(Walker, Barnett & Hill) **$117 £65**

SARTORIUS - Study Of A Race Horse - oil - 14 x 17½in.
(Thomas Love & Sons Ltd.) **$1,080 £600**

JOHN NOST SARTORIUS - Taking a Gate - signed and dated 1788 - 9½ x 11½in.
(Christie's) **$3,060 £1,700**

JOHN NOST SARTORIUS - Hunting Scenes - one signed, three signed with initials - on board - circular - diameter each 4in.
(Sotheby's) **$3,240 £1,800 Four**

FRANCIS SARTORIUS - The Finish - signed - 9½ x 13½in.
(Christie's) **$4,680 £2,600**

WILLIAM SARTORIUS - A Dead Hare, A Dead Pheasant With Other Birds, Grapes And Peaches in a wooded land-scape - signed - 29½ x 43½in.
(Christie's) **$1,170 £650**

GIOVANNI BATTISTA SALVI, IL SASSOFERRATO - The Madonna And Child - 29¼ x 24¼in.
(Christie's)   **$9,100 £5,000**

GIOVANNI BATTISTA SALVI, IL SASSOFERRATO - Head Of The Virgin - 18¼ x 15in.
(Christie's N. York)   **$2,420 £1,322**

GIOVANNI BATTISTA SALVI, IL SASSOFERRATO - The Virgin In Adoration - 18 x 14¾in.
(Christie's)   **$5,460 £3,000**

ROELANDT SAVERY - Two Horses With Grooms In An Extensive Rocky Landscape with a castle beyond - signed and dated 1628 on panel - 14 x 24in.
(Christie's)   **$39,600 £22,000**

ROELANDT SAVERY - A Still Life Of Roses, Tulips And Other Flowers in a glass vase with a lizard and a frog on a stone ledge - signed and dated 1623 - on panel - 9½ x 7in.
(Christie's)   **$145,600 £80,000**

GIROLAMO SAVOLDO, After - A Philosopher Holding A Scroll - on panel - 6¼ x 4½in.
(Christie's)   **$1,170 £650**

389

SCAGLIA

LEONARDO SCAGLIA - A Pagan
Sacrifice - inscribed - black chalk, pen
and brown ink, brown wash - 14.7 x
20.7cm.
(Christie's) $99   £55

L SCANTLEBURY - Coltishall Loch -
watercolour - 6 x 10in.
(G. A. Key) $22   £12

A. SCARNCO - Ave Maria - signed -
29 x 39in.
(Sotheby's Belgravia) $288 £160

**IPPOLITO SCARSELLA, called Lo
Scarsellino** - The Rest On The Flight
Into Egypt - on copper - 7 x 5½in.
(Sotheby's) $3,330 £1,800

H. SCHAFER - View In A German Town
with many old buildings clustered around
the river with figures and boats with a
large church steeple in the distance -
signed - 23½ x 35½in.
(H. Spencer & Sons) $1,404 £780

HENRI SCHAFER - Frankfurt am
Maine: old buildings and figures with
a church tower; and Abbeville, old buildings with figures, a church beyond - both
monogramed and dated 1882 - inscribed
on the reverse - board - 7 x 8in.
(H. Spencer & Sons) $1,710 £950 **Pair**

HENRY SCHAFER - A Canal In A Town -
15½ x 11½in.
(Christie's) $504   £280

H. SCHAFER - Metz-Lorraine. and Abbeville, Normandy - signed and dated 1885 -
oil - 13 x 17½in.
(J. Entwistle & Co.) $3,230 £1,700 **Pair**

H. T. SCHAFER - Still Life Of Lilies and
Hollyhocks - signed - oil - on canvas - 26½
x 13½in.
(Neales of Nottingham) $116 £60 **Pair**

FRANZ ANTON VON SCHEIDL - Two Dogs: A Haushund (Canis Domesticus) And A Hirtenhund (Canis Familiaris) - inscribed in German and Latin - pencil and watercolour - 35.5 x 50.5cm.
(Christie's) **$162 £90**

FRANZ ANTON VON SCHEIDL - An Ermine (Mustela Eminea) - inscribed in German and Latin - pencil and watercolour - 35.4 x 50.2cm.
(Christie's) **$198 £110**

ANDREAS SCHELFHOUT - Shipping In An Estuary By Moonlight - on panel - 11 x 13¼in.
(Christie's) **$2,700 £1,500**

F. J. SCHALL - Spring And Summer: courting couples in landscapes - both on panel - 23¾ x 14¼in.
(Christie's) **$9,100 £5,000 Pair**

WILLIAM SCHELLINKS - The Dutch Attack On The Medway 12th June 1667 - 23 x 35in.
(Christie's) **$7,200 £4,000**

JOHN CHRISTIAN SCHETKY - Capture
of the Swiftsure of 74 Guns by a French
Squadron of Four Sail of the Line - brown
wash - 7½ x 13 in.
(Sotheby's)   **$450 £250**

JOHN CHRISTIAN SCHETKY - The
Belvoir Castle out of Port - signed and
dated 1862 - brown washes - 7¾ x 12¼ in.
(Sotheby's)   **$504 £280**

ANDREA SCHIAVONE, After - Amalthea
Nursing The Infant Jupiter - on panel - 8¾ x
6¾in.
(Christie's)   **$2,160   £1,200**

SCHIDONE - Charity - black chalk,
brown wash - 19.2 x 16.5cm.
(Christie's)   **$108   £60**

ALEXANDER GEORG SCHLATER - A
Coastal Landscape With Fisherfolk - signed
and dated-21 x 35in.
(Christie's)   **$1,044   £580**

G. SCHMIDT - An Austrian Beer
Garden with two soldiers, a gentleman
and a serving girl in conversation -
signed - oil - on canvas - 31 x 24in.
(Morphets of Harrogate) **$1,425 £750**

MAX SCHMIDT - A Frozen River Landscape,
with figures and buildings - 21½ x 30½in.
(Christie's)   **$6,840   £3,800**

M. SCHOEVAERDTS - Market Scenes with towns and landscapes beyond - 10¼ x 15in.
(Christie's) **$21,600 £12,000 Pair**

MATHYS SCHOEVAERDTS - A Wooded River Landscape with elegant figures by a church and a town beyond - bears initials and the date 1647 - 16½ x 22½in.
(Christie's) **$9,100 £5,000**

M. SCHOEVAERDTS - An Extensive Coastal Landscape With A Ruined Castle, and numerous figures in the foreground - on panel - 10¾ x 16¾in.
(Christie's) **$1,980 £1,100**

M. SCHOEVAERDTS - An Extensive Italianate Landscape with numerous figures and animals - on panel - 10¾ x 17in.
(Christie's) **$2,520 £1,400**

JOHN WILLIAM SCHOFIELD - A Coastal Scene - signed - 23½ x 36in.
(Sotheby's Belgravia) **$117 £65**

KERSHAW SCHOFIELD - Chrysanthemums In A Bowl, candelabra and vases on a table - oil - 24 x 30in.
(G. A. Key) **$180 £100**

B. SCHOLDERER - The Return From The Wolf Hunt - signed - 40¾ x 49¾in.
(Christie's) **$756 £420**

MATHYS SCHOEVAERDTS - An Italianate Coastal Landscape with a market-place signed and dated 1700 - on panel - 13 x 19in.
(Christie's) **$12,600 £7,000**

MATHYS SCHOEVAERDTS, Attributed to - Figures On A Quayside On The Outskirts Of A Town - 16 x 22¾in.
(Christie's N. York) **$3,080 £1,683**

FLORIS VAN SCHOOTEN - Fraises De Bois and Gooseberries In Wan Li Kraak Porcelain Bowls, with plums and other fruits on a shaped ledge - on panel - 14½ x 23½in.
(Christie's) **$11,830 £6,500**

SCHRADER

JULIUS FRIEDERICH ANTON SCHRADER
- Portrait Of A Lady, bust length, wearing a
white dress and yellow and red cloak - signed
and dated 1848 - 30 x 23½in.
(Christie's)   **$900   £500**

ANTON SCHRANZ - An Extensive View Of
The Harbour At Mahon, Minorca, men-of-
war and other shipping at anchor, a fisherman's family on the bank in the foreground -
11 x 27½in.
(Sotheby's)   **$3,600   £2,000**

ADOLPHE SCHREYER - An Arab Horseman in a landscape - signed with monogram - on panel - 8¾ x 13½in.
(Christie's)   **$3,420   £1,900**

HEINRICH SCHUTZ - The Dog-Cart -
signed - 47½ x 39½in.
(Lawrence)   **$990   £550**

SCHWABIAN SCHOOL, Circa 1530 -
The Stoning Of Saint Stephen - on gold
ground panel - 12½ x 8¾in.
(Christie's N. York)   **$3,300   £1,803**

H. W. SCHWEICKHARDT - A Frozen
River Landscape with skaters and a
horse and sledge - on panel - 16¼ x
22¾in.
(Christie's)   **$11,700 £6,500**

HENDRIK WILLEM SCHWEICKHARDT -
An Extensive Wooded River Landscape, with
milkmaids, cows and sheep in the foreground, and a town beyond - signed and
dated 1779 - 95½ x 89½in.
(Christie's)   **$8,100   £4,500**

JOHN SCOLES - Outside The Doors -
signed with monogram and dated 1845 -
21½ x 10¼in.
(Sotheby's Belgravia) **$40 £22**

J. VAN SCOREL - The Madonna And
Child And The Infant Saint John The
Baptist In A Landscape - 19½ x 26in.
(Christie's) **$3,960 £2,200**

WILLIAM BELL SCOTT - Tynemouth,
December 1864 - signed with initials -
5 x 10in.
(Sotheby's Belgravia) **$198 £110**

THOMAS SCOTT - Melrose Abbey -
signed - inscribed and dated '96 -
10 x 14in.
(Sotheby's Belgravia) **$414 £230**

THOMAS SCOTT - The River Tweed Near
Melrose - signed - inscribed and dated '95 -
10 x 14in.
(Sotheby's Belgravia) **$360 £200**

SCOTTISH SCHOOL - A Fisher Boy
and A Fisher Girl - oil - 12 x 9in.
(Warner, Sheppard & Wade)
$1,098 £560 Pair

SCOTTISH SCHOOL - Half-length
Portrait Of A Young Man with auburn
hair - oil - 8 x 6½in.
(Warner, Sheppard & Wade) **$137 £70**

SCOTTISH SCHOOL, 19th century -
Mountain River Scene with fisherman in
pool - signed with initials and dated '66 -
oil - on canvas - 30 x 50in.
(Brooks) **$879 £460**

HENRY A. SCRIVENER - 'Harriers' Naval
Camp, Mangalawhiri Creek, Waikato River,
New Zealand with Koheroa Heights and
Redoubt in the distance - inscribed and
dated 27 July 1863 - watercolour height-
ened with bodycolour - 7 x 11in.
(Sotheby's) **$463 £240**

EDWARD SEAGO - Street Scene, Hong
Kong - signed - on board - 20 x 30in.
(Sotheby's, Hong Kong) **$8,523 £4,735**

SEARLE

E. SEARLE - Near Oban - signed and dated 1882 - inscribed on the reverse - 21¼ x 35½in.
(Sotheby's Belgravia) **$72 £40**

G. SEBRIGHT - A Bay Hunter in an extensive landscape with a hunt beyond - signed and dated 1860 - 27½ x 35¾in.
(Christie's) **$54 £30**

SEGANTINI - Arabs On A Path In A Tunisian Landscape - bears signature - 16 x 21in.
(Christie's) **$288 £160**

CHRISTIAN SELL - Prussian Soldiers Resting In A Snowbound Landscape - signed and dated 1882 - oil - on panel - 7½ x 10½in.
(Bonham's) **$1,440 £800**

LUDWIG SELLMAYR - Cattle Watering At A Stream - signed - on panel - 7 x 14½in.
(Lawrence) **$990 £550**

EISMAN SEMENOWSKY - A Ball On Board signed - on panel - 13 x 8in.
(Christie's) **$1,080 £600**

SERLIO - A Vista With Arcaded Buildings - inscribed 'Holler' - pen and brown ink, brown wash - 31.8 x 14.3cm.
(Christie's) **$144 £80**

ENRIQUE SERRA - A Venetian Wedding - signed and dated Roma 1885 - 22 x 55in.
(Christie's) **$4,500 £2,500**

D. SERRES - A Man-Of-War With Guns Run Out, by moonlight off the coast - canvas - on board - 14¾ x 16½in.
(Sotheby's) **$648 £360**

J. T. SERRES - Smugglers Unloading Boats On The Shore By Moonlight, seen through the large entrance to a cave - 27 x 35¼in.
(Sotheby's) **$540 £300**

JOHN THOMAS SERRES - A View Of Plymouth Harbour Sound with the H.M.S. 'Britannia' - signed and dated 1790 - 41 x 59in.
(Christie's) **$12,600 £7,000**

JOHN THOMAS SERRES - The Thames At Westminster From The South Bank, with sailing vessels in the foreground and the Abbey beyond - signed and dated 1811 - 23 x 33½in.
(Christie's) **$9,900 £5,500**

WILLIAM FREDERICK SETTLE -
Shipping Off Grimsby - signed with
monogram and dated - pencil, pen
and ink and watercolour - 6½ x
13¾in.
(Sotheby's)   **$324**   **£180**

FRANS VAN SEVERDONCK - A Grey
Draught Horse And Farm Animals, in an
extensive landscape - signed - 22 x 29¼in.
(Christie's)   **$1,530**   **£850**

WILLIAM SEXTIE - Fred Archer On Cherry
- signed and dated 1884 - 27¼ x 35in.
(Sotheby's)   **$2,340**   **£1,300**

EDUARD GUSTAV SEYDEL - 'Coffee-
time' - signed - dated 1859 - 14¼ x
16¾in.
(Lawrence)   **$11,160** **£6,200**

EDWARD GUSTAV SEYDEL - 'A
Warming Tot, Sir!' - signed - dated
1860 - 13¼ x 17in.
(Lawrence)   **$5,400** **£3,000**

GEORGE L. SEYMOUR - The Snake
Charmer - on panel - 23½ x 17½in.
(Christie's)   **$11,700** **£6,500**

J. SEYMOUR - The Finish Of A Race; a
grey and a dark bay racehorse with jockeys
up, at full gallop - 15½ x 24in.
(Sotheby's)   **$2,520** **£1,400**

J. SEYMOUR - Mr. Martindale's 'Regulus',
a bay racehorse held by a jockey in a
landscape - 24½ x 29¼in.
(Christie's)   **$3,600 £2,000**

JAMES SEYMOUR - A Coursing Scene: A
gentleman and a lady mounted on grey and
chestnut hunters at the kill - 32½ x 51½in.
(Christie's)   **$21,600 £12,000**

G. SHALDERS - Rural Landscape With
Many Figures Haymaking - signed and
dated '89 - 12 x 20in.
(Richard Baker & Baker) **$2,520 £1,400**

G. SHALDERS - A Mountainous Lake
Landscape with figures on a path - 30
x 44½in.
(Christie's)   **$4,320 £2,400**

GEORGE SHALDERS - "Crossing The
Ford" - 20½ x 29½in.
(Phillips, Solihull)   **$1,116 £620**

GEORGE SHALDERS - Autumn, signed -
watercolour - 13½ x 19½in.
(Christie's S. Kensington) **$234 £130**

GEORGE SHALDERS - A Highland
Landscape With Cattle Watering At A
Pond - 19½ x 29¼in.
(Christie's)   **$90 £50**

DOROTHEA SHARP - 'Watching The
Sea' - signed - 23½ x 19½in.
(Sotheby Bearne)   **$975 £500**

JOSEPH HENRY SHARP - An Indian
Brave Watching From A Bank - signed -
oil - on canvas - 19½ x 23½in.
(Sotheby's)   **$8,492 £4,400**

WALTER J. SHAW - 'The Day's Decline' - signed and dated 1881 - 33¼ x 55½in.
(Sotheby Bearne) **$741 £380**

W. SHAYER - A Busy Farmyard - bears signature - 19¾ x 19½in.
(Sotheby's Belgravia) **$864 £480**

WILLIAM SHAYER - Entitled "Near Southampton" - figures with cattle sheltering in a woodland glade - oil - 23 x 17in.
(G. A. Key) **$2,880 £1,600**

WILLIAM SHAYER, JUN - Setting Out For Market - 27 x 35in.
(Christie's) **$2,700 £1,500**

W. SHAYER, SEN - Coastal Scene With Fishermen Unloading Their Catch, in the foreground a man seated on a pony talking to a fisherman and his son - bears signature and dated 1849 - 23½ x 36in.
(H. Spencer & Sons) **$1,404 £780**

WILLIAM SHAYER, SEN - A Milkmaid With Two Cows Outside A Byre and a companion piece - signed - oil - on panel - 18 x 24in.
(Bonham's) **$7,200 £4,000 Pair**

WILLIAM SHAYER, SEN - A Country Lane with a pack horse and figures and a windmill in the far distance - signed and dated 1836 - oil - on canvas - 30 x 25in.
(Warner, Sheppard & Wade) **$4,900 £2,500**

WILLIAM SHAYER, SEN - A Country
Ale House - signed and inscribed on a
label on the stretcher - 19½ x 30in.
(Christie's) **$11,700 £6,500**

WILLIAM SHAYER, SEN - A Wooded
Landscape With A Gipsy Encampment
by a pond and a church beyond - signed
and dated '55 - 32½ x 39¾in.
(Christie's) **$12,600 £7,000**

WILLIAM SHAYER, SEN - On The Shore,
fisherfolk gathered by a quay at low tide -
signed - 29½ x 39½in.
(Sotheby's) **$5,400 £3,000**

WILLIAM SHAYER, SEN - A Coastal
Landscape with fisherfolk - bears signature
and dated 1876 - 27½ x 35in.
(Christie's) **$2,160 £1,200**

ANDREAS SHEERBOOM - A View Of A
Dutch Town, With Shipping On A Canal -
signed - 29½ x 49½in.
(Christie's) **$5,400 £3,000**

DAN SHERRIN - An Extensive Landscape with cottages by a pond - signed -
23½ x 41½in.
(Christie's) **$1,462 £750**

DANIEL SHERRIN - Country Scene,
evening, with two figures on a water-
logged track - signed - 19¼ x 29¼in.
(Sotheby Bearne) **$1,014 £520**

DANIEL SHERRIN - Showery Weather -
bears another signature and dated -
19½ x 29¼in.
(Sotheby's Belgravia) **$720 £400**

D. SHERRIN - Departing Day - extensive landscape with cottage, lade and figures - 75 x 125cm.
(Edmiston's) **$1,710 £950**

OBADIAH SHORT - St. Benet's Abbey - watercolour - 13 x 19½in.
(G. A. Key) **$99 £55**

J. SIBERECHTS - Studies Of Peasants - red chalk, watermark a Strasburg Lily - 18.5 x 28.9cm.
(Christie's) **$72 £40**

JAN SIBERECHTS - A Wooded Landscape with peasants, cattle and a haycart in a stream - 39½ x 45½in.
(Christie's) **$9,100 £5,000**

CASIMIR SICHULSKI - The Dreaming Fisherman - signed with initials and dated - gouache and pastel - 24½ x 58in.
(Christie's) **$576 £320**

SAMUEL SIDLEY - 'Saying Grace' - signed and dated 1872 - oil - on canvas - 20 x 17in.
(Bonham's) **$1,584 £880**

AUGUSTE SIEGEN - An Arab Street Scene - signed - 28 x 38in.
(Christie's) **$756 £420**

AUGUSTE SIEGEN - A State Barge Decorated With The Insignia Of Egypt - watercolour - 7 x 18½in.
(Christie's) **$54 £30**

AUGUSTE SIEGEN - A Street Scene In Cairo - signed - on panel - 20½ x 16in.
(Christie's) **$3,060 £1,700**

AUGUSTE SIEGEN - A Street Scene In Tunis - signed - on panel - 20½ x 16in.
(Christie's) **$2,880 £1,600**

GIUSEPPE SIGNORINI - A Tribesman Holding A Rifle - signed and inscribed Roma - watercolour - 27¼ x 16¾in.
(Christie's) **$756 £420**

SIMONE

TOMASO DE SIMONE - An English Yacht In The Bay Of Naples - signed and dated - bodycolour - 42.0 x 63.0cm.
(Christie's) **$144 £80**

FRANCESCO SIMONINI - The Aftermath Of A Battle below a ruined castle - inscribed on the reverse - pen and brown ink, brown wash heightened with white - 28.4 x 42.9cm.
(Christie's) **$540 £300**

F. SIMONINI - A Coastal Landscape with cavaliers in the foreground and an encampment beyond - 20 x 41in.
(Christie's) **$2,700 £1,500**

SIMSON - Fishing In The Highlands - 13¼ x 19¾in.
(Sotheby's Belgravia) **$99 £55**

J. SINCLAIR - River Landscape "On The Brathay" near Skelwith, Westmorland - signed and dated 1873 - oil - 24 x 36in.
(Richard Baker & Baker) **$252 £140**

JOSEPH SKELTON - Dunstonborough Castle - signed - 25 x 34½in.
(Sotheby's Belgravia) **$36 £20**

JAMES SKENE of RUBISLAW - The Ruins of Hermione, Moroa - signed, inscribed and dated 1838 - pencil and watercolour - 9½ x 20¾ in.
(Sotheby's) **$270 £150**

FRANK MARKHAM SKIPWORTH - Ready To Leave - signed with initials and dated '89 - 14½ x 10in.
(Christie's) **$1,657 £850**

W. V. SLATER - An Old Malthouse on the Arun, Sussex - watercolour - 10 x 24in.
(G. A. Key) **$65 £36**

FREDERICK SMALLFIELD - Inventor Of Sails - signed and dated 1877 - 32 x 41in.
(Christie's) **$50 £28**

FREDERICK SMALLFIELD - Cats! Cats! - signed and inscribed on a label on the reverse - 30¾ x 19¾in.
(Christie's) **$81 £45**

SMEAL - Scottish Children By A Watershoot - signed - inscribed 'Edinburgh' - indistinctly dated - on panel - 10½ x 14½in.
(Sotheby's Belgravia) **$117 £65**

J. SMIRSCH - Roses And Other Flowers In A Vase - signed and dated 1816 - 15½ x 12¼in.
(Christie's N. York) **$1,155 £631**

COLVIN SMITH - Portrait Of A 16th Century Provincial Lady - oil - 30 x 25in.
(G. A. Key) **$65 £36**

C. W. DYSON SMITH - Cley Mill - watercolour - 7 x 10in.
(G. A. Key) **$23 £13**

DENZIL SMITH - Shipping In Still Waters - both on board - oval - 3¼ x 2¼in.
(Sotheby's Belgravia) **$108 £60 Pair**

GEORGE SMITH - The Hayloft - signed - on board - 11¾ x 15½in.
(Sotheby's Belgravia) **$306 £170**

GEORGE SMITH - The Young Fly Swotter; and The Young Dove Collector - 13½ x 11½in.
(Christie's) **$900 £500 Pair**

GEORGE SMITH OF CHICHESTER, Manner of - A Wooded Classical River Landscape - 36 x 45in.
(Christie's N. York) **$825 £451**

ISABEL SMITH - The Gateway To The Park - signed and dated 1885 - 24 x 20in.
(Sotheby's Belgravia) **$40 £22**

ISABEL E. SMITH - Still Life Of Wild Flowers And A Bird's Nest - signed and dated 1882 - 9½ x 13½in.
(Sotheby's Belgravia) **$81 £45**

J. B. SMITH - A Wooded River Landscape with waterfall in foreground - on canvas - 14 x 18in.
(Morphets of Harrogate) **$522 £290**

JAMES BURRELL SMITH - Waterfall On The River Neath - signed and dated 1894 - 35¼ x 25¼in.
(Christie's) **$1,462 £750**

JAMES BURRELL SMITH - On The Conway - 9½ x 13½in.
(Sotheby's Belgravia) **$324 £180**

JOHN 'WARWICK' SMITH - Tregaron - inscribed and dated July 26th, 1792 on the mount - watercolour - 5¼ x 8½in.
(Christie's) **$630 £350**

JOHN 'WARWICK' SMITH - Auckland Castle, Bishop Auckland, the seat of the Bishop of Durham - pencil and watercolour - 13¾ x 20¼in.
(Christie's) **$1,080 £600**

JOHN 'WARWICK' SMITH - View Of Milford - inscribed twice and numbered - pencil and watercolour - 6½ x 9¾in.
(Christie's) **$540 £300**

JOHN 'WARWICK' SMITH - Lake of Geneva - signed and dated 1788 - 6¾ x 9¾ in,
(Sotheby's) **$1,260 £700**

JOHN 'WARWICK' SMITH - The Beach near the Stack Rock, Pembrokeshire - 5¾ x 8½ in.
(Sotheby's) **$180 £100**

MILLER SMITH - River Scenes with sailing yachts, windpump etc - watercolour - 6 x 9in.
(G. A. Key) **$94 £52 Pair**

W. H. SMITH - Deer Watering - signed - 27½ x 35½in.
(Sotheby's Belgravia) **$58 £32**

SMYTHE - Figures By A Wooded Pond - 21¼ x 29in.
(Sotheby's Belgravia) **$99 £55**

SMYTHE - A Farmyard Encounter - heightened with bodycolour - 17¼ x 26¼in.
(Sotheby's Belgravia) **$32 £18**

E. R. SMYTHE - Barges On The Orwell - oil - 10 x 7in.
(G. A. Key) **$47 £26**

EDWARD ROBERT SMYTHE - A Wooded Landscape with a ploughman resting by a tree - framed as a circle - 15½in. diameter.
(Christie's) **$810 £450**

EDWARD ROBERT SMYTHE - A Shetland Pony in a landscape - signed - 19½ x 29½in.
(Christie's) **$1,530 £850**

EDWARD ROBERT SMYTHE - Village Scene with figures unloading a horse-drawn cart and taking refreshments outside an inn - signed - oil - on canvas - 20 x 36in.
(Bonham's) **$3,060 £1,700**

EDWARD ROBERT SMYTHE - Deer In A Winter Landscape - 36 x 28in.
(Christie's) **$990 £550**

EDWARD ROBERT SMYTHE - A Pony, A Donkey And A Sheepdog in a landscape - bears Landseer signature and dated 1825 - 13 x 17in.
(Christie's) **$2,340 £1,200**

THOMAS SMYTHE - Village Scenes, Summer and Winter with timbered buildings, groups of figures and travelling tradesmen with horses and carts - one signed - on panel - 13¼ x 24in.
(Sotheby Bearne) **$12,600 £7,000 Pair**

THOMAS SMYTHE - Four Hunters Feeding From A Field Crib - signed - oil - 12 x 16in.
(Heathcote Ball & Co) **$1,098 £600**

P. SNAYERS - A Scene During The Thirty Years War with a military encampment - oil - on canvas - 30 x 84½in.
(Bonham's) **$14,352 £7,800**

PEETER SNAYERS - The Conversion Of St. Paul - signed and dated 1656 - on panel - 9¼ x 13¼in.
(Christie's) **$4,320 £2,400**

SNELLINCKS

J. SNELLINCKS - An Extensive Italianate Wooded Landscape with figures, cattle and sheep in the foreground and a church and buildings beyond - 63 x 92in.
(Christie's)   **$3,600 £2,000**

PEETER SNIJERS - A Boy With A Marmoset - signed with initials - 16 x 12¾in.
(Sotheby's)   **$5,920 £3,200**

ACHILLE SOLARI - An Extensive View Of The Gulf Of Sorento from Capodimonte - signed and inscribed - 10½ x 15½in.
(Christie's)   **$1,044 £580**

GIOVAN GIOSEFFO DAL SOLE, School of - Saint Mary Magdalene in the Wilderness - on panel - 12¼ x 10in.
(Christie's N. York)   **$396 £216**

ABRAHAM SOLOMON - 'First Class' - signed and dated 1854 - shaped top - 26½ x 37½in.
(Christie's)   **$72 £40**

ABRAHAM SOLOMON - Waiting For The Verdict; and The Acquittal - both signed and dated 1859 - 24 x 29½in.
(Christie's)   **$18,525 £9,500 Pair**

REBECCA SOLOMON - A Fashionable Couple - signed and dated 19 x 21in.
(Christie's)   **$1,755 £900**

R. C. SOMERSET - Orchard With Trees In Blossom - oil - 30 x 20in.
(G. A. Key)   **$117 £65**

R. G. SOMERSET - Keepers Cottage In Woodland Setting - oil - 30 x 20in.
(G. A. Key)   **$126 £70**

JORIS VAN SON - Still Life - on panel -
13 x 10½in.
(Sotheby's)   **$9,620 £5,200**

JAN SONJE, School of - A Wooded
River Landscape, with anglers - 25
x 30in.
(Christie's N. York)   **$825 £451**

JAN FRANS SOOLMAKER - An Evening
Landscape - signed with initials - oil on
canvas - 23¾ x 31 in.
(Bonham's)   **$4,416 £2,400**

JAN FRANS SOOLMAKER - An
Italianate River Landscape, with cattle
and drovers on a road below a ruin -
bears C. Huysmans signature - 18¾ x
22¾in.
(Christie's N. York)   **$1,980 £1,082**

A. SORBINI - A View Of An Arab
Town on an estuary - signed - 26½
x 41in.
(Christie's)   **$468 £260**

HENDRICK MARTENSZ. SORGH -
The Vegetable Market - indistinctly
dated 1660 - on panel - 19½ x 26in.
(Christie's)   **$6,840 £3,800**

SOULACROIX

FREDERIC SOULACROIX - Girl In A Pink Satin Evening Dress in a hammock - signed - oil - on canvas - 24 x 31½in.
(Bonham's) **$3,312 £1,800**

PIERRE SOULAGES - Composition - signed and dated '54 - dated 27 Dec '54 on the reverse - oil - on canvas - 76¾ x 51¼in.
(Sotheby's) **$17,385 £9,500**

SOUTH AMERICAN SCHOOL - Explorers Resting By A River in the jungle, a boat with a canvas awning moored near a waterfall, high mountains in the distance - oil - on canvas - 35 x 48¼in.
(Sotheby's) **$1,447 £750**

REUBENS SOUTHEY - Ships Lifeboat Beaching From A Wreck - watercolour - 19 x 25in.
(G. A. Key) **$97 £54**

FRANK SOUTHGATE - Ducks On The Marshes - monotone watercolour - 8 x 10in.
(G. A. Key) **$333 £185**

CORNELIS VAN SPAENBONCK - Flowers In A Vase - 23¼ x 18½in.
(Sotheby's) **$8,325 £4,500**

C. B. SPALDING - Portrait Of A Chestnut Hunter with six fox hounds - signed - 18½ x 25¼in.
(Sotheby Bearne) **$1,092 £560**

SPANISH SCHOOL, circa 1700 - The Crucifixion, after Rubens - red chalk - 46.5 x 31.0cm.
(Christie's) **$27 £15**

SPANISH SCHOOL, Early 16th century -
The Annunciation - on panel - with
embossed arched top - 39 x 33in.
(Christie's N. York)   **$1,210 £661**

SPANISH SCHOOL, circa 1650 - A Dish
Of Strawberries, A Bowl Of Broad Beans,
An Artichoke And A Parrot On A Table -
33 x 40in.
(Christie's)   **$2,880 £1,600**

R. B. SPENCER - The Nile, August 1st
1798; and Admiral Duncan's Victory
Off Camperdown - both signed, inscribed
and dated 1850 - 19¼ x 29¼in.
(Christie's)   **$4,680 £2,600 Pair**

R. B. SPENCER - Seascape With Two
Masted Sail Ships as main subject,
two other sail ships, steam and sail
ships and lighthouse in background -
signed and dated 1861 - oil - 17 x 25in.
(Richard Baker & Baker) **$180 £100**

THOMAS SPINKS - The Meeting Of The
Waters - signed and dated 1874 on the
reverse - 15½ x 23¼in.
(Sotheby's Belgravia)   **$180 £100**

S. SPODE - Portrait Of A Gentleman On
A Light Bay Hunter, with two greyhounds
and men coursing beyond - bears signature
and dated 1827 - 28¼ x 34¾in.
(Christie's)   **$16,200 £9,000**

JAN JACOB SPOHLER - Dutch Peasant
Scene with figures by a river, windmills
in distance - signed - oil - on canvas -
26½ x 16in.
(Gribble, Booth & Taylor)
     $8,640 £4,800

JAN JACOB SPOHLER - Dutch Peasant Scene with figures skating on frozen river, a cottage in foreground and windmill and Church in the distance - signed - oil - on canvas - 26½ x 16in.
(Gribble, Booth & Taylor) **$7,920 £4,400**

B. SPRANGER - A Satyr with an injured foot - on panel - 17¼ x 11¾in.
(Christie's)   **$3,600 £2,000**

BART SPRANGER, Attributed to - The Holy Family - oil - on copper - 22 x 18cm.
(Christian Rosset)   **$527 £293**

STEVEN SPURRIER - 'Tavern Scene' - signed and dated - 27½ x 35¼in.
(Sotheby Bearne)   **$370 £190**

L VAN STAATEN - Near Amsterdam; And Middelburg - both signed - watercolour - 29.0 x 40.0cm.
(Christie's)   **$576 £320 Pair**

L VAN STAATEN - Dutch River Landscapes With Windmills - signed - watercolour - 27.2 x 38.5cm.
(Christie's)   **$252 £140 Four**

NICOLAS de STAEL - Grey Bowl - 22 x 33cm.
(Auktionshaus am Neumarkt)
                 $45,750 £25,000

GEORGE STAINTON - Sunny Afternoon Off Hythe - signed - 19¼ x 29½in.
(Sotheby's Belgravia)   **$306 £170**

ADRIAEN VAN STALBEMT - A Village In An Extensive Landscape, with numerous figures and animals - on copper laid down on panel - 9½ x 14¼in.
(Christie's)   **$15,300   £8,500**

THEODORE WYNANT STALLENBERG - An Interior With A Woman At A Spinning Wheel - signed - brush and grey ink, grey wash heightened with white on blue paper - 15.3 x 19.2cm.
(Christie's)   **$81   £45**

STANFIELD - A Storm Off A Pier; On The Zuider Zee - 15 x 23½in.
(Sotheby's Belgravia) **$234 £130 Pair**

CLARKSON STANFIELD - A View Of Greenwich - bears signature and dated 1832 - 15 x 23½in.
(Christie's) **$50 £28**

G. CLARKSON STANFIELD - A View Of Heidelberg - bears signature - circular - 23¾in. diameter.
(Christie's) **$990 £550**

WILLIAM CLARKSON STANFIELD - The Bay Of Baia From Pozzuoli - signed and inscribed on an old label on the reverse - on board - 11¾ x 14in.
(Christie's) **$900 £500**

JOHN RODDAM SPENCER STANHOPE - The Grace - on panel 36 x 36in.
(Christie's) **$144 £80**

ALFRED STANNARD - A Wooded Landscape with figures fording a stream in a horse and cart - 18¾ x 24½in.
(Christie's) **$117 £65**

ALFRED STANNARD - Buckenham Ferry - signed and dated 1871 - 16 x 37in.
(Christie's) **$1,710 £950**

ALFRED GEORGE STANNARD - Sailing Vessels Off Gorleston Harbour, Norfolk, in a stormy sea - signed and dated 1848 and inscribed on the reverse - 16½ x 29½in.
(Christie's) **$2,145 £1,100**

E. H. STANNARD - Still Life Of Fruit On A Ledge, a landscape beyond - 7¾ x 9½in.
(Sotheby's Belgravia) **$54 £30**

EMILY STANNARD - Cox's Pits, Near Bedford - signed - heightened with bodycolour - 12 x 8½in.
(Sotheby's Belgravia) **$108 £60**

HENRY SYLVESTER STANNARD - Chesham, Buckinghamshire - signed - 9½ x 13½in.
(Sotheby's Belgravia) **$198 £110**

JOHN SYDNEY STEEL - A Point On The Moors - signed - 20½ x 30½in.
(Sotheby's Belgravia)   **$504 £280**

HENRY SYLVESTER STANNARD - The Shepherd Boy Near Flitwick; Dinner Time, Bedfordshire - signed - 14 x 20½in.
(Sotheby's Belgravia)   **$900 £500 Pair**

JOSEPH STANNARD - Seaboots, Sou'- Westers And Fishing Gear - pencil and watercolour - 4½ x 7in.
(Sotheby's)   **$45 £25**

SIR HERBERT HUGHES STANTON - A Hayfield Looking On To Harrow - signed and dated 1893 - on board - 8½ x 10½in.
(Sotheby's Belgravia)   **$198 £110**

M. STANZIONE - Christ Carrying The Cross - circular - on panel - 11¾in. diameter.
(Christie's)   **$684 £380**

A. J. STARK - Knole Park, Kent - watercolour - 13 x 9in.
(G. A. Key)   **$68 £38**

JOHN SYDNEY STEEL - Partridge Amongst Stooks - 19 x 23in.
(Sotheby's Belgravia)   **$684 £380**

J. STARK - Extensive Landscape with windmills and shepherds driving sheep into a pen - 17½ x 23½in.
(Sotheby Bearne)   **$4,860 £2,700**

EDWIN STEELE - Still Lifes Of Fruit And Flowers On Marble Ledges - both signed - 19½ x 15½in.
(Sotheby's Belgravia)   **$810 £450 Pair**

WILLEM STEELINK - Changing Pastures
- signed - watercolour heightened with
white - 32.0x 47.5cm.
(Christie's)   **$288 £160**

JAN STEEN - The Proverb 'Schyn Bed-
rieght' (Appearances Are Deceptive)
illustrated by a scene from Lucelle -
signed and dated 1672 and inscribed -
37 x 42½in.
(Christie's)   **$9,900 £5,500**

CORNELIS STEFFELAAR - A Winter
Landscape With Peasants On A Path And A
Castle Beyond - signed and dated 1859 - 30
x 40in.
(Christie's)   **$1,044 £580**

THEOPHILE STEINLEN - Der Ausrufer
Im Hinterhof - 100 x 81cm.
(Auktionshaus am Neumarkt)
  $35,387 £19,337

JAMES STEPHANOFF - The Rape Of
The Sabines - pencil and watercolour -
6½ x 9¼in.
(Sotheby's)   **$90 £50**

STEWART

R. MACAULAY STEVENSON - Wooded
Landscape - 30 x 37cm.
(Edmiston's)   **$378 £210**

ROBERT MACAULAY STEVENSON -
An Old Mill, Evening - signed - 16 x
19½in.
(Sotheby's Belgravia)   **$216 £120**

ROBERT MACAULAY STEVENSON -
Morning Shadows - signed - 18¾ x
25½in.
(Sotheby's Belgravia)   **$540 £300**

ROBERT MACAULAY STEVENSON -
Montreuil Sur Mer - signed - 19 x 25in.
(Sotheby's Belgravia)   **$396 £220**

W. STEWART - Fishing Boats On The
Coast - signed - watercolour - 9¼ x
19¾in.
(Sotheby's Belgravia)   **$108 £60 Pair**

STOFFE

JAN JACOBSZ. VAN DER STOFFE - A Cavalry Engagement - signed and dated 1637 - on panel - 18 x 37¼in.
(Christie's) **$3,060 £1,700**

CARL STOITZNER - A Fisherman Gutting A Fish - signed - on panel - 8 x 6in.
(Christie's) **$324 £180**

CARL STOITZNER - A Man Plucking A Guitar - signed - oil - on panel - 8 x 6in.
(Buckell & Ballard) **$432 £240**

CARL STOITZNER - An Old Sailor With A Pipe - signed - on panel - 8 x 6in.
(Christie's) **$324 £180**

C. STOJANOW - Winter Landscapes With Horse-Drawn Sleds chased by wolves - both signed - on panel - 10 x 18¼in.
(Christie's) **$1,080 £600 Pair**

P. D. STOKLE - Sailing Ships on rough seas - signed - oil - on panel - 14½ x 28in.
(J. Entwistle & Co.) **$122 £68**

M. STONE - A Girl In A Black Hat - 19¼ x 11¼in.
(Sotheby's Belgravia) **$50 £28**

MARCUS STONE - The First Love Letter - signed - 8½ x 14¼in.
(Christie's) **$3,315 £1,700**

SARAH STONE - Parrots And A Butterfly; Three Parrots In A Tree - both signed and dated 1779 - 9½ x 14½in.
(Sotheby's) **$900 £500 Two**

W. STONE - Outside A Cottage; Wintertime - both signed - 15½ x 23½in.
(Sotheby's Belgravia) **$990 £550 Pair**

ABRAHAM STORCK - Nymwegen, on the Rhine; Mainz, on the Rhine - signed - 22½ x 18½in.
(Lawrence) **$30,600 £17,000 Pair**

ABRAHAM STORCK - A Southern Port - 12 x 15¼in.
(Sotheby's) **$5,550 £3,000**

SIR ARTHUR ERNEST STREETON -
The Landing Place - signed, inscribed in
pencil on the reverse, and dated '96 -
watercolour - 12 x 14in.
(Sotheby's)   **$2,316 £1,200**

JACOBUS STORCK - A River Landscape
with Dutch sailing barges; and A Capriccio
Mediterranean Harbour - one indistinctly
signed and dated 1679 - 23¼ x 32in.
(Christie's)   **$15,300 £8,500 Pair**

H. K. STORIE - Broadland Scene - watercolour - 6 x 21in.
(G. A. Key)   **$18   £10**

STRADANUS - Studies Of A Horse And
A Bull (recto); Studies Of Putti With
Bows And Other Attributes (verso) - pen
and brown ink, brown wash - 40.5 x
27.4cm.
(Christie's)   **$99 £55**

JOHN MELHUISH STRUDWICK -
Passing Days: A man sits watching the
periods of his life pass in procession from
the future into the past - paper laid down
on panel - shaped top - 14¾ x 44½in.
(Christie's)   **$43,200 £24,000**

STRUTT - Lions Resting - 23 x 29in.
(Sotheby's Belgravia)   **$90 £50**

STRUTT - Goats On A Mountain -
12 x 24in.
(Sotheby's Belgravia)   **$36   £20**

STRUTT - Head Study Of A Lion -
35½ x 27¼in.
(Sotheby's Belgravia)   **$81 £45**

RICHARD HERMANN STREBEL -
'Anticipation' - signed and dated (18)90 -
panel - 11¾ x 15in.
(Sotheby Bearne)   **$2,827 £1,450**

ARTHUR J. STRUTT - The Wine Cart -
signed and dated Rome 1878 - 28 x 43¾in.
(Christie's)   **$900 £500**

WM. STRUTT - Three Centurions -
signed - tempera and gold - on panel -
98 x 75cm.
(King & Chasemore) **$1,666 £850**

ABRAHAM VAN STRY - An Interior
with a man writing a letter, a youth
reading nearby and a view of a town
mansion through the open door - signed
and inscribed Dordrecht and inscribed -
on panel - 26 x 22¼in.
(Christie's) **$29,120 £16,000**

J. VAN STRY - A Dutch Frozen River
Scene with figures and a sledge - oil -
on panel - 25½ x 32in.
(Warner, Sheppard & Wade)
$23,520 £12,000

JACOB VAN STRY - Cattle Grazing, A
Seaport in the distance - signed - black
chalk and watercolour - 15.0 x 21.5cm.
(Christie's) **$216 £120**

JACOB VAN STRY - A Wooded River
Landscape with peasants, cattle and
sheep and a building beyond - signed -
on panel - 14 x 18½in.
(Christie's) **$2,160 £1,200**

B. STUART - A Country House; On An
Estuary - signed and dated 1895 - 9½ x
15½in.
(Sotheby's Belgravia) **$270 £150 Pair**

GILBERT STUART - Portrait Of Commissioner Beresford, half length, wearing a buff coat, and yellow waistcoat - 28 x 23in.
(Christie's) $2,160 £1,200

GILBERT STUART - Portrait Of George De La Poer Beresford, 1st Marquess of Waterford, half length, wearing the star of the Order of Saint Patrick - 29½ x 24½in.
(Christie's) $6,300 £3,500

WILLIAM STUART - Still Life With Pineapple, red and white grapes, peaches and cherries, strawberries and white-currant - oil - on canvas - 25 x 30in.
(Bonham's) $504 £280

GEORGE STUBBS - A Grey Arab Stallion in a wooded landscape - 34½ x 44in.
(Christie's) $27,000 £15,000

GEORGE STUBBS - Julius Caesar; a bay stallion in a landscape, with a cottage beyond - signed and dated 1776 - inscribed on the reverse - on panel - 23½ x 28in.
(Christie's) $17,100 £9,500

ARTHUR SUKER - A Lake Scene - signed - heightened with bodycolour - 11½ x 17¼in.
(Sotheby's Belgravia) $108 £60

THOMAS SUNDERLAND - A Lakeland Pastoral - pen and ink and blue wash - 9¾ x 13¾in.
(Sotheby's) $504 £280

SUNDERLAND

THOMAS SUNDERLAND - In Patterdale At The Head Of Ullswater - pen and ink and blue wash - 9 x 13in.
(Sotheby's) **$324 £180**

THOMAS SUNDERLAND - From The Top Of The Mountain, Kirkstone, Looking Down On Brothers Water, Place Fell In The Distance, Westmorland - pen and ink and blue wash - 9 x 13in.
(Sotheby's) **$216 £120**

THOMAS SUNDERLAND - On The Shore Of Windermere With The Langdale Pikes, Westmorland - 9 x 13in.
(Sotheby's) **$396 £220**

THOMAS SUNDERLAND - On Windermere, Looking Towards The Langdale Pikes, Westmorland - pen and ink and blue wash - 9 x 13¼in.
(Sotheby's) **$540 £300**

THOMAS SUNDERLAND - Distant Church From A Wooded Hillside - pen and ink and blue wash - 11 x 8¼in.
(Sotheby's) **$180 £100**

JOHN SURTEES - A Sea Loch On The West Coast - signed - 14¼ x 29in.
(Sotheby's Belgravia) **$576 £320**

LUDOVICO DE SUSIO - A Roemer Of Wine And Bread On A Pewter Plate, A Stoneware Jug And A Mouse On A Table - on panel - 10½ x 15¾in.
(Christie's) **$9,100 £5,000**

GRAHAM SUTHERLAND - A Nursery Demon, after Hood and Grandville - 160 x 111cm.
(Auktionshaus am Neumarkt) **$35,387 £19,337**

HENRY SUTTON - The Thames At
Cleveden - signed and dated 1896 -
heightened with white - 12 x 18½in.
(Sotheby's Belgravia)   **$270   £150**

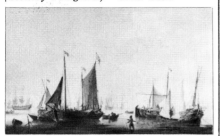

FRANCIS SWAINE - A Dutch Seascape
With Moored Fishing Boats and sailing
barges in the distance, men-o'-war lying
at anchor - signed - oil - on canvas - 31
x 47in.
(Bonham's)   **$6,120   £3,400**

MONAMY SWAINE - Shipping Off The
Coast, in a calm sea and in a stiff
breeze - both signed, one indistinctly -
on panel - 4¾ x 6¼in.
(Sotheby's)   **$612   £340 Pair**

ROBERT JOHN SWAN - The Popinjay -
signed and dated 1920 - shaped top - 30
x 24in.
(Christie's)   **$360   £200**

CORNELIS VAN SWANENBURGH -
A Wooded Italianate Landscape with
peasants and cattle on a path - signed
- 23 x 28½in.
(Christie's)   **$5,040   £2,800**

SWANEVELT - An Italian Wooded Landscape (recto) - black chalk, pen and brown
ink, brown wash; A Clump Of Trees
(verso) - grey wash, watermark - 18.3 x
26.3cm.
(Christie's)   **$126   £70**

H. SWANEVELT - A Mountainous
Italianate Landscape, with peasants
and animals on a bridge - bears
indistinct signature - 19½ x 23½in.
(Christie's)   **$1,440   £800**

JOHN WARKUP SWIFT - Shipping Off
Whitby - signed and dated 1845 - 21½ x
31¼in.
(Christie's)   **$1,560   £800**

SWISS SCHOOL, 16th century - The
Brazen Serpent - inscribed in German and
Latin - pen and brown ink, purple wash -
28.8 x 20.7cm.
(Christie's)   **$117   £65**

RUDOLPH SWOBODA, JUN - The
Carpet Dealer - signed - 37 x 21in.
(Christie's)   **$3,960   £2,200**

ANNA ALMA TADEMA - Returning
Light - signed and dated 1891 - on
board - 17½ x 6in.
(Christie's) $684 £380

FRANCIS TAILLEUX - Dieppe, L'Esplanade
du Casino - signed and dated 1936, also
signed, dated and inscribed on the reverse -
oil on canvas - 21¼ x 28¾in.
(Geering & Colyer) $378 £210

R. TALLACK - View At Pulls Ferry,
Norwich - watercolour - 7 x 10in.
(G. A. Key) $25 £14

TAMAGNI - Episodes From The Fall
Of Troy - pen and brown ink - 20.0
x 26.8cm.
(Christie's) $153 £85

TASSEL - The Crucifixion - 29 x 39in.
(Christie's) $684 £380

GEORGE TATTERSALL - The Goodwood
Cup - signed - inscribed and dated 1845 -
11½ x 20in.
(Sotheby's) $1,800 £1,000

NICHOLAS ANTHOINE TAUNAY -
Figures Merrymaking In An Encampment - signed and dated 1784 - on
panel - 6½ x 13½in.
(Christie's) $2,880 £1,600

ALBERT CHEVALIER TAYLOR -
Sir Thomas Becket Leaving Northampton
- signed and dated - 10 x 14in.
(Sotheby's Belgravia) $90 £50

JOHN FREDERICK TAYLER - Setters
In A Highland Landscape - signed with
initials - dated 1874 - heightened with
bodycolour - 17½ x 23½in.
(Sotheby's Belgravia) $306 £170

JOHN TAYLOR OF BATH - A September
Morning - signed, inscribed and dated 1793
- 36½ x 41¼in.
(Christie's) $1,530 £850

JOHN TAYLOR - Venus And Adonis; The School Of Cupid - one signed - 13 x 17in.
(Sotheby's)   **$288   £160 Pair**

F. TEHLY - Peasants Working In Fields - dated 1895 - oil - 28½ x 17½in.
(Thomas Love & Sons Ltd.)
                      $3,240 £1,800

TENIERS - Tavern Interiors With Card Players, peasants drinking and other rustic figures - oil - on panel - 11½ x 13½in.
(Heathcote Ball & Co) **$878 £480 Pair**

DAVID TENIERS, THE YOUNGER - Monkey Friars - on panel - 7½ x 10¼in.
(Christie's)   **$4,680   £2,600**

TENIERS, THE YOUNGER (After Titian) - Diana And Actaeon - on panel - 15 x 15½in.
(Christie's)   **$1,440   £800**

DAVID TENIERS, THE YOUNGER - Adam And Eve In The Garden Of Eden - signed and dated 1685 - 19¾ x 24½in.
(Christie's)   **$12,600   £7,000**

D. TENIERS THE YOUNGER - An Extensive Rocky Wooded River Landscape, with peasants, cattle, sheep and goats in the foreground and hills beyond - on panel - 16 x 20½in.
(Christie's)   **$6,300 £3,500**

D. TENIERS THE YOUNGER - A Tavern Interior, with peasants drinking and smoking - bears signature - on panel - 18½ x 24¾in.
(Christie's)   **$3,960 £2,200**

DAVID TENIERS THE YOUNGER, Attributed to - The Violinist - bears monogram - on panel - 13¼ x 10in.
(Christie's N. York)   **$3,960 £2,164**

TENIERS

DAVID TENIERS THE YOUNGER -
The Temptation Of Saint Anthony -
signed with monogram - on panel -
10 x 14in.
(Christie's) **$9,000 £5,000**

DAVID TENIERS THE YOUNGER - A
Coastal Landscape with fisherfolk and
their catch and fishing vessels offshore -
signed - on panel - 10 x 14in.
(Christie's) **$8,736 £4,800**

DAVID TENIERS, THE YOUNGER -
The Animals Entering Noah's Ark - signed
and dated 1686 - 19¾ x 24½in.
(Christie's) **$12,600 £7,000**

TENIERS - A Peasant Preparing Cabbages
in a kitchen interior - on panel - 16 x
27½in.
(Christie's) **$1,530 £850**

D. TENIERS THE ELDER - Saint
John The Baptist Preaching In The
Wilderness - on panel - 8 x 10¾in.
(Christie's) **$2,700 £1,500**

JOHN TENNANT - Fisherfolk On The
Seashore - signed and dated 1830 - 26½
x 39¼in.
(Christie's) **$5,070 £2,600**

FREDERIC CASEMERO TERRY -
"Cockatoo Island From Balmain" -
signed with initials - circa 1858 - watercolour - 20 x 43.5cm.
(Australian Art Auctions) **$814 £452**

LANCE THACKERAY - Sunrise, Damiella,
Egypt - signed and dated 1911 - watercolour
- 9½ x 6¼in.
(Christie's) **$72 £40**

JOHN THANE - Diana And Her Nymphs
Bathing - signed in full and with initials -
pen and red ink and watercolour - 7½ x
12½in.
(Sotheby's) **$288 £160**

GROSVENOR THOMAS - Autumn
Leaves - 17½ x 7½in.
(Sotheby's Belgravia)   **$504 £280**

JOHN THIRTLE - Bishopsgate Bridge,
Norwich - signed and indistinctly
inscribed on the reverse - pencil and grey
wash - 10¾ x 15½in.
(Christie's)   **$576 £320**

GROSVENOR THOMAS - The Old Mill
- signed - 13½ x 9½in.
(Sotheby's Belgravia)   **$504 £280**

JOHN THIRTLE - A View Of The
Bombarding Of Fort Shinaas - signed
and dated 1812 - 13 x 20¼in.
(Sotheby's)   **$12,600 £7,000**

ROBERT STRICKLAND THOMAS - H.M.S.
Britannia And Other Shipping in the Thames -
signed and dated 1837 - 18½ x 26½in.
(Sotheby's)   **$4,860 £2,700**

WALTER THOMAS - Galleons And Long-
Boats In Calm Waters - two signed - all
heightened with bodycolour - 11 x 13in.
(Sotheby's Belgravia)   **$18 £10 Three**

JOSEPH THOMA - A Turkish Coastal
Landscape, with fisherfolk in the foreground and a town beyond - signed -
26¼ x 41in.
(Christie's)   **$1,530 £850**

ALBERT GORDON THOMAS - Loch
Tullie, Poolewe - signed - 19 x 24in.
(Sotheby's Belgravia)   **$45 £25**

FRANK THOMAS - Landscape With
Three Horses being led into harvesting
field by labourers - signed - 16 x 24in.
(Phillips, Solihull)   **$1,476 £820 Pair**

ANDRE THOMKINS - Komposition -
signed and dated 1959 - ink - 11¾ x 16½in.
(Christie's)   **$640 £350**

JACOB THOMPSON - A Mountainous
Welsh Landscape, with figures and
sheep on a path by a stream - signed
and dated 1838 - 27 x 40in.
(Christie's)   **$2,160 £1,200**

ARCHIBALD THORBURN - A Woodcock
Resting - signed and dated 1931 -
heightened with bodycolour - 7¼ x 10½in.
(Sotheby's Belgravia)   **$1,890 £1,050**

ARCHIBALD THORBURN - Grouse On
The Alert - signed and dated 1882 -
heightened with bodycolour - 18 x
26½in.
(Sotheby's Belgravia)   **$4,320 £2,400**

ARCHIBALD THORBURN - Blackcock
And Greyhen In Flight - signed and
dated 1898 - heightened with bodycolour -
23½ x 37½in.
(Sotheby's Belgravia)   **$6,840 £3,800**

ARCHIBALD THORBURN - Ballas's Sand-
Grouse And Sociable Plover - signed and
dated 1925 - heightened with bodycolour -
7¾ x 10¾in.
(Sotheby's Belgravia)   **$2,700 £1,500**

SIR JAMES THORNHILL - A Landscape
With Classical Temples and a bridge - pen
and brown ink, brown wash, watermark
fleur-de-lys - 8¼ x 13¼in.
(Christie's)   **$1,170 £650**

WILLIAM THORNLEY - Evening - signed
- 13½ x 11½in.
(Sotheby's Belgravia)   **$828 £460**

NOEL WARNER THORNTON - Troops
On Dover Green - watercolour - 11 x
20in.
(G. A. Key)   **$86 £48**

J. THORS - Country Landscape with a
poppy field - 23½ x 35½in.
(Sotheby Bearne)   **$522 £290**

J. THORS - Wooded Landscape And River Scene with country cottage - oil - 15 x 20in.
(G. A. Key) $16 £9

JOSEPH THORS - A Woody Landscape with figures by a cottage - signed - 15½ x 23½in.
(Christie's) $1,852 £950

JOSEPH THORS - Winter Wooded River Landscape - signed - oil on canvas - 30 x 36in.
(King & Chasemore) $720 £400

JOSEPH THORS - A Peasant Feeding Chickens in a farm yard - signed - on panel - 6¼ x 8in.
(Christie's) $63 £35

JOSEPH THORS - A Wooded River Landscape - signed - 29 x 24½in.
(Christie's) $720 £400

JOSEPH THORS - An Extensive Landscape Near Worcester with a shepherd and his flock on a path - signed - 18½ x 26¾in.
(Christie's) $1,440 £800

T. VAN THULDEN - The Baptism Of Christ - on copper - 22¼ x 17in.
(Christie's) $810 £450

TIDEMANN - Studies Of Heads - pen and grey ink, grey wash - 24.0 x 17.2cm.
(Christie's) $72 £40

JAN CORNELIS TIELE - A Berber Girl Seated Cross-Legged By A Wall - signed - canvas - on panel - 19¼ x 14¾in.
(Christie's) $86 £48

TIEPOLO - The Adoration Of The Magi - black chalk, brown wash heightened with white, watermark three crescents - 40.3 x 26.5cm.
(Christie's) $216 £120

G. B. TIEPOLO - Study Of A Standing Man in a tricorn hat - pen and brown ink, brown wash - 14 x 9.2cm.
(Christie's) $180 £100

GIOVANNI BATTISTA TIEPOLO - Esther And Mordecai Before Ahasuerus - 21 x 28in.
(Christie's) $20,020 £11,000

TIEPOLO

LOUIS TIMMERMANS - Coastal Scene with fishing boats and figures, low tide - signed and inscribed on the reverse - 29 x 49¼in.
(Sotheby Bearne) **$1,014 £520**

LORENZO TIEPOLO - A Girl Playing A Lute - oval - 21 x 16¼in.
(Christie's) **$4,368 £2,400**

G. VAN TILBORCH - Figures In A Picture Gallery - 21½ x 35½in.
(Christie's) **$2,520 £1,400**

TILLEMANS - Studies Of Horsemen (recto) - black chalk; A Saddle (verso) - grey wash - 18.2 x 23.2cm.
(Christie's) **$63 £35**

WALASSE TING - Horse and Rider - brush and black and red ink on board - 49 x 88 in.
(Christie's N. York) **$2,420 £1,344**

TINGQUA, Attributed to - A View of Hong Kong, a paddle steamer, merchant vessels and junks in the foreground - gouache - 8 x 11 in.
(Sotheby's, Hong Kong) **$1,454 £808**

PETER TILLEMANS - A View Of Urley's Farm, Corscombe, Dorset - 45½ x 45½in.
(Christie's) **$5,040 £2,800**

TINGQUA, Attributed to - An extensive view of 'Whampoa' Anchorage - gouache - 8 x 11 in.
(Sotheby's, Hong Kong) **$666 £370**

TINGQUA, Attributed to - Portraits of Wong Tye, the Legendary Emperor of China and Wong Leung, Empress of China - watercolour heightened with bodycolour - 8 x 7¼ in
(Sotheby's, Hong Kong) **$1,080 £600 Pair**

TINTORETTO - The Translation Of The Body Of Saint Mark - black chalk, pen and brown ink, brown and grey wash - 19.4 x 20.4cm.
(Christie's) **$54 £30**

TINTORETTO, After - Portrait Of A Lady, small three-quarter length, in gold and white dress - on panel - 9 x 7in.
(Christie's) **$2,160 £1,200**

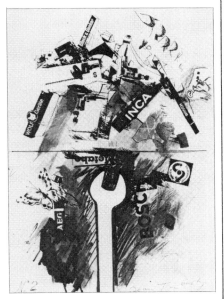

JEAN TINGUELY - Inca - signed - mixed media and collage on paper - 17 x 12¼in.
(Christie's) **$1,189 £650**

JEAN TINGUELY - Le Monstre Dans La Foret - signed and dated 1976 - ball point pen on brown cardboard - 11¼ x 11in.
(Christie's) **$1,189 £650**

DOMENICO TINTORETTO, Attributed to - Portrait Of A Venetian Senator, three-quarter length - inscribed 'Colaus Georgo Esandri' - 47¼ x 37¼in.
(Christie's N. York) **$770 £421**

TITIAN - Portraits Of Antonio De Leyva And Pietro Aretino, bust lengths, the former in profile wearing black costume and cap, the latter wearing black costume and gold chain - 30¾ x 36½in.
(Christie's) **$2,340 £1,300**

JACOPO ROBUSTI, IL TINTORETTO - The Mocking Of Christ - 51¾ x 41in.
(Christie's) **$11,830 £6,500**

W. V. TIPPET - Coming Home From Work - signed and dated - 15½ x 21¾in.
(Sotheby's Belgravia) **$162 £90**

TITIAN - The Rest On The Flight Into Egypt - 19¼ x 26in.
(Christie's) **$756 £420**

TITIAN - The Madonna And Child with the infant Saint John The Baptist - 51 x 40½in.
(Christie's) **$1,080 £600**

JAMES JACQUES TISSOT - Girl With A Fan - signed - on panel - 31 x 22½in.
(Christie's) **$22,500 £12,500**

TITIAN, After - Portrait Of A Gentleman, half length, in a black, fur-collared coat, seated in a chair - on panel - 9 x 6½in.
(Christie's) **$1,800 £1,000**

TOMAS MORAGAS Y TORRAS - The Trial Of A Murderer in the square of an Arab town - signed - 26½ x 38in.
(Christie's) **$7,200 £4,000**

LOUIS TOCQUE, Circle of - Portrait Of A Gentleman, seated, half length, in a blue coat, at a table, holding a snuff box - 29¾ x 25in.
(Christie's N. York) **$2,200 £1,202**

HENRY TODD - An Old Lady In A Wooded Lane - signed and dated 1893 - 10½ x 16¼in.
(Sotheby's Belgravia) **$270 £150**

ALDINI CASIMIRO TOMBA - Portrait Of A Girl In A Hat With An Ostrich Feather - signed and inscribed Roma - watercolour - 61.3 x 48.2cm.
(Christie's) **$162 £90**

W. S. TOMKIN - Clipper Ship Homeward Bound - watercolour - 9 x 14in.
(G. A. Key) **$90 £50**

GIULIO DEL TORRE - Feeding The Doll - signed and dated 1894 - on panel - 9¾ x 7½in.
(Christie's) **$2,700 £1,500**

CLIFTON TOMSON - A Light Bay Hunter in a landscape - signed and dated Nottingham 1818 - 27¼ x 34in.
(Christie's) **$1,440 £800**

ELLIOT BOUTON TORREY - French Riverscape - signed - oil - on canvas - 21½ x 29in.
(Richard A. Bourne Co. Inc.) **$400 £222**

ROBERT TOURNIERES, attributed to - Portrait of a Lady said to be the Marquise de Liancourt as Spring behind a parapet - 41 x 33¼ in.
(Christie's N. York) $1,650 £902

TOWNE - A Dark Bay Hunter In A Landscape - 24 x 31in.
(Sotheby's) $810 £450

C. TOWNE - Landscape With A Bull Attacked By Four Dogs - 29¼ x 24½in.
(Sotheby Bearne) $741 £380

CHARLES TOWNE - Partridge - signed with initials and dated 1820 - on panel - 5 x 6in.
(Sotheby's Belgravia) $432 £240

ALFRED O. TOWNSEND - Wooded River Landscape In Autumn - signed - oil - on canvas - 21 x 26in.
(Lalonde Bros. & Parham) $137 £75

HENRY TOZER - Shipping At The Eddystone - signed - watercolour - 32 x 24in.
(Hussey's) $130 £72

WILLIAM TRAIS - A Border Landscape - 23¾ x 31¾in.
(Sotheby's Belgravia) $3,240 £1,800

G. S. TREGEAR - The London-Dover Mail Coach - on panel - 10½ x 15in.
(H. Spencer & Sons) $360 £200

TREVISANI - The Virgin And Child With Saints (recto); Study Of A Woman (verso) - black chalk - 28.7 x 20.4cm.
(Christie's) $90 £50

HENDRIK ALBERT VAN TRIGT - Courtroom Scene - signed - watercolour - 15½ x 23in.
(Richard A. Bourne Co. Inc.) $525 £292

LOUIS-ROLLAND TRINQUESSE - Ladies Sacrificing To A Goddess - 23¼ x 28¾in.
(Sotheby's) $7,030 £3,800

J. L. TROMBETTO - Garibaldi's Red-shirts - signed - oil - on canvas - 14½ x 13in.
(Swetenham's)   **$475 £250**

JEAN FRANCOIS DE TROY, Circle of - Arachne - 40 x 34in.
(Christie's N. York)   **$462 £252**

CONSTANT TROYON - Partridges In A Cornfield - signed - 5½ x 8¼in.
(Christie's)   **$432 £240**

CHARLES PHILOGENE TSCHAGGENY - A Traveller Resting By A Path - signed - on panel - 10 x 18in.
(Christie's)   **$720 £400**

CHARLES PHILOGENE TSCHAGGENY - A Boy On A Cart Horse on a beach - signed - 11 x 18½in.
(Christie's)   **$720 £400**

CHARLES PHILOGENE TSCHAGGENY - Waiting For The Fisherman's Return - signed and dated 1839 - on panel - 23 x 31¼in.
(Christie's)   **$3,240 £1,800**

EDWARD TUCKER - The Jaws, Borrow-dale - indistinctly signed - 9½ x 14½in.
(Sotheby's Belgravia)   **$63 £35**

HENRY SCOTT TUKE - A Moored Boat - signed - 9¼ x 5¾in.
(Sotheby's Belgravia)   **$72 £40**

ALESSANDRO TURCHI, Circle of - The Temptation Of Saint Anthony - 13½ x 11¼in.
(Christie's N. York)   **$385 £210**

SCHOOL OF TURIN, circa 1755-1760 - Portrait Of Giulio Gaetano Pugnani, three-quarter length - 47 x 34½in.
(Christie's)   **$11,830 £6,500**

CLARIDGE TURNER - Hornsbridge, Near Porlock - signed and dated '98 - inscribed on the stretcher - 29½ x 19½in.
(Sotheby's Belgravia)   **$90 £50**

DANIEL TURNER - St. Paul's Cathedral From The South Bank Of The Thames With Figures in the foreground - on panel - oval - 16 x 20in.
(Christie's)   **$990 £550**

TURNER

F. C. TURNER - Portrait Of A Favourite Pony Standing in a park - signed and dated 1825 - on panel - 14 x 17½in.
(Christie's S. Kensington) **$594 £330**

F. C. TURNER - A Day's Shoot - 11½ x 15½in.
(Sotheby's Belgravia) **$1,890 £1,050 Pair**

G. TURNER - Fishermen By A Ford - 12 x 16in.
(Sotheby's Belgravia) **$234 £130**

GEORGE TURNER - A View In Derbyshire - signed and dated 1878 - 11½ x 15¼in.
(Sotheby's Belgravia) **$540 £300**

GEORGE TURNER - The Gipsies Encampment, nr. Formark, Derbyshire, a sunlit summer evening scene with gipsies, their dog and donkey beside an oak-shaded lane - signed - verso inscribed, signed and dated 1872 - oil - on canvas - 24 x 36in.
(Neales of Nottingham) **$3,348 £1,800**

GEORGE TURNER - Faggot Gatherers Near Bettws-Y-Coed - signed - signed, inscribed and dated 1893 on the reverse - 23½ x 35½in.
(Christie's) **$1,620 £900**

GEORGE TURNER - A Derbyshire Corn-field, with figures and dog in a tree shaded lane - oil - on canvas - 23½ x 35½in.
(Neales of Nottingham) **$2,943 £1,525**
GEORGE TURNER - The Trent, Barrow - signed and dated '69 - inscribed on the reverse - 9½ x 15¼in.
(Sotheby's Belgravia) **$720 £400**

TURNER, After J.M.W. - St Catherine's Hill near Guildford - sepia watercolour - 26 x 18.5cm.
(King & Chasemore) **$46 £24**

J. A. TURNER - A Professional Opinion, two prospectors examining a rock - signed and dated 1886 - oil - on canvas - 13½ x 17½in.
(Sotheby's) **$4,825 £2,500**

JOSEPH MALLORD WILLIAM TURNER - A Mountainous Landscape Between Brathy And Keswick - inscribed on the reverse - blue and grey wash - 6¼ x 8¾in.
(Sotheby's) **$1,116 £620**

J. A. TURNER - Is It Gold? - signed and dated 1886 - oil - on canvas - 13½ x 17½in.
(Sotheby's) **$6,755 £3,500**

JOSEPH MALLORD WILLIAM TURNER - The Falls Of Lodore And Derwentwater - 8¾ x 12¼in.
(Sotheby's) **$2,610 £1,450**

JOSEPH MALLORD WILLIAM TURNER - Schloss Eltz On The Mosel - pencil, pen and dark red ink and watercolour on grey papered paper - 6¼ x 9in.
(Christie's) **$14,400 £8,000**

J. M. W. TURNER - A River Scene With Hilly Landscape - pencil and watercolour - 6¾ x 8½in.
(Sotheby's) **$504 £280**

JOSEPH MALLORD WILLIAM TURNER - The Valley Of The St. Gothard - 8¾ x 11½in.
(Sotheby's) **$41,400 £23,000**

TURNER

M. A. TURNER - Harvesting Scene with figures and pond, sheep in the foreground - verso signed, inscribed and dated 1839 - oil - on canvas - 25 x 36in.
(Neales of Nottingham) **$149 £80**

W. H. De LOND TURNER - Barnet Horse Fair - signed and dated 1864 - 14¼ x 20¾in.
(Sotheby's) **$2,700   £1,500**

WILLIAM TURNER OF OXFORD - A View From The Downs Above Kingley Bottom, Sussex - signed and inscribed on reverse label - 14½ x 19½in.
(Sotheby's) **$3,240   £1,800**

WILLIAM TURNER OF OXFORD - A View Of Kingley Bottom, Sussex With Yew Tree At Dusk - signed and inscribed on reverse label - 14¾ x 21¼in.
(Sotheby's) **$2,520   £1,400**

TUSCAN SCHOOL, circa 1560 - Christ On The Cross with studies of the Marys and God The Father - pen and brown ink, brown wash heightened with white on blue paper - 23.2 x 20.8cm.
(Christie's) **$108 £60**

CY TWOMBLY - Untitled - signed, inscribed and dated 1963 - oil and pencil on canvas - 89 x 78in.
(Christie's) **$23,790 £13,000**

CY TWOMBLY - Roman Notes - signed and dated Mai 1970 on the reverse - gouache and coloured chalks - on paper - 27½ x 34½in.
(Sotheby's) **$3,477 £1,900**

J. SEDDON TYRER - A Market Place In Normandy - signed - dated 1876 - heightened with bodycolour - 17½ x 12in.
(Sotheby's Belgravia) **$144 £80**

SCHOOL OF THE TYROL, circa 1500 - A Group Of Apostles - on panel - 21½ x 11in.
(Christie's) **$4,680 £2,600**

HAO YING TZU, Style of - A Phoenix - inscribed and dated - watercolour heightened with bodycolour - 42 x 20½in.
(Sotheby's, Hong Kong) **$292 £162**

ERNEST BOYE UDEN - December's Mantle; Mermaid Street, Rye; The Inglenook - signed - two inscribed - all heightened with bodycolour - 14¼ x 16½in.
(Sotheby's Belgravia) **$38 £20 Three**

JOHANN ULRICH - A Dutch Canal Scene, thatched cottages in the foreground, boats and windmill beyond - signed - 13¼ x 20¼in.
(Sotheby's) **$630 £350**

LUCAS VAN UDEN - Landscape With Christ On The Road To Emmaus - on copper - 10 x 13½in.
(Sotheby's) **$7,400 £4,000**

LUCAS VAN UDEN - An Extensive Woody Landscape with peasants and cattle on a path - 46 x 65in.
(Christie's) **$8,100 £4,500**

FRED UHLMAN - Tuscany Farm - signed - on board - 13½ x 17½in.
(Sotheby's) **$153 £85**

JOHANN JAKOB ULRICH - Kirchenansicht - 53.5 x 40cm.
(Auktionshaus am Neumarkt) **$430 £235**

FREDERICK THOMAS UNDERHILL - The Last Piece - signed and dated 1818 - heightened with white - 10½ x 8¼in.
(Sotheby's Belgravia) **$216 £120**

F. T. UNDERHILL - Young Faggot Gatherers - 22½ x 30½in.
(Sotheby's Belgravia) **$306 £170**

FRANZ RICHARD UNTERBERGER -
A Bavarian River Gorge - signed - 16½
x 22¾in.
(Sotheby's)   **$2,520 £1,400**

UNDERHILL - April Showers - 18 x
14in.
(Sotheby's Belgravia)   **$193 £100**

UNTERBERGER - Views Of Naples -
bears signatures and inscribed on reverse -
on board - 5¾ x 8¼in.
(Sotheby's)   **$1,170 £650 Pair**
UNTERBERGER - An Alpine Landscape
with a sparkling brook, a shepherdess and
her flock to the left - inscribed - 28¼ x
23¼in.
(Sotheby's)   **$900 £500**

FRANZ RICHARD UNTERBERGER -
A View Of Amalfi - signed - 32¼ x 27in.
(Christie's)   **$6,840   £3,800**

FRANZ RICHARD UNTERBERGER -
On The Lagoons, Venice - oil - 11 x 20in.
(Bonham's)   **$3,960 £2,200**

FRANZ RICHARD UNTERBERGER -
An Extensive Coastal Landscape possibly
on the Adriatic, rustics with their cattle
and sheep by rocks in the foreground, a
rocky coastline beyond - signed and
inscribed - 35¼ x 51in.
(Sotheby's)   **$6,120 £3,400**

FRANZ RICHARD UNTERBERGER -
A View Of Capri With Fisherfolk in the
foreground - signed - 25¾ x 36in.
(Christie's) **$4,680 £2,600**

FRANZ RICHARD UNTERBERGER -
'Amalfi - Golfe de Salerno' - signed
and inscribed on the reverse - 27¾ x 49¼in.
(Sotheby Bearne) **$7,200 £4,000**

FRANZ RICHARD UNTERBERGER -
The Boat Houses, Venice: A View Of
The Bacino - signed - on panel - 23 x 13in.
(Christie's) **$3,060 £1,700**

JOHN CLARKSON UREN - Sailing Boats
Off Marazion and St. Michael's Mount -
signed and dated 1879 - pencil and watercolour heightened with white - 4½ x 10¼in.
(Christie's) **$253 £130**

STEFANO USSI - A Girl At An Oasis -
signed and dated 1872 - 33 x 23in.
(Christie's) **$1,440 £800**

SCHOOL OF UTRECHT, 17th century -
The Deposition - 77 x 61in.
(Sotheby's) **$900 £500**

MAURICE UTRILLO - The House Of
Berlioz - 55 x 46cm.
(Auktionshaus am Neumarkt)
$35,387 £19,337

MAURICE UTRILLO - La Maison Blanche -
signed - 19¾ x 25½in.
(Christie's New York) **$13,200 £7,333**

ANDRE UTTER - Landscape - 27.5 x
41.5cm.
(Auktionshaus am Neumarkt) **$1,061 £580**

THOMAS UWINS - Neapolitan Peasants
Dancing The Tarantella On The Vomizo
- signed and dated 1840 - on panel -
19¾ x 24¼in.
(Christie's) **$810 £450**

T. UWINS - The Flower Girl - oval -
15½ x 11½in.
(Christie's) **$618 £320**

ISAAC UYTENBOGAART - A Valley
Landscape with peasants returning from
market - signed - on panel - 10¾ x 13in.
(Sotheby's) **$4,810 £2,600**

J. UYTEWAEL - Lot And His Daughters
in a sumptuously decorated cave, the
city of Sodom in flames beyond - 40 x
54½in.
(Sotheby's) **$3,515 £1,900**

CHARLES VACHER - A View Of
Thebes, Egypt - signed and dated
'Thebes 1863' and stamped on the
reverse - watercolour - 13½ x 35½in.
(Christie's) $324 £180

LODEWYCK DE VADDER - An Extensive
Wooded Landscape with peasants on a path -
signed with initials - on panel - 19 x 23¾in.
(Christie's) $7,200 £4,000

VALCKENBORCH - A Hilly Landscape
With The Flight Into Egypt - on metal -
8¼ x 10½in.
(Sotheby's) $12,025 £6,500

J. VALENSI - Arabs Playing Back-
gammon - signed - 37 x 52in.
(Christie's) $1,080 £600

M. LUDOVIC VALLEE - Fete Day At
The Tuilleries - oil - 19 x 31in.
(Hussey's) $189 £105

W. F. VALLENCE - A Coast Scene with
a rowing boat - signed and dated 1868 -
watercolour - 6¾ x 10in.
(Warner, Sheppard & Wade) $59 £30

H. VALEROS - The Water Carriers -
signed - 26 x 21in.
(Christie's) $756 £420

FELIX VALLOTTON - Narcisses In A
Black Bowl - 61.5 x 50cm.
(Auktionshaus am Neumarkt) $15,165 £8,287

438

VALLOZ - Le General Bonaparte - signed - pencil and grey wash, circular - 15.5cm. diameter.
(Christie's) **$32 £18**

FREDERICK E. VALTER - An Intruder - signed and dated 1901 - signed and inscribed on the reverse - on panel - 9½ x 11½in.
(Christie's) **$468 £260**

FREDERICK E. VALTER - Moorland Sheep - signed - 15½ x 23½in.
(Sotheby's Belgravia) **$270 £150**

DOMINIQUE JOSEPH VANDERBURGH - Invaders attacking a coastal village - indistinctly signed - 23 x 27½ in.
(Christie's N. York) **$1,760 £962**

F. VANNI - Head Of A Putto - black and red chalk on light brown paper - 11.9 x 9.8cm.
(Christie's) **$36 £20**

VANVITELLI - The Tomb Of Caecilia Metella (recto) - black chalk, pen and brown ink, grey and brown wash; Figure Studies (verso) - red chalk, pen and brown ink - 21.5 x 30.7cm.
(Christie's) **$63 £35**

HENRY VALTER - A British Man-O'-War and other sailing vessels off the Dover coast - signed - 27 x 39¾in.
(Christie's) **$1,170 £650**

J. VARLEY - Conway Castle From The River - pencil and watercolour, heightened with gum arabic - 14¾ x 21¼in.
(Sotheby's) **$90 £50**

JAN VANDERBANK - Portrait Of Mary, Duchess Of Somerset, seated, three-quarter length, wearing a white dress and blue ermine lined cloak - 49¼ x 39¼in.
(Christie's) **$1,260 £700**

JOHN VARLEY - The Temple At Phylae, commonly known as 'Pharoah's Bed' - signed and dated 1878 and fully inscribed on the reverse - 20¼ x 32¼in.
(Sotheby Bearne) **$1,440 £800**

439

JOHN VARLEY - View Of Loch Ard In Scotland - signed and dated 1826 - watercolour - 14¼ x 20½in.
(Christie's) **$1,170 £650**

JOHN VARLEY - Lake Ogwen, Snowdonia - signed and dated 1835 - watercolour - 15½ x 11¼in.
(Christie's) **$540 £300**

JOHN VARLEY - Bayswater From Porchester Terrace - signed - inscribed 'Study from Nature' - dated 1831 - 9 x 12¼in.
(Sotheby's) **$2,700 £1,500**

JOHN VARLEY - Pont Aberglaslyn, North Wales - signed and dated 1805 - 25½ x 20¾in.
(Sotheby's) **$324 £180**

JOHN VARLEY - A Cottage by a Wood, figures in the foreground, a storm coming on - pencil and watercolour - 16 x 14 in.
(Sotheby's) **$324 £180**

VARLIN - London 1955 - 114 x 72cm.
(Auktionshaus am Neumarkt) **$20,221 £11,050**

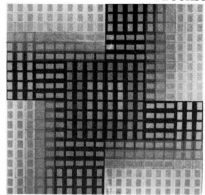

VICTOR VASARELY - "Balint" - signed - collage on board - 24 x 24in.
(Sotheby's) $5,124 £2,800

ALESSANDRO VAROTARI, After - The Mater Dolorosa - on panel - 9 x 6¾in.
(Christie's) $1,530 £850

G. E. VAUTIER - Country Landscape with a shepherd resting beside a pond - signed and dated 1849 - on panel - 11½ x 14½in.
(Sotheby Bearne) $1,548 £860

VICTOR VASARELY - Siris II - signed, inscribed and dated 1952-1958 on reverse - 76¾ x 53 in.
(Christie's) $11,895 £6,500

PALMA VECCHIO, After - Saint John The Evangelist - oil on canvas laid down on panel - 6½ x 4¾in.
(Christie's) $990 £550

VECELLIO

TIZIANO VECELLIO, called Titian -
Portrait Of Giacomo Dolfin, half length,
in Procurator's robes, holding a letter
inscribed - 40½ x 35¼in.
(Christie's) **$109,200 £60,000**

PIETER VAN VEEN - The Holy Family -
signed - on panel - 12 x 10in.
(Christie's N. York) **$1,760 £962**

ADRIAEN VAN DE VELDE - A Shepherdess At A Ford - 11½ x 15½in.
(Sotheby's) **$8,140 £4,400**

A. VAN DE VELDE - A Woody Landscape with a peasant and cattle by a
ruin - 13¼ x 18½in.
(Christie's) **$1,530 £850**

WILLEM VAN DE VELDE THE ELDER -
A Flagship (Zeelandia?) Off A Coast -
signed with initials - pen and black ink on
a prepared panel - 26½ x 35½in.
(Sotheby's) **$27,750 £15,000**

WILLEM VAN DE VELDE THE
YOUNGER - Dutch Fishing Boats and
other vessels in a stormy sea - signed
with initials - 16 x 14½in.
(Christie's) **$136,500 £75,000**

WILLEM VAN DE VELDE II - A Man-
O'-War - black chalk, grey wash - 22.0
x 13.8cm.
(Christie's) **$234 £130**

BERNAR VENET - Weather Report,
January 24, 1969 - signed, inscribed and
dated Jan. 24, 1969 on the reverse -
photographic blow-up on panel - 58 x
39¾in.
(Christie's) **$2,928 £1,600**

VENETIAN SCHOOL, XIX century -
The Grand Canal with many gondolas
and other small boats, with the
Basilica Maria della Salute and the
Lagoon in the distance - 23½ x 35½in.
(H. Spencer & Sons) **$360 £200**

VENETIAN SCHOOL, 17th century -
A Caprice View Of Venice - 24¼ x
38½in.
(Sotheby's) **$6,475 £3,500**

**A VENETIAN MASTER, After - Second Half
Of The Sixteenth Century - Portrait Of**
Francesco Donato, Doge Of Venice, seated,
half length, with a view of the Doges' Palace
beyond - bears monogram - on panel - 8¾ x
6½in.
(Christie's) **$1,800 £1,000**

VENETIAN SCHOOL, circa 1520 -
The Madonna And Child With The Infant
Saint John The Baptist - on panel - 27¾
x 24¼in.
(Christie's) **$8,100 £4,500**

VENETIAN SCHOOL, 18th century -
Many Figures on an arcade; a lover
discovered - oak panel - 8¾ x 13in.
(Woolley & Wallis) **$351 £195**

VENETIAN SCHOOL, 18th century -
Portrait Of A Little Girl - 17¾ x 13½in.
(Sotheby's) **$3,700 £2,000**

443

VENETIAN SCHOOL

VENETIAN SCHOOL, 19th century - Venice - oil - on canvas - 45 x 58cm. *(Christian Rosset)* **$959 £533**

VENETIAN SCHOOL, Late 18th century - The Piazzetta, Venice - 18 x 23½in. *(Christie's N. York)* **$1,430 £781**

ARTHUR VENTNOR - Rejected - signed and dated 1890 - 19½ x 15½in. *(Sotheby's Belgravia)* **$117 £65**

FRANS XAVIER HENDRIK VERBEECK - A Merry Company - signed - 18½ x 22¾in. *(Sotheby's)* **$6,660 £3,600**

PIETER CORNELISZ VERBEECK - A Saddled Horse Tied To A Post - bears Cuyp signature - on panel - 11 x 9in. *(Christie's N. York)* **$3,300 £1,803**

EUGENE VERBOECKHOVEN - Sheep In A Wooded Landscape - signed and dated 1878 - on board - 14 x 18in. *(Christie's)* **$1,620 £900**

444

VERNET

VERELST - Portrait Of A Lady, three-quarter length, standing in a landscape, a staff in her right hand - 48 x 39in.
(Sotheby's) **$720 £400**

LOUIS CHARLES VERBOECKHOVEN - Dutch Fishing Vessels in a choppy sea - signed and dated 1825 - on panel - 12½ x 17¼in.
(Christie's) **$8,640 £4,800**

TOBIAS VERHAECHT - A Mountainous Wooded River Landscape with travellers on a path - on panel - 20 x 30½in.
(Christie's) **$10,920 £6,000**

JAN PEETER VERDUSSEN - A Rocky Woody Landscape with sportsmen and ladies picnicking by a fountain, and horses and hounds beyond - 20½ x 24½in.
(Christie's) **$5,096 £2,800**

ANDRIES VERMEULEN - A Winter Landscape with skaters and a horsedrawn sled on a frozen waterway - signed - 16 x 19½in.
(Christie's) **$2,880 £1,600**

J. VERMEYEN - A Court Hawking Party - on panel - 22¼ x 34¼in.
(Sotheby's) **$37,000 £20,000**

VERNET, After - Extensive Classical Mediterranean Harbour Scene with Port buildings and ruins, small boats discharging cargo, fishermen and many other figures in everyday occupations - oil - on canvas - 38½ x 51in.
(Lalonde Bros. & Parham) **$1,738 £950**

SIMON VERELST - Group Portrait Of Three Young Girls, two seated full length, and one standing full length, on a terrace - 59 x 70½in.
(Christie's) **$1,800 £1,000**

VERNET

BONIFAZIO VERONESE, After - The Madonna And Child With Saint Mark And Saint Ursula - oil on canvas - on panel - 8¼ x 12¼in.
(Christie's) $2,700   £1,500

VERNET - Harbour With Ships - oil - 28 x 42in.
(Graves, Son & Pilcher) $720   £400

CLAUDE JOSEPH VERNET, Manner of - Fishermen by a Waterfall - 9 x 11¾ in.
(Christie's N. York) $440   £240

R. W. VERNON - Lowestoft Fishing Fleet leaving harbour - watercolour - 7 x 9in.
(G. A. Key) $20   £11

SCHOOL OF VERONA, Circa 1540 - A Lady Presenting A Box Of Flowers To Children, in a landscape - on panel - 9½ x 17¼in.
(Christie's N. York) $3,960   £2,164

PAOLO CALIARI, IL VERONESE, Circle of - Head Of A Bearded Man - inscribed - black and white chalk on blue paper - 15.1 x 15.3cm.
(Christie's) $270   £150

VERSCHUUR - At The Blacksmith's - 11 x 14¾in.
(Christie's) $576   £320

ANTOINE VESTIER, Circle of - The Young Soldier - oval - 25 x 20in.
(Christie's N. York) $770   £421

VAN VIANEN - A Sea God Bearing A Crowned Shield With A Moor's Head - inscribed - pen and brown ink, brown wash, indented with the stylus - 8.5 x 12.7cm.
(Christie's) $324   £180

JEAN GEORGES VIBERT - The Chieftain - signed - watercolour and bodycolour - 9½ x 13¼in.
(Christie's) $234   £130

BONIFAZIO DE'PITATI, called BONIFAZIO VERONESE - A Contest Between The Martial And The Liberal Arts - on convex panel - circular - 19in. diameter.
(Christie's) $6,840   £3,800

A. VICKERS - A Mill And Cottage beside a stream - signed - oil - on canvas - 8 x 12in.
(Warner, Sheppard & Wade) $823   £420

ALFRED VICKERS - An Extensive Landscape Near Lymington, Hants - signed - 22¾ x 39in.
(Christie's)   **$5,070 £2,600**

ALFRED VICKERS - Lake Geneva Near Lausanne, with figures in the foreground - signed and dated '52 - signed, inscribed and dated 1852 on the reverse - 7½ x 14¼in.
(Christie's)   **$90 £50**

ALFRED GOMERSAL VICKERS - Dutch Fisherfolk on the shore near a windmill - signed with initials and dated 1834 - watercolour - 21¾ x 18in.
(Christie's)   **$630 £350**

ALFRED GOMERSAL VICKERS - The Kremlin, Moscow, with figures in the Square - 10¾ x 16¼in.
(Sotheby's)   **$2,520 £1,400**

ALFRED GOMERSAL VICKERS - A View of Lubeck with figures and boats in the foreground - signed - 9½ x 14 in.
(Sotheby's)   **$2,160 £1,200**

A. H. VICKERS - River Scene With The Yorkshire Dales With Harvest Scene - oil - 8 x 16in.
(G. A. Key)   **$54 £30**

A. H. VICKERS - River Scene With Buildings And Boats - oil - 12 x 10in.
(G. A. Key)   **$450 £250**

A. H. VICKERS - Figures By A River - 9½ x 14in.
(Sotheby's Belgravia)   **$50 £28**

ALFRED H. VICKERS - A Continental Lake Scene - signed - watercolour - 10¾ x 7¾in.
(Sotheby Bearne)   **$169 £94**

VICKERS

ALFRED H. VICKERS - Ben Nevis From Corpach - signed and dated indistinctly - 15½ x 23¼in.
(Sotheby's Belgravia) **$504 £280**

H.R.H. QUEEN VICTORIA - Hagar And Ishmael in the desert - signed, inscribed and dated 1833 - pencil drawing - 9 x 7¼in.
(Sotheby's Belgravia) **$40 £22**

VICTORS - Esther As Queen, seated, small three-quarter length, - on panel - 12 x 11½in.
(Christie's) **$432 £240**

GEORGE VINCENT - Landscape With A Windmill and with two figures in the foreground - 9½ x 14½in.
(Sotheby Bearne) **$741 £380**

JAN VICTORS - Laban Searching Rachel's tent for his stolen images - 72 x 76in.
(Sotheby's) **$9,250 £5,000**

LEONARDO DA VINCI, Manner of - The Holy Family and Saint Anne with the Lamb- on panel - 38 x 28½ in.
(Christie's N. York) **$2,090 £1,142**

MADAME ELISABETH VIGEE - LEBRUN - Portrait Of A Lady, seated, half length, wearing a purple dress and white blouse, holding a folio of music - bears signature and the date 1791 - 25 x 20in.
(Christie's) **$11,700 £6,500**

DAVID VINCKEBOONS - A Kermesse Outside A Town - bears indistinct signature and the date 1622 - 42 x 60in.
(Christie's) **$10,800 £6,000**

A. LA VOLPE - A View Of Capri - signed
and dated 1870 - 20½ x 41in.
(Christie's)   **$1,080   £600**

DAVID VINCKEBOONS - A Scene Outside An Inn - 15 x 17¾in.
(Sotheby's)   **$35,150   £19,000**

VISENTINI - An Italian Piazza -
inscribed 'Canaletto 1729' - pen and
brown ink, grey wash - 35.4 x 48.4cm.
(Christie's)   **$81   £45**

VISSCHER - Head Of A Bearded Man -
black chalk - 21.9 x 17.5cm.
(Christie's)   **$40   £22**

TIMOTEO VITI - The Madonna And
Child - on panel - 25 x 19in.
(Sotheby's)   **$10,175   £5,500**

J. VIVIAN - A Capriccio View Of Santa
Maria Della Salute And The Dogana,
Venice, From The Giudecca - signed -
29½ x 49½in.
(Christie's)   **$720   £400**

A. DE VOIS - Portrait Of A Gentleman,
small bust length, wearing oriental
costume and cap - on panel - 5½ x 4in.
(Christie's)   **$720   £400**

JOHANNES VOORHOUT - A Mother
And Child With Servants before a
draped balustrade, a country mansion
beyond - signed - 17¾ x 25in.
(Christie's)   **$4,320   £2,400**

VAN DER VOORT - An Italianate
Landscape with nymphs in the fore-
ground and a town beyond - 29 x 37½in.
(Christie's)   **$990   £550**

E. VOS - A Frozen River Landscape
with figures on the ice and buildings
behind - signed - pen and brown ink,
brown wash on vellum - 19.4 x 27.4cm.
(Christie's)   **$342   £190**

J. VOYET - Two Females Leaning On
Verandah - oil - on canvas - 35 x 25in.
(The Nottingham Auction Mart)
        $87   £45

J. VOYET - Vase Of Flowers - oil - on
canvas - 28 x 23in.
(The Nottingham Auction Mart)
        $58   £30

S. VRANCX - An Ambush In An
Extensive Rocky Landscape - on panel -
19½ x 29½in.
(Christie's)   **$2,160   £1,200**

ROELOF VAN VRIES, Manner of - A
Wooded Landscape, with a watermill,
and peasants on a road - 26 x 22in.
(Christie's N. York)   **$770   £421**

HENDRIK VROOM, Attributed to -
Men Of War In Action Off-shore - bears
signature - on panel - 16¼ x 26in.
(Christie's N. York)   **$4,950   £2,705**

LOUIS WAIN - The Cats' Diamond Jubilee - signed and inscribed - pen and ink - 20¼ x 29½in.
(Sotheby's Belgravia) **$504 £280**

LOUIS WAIN - The Tennis Party - signed - gouache - 11¼ x 8¾in.
(Sotheby's Belgravia) **$180 £100**

JOHN WAINWRIGHT - A Still Life - signed and dated 1863 - oil - on canvas - 26 x 22in.
(Bonham's) **$1,890 £1,050**

JOHN WAINWRIGHT - Primroses And Blossom in a landscape - signed and dated 1862 - signed and dated 1862 on the reverse - 36 x 27¾in.
(Christie's) **$2,925 £1,500**

T. F. WAINEWRIGHT - Cattle And Sheep Resting - inscribed - 11½ x 19½in.
(Sotheby's Belgravia) **$81 £45**

THOMAS FRANCIS WAINEWRIGHT - A Highland Landscape with a young shepherdess and sheep - signed - 18½ x 27½in.
(Christie's) **$432 £240**

JAMES CLARKE WAITE - "On The Macquarie, Tasmania" - signed - oil - on canvas - 33 x 48.5cm.
(Australian Art Auctions) **$432 £240**

ERNEST WALBOURN - The Cottage By The Sea, a young woman standing by a well, watching pigeons feed in a garden filled with hollyhocks and other flowers; a bay in the distance seen through an open gate - signed - 19½ x 30½in.
(H. Spencer & Sons) **$1,584 £880**

WALKER - Portrait Of Oliver Cromwell, half length, wearing armour - 29½ x 24½in.
(Sotheby's) **$450 £250**

JOHN RAWSON WALKER - An Atmospheric Summer River Landscape with cattle watering by tree-lined banks, mountains and approaching storm beyond - oil - on board - 6 x 10½in.
(Neales of Nottingham) **$205 £110**

W. H. WALKER - Choir Practice - watercolour - 13 x 10in.
(G. A. Key) **$47 £26**

WILLIAM AIKEN WALKER - Loading Ships with bales of cotton - signed, with part of Devoe Academy Board label on the reverse - oil - on board - 4¼ x 8in.
(Sotheby's) **$3,860 £2,000**

WILLIAM AIKEN WALKER - A Negress Picking Cotton and smoking a pipe - signed - oil - on board - 8 x 4in.
(Sotheby's) **$1,737 £900**

WILLIAM AIKEN WALKER - The Old Cotton Picker in the fields with a basket on his head - signed - oil - on board - 8 x 4in.
(Sotheby's) **$1,737 £900**

H. WALLACE - A Quiet Backwater, a summer scene with angler - signed - inscribed - oil - on panel - 9 x 12½in.
(Neales of Nottingham) **$154 £80**

GEORGE WALLIS - A Minster Church - signed and dated 1850 - watercolour - 5 x 7in.
(Heathcote Ball & Co) **$22 £12**

HENRY WALLIS - Bargaining - Cairo - signed and inscribed on a label attached to the reverse - watercolour - 20½ x 14in.
(Christie's) **$72 £40**

451

WALLS

WILLIAM WALLS - The Lowing
Herd Winds Slowly O'er The Lea -
signed - 23 x 35in.
(Sotheby's Belgravia)   **$504 £280**

JOSEPH WALTER - A Fishing Boat and
other vessels at the mouth of the Avon -
signed and dated 1840 - signed and
inscribed on an old label on the reverse -
25½ x 35½in.
(Christie's)   **$3,510 £1,800**

G. S. WALTERS - Trawlers Off Beachy
Head - signed - watercolour - 19 x 12in.
(J. Entwistle & Co.)   **$153 £83**

GEORGE STANFIELD WALTERS - On
The Thames Near Sonning - signed - dated
1885 - 22½ x 36in.
(Sotheby's Belgravia)   **$1,170 £650**

GEORGE STANFIELD WALTERS -
On The Coast Of Alderney - signed -
heightened with white - 27½ x 33½in.
(Sotheby's Belgravia)   **$58 £32**

GEORGE STANFIELD WALTERS -
Leigh Boats Getting Under Way;
Lwandrecht On The Maas, Holland -
signed - heightened with bodycolour -
12¾ x 19½in.
(Sotheby's Belgravia)   **$504 £280 Pair**

SAMUEL WALTERS - The 'Glaphyra'
Off St. Kitts - 32½ x 47½in.
(Christie's)   **$5,040 £2,800**

SAMUEL WALTERS - 'The Great
Britain', a three-masted sailing ship in a
choppy sea - 23½ x 35½in.
(Christie's)   **$3,900 £2,000**

SAMUEL WALTERS - The Queen Of The
Ocean Going To The Rescue Of The Ocean
Monarch, 1848 - 32 x 47½in.
(Sotheby's)   **$1,980 £1,100**

SAMUEL WALTERS - The 'Red Jacket', a sailing ship of the Cunard White Star Line - signed and dated 1854 - 31½ x 47½in.
(Christie's) $3,060 £1,700

ELIJAH WALTON - Dahabeahs On The Nile - watercolour heightened with white - 13¼ x 19¼in.
(Christie's) $342 £190

FRANK WALTON - Feldemoor - signed with monogram - on board - 9½ x 13½in.
(Christie's) $1,260 £700

J. GELDARD WALTON - Evening On The Coast; Shipping Off A Pier - signed and dated 1892 - heightened with bodycolour - 9 x 24in.
(Sotheby's Belgravia) $18 £10 Pair

EDWARD MATHEW WARD - The South Sea Bubble: A scene in Change Alley in 1720 - signed and dated 1855 and inscribed on the reverse - 19½ x 29½in.
(Christie's) $63 £35

ENOCH WARD - Venice Square - signed - watercolour - 11 x 15in.
(Hussey's) $90 £50

FLORA WARD - Hot Punch - signed - 17¼ x 11½in.
(Sotheby's Belgravia) $270 £150

HENRIETTA WARD - One Of The Last Lays Of Robert Burns ('Oh, wert thou in the cauld blast') - signed and dated 1878 - 35 x 43in.
(Christie's) $1,350 £750

WARD

JAMES WARD - A Farm Wagon On A Country Lane - canvas - on panel - 8¼ x 11¼in.
(Christie's) $1,170 £650

JAMES CHARLES WARD - An Ayrshire Landscape - canvas laid on board - 32½ x 25in.
(Sotheby's Belgravia) $162 £90

MARTIN THEODORE WARD - Chestnut Hunters And Hounds in an extensive landscape - signed and dated 1823 - 48 x 66in.
(Christie's) $2,880 £1,600

WARDLE

ARTHUR WARDLE - The Kill - signed -
33½ x 50in.
(Christie's)   **$1,657 £850**

ARTHUR WARDLE - 'Lost In The Snow',
a study of two collies - signed - 24½ x
29½in.
(Sotheby Bearne)   **$684 £380**

J. L. WARDLEWORTH - The Letter -
signed - 40 x 29¾in.
(Sotheby's Belgravia)   **$180 £100**

WILLIAM WARDLESWORTH - Loch
Scenes - signed and dated 1889 - oil -
on panel.
(Andrew Hilditch & Son) **$68 £38 Two**

ARTHUR WARDLE - Rough Customers -
signed and dated 1885 - 23½ x 17¼in.
(Sotheby's Belgravia)   **$990 £550**

ANDY WARHOL - Jackie - signed
on reverse - silkscreen and enamel
on canvas - 20 x 16 in.
(Christie's N. York) **$3,520 £1,955**

ANDY WARHOL - Mao - signed and dated '73 on the reverse - pencil - 36½ x 36½in.
(Christie's) **$6,954 £3,800**

ANDY WARHOL - Two Dollar Bill - signed and dated '62 on the reverse - rubber stencil - on canvas - 6 x 11in.
(Sotheby's) **$1,738 £950**

ANDY WARHOL - Young Man With Flower - signed with felt pen - watercolour over print - 13¾ x 10¾in.
(Sotheby's) **$1,427 £780**

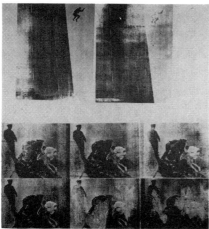

ANDY WARHOL - Suicide (Purple Jumping Man) - acrylic and silkscreen - 81 x 78½in.
(Christie's) **$73,200 £40,000**

KNIGHTON WARREN - Guarding The Harem - signed - 52 x 32in.
(Christie's) **$27,000 £15,000**

WASHINGTON

GEORGES WASHINGTON - Arab
Horsemen Crossing A Bridge by a town -
signed - on panel - 8 x 15¼in.
(Christie's) **$468 £260**

F. WASLEY - Durham Cathedral From
The River - signed - watercolour - 14¾
x 10½in.
(Warner, Sheppard & Wade) **$314 £160**

CLAUDE HENRI WATELET - Figures
In An Italian Landscape with ruins -
signed and dated 1782 - pencil, grey
and brown wash - 23.0 x 34.0cm.
(Christie's) **$126 £70**

JOHN SAMUEL WATKINS - "Survey
Camp" - oil - on board - 36 x 44cm.
(Australian Art Auctions) **$596 £331**

CHARLES WATSON - A Winter's
Evening - signed - 39½ x 29½in.
(Sotheby's Belgravia) **$396 £220**

**ARCHIBALD RUSSELL WATSON
ALLAN** - The Spanish Cock - signed -
coloured chalks and gouache - 17½ x
21½in.
(Sotheby's Belgravia) **$58 £32**

JOHN DAWSON WATSON - Portrait
Of A Girl, head and shoulders - signed
with monogram and dated 1861 - pencil
- 6¾ x 5½in.
(Sotheby's Belgravia) **$14 £8**

ROBERT WATSON - Drovers With Sheep
And Cattle - both signed and dated 1897 -
11½ x 9¼in.
(Sotheby's Belgravia) **$396 £220 Pair**

WILLIAM WATSON - Highland Landscape with cattle, sheep and drovers -
signed and dated 1882 - 23½ x 35½in.
(Sotheby Bearne) **$663 £340**

WILLIAM WATSON - Cattle And Sheep
In The Highlands - unstretched - 23¼ x
34½in.
(Sotheby's Belgravia) **$288 £160 Pair**

WATTEAU - Studies Of Negro Heads -
black and red chalk - 27.2 x 37.2cm.
(Christie's) $189 £105

WATTEAU, After - Elegant Figures At A
Dance On A Terrace, with an extensive
landscape beyond - 21½ x 26½in.
(Christie's) $3,960 £2,200

F. W. WATTS - A Wooded River Landscape with barges - 12 x 18in.
(Christie's) $684 £380

FREDERICK WILLIAM WATTS -
'Loch Fyne' - 24¼ x 31in.
(Sotheby Bearne) $3,600 £2,000

LOUIS JOSEPH WATTEAU, called
Watteau De Lille The Elder - Soldiers
And Peasants Merrymaking at tables in
extensive landscapes - one signed and
dated 1773 - 26½ x 34in.
(Christie's) $10,920 £6,000 Pair

E. WATTS - A Figure Outside A Cottage -
signed and dated '77 - on board - 7½ x
9½in.
(Sotheby's Belgravia) $216 £120

FREDERICK WILLIAM WATTS - A
Wooded Landscape Near Harrow - 23½ x
32in.
(Christie's) $1,440 £800

FREDERICK WILLIAM WATTS -
A Wooded River Landscape with boats
by a cottage - 17¼ x 23½in.
(Christie's) $3,900 £2,000

FREDERICK WILLIAM WATTS -
Chepstow Castle By Moonlight -
13½ x 20½in.
(Christie's) $126 £70

F. W. WATTS - A View Of Vanbrugh
Castle, Greenwich - 12 x 18in.
(Christie's) $630 £350

457

WATTS

GEORGE FREDERICK WATTS -
Portrait Of Henry Prinsep, small bust
length, reading - 12¼ x 10in.
(Christie's) **$1,980 £1,100**

GEORGE FREDERICK WATTS - Portrait
Of Mrs. Aglaia Coronio, Nee Ionides, half
length, wearing a white muslin dress - 23¾
x 19⅜in.
(Christie's) **$3,315 £1,700**

GEORGE FREDERICK WATTS - The
Expulsion From The Garden Of Eden -
on board - 9 x 7¼in.
(Christie's) **$270 £150**

WILLIAM HARRIS WEATHERHEAD -
A Young Fishergirl In A Cottage - signed
- heightened with bodycolour - 11½ x
7½in.
(Sotheby's Belgravia) **$117 £65**

G. WEATHERILL - On The Coast - bears
signature - 8¾ x 14in.
(Sotheby's Belgravia) **$108 £60**
GEORGE WEATHERILL - View Of
Staithes, Yorkshire - watercolour -
4 x 6in.
(G. A. Key) **$115 £64**

THOMAS WEAVER - A Bay And Two
Chestnut Hunters with a terrier in a
stable - signed and dated 1798 - 23½ x
35in.
(Christie's) **$1,350 £750**
B. WEBB - A Falcon Party by the edge
of a lake - oil - 28 x 36in.
(G. A. Key) **$630 £350**

B. WEBB - A Stag And Doe - on board -
8¼ x 6in.
(Sotheby's Belgravia) **$180 £100**

J. WEBB - Unloading Fish Near
Scheveningen - signed - signed, inscribed
and dated 1895 on the reverse - 30 x
50in.
(Sotheby's Belgravia) **$468 £260**

J. WEBB - Seascape With Fishing Smack Under Sail In Rough Waters with another sailboat and rowboat in background - signed and dated 1887 - oil - 14 x 18in.
(Richard Baker & Baker) **$225 £125**

JAMES WEBB - A View Of Saint Paul's Cathedral From The Thames - signed and dated '74 and inscribed London - 25½ x 41½in.
(Christie's) **$11,700 £6,000**

JAMES WEBB - Dutch Fishing Boats in calm water by a mudbank - signed - on panel - 11½ x 13½in.
(Sotheby Bearne) **$1,248 £640**

JAMES WEBB - A Coastal Scene, with figures unloading coal from a coaster and sailing vessels in breezy weather beyond - 39 x 59in.
(Christie's) **$3,705 £1,900**

JAMES WEBB - The Pont Neuf, Paris, with Notre Dame beyond - signed and dated 1873 and 4 and dated Paris 1870 - 25¼ x 39¼in.
(Christie's) **$10,725 £5,500**

JAMES WEBB - 'Cottages At Southend, Essex' - signed and dated 1878 - on panel - 13½ x 19¾in.
(Sotheby Bearne) **$4,680 £2,400**

JAMES WEBB - Fisherfolk By A Ruined Tower on the seashore - signed - 39 x 59in.
(Christie's) **$1,560 £800**

JAMES WEBB - A View Of Dinant - signed and inscribed on the reverse - 35¾ x 59½in.
(Christie's) **$2,730 £1,400**

WEBB

W. WEBB - Peel Harbour, Isle of Man - dated 1896 - oil - on canvas - 23½ x 36in.
(John Francis, Thomas Jones & Sons)
$1,746 £970

WILLIAM WEBB - An Estuary Scene with shipping and foreground figures, a town beyond - signed - inscribed on verso - 16 x 24in.
(Woolley & Wallis) $1,476 £820

WILLIAM WEBB - Portrait Of The Ship Kooria Mooria, a black-hulled ship under full sail in the channel off the cliffs of Dover - signed - oil - on canvas - 24 x 36¼in.
(Richard A. Bourne Co. Inc.)
$2,200 £1,222

W. B. WEBB - Fishing Boats Off The Coast - signed and dated 1875 - 11 x 17in.
(Sotheby's Belgravia) $22 £12

WILLIAM J. WEBB - The Goatherd - signed and dated 1870 and inscribed on the reverse - on board - 11½ x 17½in.
(Christie's) $2,160 £1,200

WILLIAM J. WEBB - A Dark Bay Hunter in a landscape - signed and indistinctly dated - 24¾ x 31in.
(Christie's) $63 £35

W. WEBB - Douglas Harbour, Isle of Man - dated 1896 - oil - on canvas - 23½ x 36in.
(John Francis, Thomas Jones & Sons)
$1,728 £960

HEINRICH WEBER - A Musical Gathering - signed with initials - on panel - 16 x 11¾in.
(Christie's) $1,080 £600

WEBSTER - The Oyster Stall - 23¼ x 19¼in.
(Sotheby's) $1,080 £600

GOTTHARDT DE WEDIG - Still Life With An Oil-Lamp - on metal - 4½ x 5¾in.
(Sotheby's) $11,100 £6,000

JAN BAPTIST WEENIX, THE ELDER - A Huntsman And His Dogs Resting By A Portico, in an extensive landscape with shepherds and their sheep - 31½ x 39½in. *(Christie's).* **$13,500 £7,500**

WEIR - Begging - 16½ x 21¼in. *(Sotheby's Belgravia)* **$396 £220**

HENDRIK JOHANNES WEISSENBRUCH - An Extensive River Landscape Under A Stormy Sky - signed - on panel - 3½ x 6in. *(Christie's)* **$630 £350**

JOHANN FRIEDRICH WEITSCH - A German Forest Scene with cattle near a sunlit pool - signed and dated 1874 - oil - on board - 22 x 28in. *(Bonham's)* **$4,320 £2,400**

WERNER

LUCY KEMP WELCH - Study Of A Girl Seated In A Chair - signed - pencil - 10 x 7in. *(Sotheby's Belgravia)* **$126 £70 Two**

JOHN SANDERSON WELLS - Huntsmen And Hounds moving up past a Cover - oil - on board - 8½ x 11½in. *(Phillips, Solihull)* **$235 £120**

JOHN SANDERSON WELLS - Taking The Fence - signed - on panel - 8¾ x 11¾in. *(Christie's)* **$171 £95**

JOHN S. SANDERSON WELLS - Over The Fence - signed - inscribed 'To Elsie, may you clear every fence' - heightened with bodycolour - 8 x 10in. *(Sotheby's Belgravia)* **$50 £28**

WILLIAM WELLS - Gathering Corn - 39 x 50cm. *(Edmiston's)* **$756 £420**

JOSEPH WENGLEIN - An Autumn Hunting Party - signed - on canvas - 69 x 99cm. *(King & Chasemore)* **$28,800 £16,000**

A. VAN DER WERFF - Putti With A Goat and a dog - black and white chalk on grey paper - 22.8 x 35.4cm. *(Christie's)* **$81 £45**

CARL WERNER - A Street Scene In Jerusalem - signed and dated 1863 - watercolour - 25 x 18in. *(Christie's)* **$810 £450**

WERNER

CARL WERNER - An Arab Child Playing by a house in a mountainous river landscape - signed and dated 1869 - watercolour - 12¾ x 18¾in.
(Christie's)   **$756 £420**

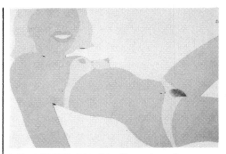

TOM WESSELMANN - Great American Nude No. 62 - signed, inscribed and dated 1965 on the reverse - liquitex polymer paint on gesso on novaply - 43½ x 60in.
(Christie's N. York)   **$16,500 £9,167**

CARL WERNER - Arabs Praying Outside The Dome Of The Rock, Jerusalem - signed and dated 1868 - watercolour - arched top - 31 x 24in.
(Christie's)   **$2,880 £1,600**

CARL WERNER - The Forum, Rome - signed - inscribed 'Rome' and dated 1853 - 15 x 11in.
(Sotheby's)   **$252 £140**

TOM WESSELMANN - Great American Nude No. 10 - signed, inscribed with title and dated 1970-73 on the stretcher - 60 x 115in.
(Christie's)   **$17,385 £9,500**

TOM WESSELMANN - Little Still Life No. 8 - signed and dated '63 - oil and acrylic varnished damar medium relief with applied photo colour printing on board - 17 x 17in.
(Christie's)   **$5,490 £3,000**

TOM WESSELMANN - Nude (Daniele And Celia) - 59¼ x 68¼in.
(Christie's N. York)   **$17,600 £9,778**

TOM WESSELMANN - Great American Nude No. 61 - signed - inscribed and dated '65 on the reverse - liquitex polymer paint on shaped panel - 36½ x 36in.
(Christie's)   **$5,490 £3,000**

ALEXANDER WEST - Pont Tragara, Italy - signed and dated 1884 - 44 x 29½in.
(Sotheby's Belgravia) **$144 £80**

BENJAMIN WEST - An Angel Rolling Back The Stone Liberating The Resurrected Christ - signed - pencil, pen and brown ink, and brown wash - on buff paper - 8¾ x 12in.
(Sotheby's) **$540 £300**

EDGAR E. WEST - 'A Country Scene' - watercolour - 10½ x 14in.
(King & Chasemore) **$162 £90**

ROBERT LUCIUS WEST - Portrait Of Alderman Richard Manders, Lord Mayor of Dublin 1801-2, standing full length with his emblems of office - 91½ x 61¼in.
(Sotheby's) **$1,080 £600**

WESTALL - A Scene From A Drama, a King seated on a bed surrounded by courtiers and Moorish slaves - oil - on canvas - 26½ x 35½in.
(Neales of Nottingham) **$232 £125**

WILLIAM WESTALL - Goats By A Waterfall - signed and dated 1825 - 21 x 14½in.
(Sotheby's) **$324 £180**

CHARLES WESTERN - A Summer Hillside with shepherd and flock - signed - oil - on canvas - 16 x 24in.
(Neales of Nottingham) **$177 £95**

J. DE WET, In The Manner Of - A Young lady being led forth by soldiers to peasants who are offering silver objects - oil - on panel - 21½ x 18½in.
(Smith, Woolley & Perry) **$1,061 £550**

HARRY VAN DER WEYDEN - The Lightship - signed and dated 1925 - 29½ x 42in.
(Christie's) **$360 £200**

HAROLD WHALEY - A Shepherd With His Flock - signed - 19½ x 23½in.
(Sotheby's Belgravia) **$162 £90**

H. WHATLEY - 'Evangeline', portrait of a young woman wearing cap and blue scarf - signed and dated '87 - watercolour - 15½ x 11½in.
(Lalonde Bros. & Parham) **$15 £8**

HENRY WHATLEY - Lady Fannie - signed with initials - heightened with bodycolour - 27 x 18¼in.
(Sotheby's Belgravia) **$360 £200**

F. WHEATLEY - The Banks Of The Medway: A Ruined Castle And Cottages on the river bank, a group of peasant women hanging washing in the foreground and a fisherman loading a boat - signed with initials - 26½ x 35¼in.
(Sotheby's) **$1,260 £700**

FRANCIS WHEATLEY - Outside The Cottage Door - 19½ x 25½in.
(Christie's) **$1,260 £700**

FRANCIS WHEATLEY - A Family Group, the father seated, the mother and daughter standing, in an interior - 39¼ x 49¼in.
(Christie's) **$21,600 £12,000**

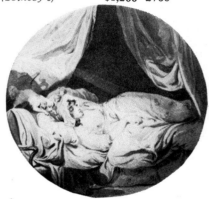

FRANCIS WHEATLEY - A Girl Asleep - signed - pen and grey ink and watercolour - circular - 7½in. diameter .
(Christie's) **$1,170 £650**

WHEELER - Coursing - canvas - on board - 8 x 15¼in.
(Sotheby's Belgravia) **$135 £75**

WHEELER - A Bay Horse In A Stable - inscribed 'Blair Athol' and dated - 15½ x 19½in.
(Sotheby's Belgravia) **$54 £30**

TIMOTHY WHIDBOURNE - A Trompe L'Oeil, cards of good fortune - signed with intials - inscribed 'London' and dated LIX - on panel - 7½ x 9¼in.
(Sotheby's Belgravia) **$36 £20**

FRANCIS WHEATLEY - Tinkers at an Irish Fair - pen and black ink and watercolours - 6¾ x 9½ in.
(Sotheby's) **$900 £500**

CLAUD WHIP - In The Casino At Monte Carlo - signed and inscribed - heightened with bodycolour - 6½ x 9½in.
(Sotheby's Belgravia) **$72 £40**

THOMAS WHITCOMBE - The Grand Harbour, Valletta, British Frigates under sail - signed and dated 1816 - 11½ x 35½in.
(Sotheby's) **$6,480 £3,600**

THOMAS WHITCOMBE - A Frigate Leaving Portsmouth Harbour with the Needles on the left and Hurst Castle on the right; and An Indiaman in a squall off the Stagg Rocks, Lizard - one signed and dated 1819 - 23 x 30in.
(Christie's) **$7,560 £4,200 Pair**

ARMSTRONG WHITTLE - An Old Bridge, North Wales, Evening - signed and dated 1866 inscribed on the reverse - on paper - 8¾ x 12in.
(Sotheby's Belgravia) **$135 £75**

ALFRED DE WIARY - Chevaux - signed - oil - on canvas - 50.5 x 72cm.
(Christian Rosset) **$155 £85**

F. J. WIDGERY - Mouth Of The Langstone - watercolour - 7 x 10in.
(G. A. Key) **$54 £30**

F. J. WIDGERY - Steperton Tor, Dartmoor - signed - watercolour - 10 x 14in.
(Warner, Sheppard & Wade) **$78 £40**

FREDERICK JOHN WIDGERY - Cawsand Beacon - signed - watercolour - 14 x 20in.
(Hussey's) **$83 £46**

CHARLES M. WIGG - Coldham Hall On The Yare - watercolour - 10 x 14in.
(G. A. Key) **$243 £135**

CHARLES MAYES WIGG - Yachts On Wroxham Broad - watercolour - 10 x 14in.
(G. A. Key) **$252 £140**

HENRY WIGSTEAD - The Village Parson; Crossing A Ford In A Carriage - pen and black ink, and watercolour - 6¾ x 9¼in.
(Sotheby's) **$252 £140 Pair**

THOMAS WHITCOMBE - A View Of Dover Castle with peasants and a horse-drawn cart on a road in the foreground - signed - 19½ x 26in.
(Christie's) **$1,620 £900**

WIGSTEAD

HENRY WIGSTEAD - The Bookseller And The Author - pen and black ink and watercolour - 9½ x 12¾in.
(Sotheby's) **$4,680 £2,600**

CHARLES WILD - St Mary's Redcliffe, Bristol: View of the North Porch; View of the Nave looking East; View of the South Transept - all inscribed - pen and brown ink and watercolour - 10 x 7in.
(Sotheby's) **$270 £150 Three**

SAMUEL DE WILDE - The Old Steyne Brighton - pencil and watercolour - 7¾ x 12½ in.
(Sotheby's) **$504 £280**

J. WILDENS - A Sunlit Summer Wooded Village scene with figures conversing and a sportsman with his dog - oil - on panel - 6½ x 16in.
(Neales of Nottingham) **$484 £260**

JAN WILDENS - Canal Scene with skaters - oil - on canvas - 27 x 45in.
(Richard A. Bourne Co. Inc.)
$27,000 £15,000

R. T. WILDING - Fishing Smacks Returning, Near Whitby - signed and dated 1915 - heightened with bodycolour - 12 x 25½in.
(Sotheby's Belgravia) **$76 £42 Pair**

WILKIE - After A Day's Hard Work - bears signature - on board - 12½ x 15¼in.
(Sotheby's Belgravia) **$81 £45**

WILKIE - The Village Festival - 31 x 45½in.
(Sotheby's) **$756 £420**

SIR DAVID WILKIE - The Chelsea Pensioners Receiving The Gazette Announcing The Battle Of Waterloo - signed and dated 1822 - on panel - 11½ x 17½in.
(Christie's) **$16,200 £9,000**

SIR DAVID WILKIE - Study For The Refusal - on panel - 12¼ x 9½in.
(Sotheby's Belgravia) **$1,170 £650**

SIR DAVID WILKIE AND THOMAS
FAED - A Highland Interior - on panel -
7½ x 9¾in.
(Christie's) **$1,350 £750**

ADAM WILLAERTS - Coastal Scene -
signed with initials and dated 1645 - oil
- on panel - 18½ x 32in.
(Bonham's) **$14,040 £7,800**

ADAM WILLAERTS - Perseus And
Andromeda - signed and dated 1660 -
24 x 29½in.
(Christie's) **$1,080 £600**

ERNST WILLERS - An Extensive Italianate
Landscape With Roman Ruins - signed and
dated Roma, 1839 - on panel - 14 x 24½in.
(Christie's) **$288 £160**

ARTHUR WILLETT - A Landscape With
Trees, bracken and deer - signed - water-
colour - 10¼ x 17¼in.
(Foll & Parker) **$144 £80**

ARTHUR WILLETT - In Full Cry; Gone
To Ground - signed - heightened with
bodycolour - 9¼ x 19¾in.
(Sotheby's Belgravia) **$576 £320 Pair**

ADOLPHE LEON WILLETTE - Putti
Disporting Over A Balcony - signed and
dated 1920 - 95 x 65in.
(Christie's) **$1,620 £900**

ADOLPHE LEON WILLETTE - A Guiding
Light - signed and dated 1920 - 98 x 46in.
(Christie's) **$2,700 £1,500**

ADOLPHE LEON WILLETTE - Pan And
A Shepherd Girl - signed and dated 1920 -
97 x 46in.
(Christie's) **$1,800 £1,000**

WILLIAMS - A River Landscape with
men in a punt; and A River Landscape
with cattle and a sailing barge - 11½ x
19½in.
(Christie's) **$50 £28 Pair**

A. W. WILLIAMS - Figures, Dogs And
Man On Horse In Wooded Lane - oil -
22 x 33in.
(G. A. Key) **$918 £510**

EDWARD CHARLES WILLIAMS - A
Wooded Landscape with figures and
cattle in the foreground and a cottage
beyond - on panel - 11¾ x 16in.
(Christie's) **$198 £110**

ELSIE WILLIAMS - Coastal Scenes -
signed and dated 1912 - 10 x 15in.
(Heathcote Ball & Co) **$40 £22**

WILLIAMS

GEORGE AUGUSTUS WILLIAMS - 'Chidingstone From The Corn Fields'; and 'Chiswick From The River' - signed with initials and inscribed on the reverse - 9¾ x 18¾in.
(Sotheby Bearne)   **$4,387 £2,250 Pair**

H. WILLIAMS - Near Glencoe, an evening scene - signed - oil - on canvas - 12 x 24in.
(Neales of Nottingham) **$52 £28**

J. WILLIAMS - By A Pond; On The Coast - signed - indistinctly inscribed - 9½ x 17½in.
(Sotheby's Belgravia)   **$108   £60 Pair**

TERRICK WILLIAMS - Wayfarers, Kairouan - signed - watercolour - 9¾ x 17½in.
(Christie's)   **$216 £120**

W. WILLIAMS - Children Minnowing - signed - 19½ x 29½in.
(Sotheby's Belgravia)   **$68 £38**

WALTER WILLIAMS - A View Near Sonning, Berkshire; and A View Near Hastings - signed with initials and dated 1878 - oil - on canvas - 7 x 9in.
(Bonham's)   **$3,060 £1,700 Pair**

WALTER WILLIAMS - Children Playing By A Stream - signed with initials - dated 1882 - 9 x 6¾in.
(Sotheby's Belgravia) **$270   £150**

WARREN WILLIAMS - Five Figures At Stone Sea Wall, waving goodbye to the fishing fleet - signed and dated 1901 - watercolour - 21 x 33in.
(Richard Baker & Baker) **$108 £60**

CHARLES WILLIS - Her Recital - signed - inscribed on the reverse - 20 x 26¾in.
(Sotheby's Belgravia) **$450   £250**

CHARLES WILLIS - Autumn - signed - 20 x 26¾in.
(Sotheby's Belgravia)   **$540 £300**

CHARLES WILLIS - Spring - signed -
20 x 26¾in.
(Sotheby's Belgravia) $540 £300

CHARLES WILLIS - Blind Man's Buff -
signed - inscribed on the reverse - 20 x
26¾in.
(Sotheby's Belgravia) $585 £325

G. WILLOUGHBY - Tavern Exteriors
with huntsmen and hounds - one signed -
13¼ x 19½in.
(Sotheby Bearne) $1,131 £580 Pair

WILSON - Parkland Cattle And Drovers
On The Banks Of A Wooded River - oil -
16 x 22in.
(Heathcote Ball & Co) $842 £460

WILSON - Mountainous Landscape With
Two Fishermen by a fast flowing stream
near a stone bridge with a herdsman and
cattle in a meadow among trees - bears
signature and dated 1773 - panel - 16 x
21in.
(H. Spencer & Sons) $540 £300

D. F. WILSON - Begonias - 25½ x 17½in.
(Sotheby's Belgravia) $68 £38

DAVID FORRESTER WILSON -
A Girl Outside A Croft - 35½ x 23½in.
(Sotheby's Belgravia) $76 £42

H. WILSON - Still Life Of Game And
Fruit On A Table - signed - 27½ x 34½in.
(Sotheby's Belgravia) $324 £180

J. WILSON - Portrait Of A West Highland Terrier - oil - 9 x 9in.
(G. A. Key) $140 £78

JOHN 'JOCK' WILSON - Sailing Vessels
Off A Jetty - signed - 4½ x 13¾in.
(Christie's S. Kensington) $576 £320 Pair

JOHN WILSON - Sailing Vessels off a
fishing village - signed - 21½ x 36in.
(Christie's) $2,145 £1,100

469

WILSON

JOHN WILSON - A Man-O'-War and other sailing vessels in a calm sea - signed and dated 1828 - on panel - 9¾ x 14½in. *(Christie's)* **$1,710 £950**

JOCK WILSON - Shipping Off A Harbour - signed - oil - on canvas - 23 x 32in. *(Bonham's)* **$1,980 £1,100**

OSCAR WILSON - A Flower Market In The Rue Du Regent, Antwerp - signed and dated 1892 - on panel - 7½ x 10¾in. *(Christie's)* **$4,680 £2,400**

R. WILSON - On The Dee - 24 x 29in. *(Sotheby's)* **$990 £550**

RICHARD WILSON - A Rural Landscape with cattle at a ford - oil - on panel - 4 x 5½in. *(Warner, Sheppard & Wade)* **$314 £160**

HENRY B. WIMBUSH - The Cuillins Of Skye - signed - 22 x 31in. *(Sotheby's Belgravia)* **$50 £28**

EDMUND MORISON WIMPERIS - A Sunlit Moorland Landscape with sheep grazing - signed and dated 1893 - oil - on canvas - 24 x 36in. *(Bonham's)* **$3,240 £1,800**

EDMUND MORISON WIMPERIS - Arundel Castle From The River Meadows - signed with initials and dated - 16 x 24¼in. *(Sotheby's)* **$360 £200**

EDMUND MORISON WIMPERIS - A Coastal View with mountains beyond - signed with initials and dated - 7 x 18¼in. *(Sotheby's)* **$117 £65**

D. WINDER - Llyn Grafant, Llyn-Y-Voel, North Wales - one signed and dated - 10 x 18in. *(Sotheby's Belgravia)* **$522 £290 Pair**

PETER DE WINT - Study Of An Elm Tree - black crayon and white chalk on blue paper - 9½ x 6¾in. *(Sotheby's)* **$288 £160**

PETER DE WINT - Landscape Near
Lincoln - 7 x 12½in.
(Morphets of Harrogate) **$243 £135**

PETER DE WINT - Moor And River,
Yorkshire - 10¾ x 15¼in.
(Sotheby's) **$5,220 £2,900**

PETER DE WINT - A Derbyshire Landscape
with trees by chalk cliffs with cattle in the
foreground - 17¼ x 24 in.
(Sotheby's) **$10,440 £5,800**

PETER DE WINT - A Country Lane -
8¼ x 12½ in.
(Sotheby's) **$1,710 £950**

PETER DE WINT - View Near Ambleside,
Westmorland, with figures and sheep on
a road and cattle watering by a bridge -
signed - 14¾ x 28½in.
(Sotheby's) **$3,960 £2,200**

PETER DE WINT - Goodrich Castle seen
from the Valley - Early Morning - 23¾ x
37 in.
(Sotheby's) **$1,800 £1,000**

WITTE

P. De WINT - Leatherhead Church, Surrey,
with figures by a wall - 15 x 19¼in.
(Sotheby's) **$1,728 £960**

HOLMES WINTER - A Ketch, North End,
Great Yarmouth - watercolour - 10 x 12in.
(G. A. Key) **$68 £38**

F. A. WINTERHALTER - Portrait Of
The Young Queen Victoria - mill board
- 12¼ x 9½in.
(Sotheby Bearne) **$253 £130**

MATHIAS WITHOOS - A Park With
Antique Sculpture - signed - 29½ x 25¾in.
(Sotheby's) **$4,810 £2,600**

E. DE WITTE - The Interior Of A Church
with grave diggers - 23¾ x 21¼in.
(Christie's) **$810 £450**

WIWA
M. L. WIWA - View On The Grand Canal, Venice - oil - 24 x 18in.
(G. A. Key) **$32 £18**

JOHANN JAKOB WOLFENSBERGER - An Overhung Cavern By Waterfalls - watercolour - 15.9 x 19.6cm.
(Christie's) **$72 £40**

J. WOOD - Horse Racing Scenes: The Saddling Enclosure, The Start and The Finish - signed - on board - 6 x 12in.
(H. Spencer & Sons) **$360 £200 Three**

LEWIS JOHN WOOD - 'Dietz on the Lahn, Germany' - inscribed on the reverse - 11¼ x 8¼in.
(Sotheby Bearne) **$1,287 £660**

PETER M. WOOD - St. Ives Harbour - signed, verso inscribed - oil - on canvas - 19 x 23½in.
(Neales of Nottingham) **$67 £36**

SAMUEL WOODFORD - Charles I In Captivity Being Visited By His Children - inscribed on the reverse - 56 x 67in.
(Sotheby's) **$1,080 £600**

C. WOODRUFFE - A Haybarge - watercolour - 10 x 6in.
(G. A. Key) **$32 £18**

CHARLES WOODRUFFE - Rescue At Sea, ship on fire - watercolour - 11 x 17in.
(G. A. Key) **$36 £20**

MRS WOODS - A Messenger To The Court Of The Butterflies - heightened with bodycolour - 22½ x 18¾in.
(Sotheby's Belgravia) **$108 £60**

R. CATON WOODVILLE - The New Sclave - signed - oil - on panel - 17½ x 12in.
(Walker, Barnett & Hill) **$468 £260**

RICHARD CATON WOODVILLE - Kandahar: The 92nd Highlanders and 2nd Gurkhas Storming Gaudi Mullah Sahibdad - signed and signed and inscribed on a label on the reverse - 50¾ x 62¼in.
(Christie's) **$4,860 £2,700**

CHARLES H. WOOLFORD - Bringing Home The Sheep, Evening - signed - 7 x 8½in.
(Sotheby's Belgravia) **$76 £42**

THOMAS WORLIDGE - Head Of A Man Wearing A Bonnet - signed with initials and dated 1751 - red pencil - 8¾ x 5¾in.
(Sotheby's)   **$81 £45**

J. E. WORRALL - Happy Thoughts - signed and inscribed on the reverse - 14¼ x 11½in.
(Christie's)   **$990 £550**

ABRAHAM BRUININGH VAN WORRELL - An Italianate Landscape With Cattle By A Fountain - signed and dated - on panel - 9½ x 12½in.
(Christie's)   **$576 £320**

FRANS WOUTERS - Landscape With Peasants and goats - on panel - 10½ x 16¾in.
(Sotheby's)   **$7,400 £4,000**

WOUVERMAN - A Cavalry Engagement Between European and Turkish Soldiers - on copper - 6¼ x 9in.
(H. Spencer & Sons)   **$864 £480**

P. WOUVERMAN - An Army Encampment with soldiers and other figures merrymaking - indistinctly signed with initials - oil - on canvas - 21 x 25in.
(Bonham's)   **$3,330 £1,850**

WOUWERMAN - Study Of A Pony - the mount inscribed in Italian - black and white chalk on blue paper - 12.2 x 10.8cm.
(Christie's)   **$126 £70**

P. WOUWERMAN - Cavalry Attacked By Infantry - bears initials - on panel - 15½ x 20in.
(Christie's)   **$1,980 £1,100**

WRIGHT

P. WOUWERMAN - A Falconer With His Dog, A Youth With A Falcon Crouching Behind - red chalk - 14.0 x 14.8cm.
(Christie's)   **$252 £140**

P. WOUWERMAN - An Extensive Wooded Landscape with travellers on a path - bears initials - on panel - 20½ x 24¾in.
(Christie's)   **$4,680 £2,600**

PHILIPS WOUWERMAN - A Harvest Scene - on panel - 14½ x 11½in.
(Christie's)   **$5,040 £2,800**

PHILIPS WOUWERMAN, Manner of - The Departure For The Hunt - on panel - 17½ x 24in.
(Christie's N. York)   **$2,420 £1,322**

G. WRIGHT - Casting About; Tally Ho; Full Cry; and The Kill - bears signatures and date '79 - 7½ x 9½in.
(Christie's)   **$1,620 £900 Four**

WRIGHT

GEORGE WRIGHT - 'Well Over' - signed - 13¾ x 17¾in.
(Christie's) **$3,120 £1,600**

GEORGE WRIGHT - A Meet At Avebury Manor - signed - 8¾ x 13½in.
(Christie's) **$2,535 £1,300**

J. M. WRIGHT - Portrait Of A Gentleman, three-quarter length, wearing armour, his left hand on the hilt of his sword, an extensive landscape beyond to his left - 48 x 38in.
(Sotheby's) **$450 £250**

R. MURDOCH WRIGHT - An Old Mill, Moonlight - signed - 29 x 19½in.
(Sotheby's Belgravia) **$40 £22**

THOMAS WYCK - An Italianate Harbour Scene with figures - signed - 18 x 20in.
(Christie's) **$4,320 £2,400**

JAN WYCK - An Upturned Barrow, a tub and other vessels - signed with initials - black chalk - 10.3 x 15.2cm.
(Christie's) **$270 £150**

N. M. WYDOOGEN - An Estuary View With Fishing Vessels In A Storm And A Town In The Distance; and A Calm Estuary View At Sunset - both signed - both on panel - 17½ x 27in.
(Christie's) **$7,200 £4,000 Pair**

WILLIAM WYLD - Figures On A French Lane, garden walls on either side - signed - 11¾ x 7¾in.
(Sotheby's) **$270 £150**

WILLIAM WYLLIE - River Scene - watercolour - 12 x 7in.
(Andrew Hilditch & Son) **$176 £98**

R. WYMER - Cavalry and Infantry Officers in varieties of regimental full dress of the period - signed and dated 1902 - watercolour - 12½ x 27in.
(Wallis & Wallis) **$396 £205**

YARNOLD - Barrow Fall - inscribed on panel - 12½ x 9½in.
(Sotheby's Belgravia) **$126 £70**
JOSEPH YARNOLD - A Mountainous Landscape with children fishing in a torrent - signed and dated '79 - 23½ x 35½in.
(Christie's) **$432 £240**

GIDEON YATES - Views Of Lancaster - two signed and dated 1809 - pencil and watercolour - 11¼ x 16¼in.
(Sotheby's) **$170 £90 Four**

J. YATES - The Lune Near Barbon - signed and inscribed - 11¼ x 15in.
(Sotheby's Belgravia) **$8 £5**

R. YATES - The Cornfield - signed - 9¼ x 13in.
(Sotheby's Belgravia) **$50 £26**

W. YATES, SEN - Pools By A Farmstead - both signed - 19½ x 49½in.
(Sotheby's Belgravia) **$811 £420 Pair**

TOMAS YEPES (HIEPES) - Flowers In A Painted Vase - both signed and dated 1664 - 59 x 38½in.
(Sotheby's) **$74,000 £40,000 Pair**

JACK BUTLER YEATS - Fine Eating Apples - signed - inscribed with title - on panel - 10¼ x 15¼in.
(Christie's) **$5,400 £3,000**

VINCENT P. YGLESIAS - At Rye, Sussex - signed - on board - 8¼ x 13½in.
(Sotheby's Belgravia) **$22 £12**

SHIH-FU CH'IU YING, Style of - Figures in Garden Settings having a meal and by a pavilion - watercolour on silk - 11¼ x 35¼ in.
(Sotheby's, Hong Kong) **$457 £254 Pair**

SHIH-FU CH'IU YING, Style of - Figures eating a meal being entertained by Musicians; Figures and Cranes in a Landscape - watercolour on silk - one 11¼ x 23¼ in. the other 11¼ x 33 in.
(Sotheby's, Hong Kong) **£499 £277 Two**

SHIH-FU CH'IU YING, Style of - Horsemen and other figures in Landscapes - watercolour on silk - 11 x 36 in.
(Sotheby's, Hong Kong) **$623 £346 Pair**

YKENS

FRANS YKENS - A Still Life Of Game
And Fruit - signed F.Y.F./1664 - 38½ x
51in.
(Sotheby's) **$7,030 £3,800**

FRANS YKENS - Christ In The House Of
Martha And Mary, a view of Antwerp beyond
- 55½ x 89¾in.
(Christie's) **$7,560 £4,200**

**VICE-ADMIRAL SIR JOSEPH SYDNEY
YORKE** - Mount Edgcombe from Stowe
House, Cornwall - 4¾ x 6½in.
(Sotheby's) **$66 £35**

HIMIDZU Y. YOSHI - Fuji San - 33.5 x
45cm.
(Auktionshaus am Neumarkt) **$152 £83**

ALEXANDER YOUNG - Crossing The
Bar - signed and inscribed - 11½ x 19½in.
(Sotheby's Belgravia) **$162 £90**

A. YOUNG - A Fishing Boat Going Out -
signed - 16¼ x 20in.
(Sotheby Bearne) **$540 £300**

JOHN MALLOWS YOUNGMAN - In
Windsor Park - signed with initials and
dated May '43 - watercolour - 9¼ x 12½in.
(Christie's) **$147 £80**

LEON ZACK - Nu Debout - signed -
81 x 60cm.
(Christie's) **$184 £100**

GIUSEPPE ZAIS, Attributed to - A Man
And Animals on the bank of a river - oil
- on canvas - 49 x 79cm.
(Christian Rosset) **$409 £227**

G. ZAIS - The Holy Family (recto); A
Man Struggling To Hold A Rearing
Charger (verso) - pen and brown ink,
grey wash - 14.4 x 20.6cm.
(Christie's) **$72 £40**

ZAIS - A Group Of Peasants -
indistinctly signed - pencil and
grey wash - 14.5 x 12.5cm.
(Christie's) **$63 £35**

ZAIS - A Wooded Landscape with a
peasant seated by a waterfall - 8¾ x
6¼in.
(Christie's) **$585 £300**

ZAMPIGHI - The Connoisseurs - indistinctly
signed - on board - 19 x 26in.
(Sotheby's) **$270 £150**

EDUARDO ZAMPIGHI - Reading The
News - signed - 20 x 40½in.
(Christie's) **$9,000 £5,000**

EDUARDO ZAMPIGHI - Tales Of The Old
Hunter - signed - 24 x 18¼in.
(Sotheby's) **$4,632 £2,400**

EDUARDO ZAMPIGHI - A Game Of
Patience - signed - 17½ x 22½in.
(Christie's) **$3,600 £2,000**

ZENALE

EDUARDO ZAMPIGHI - Bargaining - signed
- watercolour - 20¾ x 13¾in.
(Sotheby's) **$1,351 £700**

FRANCESCO ZANIN - A View Of
The Piazza San Marco, Venice - signed
and dated 1888 - 29 x 43½in.
(Christie's) **$6,300 £3,500**

KIRIL ZDANEVITCH - Contrast Of
Forms - signed and dated '17 - pencil
and pen and Indian ink - 8½ x 6¼in.
(Sotheby's) **$366 £200**

R. NOOMS, called ZEEMAN - Frigates
And Men-Of-War in a Mediterranean
Harbour - bears signature - on panel -
16 x 28in.
(Sotheby's) **$7,569 £4,200**

J. C. ZEHENDER - Landscapes With
Pheasants - both signed and dated
1775 - pencil - 13.2 x 19.5cm.
(Christie's) **$234 £130**

J. ZELGER - Extensive Swiss Landscape
with mountains and lake, figures in the
foreground - dated 1858 - oil - 40 x 52in.
(Thomas Love & Sons Ltd.) **$3,600 £2,000**

BERNARDINO ZENALE, Attributed To -
Portrait of a young man - on panel - 12½ x
9½in.
(Christie's New York) **$4,400 £2,280**

477

ZEIM

FELIX ZEIM - A Soukh In The Moyen Atlas Mountains - signed - 25¾ x 36¼in.
(Christie's) **$1,800 £1,000**

ALTICHIERO DA ZEVIO - The Crucifixion - on gold ground panel - 49½ x 55¼in.
(Christie's) **$81,000 £45,000**

J. ZICK - The Resurrection, the disciples at the empty tomb; Pentecost, the descent of the Holy Ghost - on panel - 23 x 16½in.
(Sotheby's) **$20,350 £11,000 Pair**

M. VON ZIEGLER - Alphutte - 57 x 46cm.
(Auktionshaus am Neumarkt) **$181 £99**

FELIX ZIEM - A Side Canal, Venice - signed - on panel - 21¾ x 11¼in.
(Sotheby's) **$1,080 £600**

FELIX FRANCOIS GEORGES PHILIBERT ZIEM - Venice - signed - pen and black ink - 20 x 30cm.
(Christie's) **$294 £160**

JOHANN VILHELM ZILLEN - Cattle In A Landscape - signed and dated 1854 - 15½ x 20¾in.
(Sotheby's) **$432 £240**

ZILOTTI - A Rocky Gorge - pen and brown ink - 31.2 x 21.8cm.
(Christie's) **$72 £40**

J. G. ZOBELL - A View With A Castle - signed - pen and brown ink and watercolour - 33.6 x 47.4cm.
(Christie's) **$117 £65**

ZOFFANY - Portrait Of A Gentleman Wearing A Brown Coat - on panel - 8½ x 7½in.
(Sotheby's) **$162 £90**

GAETANO ZOMPINI - A Herbseller: Erbariol; A Fruitseller: Fruitariol A Scrap Metal Dealer: Stazze Ferrut; and A Glass Dealer from Murano: Veri Rotti - signed - pen and brown ink, grey wash - 30 x 20cm.
(Christie's) **$1,710 £950 Four**

ZOPPO - The Agony Of Saint Peter - on panel - 8¾ x 6½in.
(Christie's) **$180 £100**

ZUCCARO - Portrait Of A Gentleman Standing, three-quarter length, wearing grey costume - on panel - 32½ x 26in.
(Christie's) **$1,260 £700**

F. ZUCCARELLI - The Continence Of Scipio - bears signature - 19 x 22in.
(Christie's) **$3,060 £1,700**

FRANCESCO ZUCCARELLI - A Wooded Italianate Landscape with a peasant woman and child by a torrent - 20 x 26½in.
(Christie's) **$6,324 £3,400**

FRANCESCO ZUCCARELLI - A Classical Woodland Landscape with a distant view of a village, in the foreground girls can be seen bathing their feet in a brook - oil - on copper - 14½ x 18¼in.
(Bonham's) **$14,760 £8,200**

FRANCESCO ZUCCARELLI - An Italian Landscape with figures - 12½ x 16¼in.
(Sotheby's) **$18,500 £10,000**

FRANCESCO ZUCCARELLI - An Extensive River Landscape With A Village And Numerous Figures - 56 x 79½in.
(Christie's) **$72,000 £40,000**

ZUCCERO - Portrait Of A Lady Wearing A Ruff And An Embroidered Dress - on panel - 28 x 21in.
(Christie's) **$656 £340**

A. ZUCCHI - A Capriccio Of Roman Ruins - brown wash heightened with white - 40.2 x 57.4cm.
(Christie's) **$144 £80**

HEINRICH JOHANN ZUGEL - Cattle In A Sunlit Orchard - signed and dated 188* - oil - on canvas - 27 x 34in.
(Bonham's) **$5,400 £3,000**

F. ZUGNO - The Finding Of Moses - oval - 11½ x 8¾in.
(Christie's) **$990 £550**

ROBERT ZUND - Flusslandschaft Mit Reiter Und Herde - 35.5 x 50.5cm.
(Auktionshaus am Neumarkt)
$10,110 £5,525

F. DE ZURBARAN - Saint Veronica's Veil - 42¼ x 31¼in.
(Christie's) **$6,300 £3,500**

FRANCISCO ZURBARAN, Circle of - Portrait Of A Gentleman In Armour - inscribed - 77¾ x 40½in.
(Christie's New York) **$28,600 £14,819**

ALEKSANDER ZYW - Warm Theme, Autumn 1957 - signed and dated '58 - 92 x 73cm.
(Christie's) **$221 £120**

ALEKSANDER ZYW - Abstract Composition - signed and dated '62 - 89 x 129.5cm.
(Christie's) **$460 £250**